Andrew Alexander is an award-winning journalist whose column appears weekly in the *Daily Mail*. He was previously a leader writer and parliamentary sketch writer for the *Daily Telegraph*, where he is thought to have invented the tradition of reporting irreverently on the House of Commons. Joining the *Daily Mail* in 1972, he has variously held the posts of sketch writer, City Editor and Director of Associated Newspapers. He lives in London.

ANDREW ALEXANDER

AMERICA
AND THE IMPERIALISM OF IGNORANCE
US FOREIGN POLICY SINCE 1945

Biteback Publishing

First published in Great Britain in 2011.

This edition published in 2012 by
Biteback Publishing Ltd
Westminster Tower
3 Albert Embankment
London SE1 7SP
Copyright © Andrew Alexander 2011

ISBN 978-1-84954-295-1

10 9 8 7 6 5 4 3 2 1

A CIP catalogue record for this book is available from the British Library.

Set in Adobe Caslon Pro and Steelfish by Namkwan Cho
Cover design by Namkwan Cho

Printed and bound in Great Britain by
CPI Group (UK) Ltd, Croydon CR0 4YY

To my numerous friends in the Conservative Party whose relentless belief remains to this day that the Cold War arose from the aggressive ambitions of the Kremlin, thwarted by the bold response of our American friends. Their refusal to contemplate any other explanation has spurred me on in this, my survey of US foreign policy over the last sixty-five years.

'To lose an empire is not easy. The British did it and they
learned how. The French did it and they learned how.
Then the Russians did it – and have not quite learned how.
Now I think the Americans should learn how to lose an empire.'
Hans Blix

CONTENTS

A NOTE ON THE SOURCES

Where references are made to secondary sources (which usually cite primary sources themselves) the relevant books and papers are being suggested for further reading. Frequent use is made of the Cold War International History Project website (http://www.wilsoncenter.org/index.cfm?fuseaction=topics.home&topic_id=1409). This huge American-sponsored project cannot be too highly recommended. It contains a variety of sources, principally American and Russian, and makes use of Soviet archives as they are being opened. Translations are made by scholars of international standing who also hold conferences to discuss the implications and backgrounds of the material.

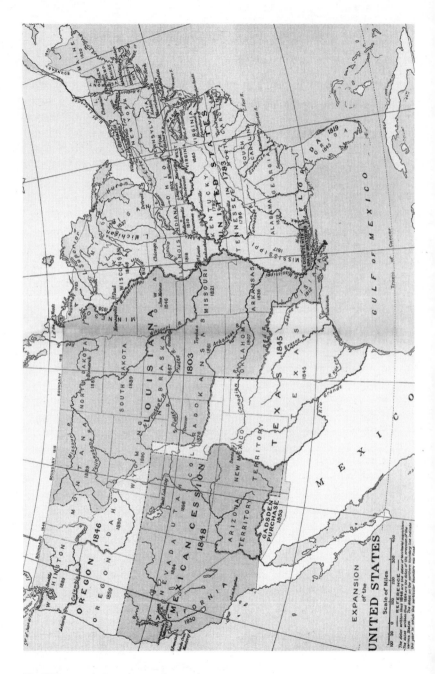

The USA expands from shore to shining shore

CHAPTER 1
THE FLAWED COLD WAR ORTHODOXY

The historical consistency of US policy – Soviet fears ignored – Stalin's fears of Communist revolutions outside Russia – Truman's view of Soviet ambitions – the Russia military threat imaginary – Stalin not a repeat of Hitler – Truman initiates the Cold War – Washington rejects Moscow's peace overtures

'One of the delightful things about Americans is that they have absolutely no historical memory.' Chinese Premier Zhou Enlai

'Scare the hell out of the American people!' Senator Vandenberg's advice to President Truman on persuading voters to accept the cost of aid for Greece and Turkey.

American incomprehension of the outside world, combined with a determination to lead it, has been the principal problem in international affairs since the end of the Second World War. The stubbornly orthodox view remains that despite 'aberrations' ranging from Vietnam to Iraq, the balance sheet remains in the USA's favour, given the triumph of the Cold War, the defeat of the Soviet Union and the collapse of Communism. America thus deserves the West's gratitude for leading it to victory after forty-five years of confrontation with an aggressive Russia. It adds some logic to the view that it is essential for the Western alliance to hold firm behind Washington as it faces the newer menace of Islamic terrorism.

However, this orthodoxy is based on the premise that the Soviet threat at the end of the Second World War was a real one.[1] But, as one of Britain's leading military

---

1 The orthodox view and its persistence is summarised in the claim in 2003 by former *Times* Editor William Rees-Mogg: 'After the Second World War, the US saved Europe from Soviet

commentators, Sir Michael Howard, observed during the last days of the Soviet Union: 'No serious historian any longer argues that Stalin ever had any intention of moving his forces outside the area he occupied in Eastern Europe.' Yet many historians, perhaps not serious but widely read, still argue that the Soviet leader had such aggressive ambitions. A proper military analysis of the situation in 1945 would have shown that the prospect of Russian armies invading Western Europe was a fantasy, like Saddam Hussein's Weapons of Mass Destruction ready for launch in forty-five minutes. Also like the domino theory reigning in Washington during the Vietnam conflict that if the North won, the whole of South East Asia would go Communist.

The opening up of the Soviet archives underlines the fantasy of the old view of the Russian 'threat'. The USA's allies today may be anxious to believe that such manifest follies as Vietnam and Iraq were uncharacteristic of a nation dedicated to peace. But both demonstrate an unmistakeable continuity of a fiercely assertive foreign policy, flourishing under presidencies of both parties. The unwinnable war in Vietnam started under President Kennedy, was stepped up by President Johnson and finally lost by President Nixon despite ferocious bombings of Laos and Cambodia, plus raids on Hanoi itself, in an effort to force North Vietnam to negotiate.

The first Gulf War, launched by President George H. Bush to expel Saddam Hussein from Kuwait, achieved its UN-legitimised end. But the subsequent programme of militarily-supported sanctions produced appalling hardship and death for the ordinary people of Iraq, whom Washington was claiming to rescue. As the death toll mounted, the sanctions were notoriously dubbed 'worthwhile' during the Clinton regime. The second Gulf War launched by President George W. Bush is only defended by those hemmed in by their former enthusiasm. Its cost since 2003 has been prodigious for Iraq, supposedly being rescued from tyranny while the Middle East and the world was simultaneously saved from Saddam's WMDs.

The prolonged and unwinnable war in Afghanistan appeared to follow the decision by the second Bush to extend the original punitive expedition launched after the 9/11 atrocity in New York. But it transpired that an attack on the Taliban regime in Afghanistan was already being planned in Washington to settle old scores with al Qaeda for previous terrorist assaults. The subsequent 'war on terror' became a general campaign against Islamic militants, extending into Pakistan and Yemen. In the case of Afghanistan it was accompanied by a high-minded claim that a Western-style democratic state was being created which would be a barrier to Jihadists. By the time Bush left office, the conflict had lasted seven years – longer than the Second World War – and the position was deteriorating. The succeeding Obama administration's policy on Afghanistan, despite pledges of a swift removal of American forces, was to leave US policy little changed. He agreed to send more troops in the hope that – reminiscent of Vietnam – they might inflict sufficient

---

rule.' See http://dailyreckoning.com/the-transatlantic-gulf. The consequences of a Third World War are not explored by him.

damage on the insurgents to ease the early US withdrawal he called for during his election campaign.

Correspondingly, Washington's almost unquestioning support for Israel in its collisions with its Arab neighbours seemed to underline a US instinct for the solution of problems by force, or the support of force by a surrogate. Washington was the vital provider of military, economic and political aid. It bore a key responsibility for Israel's prolonged assault on insurgents in the Lebanon in the late 1970s, in the brief repeat of this exercise in 2006 and similarly in Gaza in 2008 – all expeditions which aroused widespread condemnation. US policy in Latin America, regularly in assistance with notoriously brutal regimes, also demonstrated the continuity of outlook in Washington, regardless of party.

Criticism of these unfortunate chapters in American foreign policy is now commonplace. However, a readiness to recognise the folly of the Cold War and how the US began it is much harder to find, despite the high quality of 'revisionist' histories by American historians in particular. There are obviously other reasons for a reluctance to face this. It rebels against sense to accept that the world came close to nuclear Armageddon on half a dozen occasions and expended so much blood and treasure for forty years against a threat that was never real. To accept this raises serious doubt about the integrity and basic intelligence of a whole succession of Western governments and the political institutions for which they make such high claims. In mitigation of the European powers' readiness to follow the American lead, two points might be made.

The first is, ironically, that the launch of the Cold War by the USA did in due course bring into existence the very danger which had been imagined. It made frantic defence measures seem sensible. Threatened by President Truman, Russia responded by a vigorous programme of rearmament and an even tighter clampdown on Eastern Europe. With the refusal of the USA to respond to peace initiatives launched by the Soviet leadership on the death of Stalin in 1953, the Kremlin fought back under the new and more assertive leadership of Nikita Khrushchev. American and Western power in general was challenged wherever it could be found. It became rational to talk of a Communist threat and of the danger of a Soviet Union with a nuclear armoury. What was inaccurate was the assumption that a new military threat had come into being when the wartime allies finally came face to face in Germany.

A second excuse may be pleaded for Western governments following American policy: the sheer power of the dollar. What Washington decreed was little challenged by its European allies. There were dangers in objecting to the foreign policy of the USA. It was like criticising the bank manager when loans were desperately needed. Accepting the American view helped by the expenditure involved in US bases in Europe was the easiest route. The normal-give-and-take between allies declined into a subservient attitude. Britain was trying to rebuild a shattered economy with the assistance of an American loan. In 1948 it became further dependent on US aid under the Marshall Plan for European reconstruction. Britain was particularly reliant on US support for sterling, foolishly on a fixed exchange rate which was regularly in crisis.

Ironically the instability in sterling owed much to Britain's attempts to maintain its own military bases around the world, a policy warmly supported by the Americans.

This economic dependence had an inevitable effect on British policy from the start. Clement Attlee, newly elected as Labour Prime Minister in 1945, was not by instinct a hardliner when it came to the Soviet Union, though his ebullient Foreign Secretary Ernest Bevin was. His outlook was coloured by his experience of Communist manoeuvrings as a trade union leader. There were strong doubts about the American attitude in the mind of Anthony Eden, Foreign Secretary during Churchill's wartime leadership and a veteran of dealings with the Kremlin. He regarded the Soviet position after the end of the war as driven by natural motives of defence. Churchill himself with his long history of hostility to everything Soviet shared none of his deputy's reservations. But hardliners and doubters had one view in common. To defy US policy was financially perilous. The Suez crisis was to demonstrate this dramatically a decade later.

The consequences of prolonged and unquestioning support for the USA have been disastrous. It has led to friends of America being dragged into the front line of a 'war on terror' which served as a recruiting sergeant for Jihadists from all parts of Islam. The world is a much more dangerous place as a result of America's determination to save it.

✪

A wider look at history shows that a strongly interventionist US foreign policy is nothing new – though the current power to intervene globally is. A century ago, an American incomprehension of the outside world was exemplified by President Woodrow Wilson, so determined to remake countries in the American image after the First World War. His mixture of benevolence and ruthlessness may be summed up in a dispute with Mexico in 1913, when he announced 'I will teach the Latin-Americans to elect good men' followed by bombarding the town of Vera Cruz. His gunboat diplomacy intensified such feelings of nationalism and anti-Americanism that Germany hoped to make Mexico an ally in an attack on the USA in 1917 – famously exposed in the Zimmermann telegram, decoded by London.

In 1945, the USA dedicated itself in Wilsonian language to bringing 'democracy and freedom' to the countries occupied by the Soviets at the end of the Second World War. The goal was high-minded. But there was a puzzling refusal to acknowledge the Soviet claim that two invasions by Germany in twenty-seven years made the firm control of Eastern Europe essential to Russian security. Truman insisted on seeing the Soviets as the determinedly expansionist enemy of the free world almost from the day he assumed office. They were, he said, 'planning world conquest'.[2]

The United States over which he presided had emerged from the Second World War with a military and economic supremacy unparalleled

---

2   *Years of Decision* by Harry S. Truman, Hodder and Stoughton, 1955, p. 342

in history. Of the three powers which defeated the Axis alliance, the USA was unique in ending the war wealthier than when it began. By contrast, Britain's income was down by a third with much of its overseas assets sold to buy armaments from the USA. In the case of Russia, which had been responsible for destroying the vast bulk of Hitler's forces, the loss of income was immeasurable. Soviet statistics, always dubious, have never provided a wholly reliable picture of national income. But the scale of the devastation, involving at least twenty-two million and possibly twenty-seven million military and civilian deaths, speaks for itself.

There was in fact no evidence in 1945 that the Soviet Union had a sinister plan to conquer the West. The threat perceived by Truman and others was imaginary – though no less powerful for that – stoked up by years of fearing the deadly spread of Communism. We can gain a genuine insight into the Kremlin mood from opened Soviet archives. As the end of the war came in sight in 1944, the analyses of Moscow's senior diplomats anticipated a period of post-war East–West cooperation, if with reservations about possible future developments in American internal political rivalries. Nor did the Kremlin intend, as some feared, to mount a Communist takeover of Italy and France. Moscow wanted to see strong Communist parties in both countries able to influence policies in a way which would be advantageous to Russia. But having Communist governments in either country would have been contrary to the policy which Stalin always maintained: keeping Moscow as the absolute centre of the Communist world and thus something he alone could control. In any case, maintaining Communist governments in either country would have demanded the presence of Soviet troops which would have embroiled Moscow in the war which the Kremlin had every reason to avoid.

Stalin's attitude to the so-called world proletarian revolution is essential to understanding his personal and political motivation. He was, like the despot throughout the ages, principally concerned with his own survival rather than with ideological issues. He abandoned the grand global ambition of the world proletarian revolution in 1924 when he proclaimed that, henceforth, the aim was to be 'socialism in one country'. To believe that he remained at all times a devout ideologue is to misread his character.

Milovan Djilas, at one time Vice President of Yugoslavia, observed in *Conversations with Stalin*[3] that it was not altogether true, as some Communists complained, that Stalin was wholly against revolutions abroad. He was only in favour of those which he could control. He lost control of Yugoslavia. He was later to lose it in China – insofar as he ever had it.[4]

---

3   *Conversations with Stalin* by Milovan Djilas, New York, 1961, p. 114 et seq

4   Soviet archive material shows that Stalin's attitude was far from forgotten at the testy Sino-Soviet summit of July 1958. The minutes show Mao Zedong complaining about Stalin's lack of support. At the end of the Second World War he helped himself to territory which should have gone to the Chinese Communists: 'His first major error was one as a result of which the

Stalin's attitude to Communist parties abroad was really very simple. They were not there to win elections, only to act as his underlings, aiding Soviet foreign policy in all its shifts and changes, sometimes assisting one party or country, sometimes another. The overall aim was simply to promote weakness among nations which might be rivals or opponents or otherwise unhelpful to Russia. This was dramatically illustrated in the role allotted to the German Communist Party in the early 1930s. In combination with the left-wing Socialist Party it could have been enough to stop Hitler's rise to power.

But a Communist Party with real power in a German government, ruling an infinitely more advanced nation, was too much of a risk. The centre of gravity of Communism would shift away from Moscow, thus threatening Stalin's power and personal status. The German Communists were ordered not just to stay out of any coalition with the Socialists, but to attack them as 'social fascists'. George Kennan, who had been the State Department's leading Russian expert, wrote in 1962 (abandoning his famous analysis of a dire Soviet threat in 1946), 'From the bourgeois world as from his political entourage in the world of communism, Stalin only wanted one thing: weakness. This was not at all identified with revolution.'[5]

In the case of China, Stalin called on Mao to join with the Nationalists, not fight them. As the Communist forces swept south and came within sight of victory, Stalin pleaded with Mao to negotiate, not fight. The determination of the West to see every Soviet move as explicable in terms of the pursuit of the world proletarian revolution provides one of history's great ironies: the West took Communist doctrine more seriously than Stalin.

Truman claimed in his memoirs that it was at Potsdam that he finally concluded that the Soviet Union aimed at world conquest. Yet nothing that was said or done there could conceivably justify such a conclusion. The Russians were proving difficult and obstinate on certain issues but not aggressive. It was the issue of the internationalisation of waterways – a Truman obsession – which brought the President to his historically epic conclusion. The fate of the world in Truman's mind seemed to turn on, of all things, the Danube delta.

If Russia was in a demanding mood at Potsdam, it was not surprising. The Red Army had borne the brunt of the war. Of all the Germans killed, nearly nine out

---

Chinese Communist Party was left with one tenth of the territory that it had. His second error was that, when China was ripe for revolution, he advised us not to rise in revolution and said that if we started a war with Chiang Kai-shek that might threaten the entire nation with destruction ... after the victory of our revolution Stalin had doubts about its character. He believed that China was another Yugoslavia.'

'When I came to Moscow (in December 1949) he did not want to conclude a treaty of friendship with us and did not want to annul the old treaty with the Kuomintang.' (source: Cold War International History Project)

5   *Russia and the West under Lenin and Stalin*, by George Kennan, Little, Brown, 1961. p. 253

of ten perished on the Russia front. The Wehrmacht had thrown nearly ten times as many divisions at the Red Army as it did against Britain and the USA. And while Britain had been impoverished by the war, much of Russia had been laid waste. The USA – without a single bomb dropped on its mainland – had enjoyed a remarkable prosperity.

On the east European issue, it should have been evident enough at the time how Russia was driven by a desire to seek security in depth after the two devastating German invasions in twenty-seven years.[6] Moscow wanted a buffer between Russia and Germany and control over these territories. Stalin himself predicted to Djilas that the Germans would be back on their feet in twelve to fifteen years.[7] Though this seemed a daring prophecy at the time, given the wretched condition of Germany in 1945, he was to be proved too cautious. The German Federal Republic was not just back on its feet by the early 1950s, it was soon being asked to join NATO, precisely the sort of development which the Kremlin feared.

Given the German invasions, it would not have mattered whether the government in Moscow had been Communist, Tsarist or Social Democrat. It would still have insisted on firm control of these countries through which invasion had come; and bound to regard with deep suspicion any attempts to prevent it. In any case, Moscow could never forget that it was British and French policy in the interwar years to make Eastern Europe a barrier against the Soviet Union, even to consider – crucially – allowing Hitler a free hand against Russia. Colonel, later President, de Gaulle noted that even after the start of the Second World War:

> Certain circles saw the enemy in Stalin rather than Hitler. They busied themselves with finding means of striking Russia, either by aiding Finland or bombarding Baku or landing at Istanbul, much more than in coming to grips with Hitler.[8]

---

6   In the Second World War estimates of combined Soviet military and civilian deaths range widely, but 23m is a widely accepted figure, possibly conservative. Town and cities partially wrecked or burnt down: 1,700; villages destroyed: 70,000; railway lines destroyed: 65,000 kms; livestock killed or shipped to Germany: 7m horses, 17m head of cattle. Estimates of Russian deaths in the First World War vary considerably but it is widely accepted that 2m soldiers were killed. Territory lost by the old Russia ran to over 300,000 sq. miles. Much of it, most importantly the Ukraine, was recovered by Bolshevik forces with the Baltic States, including Finland, becoming independent nations. For comparison, Anglo-American deaths in the Second World War amounted to less than 1m.

7   When Djilas suggested that Germany would take a long time to recover, Stalin replied: 'No, they will recover very quickly. It is a highly industrialised country with an extremely skilled and numerous working class and technical intelligentsia. Give them 12–15 years and they'll be on their feet again.'

8   *The Collapse of the Third Republic* by William L. Shirer, Simon and Schuster, 1969, p. 544

Nor could the Soviets overlook the fact that, among its new satellites, Romania, Hungary and Bulgaria had fought on the Axis side. Moreover, Poland could be blamed for the Russo-Polish war in 1920 which followed the creation of the Soviet Union.

Only someone who had already made up his mind about Soviet intentions could have claimed that the aim was 'world conquest'. The suspicions which seemed to lurk constantly in Russian minds about the West were widely viewed as paranoid, given that the world was hungry for peace and cooperation. But it could be argued that the Kremlin had much to be paranoid about, given the history of the interwar years. British and French policy seemed so ready to solve the problem of Hitler by turning him eastwards. It is impossible to understand the Kremlin's fears without recounting those extraordinary manoeuvres, culminating in serious proposals in Britain and France that the two countries should be prepared to go to war against Russia – just after the war with Germany had broken out – in defence of Finland, then under attack from the Red Army. The country held a strategic key for Russia against Germany.

The wartime alliance of Britain, Russia and the USA certainly showed that East–West cooperation was possible. Friendly gestures by President Roosevelt made an impression on both the Kremlin and opinion at home. A friendly post-war settlement was seen as possible not just in the West but also in the extensive analyses made in the Soviet Foreign ministry by its senior diplomats. But that was while Roosevelt was alive. Once Truman took over on the President's death in 1945, it quickly became apparent that old ferocious suspicions of expanding Communism, dating back to the Bolshevik revolution, had made their return, this time with the USA indisputably the most powerful nation on earth. This made conditions all too well suited for a collision of mammoth proportions.

Yet it must be said that the great bulk of Americans, when peace broke out in 1945, were full of good intentions – though intertwined with a belief that what was good for the USA must be good for mankind, particularly where open markets and free trade were concerned. The new-found strength of the USA provided a chance to mould the post-war world, to propagate democracy, plus liberal capitalism, which, in American minds, would constitute a safeguard against future wars. This faith in democracy conveniently overlooked, among other things, the fact that Hitler had advanced to power in 1933 through a democratic vote.

The real problem at this point was not the generally benevolent intentions of the USA but its naivety about the outside world's complexities, its varied cultures, its long-standing nationalistic rivalries and in particular often strong feelings of insecurity. These were feelings hard to comprehend in a nation which could not remember any invasion and which had not suffered a single bullet or bomb fall on its mainland during the Second World War. However, it was not just the USA which insisted on misreading the post-war conditions. Some of Europe's statesmen with long histories of fearing the Communist virus also believed that the battered Soviet Union was ready to fight the West. This should have been seen as absurd. It requires no technical knowledge of military matters to appreciate the point.

Suppose, even ignoring the deterrent of the A-bomb, that the Red Army had attacked the West soon after the end of the war. It would have encountered strong resistance from the British, the Americans and hastily rearmed elements of the Wehrmacht. It would have been a hard fight but let us suppose that the Russian forces reached the Channel ports. What then?

The invasion of Britain would have been virtually impossible. The Soviets had neither the air nor sea power to make the crossing and huge numbers of troops would have been needed as occupying forces throughout Europe. Meanwhile American troops, aircraft and war supplies would have been pouring into Britain. However, let us suppose, again for the sake of argument, and against all conceivable odds, that the Russians had succeeded in occupying Britain as well as all of Western Europe. What then? The Soviet Union would have been left facing the Americans across three thousand miles of ocean. It would be the ultimate unwinnable war, a military planners' ultimate nightmare.

In short, the threat was a hallucination. The USA's Central Intelligence Agency carried out a study in 1946 which concluded that the shattered Soviet Union would not even be in a position to wage a war for fifteen years. Yet the fear of a Russian onslaught persisted. The sheer size of the Red Army, only slowly being demobilised, was regularly advanced as evidence of malign intentions. But the desire to retain large forces against the possibility of another German revival plus the need – as Moscow saw it – to maintain a grip on Eastern Europe was logical.

We have to wonder why the West was consumed by fears of Russia when the war ended. To a considerable extent, it was inspired by a seductively simple belief that Stalin was another Hitler. The USA and Britain were emerging from a war which it was generally accepted started because Hitler had been appeased. The parallel with Stalin seemed irresistible. He was no less of a dictator than Hitler and just as brutal, certainly more whimsical in his ruthlessness. Moreover Marxist doctrine in its purer and original form proclaimed the inevitability of a Communist world. Hitler had finally revealed the full scale of the Nazi menace when he seized Czechoslovakia. Now Stalin, after the war, was refusing to give up control of Eastern Europe. The parallel seemed easy enough. In fact this was another of those historical examples of 'over-learning' the apparent lessons of the day.

This simplistic view of 1945 took no account of the differences between the two episodes. Hitler had no need of Czechoslovakia, except to continue his surge eastwards. Stalin saw control of Poland as essential to Russian security against Germany. The occupation of that country and the imposition of a Communist government in Warsaw was a very sore issue for Britain which had gone to war ostensibly to save Poland. It was seen as a mark of failure and a breach of honour that the country should be left occupied by another dictator. The USA, for its part, had been dragged into the war but was eager to convince itself that it was embarking on a high-minded crusade to save democracy and all the values associated with it. Less high-mindedly, as President Roosevelt reminded Stalin at the Yalta conference, there were some six to seven million Polish-American voters in the USA to say nothing of others with links to the occupied east European countries – the so-called hyphenate vote (capable, he was warned, of turning a presidential election). Both Britain and the USA insisted on seeing Poland as the acid test of Moscow's goodwill and peaceful intentions. Minds refused to meet.

Where Truman stood on Eastern Europe was never in much doubt. His Navy Day speech in October 1945, with its declarations about firm American resistance to tyrannies and its assistance to those opposing them, sent a plain enough message to Moscow. The fact that its belligerent tone had a limited impact in the US at that moment must be attributed to the fact that the war had finally ended only weeks before. Assertions about American righteousness were only to be expected.

There was also the history of the Russian civil war which helped to stoke up the deep and at times apparently neurotic suspicions of the Soviet Union towards the West, an instinct which was also very Russian and existed well before the revolution. In the first three years after the 1917 revolution the new Bolshevik government faced military help provided by the west European powers to its internal rivals in efforts to destroy the Soviet state. This wish seemed to persist even after Stalin soft-pedalled the notion of the world proletarian revolution.[9] In the 1930s, the Russians had good reason to fear that at least part of British and French policy towards Hitler was inspired by a desire to turn him eastwards. Both Britain and the USA, but more particularly Britain, had managed to convince themselves in the interwar years that the Red Menace remained serious. Any protestations of peaceful intentions from Moscow were seen as just a disguise for the underlying purposes of revolutionary Marxism–Leninism. Besides and perhaps even more important, playing up the Communist threat was proving a serious vote winner for the British Conservatives – as indeed it was to prove a vote winner for American politicians from the late 1940s onwards.

As a consequence, the wartime alliance of Russia and the West was a brittle affair on both sides. Any sign that Britain and the USA were reluctant to throw everything they had at Germany – there were unfulfilled promises of a Second Front in 1942 and then in 1943 – fuelled Soviet suspicion. The Allies, Moscow claimed, were not seriously drawing off German divisions but were leaving Russia to do the hard fighting.

There was also the problem of Churchill's own attitude to Russia. In December 1918 he had called unavailingly for an anti-Communist crusade, to include the

---

9   Djilas recorded that Stalin felt instinctively that the creation of revolutionary centres outside Moscow would endanger its supremacy in world Communism and that of course is exactly what happened. That is why he helped revolutions up to a certain point – as long as he could control them, 'but he was always ready to leave them in the lurch'. Djilas, op. cit., pp. 114 et seq.

defeated Germans, to march on Moscow. It is true that he was one of the few Western politicians in the late 1930s calling for an alliance with Russia to contain Hitler. But as early as 1943 his old hostility resurfaced and he was saying that it might be wrong to disarm the Germans too far since they might be needed against the Russians. He repeated it in 1944. The Kremlin knew of this.

Russian fears that the West might sign a separate peace with Germany – at times reciprocated in the West by a fear that Russia might do the same – were regular. Churchill was also to write in a memorandum in 1944 that if the issues of Poland and, oddly, Soviet reparations from Germany were not settled, it would be hard to avoid a third world war. Churchill's argument over Poland was at least an obvious one. But treating the reparations issue as a potential *casus belli* was eccentric. After victory in 1918, Lloyd George had promised to 'squeeze Germany until the pips squeak'. The reparations forced on Berlin after the First World War then were a mistake which Churchill in particular recognised. He argued that a weakened Germany would hinder the economic recovery of Europe as well as leave a bitter legacy. The Russian demands for reparations from Germany after the Second World War, thought unreasonable by the USA and Britain, were no more than an echo of Lloyd George. Russia wanted revenge for the devastation caused by the Germans.

Churchill has long been associated with the start of the Cold War because of his famous Iron Curtain speech in 1946 at Fulton, Missouri. But his active role in the early years of the Cold War should not be exaggerated; he was only the Leader of the Opposition in the Commons. In mid-1945 he was voted out of office and replaced by Clement Attlee, halfway through the vital Potsdam conference. The new Prime Minister was far less inclined to see a great Soviet threat in the making. Churchill's prestige, on the other hand, even out of office, was enormous and global. He was one of history's truly great men. He had saved Britain, if not civilisation, from Nazi Germany. For many his Fulton speech – though the Labour government contemplated openly disowning it – was proof to many that the West was now faced with a new version of Hitler.

In allotting blame for the start of the Cold War, Churchill certainly has to bear some share. But predominantly, as the evidence shows, it was the Americans who must shoulder the main responsibility. They were to blame too for the continuation of the struggle when détente was on the cards. Washington, under the influence of John Foster Dulles as Secretary of State, ignored overtures from Moscow after the death of Stalin in 1953. Churchill, back in power by then, was by contrast eager to follow up these offers but was firmly warned off by Dulles.

Russia played a role, but a small one, in stimulating the onset of the Cold War. Soviet tactics in negotiations on matters large and small could be extremely tiresome, at times suggesting little desire for serious cooperation. And the ruthlessness which Stalin's forces displayed in the occupied and reoccupied territories as they swept westwards was bound to outrage Western feelings. But it did not in itself presage any intentions to occupy areas outside the sphere seen as essential to strategic defence.

Despots, though always repugnant, are not necessarily dangerous outside their own borders. The fact that Stalin was evil did not necessarily mean that his foreign policy was evil. And in the later stages of the Cold War, the USA itself was to back decidedly repressive and brutal regimes. These were vital tactics for defence, ran the argument. The Kremlin would not have argued with that general principle, though it was always ready during the Cold War to exploit the embarrassment that backing dictators was to cause within the USA.

The level of mutual suspicion which came to exist within months of the end of the Second World War was graphically illustrated by the two secret long telegrams of 1946 which travelled between Moscow and Washington as each nation's ambassador warned his government to beware of the other side's imperialist ambitions.

CHAPTER 2
TWO LONG TELEGRAMS: MUTUALLY ASSURED DISTRUST

1946: Moscow and Washington's envoys in mirror image warnings – George Kennan later regrets his message – Truman steps up military assistance to Greece and Turkey – the military-industrial complex – problems in US diplomatic methods

In the earliest years of the Cold War, George Kennan was seen as the US State Department's top Russian expert. Author of the famous Long Telegram to Washington in February 1946 – nearly 8,000 words – he was at the time *chargé d'affaires* in Moscow. (For full text see Cold War International History Project.) Kennan had not just the advantage of being fluent in Russian, a historian and a professional diplomat. He was also the sort of cultured figure who might be cited to show that it was not just untravelled, inexperienced, hard bitten individuals from business or the military who dreamt about the Red Menace.

However, as will be seen, there were two George Kennans. The first fitted the outlook if not the character of a typical Cold War warrior. The later Kennan Mk II was to prove a prolonged critic of the USA's aggressive policies, ironically so inspired by Kennan Mk I.

In his original message he argued that the Soviet Union still saw itself as living 'in a world of antagonistic world encirclement' which owed much to a traditional, 'neurotic and instinctive' Russian view of the world. Marxism was a perfect vehicle for this sense of insecurity; and the importance of Marxist dogma in Soviet affairs must not be underrated. The Soviet Union did not believe that peaceful coexistence was possible and would seek to accomplish its goals by the 'total destruction of rival power'.

America had to face 'a political force committed fanatically to the belief … that it is desirable and necessary that the internal harmony of our society be disrupted, our traditional way of life destroyed, the internal authority of our state be broken, if Soviet power is to survive'.

Kennan's views, with an initially limited circulation in Washington, were more widely aired when he wrote the next year in the magazine *Foreign Affairs* under the pseudonym 'Mr X'.[10] (His authorship was soon unmasked.) He explained how Russia with its 'aggressive intentions' could be 'contained'.

'It will be seen that Soviet pressure against the free institutions of the Western World is something that can be contained by the adroit and vigilant application of counter-force at a series of constantly shifting geographical and political points corresponding to the shifts and manoeuvres of Soviet policy but which cannot be talked or charmed out of existence.'

Between the time of the Long Telegram and Article X, the Soviet Ambassador in Washington, Andrei Novikov, settled down to a similar analysis.[11] It was to prove a mirror image of Kennan's. In September 1946, Novikov summarised the purposes and motives of American foreign policy. They had become as clear to him as the Kremlin's were to Kennan. Novikov explained in 4,000 words that 'American monopoly capitalism' was aiming at world domination.

The two warning messages encapsulate much of the tragedy of the Cold War. Each side was convinced of the other's aggressive ambitions – as convinced in fact as each was of the rectitude of its own policies, seen clearly as defensive. Both telegrams stated a number of truths, but not enough to justify their conclusions.

Kennan Mk I was surprisingly insensitive about Soviet security fears. He stated at one point that with Germany and Japan eliminated, it was 'sheerest nonsense' for Moscow to fear military attack from anyone. But as the Russians could remember, German military power had been severely limited by the Treaty of Versailles. Yet little more than a decade later Hitler embarked on a rearmament campaign which produced a vast war machine. If Kennan could not foresee the possibility of another German revival, the Russians certainly could. And with the new Federal Republic of Germany called on by the West to rearm (less than a decade after Kennan's comments), Soviet apprehension could hardly be deemed 'sheerest nonsense'.

It was certainly true, as Kennan argued, that convinced Marxists foresaw the inevitable triumph of Communism across the globe as proletariats everywhere shook off the bonds of capitalism – or in the case of Asia, of feudalism. But much as they would welcome that occurring soon, the sheer inevitability of the process meant that time and example were on their side. Communism would prove to be irresistible, both as a political system and as an economic form of organisation. True Marxist-Leninists had only to wait, meanwhile looking to their own safety, in case the capitalist world resorted to the use of military or semi-military means against the USSR. A certain missionary zeal meant that a push here or there was a duty, as was their theoretical obligation to support Communist parties across the globe. But Russia after the Second World War was not in a position to

---

10 See *The Cold Warriors*, John Donovan, Heath and Co, 1976, pp. 65–70
11 For full text see CWIHP

do much pushing. No less significant was Stalin's hostility to the establishment of Communist states which he could not directly control. He may have been a Marxist (of sorts) but he was foremost an exponent of realpolitik.

The Americans also had their own ideas about inevitability: the eventual global triumph of democracy and liberal capitalism. Like the Soviets, they too were convinced that time and example was on their side. The immediate need was safety from another war and a world in which American prosperity could continue. That meant a world where American business could flourish on the international stage, untrammelled by the tariff wars and economic chauvinism which had impoverished everyone in the interwar years.

This point was recognised in the second telegram, Novikov emphasising American ambitions to open up markets throughout the world for the access of trade and capital. The fact that the war had left the USA with military bases all round the world which it showed no sign of vacating underlined the American desire in Novikov's analysis to encircle the Soviet Union.[12]

Of the two views, Novikov's was backed up by a greater proportion of facts rather than surmise. The USA, he correctly said, was worried that the end of the war might bring a severe recession to its factories and the repetition of the trade wars of the 1930s. Fears were indeed being voiced in the administration that the impoverished post-war world might be unable to buy American goods. The need for free trade in goods and capital throughout the world was to prove a constant theme of the US government from the earliest stages of the Cold War.

Whether the Americans as a whole were quite as politically and economically ambitious in 1946 as Novikov maintained is questionable. The need for action to advance American economic interests was not questioned. An active global policy for political domination and involvement on the other hand had little popular appeal at that time. But it was to grow over the next decades to the point where the affairs of every nation came to be seen as the legitimate political (and moral) interest of the USA. Seen from the standpoint of the 21st century, Novikov had the best of the argument.

Both the Kennan documents, the Long Telegram and X Article, provided authority for views which had been taking root in most parts of the administration. Yet Kennan himself was later to say that he looked back on the Long Telegram 'with a sort of horrified amusement'. It might have been written, he said in his memoirs, for the (fiercely conservative) Daughters of the American Revolution. He was to go on in the 1950s to preach the virtues of détente with the Soviets.

He also complained that his call for Russia to be 'contained' had been taken to mean militarily. He had wanted, he said, to stress 'political containment'. It was not a very convincing argument since it was hard to see, particularly for a man of his intellectual background, how an idea or an ideology could be 'contained'. The

---

12 See CWIHP, 1990 documents collection

reality was that he changed his mind when he returned from Moscow to the State Department and saw at first hand the belligerent attitudes which were coming to dominate US policy.

Following the lines of the two telegrams each side was to attribute aggressive motives to the other. This had inevitable consequences. Every move by either side was seen as part of a plan to weaken the other – politically, economically or strategically. The USA's diplomacy was not subtle. It was often conducted in the glare of publicity which is habitual in American politics and was in many instances driven by the urge to score points for electoral purposes. If it was not for the Presidential elections, it was for the intervening Congressional elections. The so-called hyphenate vote (Polish-Americans, Italian-Americans, etc.) was strongly anti-Soviet and could swing a national result.

The Russians had no such electoral or publicity problems. But, suspicious by nature, they were among the most tiresome of negotiators, sometimes seeming like the Red Army itself, determined to wear down the other side by sheer stamina. The personality of the granite-faced Molotov as Soviet Foreign Minister played a part in this process. There was also the problem during the Cold War that no Soviet official, if he valued his position – or even his skin – would dare to take an initiative on his own. The rigidity of the system meant that clearance at the top was always necessary for any gesture which smacked of friendliness. *Niet* was always the easiest answer.

Nikita Khrushchev, who rose to the Soviet leadership in the mid-1950s, was to describe Molotov's character as showing on occasions 'unbelievable stubbornness, bordering on stupidity'.[13] Yet various issues remaining from the war were in fact eventually resolved with him through foreign ministers' conferences, such as the peace treaties with Germany's former allies. But the process was wearisome and there were rarely any displays of goodwill or friendship. The Russians, questions of defence apart, thought the USA remarkably insensitive about the huge sacrifices in men, material and infrastructure they had suffered in destroying the Wehrmacht.

The Americans found it genuinely hard to understand how Russian propaganda could ascribe imperialist ambitions to them. Had not the USA been a champion of freedom and democracy and an outspoken enemy of colonialism? The Russians, still mired in Marxism, could not understand how the USA could attribute imperialism to the Soviet Union. Was not the point of Marxism–Leninism that it liberated the proletariat? The two powers used the same word but refused to share its meaning.

The Soviets in 1945 were also convinced that they brought liberation (of another kind) to the territories they took. The governments of Poland, Hungary and Romania between the wars were hardly model democracies. The new forms of government allowed in Hungary and Romania had, at first, some elements of democracy; and Czechoslovakia returned to its fuller pre-war pattern. But after 1948 all elements of

---

13   *The Glasnost Tapes* by Tr Slector and Luchknow, Little, Brown, 1990, pp. 77, 87

democracy were removed. The full Communist pattern was imposed which – the Soviets liked to believe – would also bring clear economic progress.

KENNAN MK II

The belief that Kennan Mk I was calling for military containment was readily accepted in Washington. Indeed that seemed to be understood by him at that time. He observed the sharp rise in the defence budget and the warlike pronouncements of the administration without immediately seeking to correct the impression that containment had to be essentially military. He should not have been surprised either that the logic of his warning led to a high degree of interference by the USA in the affairs of countries close to the Soviet bloc. If the Russians had to be contained militarily, the effective frontiers against them had to be manned. He was remarkably slow to correct this impression. His doubts about his own 'X' article became evident when he pleaded later that it had only been written originally for the 'private edification' of James Forrestal, the Defense Secretary (later to commit suicide after a bout of persecution mania).

The fact that the article helped to stimulate policies of rearmament went down particularly well with what President Eisenhower later dubbed 'the industrial-military complex' in his departing address to the nation. Left so abruptly with redundant military plant when the war ended, the defence industries were delighted at the prospect of new orders and the military with rising budgets.

The policy of containment was taken up with enthusiasm by Clark Clifford, a White House adviser to President Truman. In September 1946, he wrote a memorandum declaring that coexistence was impossible and advocating a worldwide strategy based on the A-bomb to 'restrain the Soviet Union and to confine Soviet influence to its present area'.[14] The language was violent. The stage seemed to be set for a military confrontation with the Soviets, despite the CIA study suggesting it would remain militarily ineffective for some years. An updated version of the memorandum, with no dilution of its extreme views, was to become NSC-68 (National Security Council) in 1950.

Kennan's disillusionment about the effect of his earlier analyses started during his brief tenure as Ambassador to Moscow from 1952–53. He wrote in his memoirs:

> A particularly violent jolt was received one day when one of the service attachés showed me a message he had received from Washington concerning a certain step of a military nature that the Pentagon proposed to take for the purpose of strengthening our military posture in a region not far from the Soviet

---

14 The full Clifford-Elsey report was unexpectedly made public through the veteran White House journalist Arthur Krock, see appendix in *Memoirs* by Arthur Krock, Cassel & Co, 1968

frontier. I paled when I read it. It was at once apparent to me that had I been a Soviet leader and had I learned that such a step was being taken I would have concluded that the Americans were shaping their preparations towards a target of a war within six months.[15]

In 1952 Kennan was to send another telegram to Washington attempting to undo the hardline attitudes he had reinforced. He called for moderation in relations with the Soviet Union. He described this later telegram at the time as: '... The strongest statement I ever made of my views on this general subject of our responsibility for the deterioration of relations between Russia and the West in the late 1940s.'[16]

He went on to write that the USA was determined to:

Teach itself and the NATO associates never to refer to the most menacing element of our military potential otherwise than as 'the nuclear deterrent' – the unmistakable implication being that the Russians, longing for inauguration of World War III, would at once attack if not deterred by the agency of retribution. Year after year nothing would be omitted to move American air bases and missile sites as close as possible to Soviet frontiers. Year after year, American naval vessels would be sent on useless demonstration expeditions into the Black Sea – thus, by implication, imputing to the Russians a degree of patience which our own public and congressional opinion would be most unlikely to master had the shoe been on the other foot.

Time after time, as in Pakistan and Okinawa, the maintenance and development of military or air bases would be stubbornly pursued with no evidence of any effort to balance this against the obvious political costs. Political interests would similarly be sacrificed or put in jeopardy by the avid and greedy pursuit of military intelligence.[17]

One hardliner who would not repent was Dean Acheson, Secretary of State from 1949 to 1953. While Under Secretary during the Truman period, he propounded his version of what was later called the domino theory, which was so effective in entangling the USA in the Vietnam war. Acheson argued that a victory for Communism in Greece, Turkey or Iran or any of the other countries of the Near East or the Mediterranean region would lead rapidly to the collapse of pro-Western governments throughout Europe.

The seeds of the Cold War which had been sown in warlike warnings to Russia by Truman were to grow thick and fast in the wake of the Long Telegram. The influential Senator Arthur Vandenberg spoke in the Senate of the need to stop

---

15   George Kennan *Memoirs*, Boston, 1972, pp. 136–137
16   Ibid. p. 137
17   Ibid. pp. 142–143

'appeasement' of the Soviet Union. James Byrnes, the Secretary of State, delivered a warning that no country had the right to station troops in the territories of other sovereign nations 'without their consent'. That of course sounded fine and even-handed. But the point was that other countries which agreed to American bases were so much in need of US economic assistance that they could rarely resist Washington's military planners.

Byrnes also criticised the Soviets for taking, or looting, Japanese industrial equipment in Manchuria before any formal agreement had been reached on reparations. But such an agreement, as the Russians knew, would be hard to achieve with the Americans. In any case it was easy for the USA to take this high-minded attitude on reparations. It had emerged from the war with a surplus of industrial plant.

It was also time, Washington decided, to deter suspected Russian ambitions in Turkey and – as they supposed – in Greece, even though the aid for rebels there came from Yugoslavia against Stalin's specific wishes. He told Djilas:

> The uprising in Greece will have to fold up. Do you think that Great Britain and the USA – the USA the most powerful nation in the world – will permit you to break the line of communication in the Mediterranean? And we have no navy. The uprising in Greece must be stopped as quickly as possible.[18]

But Washington's view persisted that the menace in Greece was from the Soviets. Truman agreed to a proposal from Forrestal that a task force including an aircraft carrier should be earmarked for a display of American power in the eastern Mediterranean. 'The Truman Doctrine' was being created.

THE CHARACTER OF AMERICAN DIPLOMACY

Given the gap between the two powers as demonstrated by the two telegrams, it would have needed the most skilful diplomacy to bring either side to an understanding of the other's position. Sadly, the quality of diplomacy during the early years of the Cold War was lamentable – and it was to get no better with the passage of time. On the US side, the reign of John Foster Dulles at the State Department (1953–1959) was to see a foreign policy designed to scare the Soviet Union into submission. The death of Stalin and gestures of détente by the new leadership opened up new prospects which were promptly rebuffed. The British and French governments tried to redress the balance but, as decidedly junior partners in the alliance were unable to do so. There was also an inclination in Washington to listen to military hotheads in formulating policy.

---

18   Milovan Djilas, op. cit., p. 114 et seq

On the Soviet side, the interregnum of Georgii Malenkov, Stalin's immediate successor, was followed by the reign of Nikita Khrushchev whose volatile and emotional behaviour made East–West negotiations difficult. His erratic behaviour was to upset not just Western leaders but also his colleagues – and be a key factor in his ultimate downfall

The problems of American diplomacy arose from certain national psychological characteristics which lent an aggressive edge to the country's foreign policy. The USA has always been a fiercely competitive society in fields ranging from business to sport and many other fields. It has long been characterised by the unmatched flow of 'how to succeed' books. It is an important cause of the country's success as a leader in those and so many other fields.

The will to win is a fine thing but in diplomacy it can be a recipe for trouble. The United States expected not just to win but also to win demonstrably. Yet draws are the essence of successful diplomacy. Each side should be able to conclude negotiations without humiliation or loss of pride; otherwise disagreements are likely to fester. European nations with a long history of sometimes winning, sometimes losing are more ready to accept draws.

Matters were inevitably made worse in the USA by that constant glare of publicity. Positions were expounded before negotiations. The progress of talks was described in detail while they were still ongoing. And the negotiator was expected to return with the laurels of a winner. And where Eastern Europe was concerned, the importance of the hyphenate vote was never forgotten.

Rigidity was certainly a charge that stuck to both sides during the Cold War. But at least the Kremlin did not have to worry much about public opinion or announce the results of negotiations other than in the most considered form. Nor was it obliged to care about the political views of the military which were to become so marked and so well publicised in the USA. This was a problem – along with the influence of the defence industries – which was to seriously worry President Eisenhower by the time he left office.

Once the Cold War was well under way, the rigidity of American diplomacy became particularly marked. So much effort had been expended in describing the wickedness of communism that compromises were liable to look immoral in themselves – and sure to be labelled as such by numerous, rabidly anti-Soviet (and often highly religious) elements in the USA. The rigidity was certainly liable to be made worse by the American taste for military men – not given by nature to compromises – in top political or diplomatic positions. Three Secretaries of State since the late 1940s have been generals: George Marshall, Alexander Haig and Colin Powell. General Bedell Smith became Under Secretary of State. Haig sought the Republican nomination for the Presidency, withdrawing at the last minute when George H Bush was overhauling him. Air Force General 'Hap' Arnold became the Vice Presidential candidate alongside segregationist George Wallace in a third party campaign. The highly politicised CIA had three directors from the armed forces.

The practice of entrusting supreme power to military men reaches back into the 19th century when three generals were voted into the White House – Andrew Jackson, Zachary Taylor and Ulysses Grant. No other Western democracy adopted a remotely comparable practice of militarisation.

For an understanding of the deep-seated Soviet fear of the West and its response when it was stimulated, it is essential to look back beyond even the interwar years to the longer historical background. For the Cold War was a clash of two long-established empires, often mirroring each other in their urge to expand. But, remarkably, it was also a clash in which both sides made such a point of denying their imperial history.

CHAPTER 3
THE EXPANSION OF AMERICA: FROM COLONY TO SUPERPOWER

Growth of both the USA and Russia – from insignificance to global power – rising senses of mission – US ambitions extend in the Pacific – Woodrow Wilson ignores his pledges – the path to global hegemony

The freshly founded USA consisted of only three million people, occupying the original thirteen states. The expansion which followed was more than just a desire for economic survival. The American Indians were progressively displaced, regardless of various treaties. The Louisiana Purchase was made under a threat to France that it must sell or the territory would be seized. It doubled the size of the original thirteen colonies. The acquisition of the Spanish colony of Florida followed. Next came the openly expansionist war with Mexico which led to the seizure of a vast area: Texas, California, New Mexico, Nevada, Arizona and Utah plus part of what now form the states of Colorado, Wyoming, Kansas and Oklahoma.

The drive for new territories then extended overseas. After acquiring a naval base on the Pearl River, the USA took over the independent Kingdom of Hawaii. The drive for new commercial interests did not stop there. In 1845, Congress declared that Korea and Japan should be opened up for US trade, both nations being strongly resistant to outside influences. In the case of Japan Commodore Perry arrived with a fleet and a threat. If Japan did not 'open up', he would return with a larger fleet. The resentful Japanese bowed to the inevitable, adopting a policy of rapid industrialisation – which the Americans were later bitterly to regret.

The American mood was now fiercely imperialist. A leading spokesman for the Democrats, John O'Sullivan declared, in what was to become a popular cry, that it was the country's 'manifest destiny to possess the whole of the continent which Providence has given us for the development of the great experiment of liberty'.[19]

Once this frame of mind had descended on the country it was inevitable that the then Spanish colony of Cuba was soon to be in Washington's sights. Spain was soon pushed out and the territory of Puerto Rico also incorporated. The Spanish colony of the Philippines, though far away, was next on the list. American opinion had long sympathised with 'little brown brother' in fighting the Spanish rulers. Once they took over, the Americans found themselves also fighting the irregulars; and it took some time to quell them. It was not until 1935 that Washington agreed to the principle of Philippine independence, not finally granted until 1946 and only then with an arrangement for the USA to retain naval bases.

When Woodrow Wilson, the stern Presbyterian from Princeton, took over, the mood seemed to falter and he promised never again to acquire any territory by conquest. But the USA took over the affairs of the Dominican Republic and Nicaragua. In the case of Mexico, Wilson had no hesitation about interference. It was in forcing a change of government that Wilson bombarded Vera Cruz with the death of 100 or so Mexicans. Another skirmish followed with the next Mexican president.

Wilson's desire to teach others to elect good men was much in evidence when he swept into the Versailles conference. This messianic sense of mission was to be transmitted to later US Presidencies.

THE RISE OF THE RUSSIAN/SOVIET EMPIRE

Russia's growth from a primitive principality to an empire was as remarkable as the rise in size of the USA. But it was driven in part by the lack of natural boundaries and a history of constant invasion. The steppes stretched endlessly away to the east. Bloody onslaughts against the nascent Russian state came from the Huns, Avars, Kazars, Patsinaks, Cunams and most formidably from the Mongols, or Tatars, who made the small original principality into a vassal state for 200 years. The killings by the Tatars alone are among the greatest massacres in pre-20th century history.

The topography also made orderly rule difficult. To the east and south lay a series of disorderly Khanates whose borders did not hold back tribal raiders. The acquisition of these territories for security and wealth seemed natural. There were also attacks from the west. Livonia, the old version of Lithuania, was a formidable aggressor. Battles against the Teutonic Knights were a major feature in Russian children's history books. Under Ivan the Terrible, Russia became an aggressive and effective power. The bloody methods he employed against internal and external enemies naturally appealed to Stalin, who had him made the subject of an adulatory film by the film maker Sergei Eisenstein.

Modernisation of the state was extremely slow. Sheer distance made Russia a difficulty country to rule efficiently. Insofar as it produced competent administrators they had to act with constant reference to the faraway imperial court. Size only proved a real strength in invasions as both Napoleon and Hitler discovered. The state had a unique weapon of mass destruction – winter.

The growing size of Russia and an emergence of the typical 19th century appetite for territory produced excited fears in the West that Russia would impose its power on the ramshackle Ottoman empire, seize parts of the Balkans under Turkish rule and even make a grab for Constantinople – though Russia had ruled out this step. In 1852 Britain and France drifted into the Crimean War, famous for its military and organisational incompetence. It was sparked, absurdly, by a brawl between Catholic priests (supported by France) and Greek orthodox priests (supported by Russia) over rights at the Church of the Holy Nativity. In Russia the conflict was seen in terms of protection for her Greek Orthodox co-religionists under Ottoman rule. It developed with the growth of panslavism into saving their fellow Slavs in the Balkans from brutal rule by Turkey. Gladstone was to make Ottoman rule infamous in his 'Balkan atrocities' campaign which brought him back into politics and later into the premiership again.

Russia's more secular and regular demands for more entrenched rights to use the Bosphorous Straits for access to the Mediterranean were seen in London and Paris as a persistent threat. Though Britain and France won the Crimean War, it was not entirely clear what the conflict had achieved, other than promoting hostility and suspicion on both sides.

From the middle of the 19th century until 1945, Russia had little to record but defeats. Tsarist governments eyed India with interest from time to time but never very seriously. But it helped to maintain fears of the Bear, huge, powerful and primitive and with an insatiable desire to expand its poorly-ruled domain. The crumbling Ottoman empire certainly presented an easy target for more acquisitions, coloured by the usual claims that it was a rescue of Christians – including those in the Balkans – from Islamic rule. The Tsarist empire reached a peak when it consolidated its position on the Pacific coast. But territorial disputes with Japan in 1904 led to war, the sinking of the Russian fleet and total humiliation of the Tsarist government. It was forced to concede a constitution providing, in theory, for Western-style liberties under an elected assembly.

The pattern of Russian alliances changed drastically in the years before 1914. The rise of Germany since the Franco-Prussian war posed a new potential threat. Russia and France formed an alliance providing that each would aid the other if attacked by Germany. St Petersburg did little to ease relations with the central powers. Panslavism had become strong. Support in spirit, though not in arms, helped spark off two untidy wars in the Balkans in 1912 and 1913, in which Serbia, Bulgaria, Macedonia. Greece and Turkey were all involved. The conflicts were contained by the major powers through diplomacy, chiefly by the ambassadors of the major powers meeting in London. Serbia remained a problem. It was deeply resentful of the Austrian annexation of Bosnia-Herzegovina in 1908, previously only 'administered' by Vienna through an agreement with St Petersburg. It culminated in the fatal shots in Sarajevo and the outbreak of the First World War, Russia fulfilling its role in coming to the aid of France.

For two years, Russia met with successes. It had some skilful generals as well as its large, if ill-equipped, armies. But after the defeat at Tannenberg, disintegration began. In March 1917, the 'liberal revolution' swept aside the Tsar. The new government's desire to continue to fight on the Allied side was deeply unpopular in Russia and contributed to the success of the Bolsheviks in October. The need for the new government to achieve peace led to the Treaty of Brest-Litovsk. The appalled Bolshevik emissaries were confronted with total humiliation. They were forced to sign an agreement in which the old imperial Russia's losses included Poland, Finland, Latvia, Lithuania, Estonia and a large part of the Ukraine. It also meant the loss of 90 per cent of its coal mines, more than half of its industrial plants and half of its cultivated crop areas. Thus Russia ended the war with fearful losses, including some two million killed in action. Only a quarter of the army put into the field emerged unscathed. More casualties followed in the subsequent civil war, despite which the Red Army reconquered the Ukraine.

The fear that Communism would spread was very strong in the West with Churchill unsuccessfully urging his multinational march on Moscow. But British troops were to be sent to Russia to aid the Whites against the Reds. By early 1919, France, Britain, Romania, Italy, Serbia and Greece and Japan had sent troops to Russia, principally in support of the Whites' General Denikin. Much of their role was confined to controlling the areas nominally loyal to the Whites with the fighting left to Denikin's own troops. However, by the summer, most of these contingents had been withdrawn, partly because the cause was unpopular at home and partly because Denikin looked a lost cause.

Another peril faced the new Soviet government in the following year, this time from a revived Poland. Warsaw was dissatisfied with the western frontier decreed at Versailles, the so-called Curzon Line. A hastily assembled Polish army made great advances into the Ukraine, assisted by military advisers from France. But it was finally defeated by the new Red Army which pushed as far as Warsaw before the Treaty of Riga patched up a peace. Poland gained over 50,000 square miles. The Poles insisted that they had merely made a pre-emptive strike. Lenin liked to believe that a Soviet advance would inspire proletarian uprisings in Eastern Europe if not beyond.

He could certainly trumpet his claim that the bourgeois nations were united in an international effort to destroy Soviet Russia for fear of the impending proletarian revolution. This remained an essential feature of official doctrine. However room for manoeuvre was limited by Russia's desperate need for trade with the West and the repair of its prostrate economy. Communist economics were proving an abject failure. The New Economic Policy (NEP) was decreed in 1921 – lasting four years – which reintroduced limited forms of free markets.

Trotsky sternly criticised this departure from Marxist doctrine but was overruled by Lenin. The trade with the West was explained to faithful colleagues by Lenin as a sign that the capitalists were capable in their folly and cupidity of selling Russia the rope which would hang them.

After Lenin's death in 1924, there was an inevitable collision between his two principal lieutenants. Stalin ousted Trotsky and offered his new message to replace the fight for the global proletarian revolution: 'Socialism in one country'. This was such a radical departure from orthodox party doctrine that Stalin went out of his way to emphasise that all other parts of the creed remained intact. NEP was soon ended. Trotsky himself was successively removed from the party and exiled. In 1941, Stalin's killers assassinated him in his home in Mexico. Once he had removed Trotsky from power in 1924, Stalin set about eliminating all possible rivals and their supporters – real or imaginary – and enforcing a series of brutal five-year plans for industrialisation and the forcing of peasants into collective farms. The latter led to literally millions of deaths by starvation. More millions were to be added in random arrests, executions and the rise of the labour camps.

Whether the Kremlin was equally paranoid in its fears of the West is a different issue. The tactics of the European powers in the interwar years can provide an answer.

CHAPTER 4
AMERICAN ENTANGLEMENT IN EUROPE

Wilson at the peace conference – the remaking of the old world – his approach resented –
first reactions in the USA to Bolshevism – foretastes of McCarthyism

With the defeat of Germany in 1918 the victors assembled at Versailles to restore a
shattered world. The Old World was to feel the full blast of President Wilson's
self-righteousness. Though his sympathies were wholly with the Allies from
the outset of the war, he had made a point when finally embroiled in the conflict of
maintaining a moral aloofness. He insisted on classifying the USA as an 'associated
power' on the Allies' side, not a direct partner in the alliance. The USA was thus not
involved in the Allies' war aims nor did it subscribe to the Allies' views on the causes
of the war itself, which Wilson dismissed as due to the 'old system of alliances'.

The President's declaration of war aims was eloquent and naive. It was to be 'a
war to end all wars and to make the world safe for democracy'. It is hard to imagine
any European leader who could really believe that there could be a such a thing as
a 'war to end all wars' or that the aim must be to make the world safe *for democracy*
– as opposed to merely safe. The implication was that the brave new world he
envisaged would be one where the spreading of democracy's magic would banish
conflict. Indeed, he told his staff in one of his typical displays of innocence that
democracy would not just make wars less likely, it would make them impossible
since the voters would not allow them to happen. In reality pre-war Germany
had been a fairly democratic state. It did not stop the Germans entering the
war with immense enthusiasm. Wilson's trust in democracy was underlined by
his reiteration of the claim that 'the only cure for the ills of democracy is more
democracy'. More confusing was his commitment to the grand simplicity of 'self-
determination' which was to be made the world's future pattern. His Secretary of
State, Robert Lansing, privately expressed his alarm about this:

When the President talks of self-determination, what unit does he have in mind? Does he mean a race, a territorial area or a community? It will raise hopes that can never be realised. It will, I fear, cost thousands of lives. In the end it is bound to be discredited, to be called the dream of an idealist who failed to realise the dangers before it was too late.[20]

Lansing's realistic approach led to him being sidelined by the President during the Versailles negotiations.

Wilson's insistence on the USA being only an 'associated power' enabled him to enunciate doctrines at variance with those of the Allies at the beginning of 1918. The Bolshevik revolution in November 1917 was followed by Trotsky throwing open the Russian government archives and revealing the series of secret agreements reached among the European powers on the dismemberment of the Austro-Hungarian and German empires after the war. There was nothing very surprising in the fact that secret agreements were being made given the desperate nature of the struggle and the need for the Allies to recruit support wherever they could. But some of the proposals were controversial and several were liable to stiffen the resistance of the Central Powers. In response to this Wilson brought forward his Fourteen Points. They were like his war aims: high-minded, often naive and highly ambiguous. For example there was to be an end to 'secret diplomacy'. Instead there were to be 'open covenants (for peace) openly arrived at'.[21]

The difficulty of adhering to this high-minded principle was to be demonstrated when the Germans approached the USA in the autumn of 1918 in search of an armistice. Wilson could not keep the details of this from his allies. But he sent his all-important reply without consulting them. And when discussions between the major powers over future boundaries of the new nations started in Paris in 1919, Wilson agreed that these initial talks should be kept strictly confidential. There was, too, an obvious confusion about the Point which promised an independent Poland with access to the Baltic. That could only be achieved by giving the Poles a corridor through German territory, thus appearing to vitiate another of the Points. This said that an independent Poland should be 'inhabited indisputably by Polish populations which should be assured a free and secure access to the sea'. But the territory for this access was inhabited indisputably by Germans. In due course calls for clarifications and amendments to the Fourteen Points led to an additional Four Principles and Five Particulars. Ambiguities, confusion and unrealism remained.

Wilson was one of the world's least experienced statesmen – a parallel in foreign affairs might be drawn with Truman when he abruptly became president. When Wilson advanced his Fourteen Points for remaking the world, he had only been in active politics for eight years. It was only six years since he had his first

20   *Woodrow Wilson: The Lost Peace* by Thomas A Bailey, Quadrangle, 1990, p. 18
21   See Bailey op. cit., p. 23 and appendix

taste of national politics as the compromise Democratic candidate – after no less than forty-five ballots – which brought him to the White House. He showed little interest in international affairs outside the American sphere and almost none in the problems of Europe. Nor was he apparently greatly interested in the war before it became a matter of menace to the USA. In 1916 he said the USA was 'not concerned with the objects and causes of the war ... the obscure foundations from which its stupendous flood has brought forth, we are not interested to search for or explore.'

The contribution that Wilson himself made to the political instability of Europe has inevitably to be a matter of conjecture since it is hard to know whether the Allies would have made a secure peace in his absence or done better with a wiser US president in the Paris talks. But it is hard to dispute that the American combination of immense power and immense naivety was to prove dangerous for world stability, with frontiers in constant dispute. A measure of the mixture of innocence and egomania, indeed megalomania, which Wilson brought with him is evident:

> Why has Jesus so far not succeeded in inducing the world to follow His teachings in these matters It is because He taught the idea without devising any practical means of attaining it. That is why I am pursuing a practical scheme to carry out His aims.[22]

Wilson's tactics for pursuing this lofty aim were however to descend into less high-minded manoeuvrings. They sparked the memorable barb from Clemenceau, the French Premier: 'He talked like Jesus Christ and acted like Lloyd George.' Wilson also dismayed his staff on the trip to Europe by declaring that he, not the elected leaders of the Allied governments, really represented their electorates.

What emerged from Versailles was neither the Carthaginian peace which some wanted nor the magnanimous settlement which others – such as Churchill and the economist Maynard Keynes – favoured. Indisputably, Wilson had raised aspirations in Europe which could not be fulfilled. The result, though certainly not something for which he alone could be blamed, was a series of settlements of borders which left brooding dissatisfaction.

At the same time his championship of the League of Nations produced a supposed 'cure' for international differences which was to prove of dubious value. Without the USA, the League would be largely meaningless. The US Senate refused to ratify his agreement to membership, despite or perhaps because of the way he tried to browbeat the legislators on every detail. Thus the League came into force without the world's greatest power. At least as damaging was the rejection by the Senate of the proposed treaty with France as a guarantee against German aggression.

---

22 *Woodrow Wilson and Colonel House* by A. and J. George, John Day, 1956

It would be easy to see these rejections as indication of the supposed American lapse into isolationism after it rejected the League. But it could be misleading. The USA played an active international role in the 1920s and even early 1930s. When Warren Harding was elected President in 1920, Wilsonian idealism was on the wane. Even to his keenest supporters it seemed that Europe had proved ungratefully – and bafflingly – impervious to the President's idealistic master-plan, continually making difficulties, resurrecting old quarrels between resurgent nationalists and demanding reparations where the US proposed magnanimity. Washington itself showed little sign of magnanimity when it came to the British and French loans.

Others among Wilson's supporters concluded from the Senate vote that there was no hope in the foreseeable future of committing Congress to a truly 'internationalist policy'. And, for some, sheer weariness had set in. There was no immediate danger of war. Why get involved in overseas commitments in which, it was frequently reckoned, wily Europeans would outsmart the straightforward Americans?

Isolationists and Internationalists could be found on both sides. The Democrats were associated more closely with interest in European issues. Harding himself had talked vaguely of an Association of Nations as a peace-preserving alternative to the League. He wanted 'the middle ground between aloofness and 'injurious commitment' – a sort of political no man's land. His landslide victory was, like most political triumphs, attributed to domestic and international issues according to taste. For those who disliked the League or European connections it was a mandate for selective isolation. In the increasingly important area of the Pacific and Asia they favoured a forward policy. As to overseas business activities in general, Harding urged Americans to 'go on to the peaceful commercial conquest of the world'.[23]

Washington participated in numerous League conferences. In disarmament, the Americans called the Washington conference which secured eventual agreement between the USA, Britain and Japan over warships. In the remaining interwar period, the USA confined its foreign concerns largely to the south and the east becoming preoccupied with its own economic troubles and, as Hitler grew stronger, committing itself to formal neutrality.

In the 1930s, after the Wall Street Crash and the subsequent banking crisis, the USA adopted stern tariffs which precipitated tit-for-tat measures which deepened and prolonged the international depression. The folly of this was, by the 1940s, to convince Washington that post-war settlements must vigorously promote international free trade with equality of access to raw materials. It was inevitably to cause tension with the Russians and the closed Soviet economy.

The menace of Bolshevism added to American distrust of the outside world. At home, the self-proclaimed quality of tolerance collapsed. What the historian

---

23   *The Tragedy of American Diplomacy* by William Appleman Williams, Delta, 1962, p. 93

Richard Hofstadter called 'the paranoid style in American Politics'[24] came swiftly to the fore. The New York State legislature expelled five Socialists as dangerous revolutionaries. The *New York Times* described the move 'as clearly a measure of national defence as the declaration of war against Germany'. It further claimed that the Attorney General in Chicago had uncovered a huge conspiracy to overthrow the government and, after seizing all businesses, to establish a Soviet government.

On the orders of the US Attorney General himself, Mitchell Palmer, nearly 4,500 supposed or actual Communists were arrested in 1919. He declared: 'like a prairie fire the blaze of revolution was sweeping every American institution of law and order.' In Boston, about 1,000 were arrested on the score of their left-wing connections, though mostly released since no charge could stick.

Tolerance was little in evidence in the interwar years. Ku Klux Klan membership reached 4–4.5 million in the 1920s. In the 1930s, the weekly broadcasts of Father Coughlin, the rabid Catholic priest, achieved an audience of 30 million. He consistently warned his fellow countrymen against Communism, Jews, bankers and Freemasons.

Hysteria was of course to resurface many years later in a virulent form as Senator McCarthy played on rising fears of the Red Menace. And in a milder form it appeared in Truman's 'loyalty' legislation.

---

24 *The Paranoid Style in American Politics* by Richard Hofstadter, Univ. Chicago Press, 1979

CHAPTER 5
THE RED MENACE AS A POLITICAL TOOL

Instability in Europe – outside attempts to destroy the Bolsheviks fail – Britain and France see Hitler as less menacing than Communists – Soviet searches for anti-Hitler alliance rebuffed – League of Nations fails its tests

The years between 1917 and 1919 had seen the fall of three of Europe's oldest dynasties: the Habsburgs in Austria, the Hohenzollerns in Germany and the Romanovs in Russia. The titanic struggle of the First World War had proved a bloodbath. Revolution was in the air. The ends for which the great sacrifices had been made seemed almost trivial. Serbian nationalism had dragged France and Britain into a war which devastated a generation. Belgian neutrality seemed a poor excuse for all the war dead. Russia had joined battle on what was to prove the winning side but had been routed by Germany and fell under Bolshevik control.

Confidence in traditional parliamentary institutions, traditional parties and their leaders was low. Even in Germany, a country so addicted to *ordnung*, defeat on the battlefield gave way to chaos as unofficial armies brutally repressed rebels with Communist leanings. Hungary had a brief Communist regime. The Bavarian regional government succumbed, only for the military to intervene and swiftly remove the Communists. Though Russia was trying to restore diplomatic and trading links with the West, it persisted with the Comintern, established by Lenin in 1919 to 'coordinate' the activities of Communist parties throughout the world, and which kept up a constant cry for the end of the capitalist order.

Not surprisingly it fuelled the anti-Communist rhetoric of many Western leaders, proclaiming the new peril. Apart from the openly declared Communists, electorates were warned that many Socialists believed in the Marxist analysis of the weaknesses of capitalism and its eventual doom. A new label – 'fellow travellers' – was applied to those Communist supporters who traded on the more respectable credentials of Socialists in a programme to infiltrate the Left.

The advantage to the Conservatives in Britain of the Communist threat, real or imagined, was dramatically illustrated when the country's first ever Labour Government in 1924, under Ramsay Macdonald, called an election after losing a crucial Commons vote. It had recognised the Soviet government and started on a round of economic negotiations. Shortly before polling day, the press revealed the forged 'Zinoviev Letter'. Supposedly secret, it was a call from the head of the Comintern to British comrades to prepare for the revolution. Whatever its dubious authenticity, its impact was immense, with Macdonald having played a major role in bringing Russia in from the cold. The Tories swept to power with 412 of the 611 seats in the Commons. Communists retained one seat.

Clearly, the anti-Communist card was a trump. This helps explain a curious feature of the interwar years. Conditions had never been so propitious for the Left. There was an economic slump, very high unemployment and a crisis for capitalism in general. Yet during the twenty-year interwar period Labour enjoyed only three years of power. The second period of Labour power, from 1929 to 1931, gave way to a coalition government nominally led by Macdonald. But it was to all intents and purposes a Conservative administration. In the 1931 general election the Labour Party, flying under its own colours, was reduced to a fity-five seat rump.

There was a widespread distrust of the Socialists as too sympathetic to Communism, which was proving an economic failure in Russia alongside tales of starvation and brutality. It must have seemed to the Tories as if playing the Red Card provided them with the elixir of eternal political life.

How many of the Tories believed their own noisy protestations of danger is impossible to say. Some, such as Churchill, were passionate in their fears of the Bolshevik menace. Others who looked at the weakness of the Soviet Union and understood that a sea change of policy had taken place in the new Stalin doctrine of 'socialism in one country' regarded the threat as insubstantial. It hardly mattered. It was an eminently exploitable issue. The upshot was relentless anti-Communist propaganda from the Conservatives while many Socialist politicians hastened to proclaim that they too saw the Communist danger.

The effect of propaganda on the propagandists themselves is regularly underrated. As those with experience of politics know, it is often greater on those who propound it than on the public which receives it. The messengers become prisoners of their own propaganda. For all their shortcomings, politicians prefer to believe that what they say is true. After a long period of proclaiming some danger they can easily convince themselves of its reality. By the time that Hitler had established himself in power, claims about the Red Menace had been running for many years. They qualified as handed-down wisdom. The belief had become widespread that Stalin and not Hitler was the real menace. At least Hitler's revolution was not for export while Stalin's was – or could credibly be described as such with many references to Marx and Lenin. This attitude was to have an ominous effect on British decisions throughout the 1930s.

Whether Stalin had ever in his life been fanatically devoted to the doctrines of Marxism–Leninism or was just another revolutionary who found a mechanism for self-advancement is something we shall never know. He may have been a once ardent doctrinaire who merely succumbed, as so often happens, to the relish of power for its own sake. Political fanatics who remain fanatics over their lifetimes are very rare. Once in power, their ideals rarely survive intact. The enjoyment of power itself, changes in personal attitudes, the discovery of the practical problems of government and diplomacy, to say nothing of simple age – all combine to dilute fanaticism.

Among those warning of the perils of Soviet expansion were not just politicians but also academics who claimed a special pre-eminence because they had studied the sacred texts of Marxism. A belief that Soviet foreign policy could be assessed through studies of Communist doctrine was naive. It was like arguing that the foreign policy of Christian Britain in the 17th century could be understood by studying the New Testament. In practice, diplomacy is almost invariably driven by national or personal self interest.

Communist parties abroad had to go through changes of line and alliances according to Moscow's commands. If the most striking was the German case when Communist and Socialist parties combined might have stopped Hitler, there was also a remarkable about-turn in France. The party had been attacking France's military preparations in the early 1930s as anti-working class. Then, as Hitler's policies became more threatening, the line was abruptly switched to combining with Leon Blum in the Popular Front and pressing for greater military preparedness. However the apparently erratic moves of Communist parties never presented the determined anti-Communists with too serious a problem. They were always ready to see each move as some clever manoeuvre to advance the proletarian revolution.

THE PATH TO MUNICH INSPIRES SOVIET FEARS

It is impossible to understand the apparent paranoia of Moscow in its dealings with the West during and after the Second World War without an appreciation of the events up to the war itself. The analysis of British and French policy as a desire to steer Hitler into attacking Russia was likely to be reached by any observer in Moscow, whether Communist or not.

Throughout the 1920s and into the 1930s, the Soviet Union set out to normalise relations with the rest of the world. It was determined to secure proper diplomatic status. With the twin benefits of official recognition by the USA and admission to the League of Nations in 1934, the Soviet government embarked on a search for alliances to confront the rising Nazi menace. With Britain and France unprepared to take a firm line, Russia became the only major power to support the idea of collective security – joint action by Britain, France and Russia against Germany and at one point Italy.

A non-aggression pact between Poland and Germany in 1934 did nothing to reassure the Soviets. Both countries had been so recently at war with Russia. Maxim Litvinov, the Russian envoy at the League, set about forging protective links. The Comintern also replaced its warlike rhetoric against the capitalist world at large with the new policy that Communists and Socialists should form a united front against Fascism. At the League, Soviet Ambassador Maxim Litvinov declared that 'Peaceful coexistence' could prevail but only with the non-fascist West.

Before formal admission to the League, he established a cordial working relationship with Louis Barthou, the French Foreign Minister, who had battled with several countries about overdue Soviet membership. Litvinov and the old-fashioned French conservative may have had little in common politically but they were united in seeing the vital need for an alliance.

Hitler, achieving power in January 1933, lost little time in demonstrating his aggressiveness. Within months Germany left the League as well as the two-year-old Disarmament conference. He went another step in 1934, attempting to provoke a Nazi coup in Austria. It failed when an alarmed Mussolini, unexpectedly the strong man of the moment, mobilised four divisions on the Brenner Pass between Italy and Austria. Hitler backed down.

Barthou envisaged that Russia should, as before the First World War, become France's ally in the east. Each would come to the other's assistance in the event of either being attacked. But in a major tragedy, Barthou was mortally wounded during the assassination of King Alexander of Yugoslavia in Marseilles in October 1934. He was to prove irreplaceable. Another assassin's bullet, as at Sarajevo, set in train a series of disasters.

The Franco-Soviet pact which Barthou had negotiated was finally signed by a new Foreign Minister, unfortunately the notorious Pierre Laval, at that time a Socialist and later Premier in the Vichy government – executed eventually for his collaboration. He set about diluting the pact. Throughout 1935, Moscow pressed for a detailed military accord to put teeth into the alliance but was ignored by France. The Treaty was not even presented to the French Assembly until 1936, when it was finally approved. The impetus was then Germany's 1935 decision to reintroduce conscription.

The French had the strength at that point to move in and stop Hitler. They were entitled to do so under the terms of Versailles. But they settled for a protest to the League. Britain sent Sir John Simon, the Foreign Secretary, to ask Hitler to behave better. Litvinov provided the strongest attack, warning that Germany was rearming 'not for defence but for the violation of frontiers with the idea of revenge by forcible methods, for the violation of the security of neighbouring or remote states, for the violation of universal peace'.[25]

---

25 *Litvinov* by Arthur Pope, Secker and Warburg, 1943, p. 354

Moscow gave the French Communists their about-turn orders. The party line in early 1934 was that the Communists would not support a war 'initiated by capitalist and imperialist powers'. Within months, following orders, it was calling on the Socialists to form the Popular Front against Fascism. The defence budget which had been attacked as too large was now suddenly criticised as too small. The Socialists who had been betrayers of the working class were now seen as badly needed allies. This at least relieved the French military who regarded Communist influence among conscripts as a menace to discipline. It now became a duty for party members to convert the Socialists who remained still resisters to what their leaders had been characterising as 'the military planning of the bourgeoisie'.

The Popular Front won power in the 1936 elections, led by Leon Blum. It was to last only a year, though Blum was to take office as deputy premier in the next coalition. The revolving door of French politics revolved again and it was Edouard Daladier who, except for a brief interlude, was to be Premier until 1940.

France was riven by every sort of division. On the Left there was little or no agreement on anything except the horrors of the Right. On the Right, proto-fascist groups led street fights against the supposed danger of Communists and Jews and the Left in general. The country was in a poor condition to deal firmly with external enemies. The army was in a poor state. Equipment was not in fact that bad – enough for the French to have more tanks than the Germans when war came. But morale was pitifully low and the high command was sunk in a mood of pessimism. The government was not strong enough to remove the demoralised generals; and the generals were not tough enough to make the government appreciate the impending danger.

It was against a background of political weakness at every level in France that the British government set out on its own independent but still weak line with the Anglo-German Naval Agreement of 1935. This allowed Hitler a naval building programme which kept his shipyards busy till the outbreak of war. It was a breach of the Versailles Treaty as well as a breach of trust with France. The new agreement would still leave the Royal Navy significantly stronger than the German fleet – on paper. But it provided a strong enough German navy to dominate the Baltic, as an alarmed Moscow realised.

Hitler next set out to defy both Versailles and the 1925 Locarno Pact whereby Britain, France, Czechoslovakia and Germany agreed the then existing border. It had allowed Germany into the League. In early 1936, Hitler's forces reoccupied the Rhineland, hitherto designated as a German area but not to be allowed a military presence. As the intelligence reports of this impending move increased, the French Foreign Minister, Pierre-Etienne Flandin, consulted Anthony Eden, his London counterpart. Eden provided a taste of the indecision which was to surface regularly during his long political career. France wanted to know what Britain would do. Eden batted back the query. What did France propose to do? Did it regard the demilitarised zone as of paramount importance? The area (without which

Germany could not directly invade France) was primarily a matter for France. Perhaps Paris would prefer to negotiate while the area was still unoccupied?

He was later to accuse the French of avoiding the key decision – having done just that himself. Eden told the Cabinet that it might be best for Britain and France together to negotiate with Germany. The French government turned to the military to ask what strength the armed forces had to eject German forces should they occupy the area. The timid answer was that the French forces were primarily organised as defensive. It was an answer which boosted the position of the do-nothing-but-protest group in the French government. In reality, the German forces were so weak at that point that France or Britain or both together could easily have sent them scuttling back.

When Hitler finally made his move, the French government once more asked the military if it had the strength to act, with or without Britain. General Gamelin hesitated. It would need a general mobilisation, which would take time. And alone, France would have the advantage at first but in a lengthy war, German manpower and industrial strength would tell. Since the French High Command knew from its intelligence sources how small were the German forces in the Rhineland, this was simply an answer from a High Command which had no appetite for war, short or otherwise. Nevertheless France insisted that the Locarno powers should meet. Accordingly they gathered. Eden was opposed to unilateral French action.

Italy, which had signed the Locarno Treaty, had also walked out of the League, after its widely condemned invasion of Abyssinia in 1935. The subsequent sanctions by the League were emasculated by Britain and France which refused to embargo oil supplies. Italy took advantage of the moment and declined to back action against Germany unless all sanctions were lifted.

Locarno was dead. So the onus for action was transferred to the League. There only Litvinov proved a strong voice. This was the third time in eighteen months since Russia had joined the League, he declared, that he had had to complain about the violation of international obligations – the Italian attack on Abyssinia being the second and German conscription the first. He insisted at Geneva that Russia for its part was ready: 'To take part in all measures that may be proposed by the council of the League … which were acceptable to other council members.'[26]

But the council had no measures to propose, only protests to voice.

The Spanish civil war did nothing to allay suspicions in Moscow that Britain and France were more sympathetic to Germany and Italy than to Russia, or at any rate less fearful of them. The civil war followed a military revolt against the republican government, a mixture of left wingers, similar to the Popular Front in France though notably more anti-clerical.

Mussolini and Hitler provided aid to Franco's rebels. The Soviet Union countered

---

26   Pope, op. cit., p. 389

with aid to the other side. Moscow offered, though how sincerely we cannot know, to end its involvement if Italy and Germany did the same. Nothing came of it. Volunteers, mainly to the republican side, came from a long list of countries. The struggle, which lasted two years, became a great romantic cause of the time, not least because Hitler was testing his new air force by bombing civilians.

The British and French governments seemed simply motivated by a hope that the war would soon be over. This led them to incline to Franco as the inevitable victor. Moscow's intervention was widely seen as another sign of serious Communist ambitions. This seemed to be born out with the failure to adopt a strong line with Hitler even when he threatened Austria in 1938. Britain and France could reach little agreement on what should be done. The Foreign office vacillated. Alexander Cadogan, Permanent Under Secretary at the Foreign Office, recorded in his diaries:

'Personally I almost wish Germany would swallow Austria and get it over. She is probably going to do so anyhow – anyway we can't stop her. What's all this fuss about?'[27]

The French Prime Minister, Camille Chautemps, had no stomach for a showdown. He nervously resigned when it became clear that the *Anschluss* was about to take place and he might have to make a decision. Blum quickly formed a government and appealed for national unity from the far Left to the far Right. Paul Reynaud (later Prime Minister when France fell) was one of the few outspoken supporters of this appeal. His anguished cry was: 'It is not Stalin who enters Vienna today, who will menace Prague tomorrow – it is Hitler.'[28]

A despairing Litvinov forecast that Hitler would attack Czechoslovakia in the summer of 1938. That country would give in because she had no confidence that France, though treaty bound, would come to her rescue. He delivered his by now regular protest at Geneva at the lack of concerted action. Again his voice was ignored.

The motives behind the policy of appeasement have been analysed on countless occasions, usually with the conclusion that they were based on a failure of nerve and a horror of war, given the experience of 1914–1918. These factors certainly dominated many minds. However, the failure to stop Hitler when he was militarily so weak, thus averting the menace of a general conflagration, was easy to see from Moscow as aimed against the Soviet Union.

In 1936, a group of Conservative MPs went to see Stanley Baldwin, the Prime Minister, to voice their alarm about Hitler and Britain's defences. He told them that he thought it possible that Hitler's real intention was to make his move eastwards against Russia; and it would not 'break his heart' if it proved so. He would be happy to see a fight between 'the Nazis and the Bolshies'.[29]

---

27   *Diaries of Sir Alexander Cadogan* edited by David Dilks, Cassell & Co., 1971, p. 47
28   *The Collapse of the Third Republic* by William L. Shirer, Simon and Schuster, 1969, p. 332
29   *Churchill: the End of Glory* by John Charmley, Hodder and Stoughton, 1993, p. 309

This supposedly attractive outcome was a perfect example of political blindness driven by anti-Soviet nervousness. What Baldwin and others had not thought through was the possible outcome of such a conflict. If Germany conquered Russia, the Nazi empire would extend from the North Sea to wherever it chose to stop – somewhere in Asia, even the rim of the Pacific. With such power and access to Russia's unique resources of raw materials, Hitler would become the most powerful ruler in the world. The alternative if improbable outcome, a Soviet victory, would bring the Red Menace to the borders of the North Sea.

France's attitude was little better than Britain's. Governments rose and fell and the French approach veered between displays of determination and relapses into nervousness. In the final debacle of Munich, Moscow was to discern yet further evidence that British and French policy was influenced by a wish to see Russia the target of Hitler's ambitions.

CHAPTER 6
HITLER PRESSES ON

Hitler aims at Czechoslovakia – British and French indecision – Soviet Union presses more strongly for an alliance – distaste in London and Paris for an association – Chamberlain surrenders at Munich – Hitler takes Sudetenland – Kremlin's worst fears realised

Having feasted on Austria, Hitler's appetite turned to Czechoslovakia. The supposed plight of the German-speaking inhabitants of the Sudetenland was his chance for another gamble. As he fulminated about the Czech government, the British and French governments asked their military chiefs to analyse the forces at their disposal. They returned discouraging answers.

But there were also cautious, indeed alarmed, voices among the German generals. The military attaché in Prague warned Berlin that the thirty-four well-trained and well armed divisions that the Czechs could put into the field amounted to about the same as Germany could muster for an invasion – but in the Czech case with only one well fortified frontier to defend. A plot was hatched by Hitler's generals to remove him if he went too far.

The threat to Czechoslovakia raised a new issue in East–West relations. France still had its pact of mutual assistance with the young republic. So had the Soviet Union. But in the latter case, it only came into effect if the French fulfilled their obligations. The French Foreign Minister, Georges Bonnet, raised the issue with Litvinov. If Germany were to attack, what would the Soviet Union do? Litvinov's answer was that Moscow would stand by its commitments. But there was no common frontier, the French reminded Moscow, Russia being separated from Czechoslovakia by 100 miles of Polish and Romanian territory. To this the reply was that Russia had no desire to go to war with either of those countries. But it trusted that France, which had extensive influence with both of them, would use it to secure a right of passage. Bonnet was to raise the issue with both governments but more in the spirit of inquiry than pressure. The replies were not encouraging.

An alliance of Britain, France and Russia to save Czechoslovakia – proposed by Churchill as 'the Grand Alliance' – could certainly have stopped Hitler. But Chamberlain would have none of it. In March he wrote to his sisters (regular recipients of his political thoughts):

…With Franco winning in Spain by the aid of the German guns and Italian planes, with a French government in which I cannot have the slightest confidence and which I suspect is in closest touch with our Opposition, the Russians stealthily and cunningly pulling all the strings behind the scenes to get us involved in a war with Germany (our Secret Service does not spend all its time staring out of the window) and finally with a Germany flushed with triumph and all too conscious of her power…

As a matter of fact the plan of the 'Grand Alliance' as Winston calls it had occurred to me long before he mentioned it … I talked to Halifax and we submitted it to the Chiefs of Staff and the FO experts. It is a very attractive idea. Indeed there is almost everything to be said for it until you come to examine its practicality. From that moment the attraction vanishes. You have only to look at the map to see that nothing we could do could possibly save Czechoslovakia from being overrun by the Germans, if they wanted to do it. The Austrian frontier is practically open, the great Skoda munitions works are within easy bombing distance of the German aerodromes, the railways all pass through German territory, Russia is 100 miles away. Therefore we could not help Czechoslovakia – she would simply be a pretext for going to war with Germany. That we could not think of unless we had a reasonable prospect of being able to beat her to her knees in a reasonable time and of that I see no sign. I have therefore abandoned any idea of giving guarantees to Czechoslovakia.[30]

Chamberlain's analysis was unconvincing. Threats without the ability to bring direct aid to a country was precisely the route he chose in 1939 when he gave guarantees to Poland and then Romania against Germany. Geography made it out of the question that Britain, or indeed France, would be able to provide serious assistance to either country.

The Grand Alliance of Britain, France and Russia would have been one of clear military superiority and it would have threatened Germany with the intimidating prospect of war on two fronts. Even if no arrangement could be made for getting substantial Russian forces to Czechoslovakia, Hitler would still be fighting the well-armed Czechs behind strong fortifications while facing an attack from France and Britain. Germany was also without any effective oil resources of her own. An economic blockade alone would have been ruinous for her. A warning

---

30 *Neville Chamberlain* by Keith Feiling, Macmillan, 1946, pp. 347–348

that such an alliance would resort to force would have forced Hitler to abandon his claim to the Sudetenland.

The crisis rumbled on throughout the summer. In May, London warned Berlin that if France became involved in aiding Czechoslovakia Her Majesty's Government could not guarantee that 'it would not be forced by circumstances to become involved also'.[31] This was not as stern a warning as it might seem, given French nervousness. Lord Halifax, the Foreign Secretary, underlined the feebleness of London's stand by cautiously reminding the French that Britain was not bound to get involved on their side save in the event of an unprovoked attack by Germany on France itself. The crisis was fuelled by news from London that an increasingly nervous Chamberlain had been briefing journalists along the lines that neither Britain nor France would be prepared to fight for Czechoslovakia and probably Russia would not either.

Hitler's pawns in the Sudetenland staged well-prepared riots. The Czech government's determination to maintain law and order led to wild German claims about brutality and of hundreds being shot. The crisis came to the boil in September. There was a brief flourish of determination in Paris and London. The Foreign Office warned that Germany should be under no illusion. An attack upon Czechoslovakia would mean 'the possibility' of British and French 'intervention'.[32] No mention was made of Russia which was to be systematically kept out of the subsequent negotiations, causing understandable fury in Moscow.

Hitler was unimpressed by this passing phase. Daladier met with Lord Halifax, the Foreign Secretary. The two frightened men agreed to propose a 'reorganisation' and guarantee of Czech frontiers. In Geneva Litvinov reaffirmed the Soviet commitment to its pact with the Czechs. The Soviet embassy in Paris, informed General Gamelin that Marshal Voroshilov had thirty divisions, plus cavalry and the bulk of the air force, ready for intervention to the west.

The lack of will on the part of Chamberlain and Halifax permeated their colleagues. Cadogan recorded: 'FPC (the Cabinet Foreign Policy Committee) unanimous that Czechoslovakia not worth the bones of a single British grenadier. And they are right!'[33]

However, Britain felt the need to put on a show of firmness with an official communiqué in late September showing the limits of British patience:

> The German claim to the transfer of the Sudeten areas has already been conceded by the British, French and Czechoslovak governments. But if in spite of all the efforts made by the British Prime Minister, if a German attack is made upon Czechoslovakia the immediate result with be that France will be bound to come to her assistance and Great Britain and Russia will certainly stand by France.[34]

---

31 *Documents on British Foreign Policy* by Sir Llewellyn Woodward, Third Series, Vol. 1, p. 237
32 Ibid.
33 Cadogan diaries p. 63
34 Llewellyn Woodward, op. cit.

That being the case, an open and proper alliance with Russia would immeasurably strengthen the British hand. Chamberlain was very reluctant to pursue it. As late as May 1939, when Hitler had seized the whole of Czechoslovakia, Cadogan was to write that the chiefs of staff were now favouring 'whole hog alliance with Soviet. PM annoyed'.[35]

Negotiations by the French and the British in the period up to Munich over Hitler's threat to the Sudetenland went through their typical bouts of oscillation and prevarication. Sometimes it was the British who tried to impress on the French the need for firmness, sometimes it was the other way round. Each side discovered new reasons to hold back when the other side showed an inclination to stand firm.

Chamberlain flew three times to meet Hitler. His caution allowed the German leader to assess how easily the Prime Minister could be intimidated by yet further demands. The Sudetenlanders must not just come under the protection of the Reich, but German troops must be allowed to occupy the area. The mood was black. The British Fleet was mobilised. Trenches were dug in London parks, schoolchildren began evacuation. The two sides really did seem to be settling down for a conflict. Chamberlain wired a request to Hitler for another personal meeting. Hitler agreed. The ignominious Munich settlement followed, with the Sudetenland allocated to German occupation and the Czechoslovak defensive line outflanked.

Litvinov drew a predictable conclusion. No doubt the British and the French genuinely preferred that Czechoslovakia remain independent. But if it came to a choice, they preferred that Hitler should move east rather than risk seeing the country rescued by Russian military forces moving west. The assumption by various British and French ministers was that Russian forces, once in Czechoslovakia and passing through Poland and Romania would probably stay there.

Litvinov was in despair and, after Munich, recognised his failure in trying to persuade Stalin that Soviet policy should be based on supporting London and Paris. The problem was underlined in the French press. *Le Matin* advocated that France should be protected by giving Hitler the green light to move eastwards against Russia. Litvinov returned to Moscow and resigned in 1939. He predicted to Stalin that the Germans would soon march on Prague. An obvious but vital point was that the elimination of the Czech army and the country's fortifications would mean the loss of one of Russia's first lines of defence.

The episode was seared on Russian memory. There were to be two very different echoes of Munich in 1945, as the USA and Britain negotiated over Eastern Europe. To the two allies, the lesson of Munich was that brutal dictators had to be faced down. To Russia, the lesson was that defences against Germany could not be relied on unless they were either directly under Soviet control or in the hands of a nation which was manifestly friendly – as Czechoslovakia was in 1945 and Poland was not.

---

35   Cadogan diaries, p. 180

CHAPTER 7
WAR BEGINS

Hitler seizes Prague – Moscow redoubles pleas for anti-German alliance – London and Paris still hesitant – low grade missions sent to Moscow – high grade mission sent by Berlin – Molotov-Ribbentrop pact – war begins – Britain and France plan for war with Russia as well as Germany when Soviet troops invade Finland – USA seeks to stay apart

When Hitler seized Prague in March 1939, Poland and later Romania were given their guarantees by Britain and France. From the USA there came condemnation of Hitler and widespread sympathy for the democracies. But several Neutrality Acts had bound the country to non-interference.

The big question now was whether Britain and France would enroll Russia as an anti-Hitler ally. Would Moscow be satisfied that London and Paris no longer hoped that Hitler would concentrate on Russia alone? The Foreign Office asked what Russia's attitude was to the new danger. Moscow swiftly proposed a conference of the British, French, Russian Polish, Romanian and Turkish governments to discuss how resistance could be organised. The Russian proposal was rejected as 'premature'. Instead Chamberlain proposed that Britain, France, Poland and Russia would act together in the event of further German aggression. This time it was Poland which stood in the way of action, dismayed at the thought of any alliance which might bring Russia into Polish Territory.

A month later the Foreign Office put forward a new proposal. Russia would declare that in the event of an attack on one of her European neighbours, it would offer armed assistance if desired. However, this seems not to have been meant too seriously. Cadogan referred to this proposal as 'made to placate our left wing in England rather than for any solid military advantage'.[36]

36 Cadogan diaries, p. 174

The Russians countered with their own suggestion. Britain, France and Russia should agree to offer all help to states lying between the Baltic and the Black Sea. The three nations would discuss 'promptly' the means of giving such help. This was a proposal with real teeth. But Cadogan got no satisfaction from receiving it. He minuted: 'We have to balance the advantage of a paper commitment by Russia to join in a war on one side against the disadvantage of associating ourselves openly with Russia.'[37]

By mid-May the Chiefs of Staff were pressing for a full alliance with Russia. Cadogan commented that 'perhaps' Britain should go 'the whole hog' with Russia, but only to ensure no German–Russian alliance.

Moscow's stated attitude was that without direct guarantees from Britain and France to the Baltic states and Finland, a German attack could be aimed at Russia through those countries. The Foreign Office view was that perhaps Britain would need to offer some commitments to allay this Soviet fear. He was reluctantly coming round to favouring the proposal. But 'the PM hates it' he recorded. 'In his present mood the PM says he will resign rather than sign an alliance with the Soviet.'[38] A few days later Chamberlain's view changed. He was apparently resigned to an alliance.

It was by then over two months since Hitler had taken over Prague. The hesitancy in London led to Molotov insisting to the British Ambassador that Britain and France wanted to spin out the exchanges indefinitely. Within a fortnight, however, Chamberlain was in a firmer mood and able to announce that general agreement had been reached on the 'principles'. Britain and France would give immediate assistance to Russia in the event of German aggression.

The negotiations dragged on. Cadogan dismissed the Russians as 'mulish'. London saw Russia as looking for an excuse to interfere in the Baltic states and Finland. But Molotov was for military talks to start immediately. Chamberlain agreed on a fresh effort to find a formula to deter Russia from any Baltic States moves. It was finally agreed that British and French military missions should go to Moscow – but not too quickly.

This was the basis for the notorious 'Slow Boat to Leningrad' mission. Meanwhile Hitler was making aggressive noises about Danzig and the Polish Corridor which passed through German territory. Britain, though now committed to a firm line against Germany, was urging the Poles to find some means for a peaceful solution. The spirit of appeasement was not dead. The British and French teams did not reach Moscow until 11 August. They were not impressive. The much-hyphenated but diplomatically inexperienced Admiral Sir Reginald Plunkett-Ernle-Erle-Drax headed the team from London with a relatively junior Foreign Office official. General Doumenc headed a more powerful team from

---

37　Cadogan diaries, p. 175
38　Ibid., p. 182

Paris. A serious point emerged when Admiral Drax told his hosts aide that he had no authorisation to reach an agreement. At least the French had that.

The Russians were pressing on a vital issue. Britain and France must persuade Poland and Romania to open their territory to Soviet forces if the situation deteriorated. Both Western teams failed to provide an answer. By 20 August, no points of agreement had been reached. Meanwhile, Hitler had not been idle. Britain had offered the Russians the retired Admiral. Hitler now offered the Russians his Foreign Minister. On 23 August, the Molotov-Ribbentrop Pact was signed.

The news was received with disbelief in Britain and France. The pact was widely denounced as an act of unparalleled cynicism. In reality it was a great diplomatic coup by Russia. After years of watching Britain and France ready to encourage Hitler to attack Russia the Kremlin had now given him carte blanche to attack *them*. The pact not only provided him with the ideal opportunity to wage such a war, it also gave Russia time to prepare for an eventual German onslaught – assuming that a war in the West would still leave the Werhmacht strong enough to make such an attack. The pact also won time and new territory which any German attack would have to cross. Under the secret clauses, Russia was to advance its frontiers by occupying the eastern half of Poland, overpowering the Baltic states and taking Bessarabia from Romania. The trade agreements in the pact would ensure Germany of important war materials. And while Hitler made war in the West, Russia would have more time to train and enlarge its armed forces and boost war production and to shift armaments plants to the east.

Matters now raced to a climax. The German forces poured into Poland. The British and French declarations of war followed. Yet within weeks, both countries became involved in a bizarre diversion. It was to be of little significance militarily but it casts an intriguing and usually overlooked light on the attitude of the Western powers towards Russia.

Tragedy and Farce over Finland

After the Germans had shattered Poland, Russia took over the eastern half of the country, restoring more or less Versailles' Curzon Line as the limit of the Polish boundary. At the same time, Moscow proposed a territorial exchange with Finland to allow control over the sea approaches to Leningrad. Moscow called for the grant of a thirty-year lease of the major port of Hanko and a withdrawal of the Finnish border by twenty-five kilometres where it approached Leningrad. In exchange, Moscow offered a substantial area of Russian Karelia. The Finns rejected the plan. The David and Goliath war started in November.

The prime motive was certainly strategic, since Leningrad was within artillery range of Hanko. But if fighting occurred Moscow would have a chance to try out the Red Army after the drastic and brutal purges of senior officers starting in 1936.[39]

---

39 Stalin had removed and in many cases murdered over 4,000 senior officers including the

Despite their small numbers, the Finns threw back the Russians in the initial stages. The British government proved remarkably pugnacious. Britain had entered the war under-equipped and poorly prepared. The success of the Polish invasion showed Germany to be even more formidable than had been feared. The government asked the Chiefs of Staff about the consequences of Britain fighting alongside the Finns' side. The predictable reply was that the armed forces were not in a position to undertake 'additional burdens'.

Nevertheless, the British government, urged on by the aggressive Northern Desk of the Foreign Office, decided that at least it could send aid to the Finns, desperately little though it had to spare. It was decided to send aircraft and men and general military supplies. Military personnel, especially those required to service the aircraft, would be demobbed first and officially designated 'volunteers' – a device later used by the Kremlin during the Cold War and much denounced by the West. Any *genuine* volunteers would have to be carefully vetted, it was concluded in London. Clumsy amateurs, such as those who fought in the Spanish Civil War, should be avoided.

If London had its doubts about this remarkable operation, Paris did not. The nervousness about standing up to Hitler gave way to vigorous demands to come to the aid of Finland, even if it did mean war with Russia. William Bullitt, US Ambassador in Paris, was duly informed by Alexis Leger, head of the Foreign Ministry: 'The French Government had proposed to the British Government that the British and French fleets should enter the Black Sea and bombard Batum and send airplanes to bomb Baku and thus cut off both Germany and the Soviet Union from supplies of oil.'[40] The Finnish government was informed that Britain and France stood ready to despatch a force of 57,000 men with the first 15,000 to arrive by the end of March.[41] In fact this was too late. The heavily outnumbered Finns were negotiating peace terms with the Kremlin.

But one plan remained on the table – bombing the Caucasus oil fields. The Foreign Office supposed this would bring Russia to its knees. The Inter-services Project Board in London was still studying this plan. The RAF undertook area reconnaissance of the site and prepared target plans. A month after the Finns surrendered, General Gamelin suggested that Baku should not only be bombed but also that the British Fleet should get involved if it could get into the Black Sea.

---

heroic Marshal Tukhachevsky. They were accused of planning a coup. There is some evidence that the information about a plot was fed to the Kremlin via the Czech government – possibly as a manoeuvre by German intelligence to weaken the Soviet forces. There also remains the possibility that there really was a plot. Given the brutality and incompetence of Stalin's rule, it would be unfair to the Marshal and his senior colleagues to say that the thought of a coup never came into their minds. The purge was accompanied by a series of show trials of old Bolsheviks, made to confess to a variety of improbable plots.

40   *The Collapse of the Third Republic* by William L.. Shirer, Simon and Schuster, 1969, p. 545

41   Ibid., p. 544. For wider discussion see *The Impact of Hitler* by Maurice Cowling.

Captain Paul Stehlin, former assistant air attaché in Berlin and now on the mission to Finland, recorded that he was 'stupefied' by the apparent loss of sense in the French High Command when briefed on its plan for attacking Russia.[42] These ambitious plans were only finally discarded after the Finns made peace with the Soviets in March.

From the Soviet perspective, this episode was bound to raise doubts about whether Britain and France were serious about fighting Germany. The military unpreparedness of Britain and France in late 1940 was all too obvious. Yet despite that an assault on Russia could be contemplated. Meanwhile the British army in France, like the French army itself, had taken no advantage of the German forces being so heavily committed in Poland. It was only the German invasion of France in May 1940 that brought the Allied land forces there into action. It seemed hard to believe until then that the two allies were serious about fighting Germany. But, ran the assumption, they would be happy to see 'the Nazis fighting the Bolshies' as Baldwin had favoured. Britain soon forgot the Finnish episode. The Kremlin could hardly do so. Why did Hitler risk leaving such small forces facing France and Britain when invading Poland? Because, Moscow could argue, Hitler knew that Britain and France were not serious about fighting Germany.

America tries to stay on the sidelines

The interwar years found American opinion in an isolationist mood towards Europe. Asia was another matter since Japan was mounting a serious challenge. Wilson had made a great impact at Versailles but he had failed to persuade Congress that the USA should join the League or support a proposed treaty with France against a German invasion. The USA had not come voluntarily into the First World War as was also to be the case in the Second. The American public listened more readily to the old isolationists, resurfacing after the Wilson period. Franklin Roosevelt as the Democratic candidate in 1932 succumbed to pressure to disavow the League. He was also, though charged with being an internationalist, to torpedo (at very short notice) the London economic conference of 1933. This was called to prevent the tariff wars which were making the world depression worse. Plans for economic recovery, he said, should be on a national not an international basis. On the other hand, he was prepared to take the adventurous step of establishing diplomatic relations with the Soviet Union – seen as morally indefensible by his critics.

Anything to do with the League was so adverse to isolationists that his attempt to bring the USA into membership of the World Court failed. It had been established under one of the League's covenants in the hope that international differences could be solved by arbitration. It was not an instrument of the League but the idea of membership was attacked as a sly prelude to back door entry.

---

42   Ibid., p. 544

The USA did participate in a number of conferences held under League auspices, in particular the naval agreements which limited the building programmes of the main powers' warships. But since this involved Japan, Washington would hardly fail to take part. The problem of Japan's continual encroachment on China and American interests there was the most important issue in American foreign policy. The rise of Hitler produced only the Neutrality Acts by which Congress was determined not to be embroiled in the darkening affairs of Europe. Roosevelt himself took a much clearer view of the menace. But he was powerless to involve the USA against the will of Congress.

The first Neutrality Act in 1935 was passed as Mussolini prepared to invade Ethiopia. It required the President to declare an embargo on arms sales to any belligerent whether attacker or attacked. A further Act in 1936 prohibited loans or credits to any belligerent nations. A third Act passed one year later authorised the President to make a 'cash and carry' order for any materials bought in the USA by a belligerent, i.e. they must be paid for on production or in advance and must be transported by that nation's own ships.

These were far from neutral acts. Only Britain and France could provide a merchant marine sufficient to carry large quantities of arms or indeed other materials in the event of war. Only they could provide the fighting ships to protect convoys. They were thus the only potential purchasers. The effect of the Acts' financial prohibitions was to throw US support, wittingly or unwittingly, on the German side. The continuing power of the isolationists was displayed in August 1939, on the very eve of the outbreak of war, when Roosevelt failed to persuade Congress to agree to a swift repeal of the arms embargo provisions within the Neutrality Acts. He tried again and won the support of Congress, despite strong resistance, for his amendment in November, by which time Germany was overrunning Poland. But the provision that sales must be on a cash and carry basis remained.

Roosevelt had few illusions about the menace though he said little of that in public. He called on Sumner Welles, Assistant Secretary of State, to visit the warring nations' capitals to see if there was a basis for an American diplomatic initiative. Welles recorded that Roosevelt saw one of two dangers, unless by some 'miracle' the conflict was ended.

> The first that a victory by Hitler would immediately imperil the vital interests of the United States. The other an eventual victory of the Western powers could only be won after a long and desperately fought contest which would bring Europe to total economic and social collapse with disastrous effect upon the American people.[43]

---

43   *The Years of Decision* by Sumner Welles, Harper and Harper, 1941

Unfortunately the President was still fighting uphill so far as the American public was concerned. Welles records his own view that except perhaps in one or two sections of the country, general opinion had 'reached another climax of out-and-out isolationism'.[44]

---

44   Ibid., p. 75

CHAPTER 8
A STRAINED COALITION

Germany invades France - Churchill becomes Premier - seeks American aid and agrees Atlantic Charter - economic rivalry an issue - Russia invaded - Eden visits Stalin - assesses his character - post-war frontiers arguments - Japan bombs Pearl Harbor - Germany declares war on USA - promises of Second Front abandoned - Churchill flies to pacify Stalin

The arrival of Churchill in May 1940 as Prime Minister, the fall of France and the Battle of Britain followed in quick succession. Now at least the fighting was real and the determination of Britain to fight was beyond doubt. Hitler ditched his plan for a cross-Channel invasion in September. The land fighting against the Axis powers was confined to North Africa. Sweeping victories there over the Italians provided an exaggerated picture of British power until the arrival of General Rommel and the Afrika Korps.

The problem of war supplies loomed large. Britain could get arms and raw materials from the USA if it paid cash. It could also barter. The mothballed fifty First World War destroyers which President Roosevelt was ready to offer came in exchange for a series of military bases in the West Indies, Newfoundland and Bermuda, a transaction he regarded as a bargain since it substantially advanced the American frontier against a possible German attack. At one point, the suggestion was made that the British might care to part with the whole West Indies; Eden was appropriately irritated. The President also authorised the despatch of over 600,000 US army rifles to Britain through the legal device of selling the equipment to armament firms to sell to Britain, with the assurance that Washington would provide the firms with new orders. The destroyers had some use in the battle of the Atlantic but many had to be refitted in British shipyards at the expense of building other warships. Nonetheless, the destroyers were seen as a heartening gesture.

Britain was, however, running out of money. In the autumn of 1940, Churchill sent Roosevelt a plea for help. The President had every sympathy. But the public, though also predominantly sympathetic to Britain, was not enthusiastic about deeper involvement in the war. Roosevelt proposed a Lend-Lease Bill which would allow Britain large credits to buy arms and material. Two months of bitter debate followed. Roosevelt put forward the simple argument of self-interest:

> The best defence of the United States is the success of Great Britain in defending itself … I go back to the idea that the one thing necessary for American national defence is additional productive facilities; and the more we increase these facilities – factories, shipbuilding ways, munitions, plant etc and so on – the stronger American defence is. Orders from Great Britain are therefore a tremendous asset to American national defence because they automatically create additional facilities. I am talking selfishly from the American point of view – nothing else.[45]

Truman was to point out that for every extra British or Russian soldier armed through Lend-Lease, it meant one less American likely to face action on the battlefield.

There was certainly a problem pointed out by various critics of Lend-Lease that Britain could well be too impoverished to eventually repay the cost of the programme. Roosevelt said, perhaps with studied vagueness, that he would expect payment 'in kind'. In practice the USA was to make two substantial fifty-year loans to repay the aid, with an allowance to waive the repayment in certain circumstances. This was done on six occasions, though the cost of repayment increased as the pound slumped against the dollar. The concluding repayment was made in 2005.

The Lend-Lease Bill was finally passed by the Senate with a majority of nearly two-to-one and in the House with a majority of five-to-one. The availability of arms for Britain was now assured, provided the British merchant fleet and its Royal Navy escorts could survive the U-Boats. When the battle of the Atlantic looked like being lost, the USA provided facilities and eventually escorts which greatly strengthened the British position.

With the invasion of Russia in mid-1941, the whole pattern of the war was to change, including the Lend-Lease programme. In Britain, the sudden acquisition of the new ally produced a wave of pro-Soviet feeling, though alongside fears that Germany might win a quick victory against an army so weakened by Stalin's purges. The surge of goodwill in Britain was not reciprocated in the Kremlin. There was little reason why it should be after so many years of a British policy which hoped that Hitler's ambitions could be directed eastwards. Now it had happened – though in circumstances very different from those hopefully assumed by the inveterate anti-Soviets in the pre-war years. The Nazis were now fighting the Bolshies – but Britain as well.

---

45   Spartacus.schoolnet.co.org. The site usefully includes the Bill itself, Eden's complaints about negotiations with the USA, and the views of leading supporters and critics of Lend-Lease.

From the Kremlin's point of view there was no particular reason to believe that the underlying hostility of so many British politicians towards the Soviet Union had undergone any great change even if the countries found themselves unexpected allies. Seen from Moscow, the fact that Britain and France had found themselves at war with Germany looked less like a determined attempt to destroy Hitler than a miscalculation.

And could the Kremlin now trust the British government? Moscow was constantly to fear that London would make a separate peace with Hitler. The fact that the country was now led by Churchill did little to reduce Soviet alarm. Russian policy was shot through with suspicion. And since the British Government never lost its own fear that Stalin might make a separate peace with Hitler, the stage was set for a touchy relationship.

Churchill's initial enthusiasm for the new and desperately needed ally was soon qualified. The surge of public support for the Soviet Union proved such that he suggested to the Ministry of Information that something should be done to counteract 'the present tendency of the British public to forget the dangers of Communism in their enthusiasm over the resistance of Russia'.[46]

Perhaps he thought Eden too had forgotten the dangers of Communism. The Foreign Secretary was more relaxed about the Red Menace than the Prime Minister. The differing attitudes of the two men were to cause considerable tension, especially in the late months of 1941. Eden managed to persuade Churchill to sanction an ultimatum to neutral Iran to expel German citizens living there – a potential danger to Britain's oil supplies. When Iran refused, there was a joint action by Britain and Russia which led to a partition of the country between the two powers. It became a bone of contention in the early days of the Cold War.

Two major issues divided Eden and Churchill: aid to Russia and her post-war borders. Military assistance was obviously vital. Stalin, with his back to the wall and facing possible defeat, had called for twenty-five to thirty British divisions to be sent to Russia to fight alongside the Red Army. This was a wild demand given Britain's limited resources. Churchill would not agree even to a token force. Nor would he agree to anything like the supply of war materials that Russia called for. This concerned Eden. Sir Stafford Cripps, Britain's Ambassador in Moscow, was to threaten resignation because the flow of aid was so small.

The Atlantic Charter
Churchill and Roosevelt met in warships off the Newfoundland coast in August 1941, and as their staffs discussed all-important strategic issues, the American side proposed a declaration, to be called the Atlantic Charter. It grew out of little more than their desire for an inspiring press release. The Russians, in the war for six weeks were, as so often, not consulted about the draft. Much was to be made of the

---

46   Charmley, op. cit., p. 469

document, Roosevelt emphasising the high moral purpose of support for Britain. The President was concerned about the continuing support of Congress for Lend-Lease to Britain and the looming problems if it was extended to Russia. Senator Robert Taft spoke for many when he declared: 'A victory for Communism would be far more dangerous to the United States than a victory for Fascism.'[47]

The Charter, to the dismay of the Foreign Office, was soon in danger of being transformed into a premature declaration of war aims such as had bedevilled President Wilson. There were eight points in the Charter, mainly pieties, of which three were significant. Neither Britain nor the USA sought aggrandisement, territorial or otherwise. All peoples had the right to choose their governments. All countries should have access on equal terms to the trade and raw materials of the world. Since this last point conflicted with the British system of Imperial Preference, Churchill had it qualified – backed by a hastily summoned Cabinet in London – as allowing 'due respect to existing obligations'. But an equal access provision, so relentlessly pursued by the USA, was inserted into the Lend-Lease agreement.

The 'right to self-government' item was awkward. Churchill had to explain in the Commons that it did not apply to the British Empire's colonies. The Poles complained in due course that the Charter did not guarantee a Polish outlet to the sea. The Free French, because of their own country's colonial empire, disliked the self-government item as much as Churchill. The Russians complained to Eden that they had not been consulted. They were later to point out to Britain and the USA, with pleasant satisfaction, that the two countries were not living up to the Charter, for example in their indifference to the regime in Spain and their readiness to admit Argentina to the United Nations.

The Russians in due course agreed under US pressure to sign up to the rashly drawn up Charter. They added a cautious codicil: 'Practical applications of these principles will necessarily adapt to the circumstances, needs and historic peculiarities of particular countries.'[48]

Eden confronts Stalin

Anglo-Soviet relations were under such strain as the months passed for Eden himself to be despatched to Moscow. But he was strictly instructed not to make any firm promises about post-war borders. Stalin was already demanding there should be and that they include recognition of the 1941 borders of the USSR, incorporating the Baltic States and a chunk of Poland. While Eden was still travelling the news came of the Japanese attack on Pearl Harbor. When Roosevelt's Cabinet was hastily convened, some favoured declaring war on Germany as well as Japan. Roosevelt vetoed the suggestion. The dilemma was solved four days later when Germany and Italy declared war on the USA. Pearl Harbor brought new

---

47 *The Cold War and its Origins* by Donald Fleming, Allen and Unwin, 1960, p. 136
48 *Spheres of Influence* by Lloyd C. Gardner, John Murray, 1993, p. 103

hopes – and further complications about post-war borders which Americans were no less reluctant than Churchill to accept.

Eden found himself talking to Stalin within earshot of German guns. This did not stop the Soviet leader focusing sternly on the post-war settlement. Britain must accept his demands. There was an accompanying and remarkable proposal from the Soviet leader. He thought that the way forward would be to see Europe divided up into Russian and British spheres of influence. Britain would recognise the Soviet right to establish military bases in Finland and Romania. Germany would be divided and Britain would be welcome to establish her own military bases in Scandinavia and perhaps in Belgium. The Americans, Stalin seemed to think, would not be involved in these matters.

Eden insisted that he was not authorised to enter into any arrangement. He was in fact fairly sympathetic in his own mind to the borders request on grounds of realpolitik. What the Russians already had or would regain they would obviously be able to keep. If they were defeated the issue would not arise. But, he explained to Stalin, Churchill had agreed with Roosevelt some time before that no arrangement about European borders should be reached without consulting Washington. Besides, Stalin's proposal would conflict with the Atlantic Charter. 'Why does the restoration of our frontiers conflict with the Atlantic Charter?' came the demand. Eden's attitude eventually drove an increasingly suspicious Stalin to comment: 'I thought the Atlantic Charter was directed against those who were trying to establish world domination. It now looks as if the Atlantic Charter was directed against the USSR.'[49]

Eden contented Stalin with a promise to press the question of borders when back in London. He was to receive no encouragement from Churchill. Eden pointed out that if the Allies won the war 'Russian forces would probably penetrate into Germany and that at a later date she will want more than her 1941 frontiers.'[50].

Churchill's reply was scornful. To say that 'nothing we or the US can do or say will affect the situation at the end of the war' was to make very large assumptions. In the optimistic view of the Prime Minister:

> It seems probable that the United States and the British Empire, far from being exhausted, will be the most powerfully armed and economic bloc the world has ever seen, and that the Soviet Union will need our aid for reconstruction far more than we shall need theirs.[51]

Eden persisted and found an ally in Halifax who, for all his former anti-Soviet thinking, was now in a realistic mood about how Stalin's mood depended on

---

49   Ibid., p. 114
50   Gardner, op. cit., p. 115
51   Foreign Office documents, January 1942, n371/32874, Public Record Office

post-war security. In reply, Eden agreed and added of Stalin: 'He seemed to me a man with a complete "realpolitik" outlook and a descendant of Peter the Great rather than of Lenin.' He added that it was easy to spot the mentality of international socialists and Communists. 'But I can say that it never peeped out at any time.'[52]

Churchill's bullish attitude about the combined power of the USA and Britain underwent a sharp change as the military position deteriorated. Japan was threatening Singapore. In the Atlantic the losses were rising. In North Africa Rommel continued his successes. So Churchill wrote to Roosevelt in early March as the Russians were pressing for a treaty to recognise their 1941 boundaries:

> The increasing gravity of the war has led me to feel that the principles of the Atlantic Charter ought not to be construed so as to deny Russia the frontiers she occupied when the Germans attacked her ... I hope therefore that you will be able to give us a free hand to sign the treaty which Stalin desires as soon as possible.[53]

The President was not ready to do so, though he was prepared to give the Russian Ambassador some ambiguous undertakings about Soviet 'security' after the war. The issue now became entangled with that of the Second Front for which Stalin was to make frantic demands. They were continuous from the moment the German invasion began. Before Pearl Harbor, Churchill pointed out that a cross-Channel invasion by British forces was out of the question. Britain did not have the resources. Such an enterprise might temporarily draw off German forces but after its predictable failure, Hitler would transfer large forces to the eastern front. When the USA came into the war, the Soviet demand for an early cross-Channel invasion seemed less unreasonable. It met with a sympathetic hearing from Roosevelt. He expressed his hope to Churchill in March for 'a new front on the Continent' in the summer.

By May the President was complaining about the difficulties being raised by both the British and the American military to any sort of Second Front before 1943. Conditions and material were never ideal, he recognised (a major problem being the absence of landing craft). But he regarded it as 'essential' to have active operations in 1942.

The definition of Second Front action was at that point vague. The President talked of establishing air superiority followed by commando raids of up to 50,000 men. The Soviet Union must be helped. It was killing far more Germans than everyone else put together. The President was prepared to face heavy losses. However, the losses would be primarily British. The USA lacked both troops and commanders with

---

52   Gardner, op. cit., p. 121
53   FO Policy towards Russia, op. cit., 28 Jan 1942

battlefield experience. Churchill and General Alan Brooke (later Lord Alanbrooke), Chief of the Imperial General Staff, were understandably alarmed.

Harry Hopkins, Roosevelt's special envoy, and General George Marshall, Chairman of the Joint Chiefs of Staff, came to London in April with plans for a cross-Channel invasion for 1943 – or possibly late 1942 if Russia's position was deteriorating. Hopkins told Eden that 'our main proposal here should take the heat off Russia's diplomatic demands upon England'.[54] But Churchill thought Roosevelt was being 'very foolish' in trying to substitute an ill-advised military venture for agreement with the Soviets on post-war borders. Churchill himself was now firmly in favour of recognising the demanded borders as the lesser evil than a rash cross-Channel invasion.

Molotov arrived in London with a draft Anglo-Soviet Treaty involving all that Roosevelt feared. Russia's pre-1941 borders would be recognised. A secret protocol would involve British consent to Soviet plans for bases in Finland and Romania. Britain would have Soviet support in establishing bases in Holland and Belgium. The Americans strongly protested that this was an attempt to carve up Europe into spheres of influence.

Gilbert Winant, American Ambassador in London, called on the visiting Molotov to emphasise the President's view on the proposed treaty. But he also wanted to underline how keen Washington was on a Second Front. Molotov was under pressure from Moscow not to press his case too far. He abandoned the proposed treaty in favour of a straightforward military alliance. One problem had been solved. But in its place was another: the Russians now felt they could regard talk about a cross-Channel invasion as a promise.

Molotov went on to Washington determined to firm up this undertaking. The President pointed out that both the American and British military advised against 1942. They preferred 'a sure thing in 1943'. Molotov argued on. Finally Roosevelt authorised him, to Marshall's alarm, to tell Stalin 'we expect the formation of a Second Front this year'.[55]

It remained a wholly unrealistic idea. Molotov said in an interview after the end of the Cold War that Russia realised this at the time. But at least he had the commitment which, if unfulfilled, could be a useful negotiating lever. By August Churchill decided that he should tackle the bear in his own lair and set off for Moscow to tell Stalin that there would be no Second Front in 1942.

Churchill flies to Moscow

This was the first time the ancient enemies and now allies had met. Relations between the two were to range from friendship and admiration to distrust and scorn, ultimately total hostility. Churchill was volatile by nature. Stalin was relentless

---

54   Gardner, op. cit., p. 133
55   Foreign Relations of the US, 1942, State Department III, p. 575–578

in his pursuit of Soviet interests. He was dealing with one of Bolshevism's oldest enemies whom he suspected, rightly as it eventually turned out, might revert to his ancient hostility. American–Russian relations were easier. Roosevelt believed, unlike Truman, that post-war cooperation with Russia was eminently possible once good relations with 'Uncle Joe' were established. Churchill thought so too – at times.

The meeting in Moscow started badly when Churchill explained the postponement of the Second Front. Stalin protested that the British attitude was excessively cautious, even, by implication, cowardly. He would not believe that the German forces in France were strong. Anyway, there had been a promise.

The Prime Minister spent some time arguing in detail that an unsuccessful Second Front would do more harm than good. He appeared to satisfy Stalin with his revelation of Operation Torch, the American landing in North Africa scheduled for October. It would make it possible to attack the 'soft underbelly' of the Axis via Italy. The Soviet dictator was impressed and made his own analysis of the strategic possibilities finally adding: 'May God prosper this undertaking.'

Churchill's record of this was positively glowing:

> I was deeply impressed with this remarkable statement. It showed the Russian dictator's complete mastery of a problem hitherto novel to him. Very few people alive could have comprehended in so few minutes the reasons we had all so long been wrestling with for months. He saw it all in a flash.[56]

But Stalin was in a more critical mood the next day. Evidently his colleagues did not think he had made enough of the failure to launch a Second Front in 1942. Churchill declared, rashly, that a cross-Channel Second Front would still be possible in 1943. (He would have to explain away in due course that this timetable could not be met.) The Moscow meeting concluded with some badinage about their ancient enmities.

Churchill's relationship with Stalin was, however, soon back on the roller coaster. The Red Army needed massive supplies. The USA could provide them but transporting them was left to Britain which had to use the notoriously dangerous Arctic route. Transportation through Iran via the Mediterranean could not be substantial. Supply could never meet demand.

The disasters which befell the British convoys made little impression on Stalin whose scornful comments roused Churchill to fury. Two other developments strained relations to the limit. The slow Italian campaign was siphoning off fewer German divisions than expected. Worst of all, the Second Front was now being postponed until 1944. Churchill had later to tell Stalin that D-Day might need to be delayed from the spring of 1944 to the summer.

Stalin was furious. At one point relations were so bad and the German resistance to the Russian steamroller still sufficiently strong to renew London's fear that

Stalin might make a separate peace with Hitler. Churchill's age-old hostility to Communism surfaced again in 1943. In October Eden's private secretary, Oliver Harvey, records the Prime Minister saying: 'We mustn't weaken Germany too much, we may need her against Russia'.[57]

Relations between Churchill and Roosevelt, though generally warm, did not always run smoothly. Roosevelt constantly feared that Britain wanted a 'spheres of influence' division of Europe with Russia. There was also a strategic divide. Churchill wanted an Allied assault through the Balkans to forestall Soviet advances. His own military resisted and the Americans gave the proposal a decisive thumbs down.

TEHRAN: THE FIRST MEETING OF THE BIG THREE

The first Big Three meeting came in November 1943 in Tehran. To Churchill's dismay, Roosevelt was determined to show the Russians that the USA and Britain were not going to 'gang up' against Moscow. The President saw Stalin alone at the outset of the conference.

Roosevelt proved also markedly keener than Churchill to discuss plans to weaken post-war Germany. The mistakes after the First World War were in the Prime Minister's mind. He thought that the Germans would prove pacific after the war. Stalin insisted that the German characteristic of obedience would keep them a danger. He seriously upset the Prime Minister by suggesting the execution of 50,000 officers of the German General Staff. Roosevelt tried to make a joke of it; Churchill remained horrified.

The details of Operation Overlord, the invasion of France, were now explained to Stalin. He bluntly asked the simple question: 'When?' He did not get a firm reply. Who would command it? This had not been decided. Stalin scornfully dismissed the whole enterprise.

More promisingly from the Russian point of view, Roosevelt said that he wanted to remove American troops from Europe within two years of the war's end. Stalin readily approved. Roosevelt implied also that he would not fuss about the Russian occupation of Eastern Europe. As for central Europe – Poland – he hoped for Stalin's help with so many Polish-descended voters to satisfy. Stalin wanted the Russian border to be the old Curzon Line. In return the Poles would be getting a chunk of eastern Germany. Churchill accepted the plan, though later complaining bitterly of the number of displaced Germans it caused.

What pleased both Western leaders most was Stalin's assurance that Russia would come into the war against Japan after the defeat of Germany, though it

57   *Eden* by David Carlton, op. cit., p. 225

would take months to move the troops the 6,000 miles between the western and the eastern front. At that point the fear was that the final subjugation of Japan would involve horrendous casualties. The A-bomb was only a secret project and far from certainty or completion. Stalin inevitably wanted his compensation for his assurance. Outer Mongolia must be officially recognised as Soviet, the southern half of Sakhalin (lost to Japan in the war of 1904–5) must be yielded, also certain strategically important Kurile islands. There were further demands but as these were compensation for losses in the 1904–5 war they seemed reasonable enough.

The Polish Problem

Poland was an issue of honour which haunted the Prime Minister. Roosevelt had his voters; Churchill had his conscience. Britain had gone to war to 'save' Poland and failed. He also had a warm admiration for Poles who fought with the British forces. Dealing with the Polish government in exile at its London base was, however, difficult. As Churchill remarked to Stalin, two Poles would always find something to argue about. Stalin replied that a Pole on his own would quarrel with himself.

Moscow had prepared for the post-war period by setting up a tame administration, the Lublin Committee. This was inevitably despised by the London Poles. When the graves of some 10,000 murdered Polish officers were unearthed by German forces in the Katyn Forest in 1943, the London Poles raged at Stalin. He had in fact been ruthlessly culling the Polish middle class and the total of this massacre was later established at over 20,000. Stalin dismissed the discovery as a German plot and broke off relations with the London body. Churchill tried unsuccessfully to persuade the government in exile that it must somehow work with Moscow. He bit his tongue and took an emollient line with Stalin himself. To worsen matters, the uprising by the Polish underground in Warsaw in 1944 was cruelly left unaided by Russian forces at hand.

The dilemma for Churchill was acute. His natural sympathy for the Poles apart, he was also to be haunted by the fear that history would see him as the man who fought appeasement at Munich, only to accept it for Poland. But he had to maintain a working relationship with Stalin. These conflicting desires contributed to the increasingly erratic nature of the view he took of the Soviet leader.

He was in due course able to persuade Moscow to add some London Poles to the Lublin Committee as it became the de facto government of the country during the Red Army's advance. In the event only one man was added from that source – and soon dropped. The Lublin group were to be eventually but reluctantly recognised as the official government by both Britain and the USA in June 1945, shortly before the post-war Potsdam conference, the last meeting of the Big Three. The taste left was very bitter. After Yalta in early 1945, Churchill declared: 'I have not the slightest intention of being cheated over Poland, not even if we go to the verge of war with Russia.'[58]

---

58   *The Fringes of Power* by John Colville, Hodder and Stoughton, 1985, Vol. II

But it was a hollow threat. When the House of Commons came to debate the Yalta arrangements, the Prime Minister was fiercely criticised. Ironically, various Munich appeasers were now mounting onslaughts against the Prime Minister's 'appeasement'. Eden, at a Moscow conference, kept asking members of the Moscow Embassy staff whether he might 'go down in history books as an appeaser'.[59]

Washington's fear about a spheres-of-influence deal by Britain and Russia were to mount after Churchill made a second visit to Moscow in late 1944. He made a remarkable proposal in what he later dubbed 'the naughty document'. He wrote on a half sheet of paper that the division of power in the Balkans should be:

Greece 90% Britain, 10% Russia
Romania 90% Russia, 10% Britain
Yugoslavia 50-50
Bulgaria 75% Russia, 25% Britain
Hungary 50-50

The list was studied by Stalin who then ticked it and passed it back. Churchill was to write of this moment with becoming candour:

After that there was a long silence. The pencilled paper lay in the centre of the table. At length I said, 'Might it not be thought rather cynical if it seemed we had disposed of these issues, fateful to millions of people in such an offhand manner. Let us burn the paper.' 'No, you keep it,' said Stalin.[60]

The Americans were sternly critical when they heard about it, Churchill suggested that it would only apply during 'war conditions'. But Stalin could hardly be blamed for concluding that Britain certainly, the USA possibly, had understood that various countries were going to be allotted to the control of the main powers. In the case of Greece, British troops had already landed to support King Paul's regime against left-wing rebels.

Talk of nations being free to choose their own destinies and, by extension, their own governments would be interpreted by a man like Stalin – and perhaps by others too in the light of the naughty document – as largely window-dressing. Lord Moran, Churchill's personal doctor and confidant who accompanied him on all trips foreign, summed it up: 'He [Churchill] would hold on to Greece – Stalin could have the rest of the Balkans'.[61]

59 Carlton, op. cit., p. 246
60 Churchill memoirs, op. cit., also *Meeting at Potsdam* by Charles Mee, Evans and co. Inc, 1975, pp. 118–9
61 *Churchill: the Struggle for Survival* by Lord Moran, Sphere Books, 1968, p. 230

He seemed to confirm this later: 'Winston's emotional nature, to be sure, has been deeply touched by the faithful manner in which Stalin has discharged his undertaking not to interfere in Greece. He has stuck to his bargain to the letter.'[62]

Vladimir Dedijer, Tito's biographer,[63] adds that Stalin discouraged aid from Balkan countries to Greek Communists as part of the October bargain. He claims that Stalin tried to honour the 50-50 arrangement over Yugoslavia by urging Tito to bring back King Peter. Churchill's attitude to Russia throughout 1944 and into 1945 remained erratic. He veered between excessive credulity and excessive suspicion. In August 1944 Moran writes of Churchill when in Rome: 'Winston never talks of Hitler these days. He is always harping on the dangers of Communism. He dreams of the Red Army spreading like a cancer from one country to another. It has become an obsession and he seems to think of little else.'[64] Yet in February 1945, at Yalta, Moran was to record Churchill saying: 'I find he (Stalin) does what he says he will do.' Moran added: 'The PM spoke once more of the disaster it would be if anything happened to Stalin. His human understanding and moderation, on many occasions made a deep impression on him.'[65]

---

62   Ibid., p. 257
63   *Tito*, Milovan Djilas, Weidenfeld & Nicholson, 1981, pp. 233, 292–3, 321–323
64   Moran, op. cit., p. 193
65   Ibid., p. 258

CHAPTER 9
SOVIET DIPLOMATS IN OPTIMISTIC MOOD

Soviet foreign ministry assembles three groups to study post-war prospects - experienced diplomats in charge - reasonable prospects for peace seen by all groups - Marxist doctrine gives way to realpolitik - Gromyko has last-minute second thoughts

In the long run-up to the Big Three Yalta conference in February 1945, leading Soviet diplomats, with committees of advisers, were drawing up an assessment of the post-war prospects for East–West relations. Their views, which only came to light with the opening of the Russian archives, were notably optimistic. The Soviet side contemplated a post-war relationship with the West which, though occasionally difficult, would be based on cooperation not conflict. In 1944, Molotov instructed 'the Big Three' in Soviet diplomacy to prepare analyses: Ivan Maisky was a former Ambassador in London; Litvinov had become Molotov's deputy; Andrei Gromyko had been Ambassador in Washington since 1943. The memoranda suggest at moments an almost starry-eyed vision. There is, on the whole, a remarkable lack of Marxist jargon in the documents.

Maisky: 'The next thirty to fifty years'
This memorandum sent to Molotov in early 1944 outlined a long-term programme for the next thirty to fifty years. Though foreseeing problems about East–West relations, his overall vision was cheerful. A problem could be the rise of American 'imperialism' as and when Republicans replaced Democrats. An expansionist policy could develop in Washington. Another difficulty might spring from 'proletarian revolutions' across the globe increasing tensions between the USA and the Soviet Union. In Maisky's eyes, proletarian revolutions might prove a problem rather than a Marxist blessing. In principle, his programme advocated that the Soviet Union should strengthen friendly relations with both the USA and Britain.

'Our cooperation with the two countries is an absolute necessity,' he wrote. 'It should take advantage of any Anglo-American differences, so as to improve relations with Britain as a counter-balance. Soviet influence in China should be increased and Moscow should remain the centre for "truly democratic" countries and forces. Germany and Japan should be kept down firmly.'

The conquest of Japan should be left to the USA and Britain. Maisky thought that the price in blood which would have to be paid would 'cool American imperialist ardour'. Soviet interests in Europe would be served by having just the USSR as the one land power and Britain as the sea power. In the long term, it would provide time for the Soviet Union to become so strong as to not be threatened by any aggression in Europe or Asia. Alternatively, continental Europe 'becomes socialistic excluding the possibility of war itself in this part of the world'.

The Anglo-America clashes he foresaw would arise from the USA seeking to replace Britain as the economic power in her crumbling empire. But while he warned about a new and dynamic American imperialism, he stressed that it was a new brand, 'not so much territorial or military as financial and economic annexation'. That should not preclude the 'absolute necessity' of East–West cooperation.

In Europe itself, he foresaw France, Czechoslovakia, Denmark, Norway, Holland and Belgium producing popular front governments which would mean no problems for the Soviet Union. But in Eastern Europe, it would be necessary, in conjunction *with Britain and the USA* (italics added) to impose what he called 'real democracies', given the history of those countries.

A long-term problem still nagged Maisky. The 'acute contradiction' between the USA and the Soviet Union might one day cause serious problems by 'stimulating the resurrection of Germany and Japan ... by building up an anti-Soviet bloc in Europe... [E]ven more dangerous would be a US-Chinese alliance spearheaded against the USSR'.

The Gromyko analysis

This report, drafted in July was still more optimistic than Maisky's. He thought the USA would be ready for economic and political cooperation. There was strong support for Roosevelt's general approach and it would be in American interests to maintain it even if the Republicans came to power. The USA would not only be keen on the 'military enfeeblement' of Germany, it would also want to see it kept down economically because: 'The industrial-bourgeoisie of the USA in any case would be interested in the prevention of Germany's re-emergence as a serious economic competitor.'

Peace would be an American interest because the country had emerged with such predominance in trade, finance and technological development that it would wish to put to profitable use. Alongside this Gromyko predicted that: 'The US would be sympathetic to and facilitating in establishing bourgeois-democratic regimes in Western Europe and first of all in Germany.'

So the Americans would be enemies of fascist-type governments, 'at least for some time'. He also believed that the USA and the USSR would have mutual economic interests. The Americans would be looking for new markets and raw materials while the Russians would be seeking credits, technical assistance and scientific cooperation.

Problems? Gromyko feared the Americans would be too soft on Germany. He was also worried about the Catholic Church, the anti-Soviet press and the 'general ideological hostility of the US ruling class towards the USSR'. As to Eastern Europe, the establishment of Soviet-type regimes would produce concerns in 'domestic political circumstances' (the hyphenate vote issue). It would be hard to have the Baltic States recognised as part of the USSR.

The Middle East was also a possible problem area. It would not be in the Soviet interest to see American influence in that area consolidated, particularly in Iran. However, he concludes: 'In spite of possible difficulties which from time to time might emerge in our relations with the United States, the necessary conditions are clearly present for a continuation of cooperation between our two countries in the post war period.'

But at the last moment, he sent a cautioning cover note to Molotov. Apparently fearing his committee had been too optimistic, he added that serious clashes could not be excluded, even military ones because 'the political and ideological hostility of the ruling classes of the USA and other countries would remain'.

The Litvinov view

The memorandum from the old League of Nations warhorse shows that his own committee of experts were fairly optimistic. The analysis is concluded in January 1945, just before Yalta.

Litvinov quotes with approval the comment of Sumner Wells, a key voice in the State Department: 'With no other country have our interests clashed as little as with Russia.' Litvinov was confident about the 1941 western borders because the USA did not have major interests in that part of the world. Roosevelt would show some sign of disapproval but being a realist would 'recognise boundaries adequate to our aspirations'.

He did foresee clashes but primarily between the USA and Britain. America would press for compensation for its wartime role. Washington would expect Britain to open up her empire to trade, markets and investment. But both the Western allies would want: 'A normalisation of life in European countries, their full stabilisation by means of establishing such bourgeois, democratic or even conservative forms of government which would remove fears of social upheavals.'

China might provide a point of conflict since the USA was seen as likely to increase its influence there to the level of a protectorate. There could also be arguments about Lend-Lease since the Soviet Union could not repay. The Americans might press for some sort of political compensation. However the

Americans and the Soviets might combine against Britain on the issue of the latter's desire to hold on to the colonies. But Litvinov adds a cautious note which Molotov underlined in blue pencil:

> While there are no deep reasons for serious and long term conflict between the USA and the USSR in any part of the world (with the possible exception of China) it is difficult to outline some concrete basis for their positive political cooperation apart from a mutuality of interest in the preservation of world peace.

Like the other analyses this was written well before the A-bomb was tested. Had Litvinov been able to foresee that he might have laid more emphasis on the 'mutuality of interest' to which he refers in a rather offhand way. In the case of Soviet-British relations, he did not see the same historical basis for common interests. He singled out the conflict of interest over Iran but thought that could be managed. Britain was also unlikely to make difficulties about Moscow's wish to have a greater say in the control of traffic through the Dardanelles.

Where the two counties had a complete common interest was in the need to curb Germany as a military power. The USSR would now be the only major Continental power. This was such an important development that Britain would seek: 'An amicable settlement of security issues according to the principles of geographic proximity.'

He saw Russia enjoying predominance in Finland, Sweden, Poland, Hungary, Czechoslovakia, Romania, the Slav countries of the Balkans and Turkey. 'The British sphere should undoubtedly include Holland, Belgium, France, Spain, Portugal and Greece. Norway, Denmark, Germany, Austria and Italy should constitute a "neutral" zone.'

He later suggested that Norway, Turkey, Yugoslavia, Denmark and Italy might be 'subject to bargaining and compromise'. He thought Britain would agree to such a division of interests because of likely post-war rivalry between it and the USA. That could see American ambitions in the British Dominions where they would want territory or at least bases, with the competition between the two countries intensifying over the struggle for oil and rubber: 'Faced with such a cheerless prospect England cannot avoid thinking about the expediency of securing long term tranquillity in Europe by way of reaching an accord with the USSR.'

Both Russia and Britain would have a mutual interest in opposing American expansionism in the Far East and in settling the Lend-Lease issue. He defined security spheres as meaning zones where a major power would exclude another major power from entering into 'particularly close relations or reaching agreements with countries' in another's security sphere and establishing military bases there. He did not see these spheres of interest being 'detrimental to the independence of the states included in them'. But he expected a demand by Britain for: 'Guarantees regarding the nature of government and independence for the countries in the Soviet security sphere.'

Molotov used his blue pencil on this passage. Clearly, demands from Britain on any Soviet withdrawal of this matter would get short shrift from him.

Litvinov recognised that the 'spheres of influence' approach would encounter difficulties. Britain had traditionally resisted the growth of a single major power dominating the Continent. Also, the Americans had been openly opposed since the time of Woodrow Wilson to spheres of influence – though not, Litvinov noted, that this stopped the USA insisting on Latin America as its own area of interest.

These documents must have influenced Stalin and Molotov. But they dealt with a Rooseveltian USA. The Soviets soon found themselves dealing with Truman.

Open protestations of friendship and peaceful intentions were common enough on the Soviet side at the end of the war. But they were widely distrusted by Washington and later London as outright hypocrisy. Orthodox Marxist thinking does creep in on the issue of expected Anglo-American rivalry. Capitalist countries were expected to fall out as they pursued their own economic interests. The role that economics was to play in Anglo-American relations was seen as very significant. But it was such as to bind the United States and Britain, not separate them.

The Kremlin's analysts were remarkably united in seeing Britain continuing as a major power in the post-war years. It was not to be. Thus the idea of utilising British interests from time to time to keep American expansion at bay was a chimera. The post-war Big Three of the wartime alliance was soon to subside into a Big Two-and-a-half.

We have to wonder, given post-war events, how far Stalin and Molotov agreed with their subordinates' views. There is no reason to think they did not see them as reasonable at the time, though Litvinov and Maisky fell into disfavour later when their optimism was discredited.[66] Russia's behaviour at Potsdam and in the later foreign ministers' conferences does not suggest that the realpolitik strategy outlined in the documents had been dropped. And Western representatives who saw Stalin himself during the end of the war period always found him concerned about security and power rather than ideology. Churchill had offered Stalin his spheres of influence deal in his 'naughty document'. It was American objections which killed it.

It was to prove another historical irony that while the supposedly ideology-driven Soviet side negotiated and argued about frontiers and security, it was the Americans who regularly invoked ideology, in the form of liberal, capital, democratic and economic principles, to justify their rising conflict with Russia.

---

66   Both men were sent into retirement with a very low grade Soviet honour, the equivalent to a top British diplomat being retired with no more than an MBE.

CHAPTER 10
FALSE HARMONY AT YALTA

Roosevelt's last Big Three meeting – supposed settlements rouse British and US delight – Stalin's firm promise to join war with Japan – German reparations to USSR promised – Poland unresolved but Roosevelt confident it will be – after the conference Churchill backs Russia in tough measures for Romania – Roosevelt returns with only weeks to live

With the defeat of Germany in sight, the Allied leaders and their military advisers met at Yalta in February in the rather battered surroundings of the former Imperial summer palace of Livadhia. It was to prove the high point in East–West amity. It was also Roosevelt's last meeting with Churchill and Stalin. He was already a sick man and was to die before the Potsdam conference in July where American policy took a harsher note.

Most issues were resolved, so the participants thought, or were postponed for later discussions but still with the belief that they too were soluble. At times the atmosphere became almost euphoric. Cadogan, the least likely admirer of the Soviet leader, wrote 'Stalin is a great man.'[67] Hopkins, when the topic of reparations was threatening this harmonious atmosphere, passed a note to Roosevelt suggesting it be postponed for later talks: 'The Russians have given in so much at this conference.'[68]

The President remained more suspicious of British than Russian ambitions. He told Stettinius, his Secretary of State, that there was no land 'not even a sandbar' which the British would not seize if they were given the chance.[69] The US Chiefs of Staff had also argued that Britain should be allowed no role in the conquest of Japan. They were welcome to evict the Japanese from former

---

67 Cadogan diaries, op. cit., p. 708
68 *Special Envoy* by Averell Harriman and Elie Abel, Random House, 1975, p. 404
69 *Roosevelt and the Russians* by Edward Stettinius, Doubleday, 1949

British territories but no more than that. They had also fiercely resisted some months earlier Churchill's offer to transfer a large part of Bomber Command and the bulk of the Royal Navy's battle fleet to the Pacific. This was despite the serious concern of the Americans about the high casualty rates their own forces were enduring.

Of the Russians at that stage, Roosevelt had little fear. The two great powers had to get along and would do so as the details of a peace settlement were worked out. But Poland proved a major stumbling block, even though the American side was anxious to play down Soviet suspicions that the USA wanted a government there hostile to Russia. The President told Stalin: 'The United States will never agree to lend its support in any way to a provisional government in Poland which would be inimical to your interests.'[70] Differences about other East European countries seemed to be settled by comforting Soviet promises of genuine elections. Churchill was later to assure a restless House of Commons: 'I know of no government which stands in its obligations, even in its own despite, more solidly than the Russian Soviet Government. I decline absolutely to embark here on a discussion of Russia good faith.'[71]

In the Pacific war the President had been warned that it could yet last a long time and involve huge casualties if Japan had to be invaded. Work on the atomic bomb, supposedly secret from the Russians, was far from complete or guaranteed of success. It was a great relief when Stalin firmed up his original Tehran promise to join the war against Japan. He promised to attack Japan within two or three months after the end of the war in Europe. In return, the conference firmed up Soviet rights in Manchuria and the return of territories lost in the 1904–5 war, plus some minor but strategically significant islands. This was a breach of the Atlantic Charter which promised no territorial aggrandisement. But no one was inclined to dwell on that.

The Russian desire for improved rights in the Dardanelles was referred to the subsequent meeting of foreign secretaries planned for London. On Iran, the Russians would make no concessions from the position it had taken up at Tehran. But since it appeared to involve a question of horse-trading over oil rights, serious problems were not anticipated. The strong feelings aroused over reparations found Stalin in a determined mood with Roosevelt and Churchill, particularly the latter, anxious to avoid the errors of Versailles. The Western leaders thought Germany should be allowed a relative degree of prosperity otherwise the seeds of another conflict could be sown. This cut little ice with the Russians. They wanted as much compensation as they could get for their devastated country. They also regarded tough not magnanimous measures as the effective means of curbing German militarism.

---

70 *Roosevelt and the Russians* by Edward Stettinius, Doubleday, 1949, pp. 149, 157, 158
71 Hansard, 27 Feb 1945

A figure of $20bn was put forward by the Soviet sides as the total value of plant and machinery which would be sequestered, half to go to Russia. Churchill was particularly resistant. It was agreed after warm debate that the matter should be referred to a Reparations Commission. The general principle that – as a basis for 'discussion' – the total of reparations should be $20bn and that 50 per cent should go to the Soviet Union. It was a usefully ambiguous arrangement for Soviet diplomats to exploit later.

The Russians claimed in subsequent negotiations after Roosevelt's death that this meant they were indeed entitled to $10bn and angrily resisted anything less. Churchill's resistance was to remain extremely strong and, in many ways, eccentric. It was in the light of these talks that Churchill wrote his private memorandum saying that this was such an important issue between the two sides that, together with Poland, it could mean another war.

A more harmonious settlement was reached on arrangements for the establishment of the United Nations Organization. Stalin had originally been in favour of the Big Three settling the world's affairs. But he was persuaded to accept the US-British proposal which provided UNO in its basic form. All three could agree on the need for the veto in the security council since none wanted a large group of smaller nations to be able to impose its will on the major powers.

After some hard and successful bargaining by Stalin the conference agreed to three votes for Russia – adding in the Ukraine and Byelorussia as supposed independent republics. He had argued that Britain had the Dominions which would always vote alongside the mother country. The Soviet leader even suggested that the USA could have an extra two votes if it wanted them. The offer was declined with thanks. San Francisco was set down for the first meeting of the new organisation.

For the future of the 'liberated areas' of Eastern Europe the principal was accepted that interim governments would be formed 'broadly representative of all the democratic elements in the population'. Thereafter there would be free elections.

But it was the continuing problem of Poland – treated as a separate issue – on which a satisfactory arrangement had not been achieved in 1944, which was to prove the circle that could not be squared. Agreement proved possible on the new boundaries for this unhappy country. In the east it would be the Curzon Line, or the 'Curzon–Clemenceau' line as Stalin called it, anxious to point out that it was more than just the work of a British foreign minister. This massive loss of territory compared to the area which the Poles had carved out in the 1920 war would be compensated for by a substantial but still not equal area of eastern Germany. Churchill was still worried about German refugees.

As for the Soviet-backed Lublin administration, there was an agreement that it should be more broadly based, with representatives from 'Poles abroad'. It would then be pledged to hold free elections. But the Russians, ominously, refused a request from Churchill that there could be Western participation in the supervision of the elections or even their observation. When the Polish question was raised, Churchill pointed out that freedom for Poland was 'a matter of honour' since that country's independence had been the issue over which Britain had declared war. Stalin's declaration was vehement and he rose to his feet to make it:

> For the Russian people, the question of Poland is not only a question of honour but a question of security. Throughout history Poland has been the corridor through which the enemy has passed into Russia. Twice in the last thirty years our enemies the Germans have passed through this corridor ... Poland is not only a question of honour but of life and death for the Soviet Union.[72]

He called for a Poland strong enough to resist another attack. It should be a country both 'free and friendly' to the Soviet Union. This was in itself an obvious contradiction. Given the traditional hostility between the two states, Poland could either be free or friendly to Russia. It could not be both. It was finally agreed that the Polish issue could be taken up again by a forthcoming foreign ministers' meeting in London.

Both Western leaders returned home from the Crimea anxious to make claims for their success. Roosevelt was extravagant in his review of the conference, branding it as a 'turning point I hope in our history and therefore in the history of the world'. In an echo of Woodrow Wilson's words – and equally misplaced optimism – the President argued that the decisions taken:

> Ought to spell the end of the system of unilateral action, the exclusive alliances, the spheres of influence, the balances of power and all the other expedients that have been tried for centuries and have always failed.[73]

It is an ironic thought that the elite of the Soviet Foreign Office, as we now know from the archives, was proposing spheres of influence arrangements precisely because they were seen as holding out good prospects of peace and cooperation. In any case, as might have been easily foreseen by Washington, the post-war situation in Europe was bound to give a further impetus to spheres of influence arrangements. And of course the USA had no intention of giving up on Latin America.

As for the Polish issue, the President said that the talks had produced 'the most hopeful agreement possible for a free, independent and prosperous Poland'. No doubt he hoped this might quell any alarm at home. But it was putting a very high gloss on a very limited agreement. He commented privately that it was simply the best he could do for Poland at the time.

---

72   *The Cold War and its Origins* by Donald Fleming, Allen and Unwin, 1961, pp. 202, 203
73   See *Special Envoy* by Harriman, op. cit., p. 418

Both the Western leaders were to face charges that they 'gave away Poland' at Yalta. But the reality was that it was not theirs to give. The Russians were already the occupying power. There was little the West could insist on, they could only beg for concessions about the prospective composition of a Polish government.

Churchill had to face restless MPs when he returned from Yalta, privately conceding his fear of being seen as the author of an east European Munich. He refuted claims that the Polish state had been effectively halved – it was to gain territory from Germany: 'And I repudiate and repulse any suggestion that we are making a questionable compromise or yielding to force or fear ... The Poles have their own future in their hands with a single limitation that they must honestly follow, in harmony with their allies, a policy that is friendly to Russia. That is surely reasonable.'[74]

His statement was regularly interrupted by protests, mainly from his own back-benchers. When he came to ensuring a democratic Poland, he acknowledged difficulties. But his peroration took him well out on a limb: 'The impression I brought back from Crimea and from all my other contacts is that Marshal Stalin and the Soviet leaders wish to live in honourable friendship and equality with the Western democracies. I feel also that their word is their bond.'

Churchill's doctor diagnosed a rising weariness in his patient:

> All this hovering, all these conflicting and contradictory policies are, I am sure, due to Winston's exhaustion. He seems torn between two lines of action: he cannot decide whether to make one last attempt to enlist Roosevelt's sympathy for a firmer line with Stalin in the hope that he has learnt something from the course of events, or whether to make his peace with Stalin and save what he can from the wreck of Allied hopes. At one moment he will plead with the President for a common front against Communism and the next he will make a bid for Stalin's friendship. Sometimes the two policies alternate with bewildering rapidity.[75]

Churchill proved to be in no mood to make difficulties for Stalin when the matter of Romania came to the fore within weeks after Yalta. The Russians forced King Michael to dismiss the government of General Nicolae Radescu and replace him with a Communist. Churchill told Eden that it was wrong for the Foreign Office and British representatives to make a fuss about the new Prime Minister in Bucharest. After all the Russians' southern military supply lines passed through Romania. And Britain had no justification in protesting while Russia was acquiescing in Britain's role in Greece.

When Eden told him that Washington was invoking the Yalta agreement about the liberated countries of Eastern Europe and suggesting that Britain

74   Hansard, 27 February 1945
75   Moran, op. cit., p. 229

should follow suit, Churchill dismissed Romania as an 'ex-enemy state'. In his memoirs Churchill implied that he took a more robust view of the Soviets' breach of the Yalta principles in this case. His memorandum to Eden does not bear this out. There he told Eden that if Britain pressed the Soviets too hard, it would damage the spheres of influence agreement with Stalin which he believed still held, whatever Washington might think.

The Americans were in fact too hasty to complain about the Soviet moves in Bucharest. Romania had been an enemy during the war and after the Fascists had been ousted as the Russians advanced, the king installed a coalition, including three Communist ministers, with General Radescu as the new Prime Minister. But Radescu was strongly anti-Communist and anti-Russian. Disorders soon followed as his and the Communists' supporters clashed. As Churchill himself pointed out, the Red Army's southern supply lines ran through Romania. Moreover, the Germans were still in control of neighbouring Yugoslavia. The Russians had a case for insisting on the removal of Radescu.

The Russians were to prove not wholly duplicitous on east European elections. Czechoslovakia and Hungary were allowed relatively free elections. Communists did quite well in the former and very badly in the latter. In Bulgaria and Romania there were merely gestures in allowing some non-Communists into government. All such elements were later removed in the wake of the East–West fallout over the American Marshall Plan of 1948 for economic assistance to Europe.

CHAPTER 11
A NEW US PRESIDENT MEETS HIS ALLIES

Truman succeeds Roosevelt – no knowledge of foreign affairs or Yalta – is briefed by hawks – treats visiting Molotov harshly – sends Harriman to Moscow – is plunged into Potsdam conference – Stalin in indignant mood – Truman drops hint about A-bomb – foreign ministers tussle – Japanese peace feelers rebuffed – Eastern Europe troublesome – Truman dismayed

Roosevelt died in April 1945. That this was to cause such a shock is hard to understand. It was well known that his health had been failing badly. Strangely little thought had been given to the daunting task that would face his successor, Vice President Harry Truman. The new President seemed as surprised and unprepared as everyone else. He had remained deeply involved in domestic issues. He had not been briefed about Yalta, despite its immense significance or on the unsolved problems that remained: 'They did not tell me anything about what was going on.'[76] Nor had he asked to be briefed. He did not even know about the development of the atomic bomb until he had been nearly two weeks in office.

He never denied his lack of knowledge about the great issues being decided by the President. One of his few recorded comments about the problems the USA faced when Hitler spread the war to Russia was:

If we see that Germany is winning we ought to help Russia and if Russia is winning we ought to help Germany and that way let them kill as many as possible although I don't want to see Hitler victorious under any circumstances.[77]

The President had now to arrive at a more sophisticated view than this. Among the documents which landed on his desk was a memorandum which the Office

---

76 *Conflict and Crisis* by Robert Donovan, Norton, 1977, p. 18
77 *Roosevelt the Soldier of Freedom* by J. M. Burns, Harcourt Brace, 1970, p. 96

of Strategic Services (the OSS, forerunner of the CIA) had already sent the dying Roosevelt. It made grim reading. According to the OSS, if the USA stood aside, Russia would emerge as so strong that it could dominate Europe 'and establish its hegemony over Asia'. It was easily foreseeable, claimed the excitable OSS, that Russia 'may well outrank even the US in military potential'. It was just the first of many wild overestimates of Soviet strength.

Truman quickly arranged meetings to brief him on policy towards Russia. Within ten days he was to meet Molotov, stopping off to pay his respects at the White House on his way to the San Francisco conference to discuss the proposed United Nations Charter. The UN was very much a Roosevelt creation. The Soviet view had been that when peace came the Big Three, with their own spheres of influence, should maintain order in the world. Stalin reluctantly yielded to Roosevelt's plea for a large international organisation, to replace the discredited League but with clearer rules and obligations. He regarded sending Molotov himself to San Francisco as a gesture to Roosevelt's memory.

The team of civilians and military heads arranged to brief Truman that day represented a mixed bag of views. Admiral Leahy, who doubled as Chief of Staff to the President and the effective chairman of the Joint Chiefs of Staff, was a powerful personality and a typical Washington hawk, as was the naval head Admiral King, though not General Marshall. He sided with Stimson, the War Secretary, against taking too strong a line with the Russians.

Both were cautious about the President being outspoken. But the hawkish view prevailed. This fitted with Truman's own instincts. He was decisive and impatient by nature and given the analysis by his staff, he wanted a showdown over the Russian failure to live up to the Yalta accords. According to Forrestal's diaries the President's mood was that arrangements with the Soviet Union had so far been a one-way street. He intended to get on with the San Francisco conference and if the Russians 'did not care to join us they could go to hell'.[78]

The subsequent meeting with Molotov was a rough one. Truman at once upbraided him for failing to keep to agreements on Eastern Europe. The message he should take to Stalin was that if the Yalta agreement was not observed, it would seriously shake confidence in the unity of the Big Three. He interrupted Molotov's reply four times with increasing sharpness and concluded with the comment that Stalin must keep his word.

'I have never been talked to like that in my life,' complained Molotov. 'Carry out your agreements and you won't be talked to like that,'[79] concluded the President, indicating that the meeting was over. This highly undiplomatic exchange was a great source of pride to Truman who later commented to Joseph Davies, former Ambassador to Moscow, that he had given Molotov 'the old one-two, straight to

---

78   Fleming, op. cit., p. 267
79   Ibid., p. 268

the jaw'.[80] Leahy, though he had been cautious about the meeting, said he much enjoyed observing this confrontation. How much damage this had done to East–West relations is hard to say. Few forget personal humiliation. However, better sense was to prevail when Truman later despatched Harry Hopkins, Roosevelt's personal envoy to Moscow, to try some fence mending.

The Hopkins Mission to Moscow

In Moscow Hopkins complained to Stalin that there had been a deterioration in the previous six weeks in the two countries' relations. Washington wanted to reverse that. He wanted to state 'as forcibly as I know how' that the situation would get worse if the Polish question was not settled satisfactorily.

It was not; matters did get worse. Hopkins and Stalin sparred over the impossible formula that Poland should be friendly to the Soviet Union and have a freely chosen government. Indeed, Hopkins seemed keen to half write a constitution for a liberated Poland. The basic freedoms should include, apart from adult suffrage, the right of all citizens to public trial, choice of counsel and habeas corpus. Stalin replied, no doubt with inner amusement, that these were well understood principles but they could not be applied in war conditions, as the USA and Britain had demonstrated in their own suspension of normal legal rights in time of war.

Poland, he went on, could not be settled so long as it was the principle of British Conservatives to re-establish the cordon sanitaire of pre-war years which had led to a weak and hostile Poland and made it the path for the second German invasion in twenty-seven years. It was all very well for the USA and Britain, they had not been invaded. The German incursion had been like the onslaughts of the Huns.

He was prepared to see some non-Communist additions to the Lublin government but was very wary of the London Poles. Ambassador to Moscow Harriman intervened to say that he agreed. He did not think the British would press the case for the (troublesome) London Poles. However, prospects for any movement on the main question abruptly vanished when the news came through during Hopkins' stay that the Soviets had arrested fourteen representatives of the London Poles. Stalin claimed that they were using illegal transmitters and that the Russian supply line through Poland could not be threatened in that way.

Apart from his agreement about the additions to the Lublin government, Stalin was not yielding. He was irked too by the issue of reparations. Why had France been included in the Reparations Commission? She had surrendered to Germany. This was an attempt to humiliate the Soviet Union. With the Americans so determined to play up the importance of democracy, Stalin demanded to know why Argentina, with its fascist regime, had been invited to join the United Nations. He complained that this, among other things, breached an understanding that only those who had declared war on Germany before 1 March should be invited.

On other matters, there was less bad blood. Stalin said he was prepared to understand the abrupt termination of Lend-Lease which had occurred the moment that Germany surrendered. Given that Russia had committed to join in the war against Japan, this had been particularly resented. The American explanation was that it had been an administrative blunder. The shipments had been swiftly restored. Hopkins also contented Stalin with an assurance that, though not one German ship had yet been handed over to the Russians, he saw no obstacle to fulfilling the one-third formula which had been reached in previous discussions.

The visit ended with the usual declarations of goodwill. The report by Hopkins was enough to delight Truman, who declared at a press conference that the results had been 'completely satisfactory and gratifying'. He still had much to learn. The stage was now set for the momentous Potsdam conference arranged for July, just weeks after the German surrender.

POTSDAM: TRUMAN MAKES UP HIS MIND

I am afraid Stalin does not and never will understand our interest in a free Poland as a matter of principle. He is a realist in all of his actions and it is hard for him to appreciate our faith in abstract principles. It is difficult for him to understand why we should want to interfere with Soviet policy in a country like Poland, which he considers so important to Russia's security, unless we have some ulterior motive.'
Harriman to Truman after visiting Stalin.[81]

Potsdam opened in an atmosphere of triumph. Germany had been soundly beaten. Japan's defeat was only a matter of time. The bands of the three powers played noisily. The hospitality of the Russians – Potsdam was in their zone – was as usual on an impressive scale. Each leader had brought large numbers of advisers with him. There was constant dining and talking outside the formal sessions. In a fine display of democratic rectitude Churchill had brought the Labour leader Clement Attlee with him, just in case the general election went badly. It did and the new Prime Minister took over Churchill's role. It made little difference to British policy, though the new leader's quiet style was a welcome change to his predecessor's lengthy discursions.

The conference was to mark the turning point in East–West relations. It did not start the Cold War itself in any clearly visible way. But it was the end of a recognisable alliance. Truman wrote in his memoirs that this was the moment when he concluded that the Russians were 'planning world conquest'.[82]

---

81   Harriman and Abel, op. cit., p. 494
82   *Memoirs* by Harry S. Truman, Hodder and Stoughton, 1955, Vol. I, pp. 411–412

The conference certainly threw up problems and some moments of ill temper. But East–West relations did not reach anything like an irretrievable breakdown. Some issues were resolved and others were left to sub-committees and to a series of formal foreign ministers' conferences.

The first day of the conference was an untidy affair. Stalin proposed Truman as chairman. This gesture was repaid by the President taking the chair only to launch an immediate attack upon Soviet policy in Eastern Europe. He read from a prepared note that the Yalta agreement on 'free and fair elections' had not been adhered to and 'must' be resolved. He did not, however, include the ambitious suggestion of the State Department that US nationals should be free to move about freely and carry on commercial operations in Eastern Europe.

Other matters which the President said should be tackled were setting up a council of foreign ministers, arranging the Control Commission for Germany and next steps for Italy. The foreign ministers' council, he suggested, should include China. Since that country was heavily dependent on the USA, Stalin reacted sharply. Why China? The foreign ministers meetings were supposed to deal with Europe, were they not? Truman retreated. The Big Three would have to talk it over. Stalin seemed satisfied. He made no immediate comment about Eastern Europe. With the talk seeming to wander, Stalin proposed an agenda:

The division of the German fleet and merchant marine
Reparations
Trusteeships under the UN
Relations with the Axis satellite states
The Franco regime imposed on Spain by the Axis
Syria and Lebanon
The Polish border.

Stalin's agenda, to which the conference agreed in principle, was carefully devised. On the first two items the Soviet Union seemed to be on very strong ground. But resistance was to emerge.

Churchill was agreeable about the German battle and merchant fleets. Russia should have its one-third share. This upset Eden's negotiating instincts. He urged Churchill not to 'give up our few cards without return'.[83] This had some effect and the next day Churchill started to row back. He suggested the submarines should be outside the arrangement – all should be sunk. As for the rest, they could be equally divided. But that should in turn be subject to the proviso that there was general agreement on 'all the other questions and we leave here on the best of terms'.[84]

Now Truman was starting to row back too. More ships might be needed for the

---

83   *Meeting at Potsdam* by Charles L. Mee, Evans & co, New York, 1975, p. 104
84   Ibid.

war with Japan and later with supplying Europe's economies as they were rebuilt. But Russia was to be part of the war on Japan, replied Stalin. Churchill suggested that ships could be earmarked for subsequent distribution, at any rate the merchantmen. Truman irritated Stalin with the suggestion that the issue be postponed until after Japan's surrender. Besides, he said, the USA would have many ships which could be 'sold' to interested parties. Sold? Stalin insisted that Russia was automatically entitled to a share of the German fleet. It was not a gift. Truman and Churchill gave in.

The reparations issue proved contentious. The $20bn figure accepted at Yalta as a 'basis for discussion' – half to go to Russia – worried Truman and Churchill, in particular the latter. They did not want Germany to be pauperised. The Russian side bridled at the suggestion that the sums were up for debate. It was finally agreed that the foreign ministers should discuss the matter later that day. Lacking agreement, the ministers referred it to an ad hoc economic subcommittee. Its meeting cast an interesting light on the attitudes of both sides.

Maisky argued that eliminating German war potential should mean eliminating German heavy industry. The Americans argued that reparations would become more likely from a rebuilt economy. The Germans would need imports to survive. What was taken out of the country should be used to pay for these. But this was clearly against Russian interests since they had no intention of having to export anything to Germany – even if they could – to pay for the machinery they saw as their right. Maisky saw this as an example of capitalists wanting profits from foreign trade and not caring 'for those who have suffered'.

There was a commercial view offered by Will Clayton, an assistant secretary of state and former textile industrialist. He tried to liken the need to put Germany on her feet with a company threatened with bankruptcy. 'If a railroad company can't pay its debts the receiver keeps that road going otherwise the creditor would get nothing.'[85] In a tactless conclusion, he added that bankers would not have it any other way. This roused Maisky: 'We can never get the Russian people who have suffered so much to understand why Wall Street bankers have to be paid before they are.'[86] Finally the subcommittee referred the matter back to the foreign ministers.

On the issue of trusteeships, the Russian side was not seriously interested at that point except to strike attitudes and score possible bargaining positions by agreeing to give up such claims. The Syria/Lebanon matter was dropped when Britain insisted that these were matters for herself and France. When these matters were referred to the foreign ministers' committee, Molotov abandoned the matter. It should have struck Truman as odd that a country bent on 'world conquest' should have so readily given up claims to potential bases anywhere.

The issue of Spain was raised by Stalin only as a counter to Truman's initial charges. If the Allies were so keen on free elections why were they not demanding

---

85   Ibid., p. 127
86   Ibid., p. 127

them in Spain? Churchill insisted that it would be wrong to interfere in the internal affairs of another country. In any case, he added, Spain was an important trading partner for Britain.

Stalin replied that the point about Spain was that its government was Axis-imposed, making it an international threat. Churchill maintained that he could not advise Parliament to interfere in another country's internal affairs. Truman said it would of course be a good thing if there was another Spanish government to recognise but there wasn't. Stalin proposed referring that matter also to the foreign ministers. Churchill preferred that it should be agreed by the heads of government. But the President insisted that the conference needed to move on to other matters. In the event, the foreign ministers were to agree on a statement. While the Madrid government was not to be openly condemned, it was not to be invited to San Francisco.

Truman moved on to Eastern Europe, specifically Yugoslavia whose regime Churchill wanted to condemn. In that case, said Stalin, Tito should be invited to Potsdam to hear these accusations. This would be very inconvenient, said Truman. He had not come over to discuss each separate country in Europe. If Tito was not to be invited, said Stalin, the matter should be withdrawn. It was.

The President wanted to discuss bringing Italy into the UN, no doubt influenced by the many Italian-Americans among his voters. Stalin agreed to talk, suggesting it could be considered alongside Finland, Romania and Bulgaria. He avoided mentioning Poland where the biggest differences were liable to emerge. At that time Italy was ruled by a Cabinet dominated by a US nominee. Churchill had backed the rival Marshal Badoglio. The Prime Minister waxed eloquent about the losses suffered by Britain through Italy's role in the war. He also pointed out that the Rome government had not yet had an election and thus could only be ruled by a government of nominees.

Stalin took this argument a step further. He could not see why Italy, without a popularly elected government, deserved any better treatment than Romania, Hungary, Finland and Bulgaria. Romania had contributed twenty-two divisions to the German attack on Russia, Hungary twenty-six and Finland twenty-four. Italy's only special claim was that it been the first to surrender. It had however caused enormous damage while its forces had been fighting on the German side. Yet its government had been recognised by the USA and was being seen as an appropriate candidate for the UN. In that case, he went on, diplomatic recognition could be afforded to the Eastern European countries as well.

Truman hovered, claiming that diplomatic recognition would have to be preceded by freedom of movement and of information. The governments concerned would have to be 'reorganised' before recognition. He persevered. No application for membership of the UN would be supported by the USA unless the government was 'responsible and democratic'. That certainly did not seem to apply to Argentina, was Stalin's reply. Churchill now changed his line, praising Italy for having come out of the war and since fighting on the Allies' side. The upshot was that there would be a statement recognising the need for the preparation of peace treaties with the countries concerned.

Atomic Interlude

The problem of Japan soon arose – and showed that Truman could be as devious as Stalin. The latter reaffirmed the commitment at Yalta to attack Japan from the west within three months of Germany's surrender. Russia wanted to claim its promised prizes there. Truman however, with the atomic bomb now nearing testing, was hoping to defeat Japan without Soviet assistance.

On 17 July, Stalin told Churchill that Japan had put out a peace feeler through Moscow – with which it was still officially at peace – asking if the formula of unconditional surrender could be modified? Churchill thought this possible. Stalin handed Truman the same message. The President showed keen interest though he already knew the position because the USA had broken the Japanese diplomatic code. Truman was anxious to resist any peace feelers. The A-bomb test at Alamogordo was imminent. With the bomb he could force a total Japanese surrender without Russia being involved.

Stalin asked Truman for his views on a reply, observing that a general answer might be returned asking for details. Alternatively, he suggested – no doubt anxious for Russia to be in at the kill – the note might be ignored. Truman had little choice but to seem reasonable and anxious to save American lives. He agreed that details should be pursued. Before he left for Potsdam, Admiral Leahy had in fact urged the abandonment of the unconditional surrender formula and had been supported in this by Admiral King. The Japanese in the view of Leahy – and many others – were already close to defeat; and King thought that the USA could handle the matter without Russia. Or indeed the A-bomb. Secretary of State Byrnes however was to take the view that using the bomb would make Russia 'more manageable'[87] in Europe. Churchill later said that a new, tougher mood in dealing with Stalin came over Truman when he knew he had the Bomb and did not need Russia.

Later that day, 17 July, Stimson took the message about the successful test. His own suggestion was that the Japanese should be warned of its existence while at the same time amending the unconditional surrender terms to allow Japan to retain the Emperor. Byrnes rejected both suggestions. Churchill favoured not telling the Russians about the bomb.

Stimson soon received another cable, to say that preparations for a bomb which could be dropped were going ahead. But at a meeting that evening Byrnes found

---

87   According to Stimson, Byrnes was 'full of his problems with the coming meeting of the foreign ministers and he looks to having the presence of the bomb in his pockets, so to speak, as a great weapon'. *The Tragedy of American Diplomacy* by William Appleman Williams, Dell Publishing company, 1962, p. 256

resistance to the idea of using the weapon – from Stimson, Leahy, Marshall and General Arnold of the Air Force. The Secretary of State said he would consider the matter. Meanwhile reports came in of the ability of US forces to shell the Japanese homeland without any response, bringing closer the prospect of surrender.

On 18 July, Truman persuaded Churchill that Stalin should be told about the new weapon. Churchill added that to insist on unconditional surrender might lead to a great loss of life. Stimson, the War Secretary, suggested that the reply to Japan in the final communiqué from Potsdam should indicate that the Emperor could be retained – a vital point for Japan. But Truman and Byrnes removed the suggested phrase from the US reply to Tokyo. Truman wanted to delay a Japanese surrender until he was in a position to deploy the awesome Bomb. It was also argued by some that any dilution in the unconditional surrender policy would be a sign of weakness. It is also suggested that Truman delayed peace talks not just to show he had the Bomb but that he had the will to use it on civilian centres. Which he was to do twice in quick succession.[88] The idea of using it on some deserted South Pacific island as a demonstration was ignored. It was not until 24 July that Truman told Stalin about the Bomb. He did so in a way which he obviously hoped would not stir Stalin into any move which would enhance his claim to the spoils when Japan surrendered. At the end of the day's session, Truman records that he strolled over to Stalin to tell him that 'we had a weapon of unusual destructive force'.[89] Truman recorded that Stalin showed no special interest, only saying that he was glad to hear of it and hoped it would be put to good use against Japan. Truman's anxiety to avoid the complete truth was in fact being matched by Stalin's display of little interest. The Soviet leader already knew about the Bomb through his own spy ring.

Byrnes' hope that the possession of the Bomb would make Russia more manageable in Europe was severely disappointed. Stalin saw the aim and was not prepared to be threatened. He told Gromyko at the conference, 'Washington and London are hoping we won't be able to develop the Bomb ourselves for some time. And meanwhile using America's monopoly … they want to force us to accept their plans on questions affecting Europe and the world. Well, that's not going to happen.'[90]

The Economic Angle

The emphasis put on economic issues by the Americans at Potsdam was to become a regular feature of their souring relations with the Soviets. Washington was keen, even obsessed, with the idea that free trade had to be established everywhere in

---

88   *Major Problems in American Foreign Policy*, edited by Paterson, DC Heath, 1978, Vol, ii, p. 260–266

89   Fleming, op. cit., p. 221

90   *Memoirs* by Gromyko, Doubleday, 1990

the post-war years. Britain had already been pressurised through the conditions of Lend-Lease and the Atlantic Charter to abandon Imperial Preference, if not immediately then soon.

There was much to be said for the American vision. Today, few economists would deny that all-round free trade is a general benefit. But things were not seen this way in 1945 in Britain, let alone in Russia. They were two very different economic models in any case. At least, Britain had an advanced economy which could benefit from more open trading. Russian industry was not competitive by any stretch of the imagination.

Molotov was later to express the fear that if Yugoslavia and Romania were open to US business, the best industries there would be taken over by Americans. In an interesting prophecy about cultural trends, he forecast that this would mean that, before long, the radio in those countries would carry just a succession of 'American gramophone records'.[91]

The USA, in these discussions, was talking from a position of extraordinary strength. The two powers seemed mirror images. The USA had a surplus of factories; few of Russia's were left standing. The Soviets wanted only loans, not American direct investment. Given Russian suspicions of the outside world, this was not surprising. Loans were certainly a possibility but the Americans attempted to use this prospect as a political bargaining counter.

'Prolonged and Petty Bickering'

The meetings went on. At the next discussions of the foreign ministers, Molotov agreed to drop any arguments about trusteeships which the United Nations might set up – and which chiefly concerned Italian and former French colonies. He proposed that the agenda deal with Italy, liberated Europe and Romania.

Byrnes said the President's comments had settled Italy. Molotov did not dispute the principle. But he wanted to know about Italian reparations. Byrnes wondered what they would pay with. Eden suggested that would be dealt with in the peace settlement. Byrnes pointed out that Italy had been advanced large sums by the USA and more would be needed. Reparations did not seem to be 'an immediate problem'. The Russian side queried the anomaly of little Finland being asked to pay reparations while large Italy was not. Byrnes thought it might be possible to work out something for future years. But the USA certainly did not intend to make payments to countries so that they could in turn pay reparations. Molotov insisted that he had not suggested this. The economic subcommittee might consider the matter. Byrnes thought they had just settled the issue. Perhaps, was Molotov's answer, but when the subcommittee got to work it could still discuss Italian reparations.

The Americans said that if the committee could not agree, the matter should be referred back to the heads of government. Meanwhile a subcommittee should

91   Mee, op. cit., p. 306

be set up to draft a statement' on the admission of Italy to the UN. Molotov agreed and when the foreign ministers reported back to the heads of government, they could suggest that reparations be referred to that or another subcommittee. Byrnes was silent.

Next the ministers discussed the Yalta Declaration on Liberated Europe. Since Truman had attacked Soviet behaviour in Eastern Europe, Molotov proposed a counter-blast which would criticise Britain over Greece. London was providing military and economic support for a right-wing regime centred around King Paul, fighting a coalition of the Left, much of it dominated by Communists with supplies provided from Yugoslavia. There had been no elections and Molotov insisted that the British were keeping down the genuinely democratic forces of Greece.

Eden denounced this as a travesty. The world's press was free to go to Greece and report. The Greek regime was in favour of open elections. Observers could watch them which they could not in Romania or Bulgaria. Molotov pointed out that there were Allied missions in both countries. Byrnes insisted that the East European governments could not be recognised unless the Western press had freedom of movement. Molotov claimed there were no excesses in Romania or Bulgaria to compare with those in Greece. He knew this, he said. His authorities on Greek excesses were the British and American press.

The USSR, went on Molotov, could not long delay recognition of Eastern European governments. Byrnes said the USA too would recognise them once free elections had been held. There would soon be elections, was the Russian's reply. Yes, said Eden, but in Greece they would be open to all parties, not as in Eastern Europe where there was going to be a set list. Molotov insisted there was no reason to fear the latter elections. Greece was another matter. He quoted warlike speeches made in Greece against neighbouring countries. Eden said this was in response to Yugoslav accusations of aggressive intentions which were unfounded. The Greeks did not have the resources for any actions against other countries.

Molotov accepted Eden's logic – that Greece did not have the resources to be aggressive – was correct. Warlike speeches were being made, nevertheless. Eden referred to the storm of abuse against the Greek regime coming from Moscow and Yugoslav radio. Molotov persisted that his facts came from the Western press. Eden said he wished to report on Molotov's statement to Churchill since it contained grave charges against the British government. No, said the agile Molotov, the charges were against the Greek government.

It was this sort of argument which later led Truman to dismiss Potsdam as 'prolonged and petty bickering'.[92] His fears about Russia's global ambitions seemed to be based, at any rate in his memoirs, on minor items. The first was the Soviets' desire to control the Dardanelles. The second, and related to the first, was the way Stalin blocked Truman's ambition for 'the internationalisation of all the principal waterways'

92 Truman memoirs, op. cit., p. 65

in particular the Danube. A third alarm point arose from Russian claims on the Turkish provinces of Ardahan and Kars. This, in his over-excited imagination, signalled a possible full-scale invasion.

It was true that Moscow was calling on Turkey to yield the two provinces, once part of Imperial Russia, to the Soviet Union. This demand had in fact only arisen because the Turkish government, worried about the hostility which their neutralism had aroused during the war, approached Russia for a treaty. Moscow's reply was that this was not possible while Turkey retained the two provinces which it had gained from the Bolsheviks during their period of maximum weakness. They were also adjacent to the Baku oilfields which made them strategically important.

It was true too that Stalin had been calling for a Russian role in the military control of the Dardanelles, Russia's only outlet to the Mediterranean. But this was no novelty. Tsarist Russia had been agitating for that for over a century. Indeed Churchill was sympathetic on this point. He suggested a revision of the Montreux agreement to ensure that the Soviet Union had free passage through the straits for her naval and merchant shipping at all times. Truman was obliged to concede that a revision of Montreux should be discussed in due course, with UN control of the straits in mind. But, Churchill added, Russia should not be allowed to press for the return of the two provinces, which Stalin claimed were needed because a weak Turkey could not guarantee the straits.

In reality, no serious threat of an invasion existed. Nor would it have made sense for the Soviets to launch an invasion and set in train another major conflict which they were in no position to fight, least of all on such a minor issue. In due course the disputed area was to become a site for military bases – but ironically for the USA, not Russia.

The international waterways issue which Truman refers to mainly concerned the Danube and became something of an obsession with him. The State Department had urged the internationalisation in a briefing paper prepared for Potsdam, proposing a Western majority on the controlling board. For Russia, however, this was strategically a very important area. The Danube delta faced southern Russia across the Black Sea. It had been the jumping off point for one of the major German offensives.

In London, *The Times* explained, no doubt after a briefing in Potsdam, that internationalisation could bring about a supervisory body which would establish the benefits of free trade along the banks of the river and in the area generally. Soviet alarm was increased. Moscow did not want capitalists or capitalism in the Soviet Union's own sphere and jeopardising its control over an area important to Russian security. It was not a surprising view. Yet the President regarded Soviet hostility over the Danube issue as truly sinister.

Molotov was not slow to make the obvious reply in the foreign ministers' council. Perhaps they should discuss the internationalisation of the Panama and Suez canals? This effectively kicked the issue into touch, though Truman maintained in his memoirs that he had in mind all the principal waterways of the world. The proceedings at Potsdam do not bear this out. In any case, an American government which suggested ceding control of the Panama Canal would have faced domestic uproar.

Other matters, especially about Eastern Europe, had irritated the President at Potsdam though it was hard to see why they should have alarmed him so much. The Polish question had been settled to the extent that the Communist-dominated government had been recognised by the USA and Britain, if reluctantly, a month before. Some arguments about the precise new western border of Poland, incorporating a large chunk of eastern Germany, continued at Potsdam. But with possession being nine points of the law there was little choice other than to accept the Soviet position.

The Soviets' concerns about their security after the war and their desire for buffer states between them and Germany appeared to have made no impression on the President's mind. Harriman's wise warning about how Poland exemplified this problem seemed to have made no impact. The President wrote:

> It did not seem possible that only a few miles from the war's shattered seat of Nazi power, the head of any government could not bend to every effort to attain a real peace ... I was not altogether disillusioned to find now that the Russians were not in earnest about peace ... 'For the first time in the history of the world a victor was willing to restore the vanquished as well as to help its allies ... But one of our allies took the conqueror's approach to victory.[93]

What had been settled, apparently, at Potsdam would have to come at a price for the Soviets. Truman further records: 'The experience of Potsdam now made me determined that I would not allow the Russians any part of the control of Japan ... force is the only thing the Russians understand.'

The point about Japan was a serious matter because it ran counter to the understanding that Russia (along with Britain and China) would be among the forces occupying this historic foe. Truman's intransigent attitude on one issue after another was to play a major role in the breakdown of the foreign ministers' conference in London in September, convened in what was to prove a pious hope that it could settle the issues unresolved at Potsdam.

---

93 Truman memoirs, op. cit., p. 110

CHAPTER 12
HIROSHIMA ENDS THE WAR BUT PEACE SEEMS DISTANT

US motives for dropping A-bomb – the sincerity of Japanese peace feelers – foreign ministers in bitter arguments – Truman exasperated – Stalin threatens Molotov – Eden calls for understanding of Soviet position

Having made his disingenuous comment to Stalin about the Bomb's discovery and test, Truman set about ensuring that Japan did not pre-empt this demonstration of supreme military power by surrendering first. This would also minimise Russian involvement in Japan's final defeat. While the atomic bomb was still only under development, Stalin's promise at Yalta to declare war on Japan was crucial. But by the time the Bomb had been tested, the picture was very different. The menace of an invasion of Japan with huge American casualties was fading fast. US bombers were roving at will over Japan which had not even the aviation fuel to fight back. Essential raw materials were no longer available for the military and the islands faced starvation.

Truman already knew in detail what Stalin told him about Tokyo putting out peace feelers through Moscow. On 11 July, Ambassador Sogo was told to approach the Soviet government and ask for its mediation. The American intercept 'Magic' was decoding all the traffic. In a message labelled 'very urgent', it was explained that the Emperor was mindful of the 'evil and sacrifice' the war was imposing and desired 'with all his heart' that the war could be terminated so long as the terms of 'unconditional surrender' were withdrawn.

On 25 July, there was another and more pleading message. Would the Ambassador try to convince Stalin that he could achieve a reputation as 'an advocate of world peace' if he would receive a special envoy. It seemed to Tokyo that discussions in the USA and Britain were moving towards some relaxation of the unconditional surrender conditions which were unacceptable to Japan. The USA and Britain should not believe this was a stratagem, it was not 'merely a peace feeler'. The proposal was sugared with the assurance that all the Russian demands in the East would be accepted.

As was understood, the crucial point to Japan was the continuation of the monarchy. The proposal from the State Department that the Potsdam communiqué should include some possibility less than 'unconditional surrender' was put to Truman. But the President and Byrnes decided to strike it out.[94] In Tokyo the Cabinet was split between the military who wanted to fight on and the civilians eager for peace. The Americans were manoeuvring for a Japanese refusal to surrender. Tokyo was manoeuvring for the essential condition about the monarchy. The terms which the Japanese were left with might conceivably be interpreted as allowing maintenance of the throne. It was hard to see whether Tokyo took the point. It declared that the final terms had no important value. Japan would fight for 'a successful conclusion of the war' – in itself an ambiguous phrase since no one in Tokyo was so deranged as to think they could win. Had they known what they were threatened with they would have been more cautious. The question of whether Tokyo was despatching a flat rejection or was playing for time has long been debated. Eden concluded that the Americans did not want Soviet participation in the defeat of Japan. The Russians, significantly, were never consulted about the final ultimatum, even though they were supposed to enter the war within a fortnight. The technical grounds were advanced that they were not combatants at the time. In reality, Truman did not want to offer Stalin any chance to disrupt the A-bomb timetable.

On 25 July, Truman's secretary records that 'the weapon is to be used against Japan between now and 10 August.' Russia's declaration of war was expected about that time. Truman's timetable had been settled in his mind well before the last messages to and from Tokyo.

Truman recorded that he had talked to Stimson about a target and they had agreed that it would be a 'purely military one and we will issue a warning to Japan asking them to surrender and save lives'. In the event there was no warning and Hiroshima and Nagasaki were mainly industrial and civilian targets. The President was displaying a surprisingly ruthless streak. The list of military figures that were to deplore his decision is substantial. It includes Generals Eisenhower and MacArthur. Other opponents at the time included Stimson and his Assistant Secretary as well as the normally so stern Admiral Leahy, who described the Bomb as 'a barbarous weapon'. USAAF commander 'Hap' Arnold condemned the decision. The intelligence general who intercepted Tokyo's messages to Moscow later wrote: 'When we knew we didn't need to do it and we knew we didn't need to do it and they knew we didn't need to do it, we used them as an experiment for two atomic bombs.'[95]

A contrary voice was that of Byrnes with his later famous belief that using the weapons would make the Russians 'more manageable' in Europe. The casualties

---

94   Robert J. Donovan, op. cit., p. 91
95   *The Decision to drop the Atomic Bomb* by Gary Alperovitz, Praeger Publishers, 1996, p. 359

at Hiroshima and Nagasaki were in effect the first victims of the Cold War. The conclusion of the US Strategic Bombing Survey of 1946 deserves to be quoted.

Based on a detailed investigation of all the facts and supported by the testimony of the surviving Japanese leaders involved, it is the Survey's opinion that certainly prior to 31 December 1945 and in all probability prior to 1 November 1945, Japan would have surrendered even if the atomic bombs had not been dropped, even if Russia had not entered the war and even if no invasion had been planned or contemplated.[96]

The Foreign Ministers Confer; Truman Tires of 'Babying the Soviets'

Two foreign ministers' conferences were held before the end of 1945. London was a total failure. A second was arranged in Moscow in December adding France and China. Modest progress was made. Soviet archives provide a vivid picture of the difficult and, at moments, perilous relationship between Molotov and Stalin on both policy and personal grounds. The material shows Stalin rebuking Molotov for being 'liberal' in the face of US demands at both conferences. A similar charge of being too soft was levelled at Byrnes by his President. After the second meeting in Moscow. Truman fumed that he was tired of 'babying the Soviets'.[97] He also made his bellicose speech on US Navy Day (see Chapter 13) between the two meetings which could only ring alarm bells in the Kremlin, cause traditional Soviet suspicions to resurface and make difficulties for the foreign ministers' conferences. Before the London talks, the Russians had tightened their grip on Romania and Bulgaria while allowing reasonably free elections in Czechoslovakia and Hungary. Civil war continued to rage in Greece and of course in China.

How did the outside world, and in particular the balance of forces, look to Moscow as Molotov headed for the London conference? The USA had been demobilising rapidly but the American navy remained by far the most powerful in the world. Moreover, Washington was showing no signs of wanting to leave its various air force bases, many of them not far from Russia itself. South Korea was on its way to becoming an American client state. In China the Nationalists were more than ever dependent on aid of every sort from the USA as Mao Zedong drove south. And the Americans now had the A-bomb – which had sparked off a frantic programme in Russia to become an atomic power.

Byrnes arrived at the first conference, held in London accompanied by the later famous Cold War warrior, John Foster Dulles, there to demonstrate cross-party support from the Republicans. The Secretary of State was predictably to press for free elections in the countries bordering the Soviet Union. It was the President's line, laid out in his report to the public on Potsdam. The existing

---

96 See SAC/anesi.com/ussbs01
97 *Harry S Truman* by Margaret Truman, Hamish & Hamilton, 1973, p. 298

regimes would have to be changed, the Americans said. Since these countries were, in the view of Harriman, about 80 per cent anti-Communist and 80 per cent anti-Russian, Molotov was clearly not going to allow any serious progress on that matter. The American attitude was in some contrast with Attlee's approach. More tentatively the British Premier 'looked forward to the emergence in these countries of democratic governments based on free elections'. The issue of Japan where the Americans were taking total control continued to be an irritant. The American attitude could only add to traditional Russian fears of encirclement. The first meeting, held in London, and the subsequent report to the Senate by Byrnes gave the flavour of the problems to come.

The conference opened with Molotov readily accepting, to general surprise, a procedural proposal that France and China should participate in all meetings, including those to discuss the proposed peace treaties. Unfortunately for Molotov this surprised Stalin too.

After a period of unsuccessful bargaining over reparations from Italy – the Americans knew this would involve them providing more aid – slow progress was made on the peace treaty with that country. Stalin cabled to Molotov that no peace treaty on Romania should mean no peace treaty on Italy. The Soviet Foreign Minister also now called for a UN trusteeship for Russia in the former Italian colonies in North Africa, something which had been dropped at Potsdam. This was resisted and Stalin told him to press the point because, he claimed, there had been American-Soviet agreement on the point when Stettinius had been Secretary of State before Byrnes.

It became clear that the Soviet Union was in danger of being outvoted four-to-one on all the issues, the most important of which were Romania and Bulgaria. Eleven days after the start of the conference, Molotov abruptly announced that he had made a serious procedural error on the first day. The agreements at Potsdam had stipulated that only those who had been at war with these two Eastern European nations should draw up the peace treaties. France and China, not having been at war with either, should withdraw from those discussions.

This infuriated Britain and the USA. Molotov offered Byrnes a bargain. He would withdraw his procedural objection if the USA would withdraw its complaints about the Romanian government. The bargain was declined. So Molotov raised the issue of Greece, still deep in civil war. He was able to enjoy using virtually the same phrases to describe the regime in Athens that his rivals had used to describe the one in Bucharest – quoting British press reports.

Molotov's about-turn on procedure raised the temperature of the conference. This was the Russian foreign minister at his most tiresome and it raised doubts about whether he really wanted to make any progress. Byrnes believed that he was trying to break up the conference and considered appealing to Stalin over Molotov's head. In fact it was Stalin who had ordered the about-turn. He did not like the way the conference was going on Romania and told Molotov he was being far too 'defensive'.

The Soviet leader was prepared to see the conference broken up if Britain and the USA would not agree progress on the Balkans. He was also, unlike Molotov, hostile to a suggestion from Byrnes that the victorious powers might agree a treaty to demilitarise Germany for twenty to twenty-five years. He despatched a sharp cable to Molotov warning him that the Americans were pursuing four goals:

> First to divert our attention from the Far East where America assumes the role of tomorrow's friend of Japan, and to create a perception that everything is fine there; second to receive from the USSR a formal sanction for the US playing the same role in European affairs as the USSR so that the US may, hereafter, in league with England, take the future of Europe into their hands; third to devalue the treaties of alliance that the USSR has already reached with European states; fourth to pull the rug out from under any future treaties of alliance between the USSR and Romania, Finland, etc.[98]

However, he went on to suggest that an anti-German pact might be acceptable if the Americans would agree to an anti-Japan pact at the same time. He was deeply suspicious of US ambitions in the Far East. Byrnes said he would think about this when it was suggested by Molotov but he and the rumbustuous British Foreign Secretary Ernest Bevin refused to have the matter attached to the conference agenda. Stalin called this 'the height of impudence'. He added that he had information that the Americans were about to lay their hands on $1–2bn worth of Japanese gold reserves. That was why the USA and Britain were trying to prevent a discussion on Japan. When charged with the gold accusation by Molotov, Byrnes and Bevin denied it vigorously.

The bargaining went on fruitlessly. The issue now became who could be blamed for the breakdown of the talks and whether the prospect of failure would lead either side to make concessions. Tempers were stretched on the Western side. When Molotov came up with another tiresome procedural proposal, an increasingly irate Bevin accused him of sounding like Hitler. Molotov headed for the door. He was only turned back when Bevin hastily apologised. When discussions reached another low point, the Russian muttered that the reason the foreign ministers had made better progress in previous talks was that the West had then been represented by Cordell Hull and Eden.

Bevin's role as a negotiator with the Russians was an interesting one. It had been widely assumed that, as a prominent trade unionist of unimpeachable proletarian origins, he would prove ideal. The cry that 'Left can talk to Left' had been heard in the general election when Labour was accused of lacking experience in foreign affairs. The assumption was wrong. Communists were widely detested by traditional Socialists. Bevin had spent a considerable part of his life in the

---

98 See CWIHP

Transport and General Workers Union opposing Communists whom he regarded as a menace. He was inclined to see the Soviet government in an equally poor light, excluding the possibility, or at any rate diminishing it, that totally different issues were at stake than leadership of trade union branches. His colleague Chancellor Hugh Dalton thought him 'dangerously obsessed with Communists'.[99]

Byrnes had been surprised to find Molotov in such an obstinate mood on one issue after another. He had thought that the possession of the A-bomb would prove diplomatically as well as militarily irresistible. Stimson recorded his apprehensions about Byrnes's attitude after a long talk with the novice Secretary of State before he left for London. He wrote: 'I found Byrnes very much against any attempt to cooperate with Russia. His mind was full of his problems ... and he took to having the presence of the Bomb in his pocket to get through the thing.'[100]

Further meetings in London were abandoned and the foreign ministers could not even contrive a communiqué. But Byrnes had achieved one success. He did not want the Russians to mount a strong case for a role in Japan. It would have been difficult to resist, both because of the previous understanding and because, as Byrnes himself admitted, it would have been difficult to demand a US say in Romania and Bulgaria while denying any role for Russia in Japan. It was not a coincidence that the following year, when the Soviets dropped their claims to a role in Japan, the USA went ahead and signed the peace treaty with Bulgaria despite the Sofia government being more obviously by then a Soviet puppet.

Blame for the conference's failure was placed fair and square on Molotov when Byrnes reported to the Senate. He concluded with an assurance to his audience with a familiar refrain that God was on the side of the USA.

Stalin Threatens Molotov

Meanwhile a remarkable drama of personalities was being played out in Russia, which at least sheds some light on the tightrope which Molotov walked. Stalin went off for a holiday on the Black Sea. Western Kremlinologists went into top gear. Clearly matters could not be that straightforward. The Soviet leader must be in bad health. The Western press proffered a variety of illnesses – claiming good authority, of course – and speculated about his impending retirement with Molotov or Marshal Zhukov as the likely successors.

Nothing was more likely to stir Stalin's paranoid instincts. Who was circulating these rumours in Moscow? Why were they allowed to circulate? Stalin seized on an incident about censorship of the Western press when Molotov had allegedly suggested to a correspondent that it might be less strict in future. Stalin had the foreign minister humiliated by ordering his top colleagues to read him a lecture cabled from the Black Sea. He was further assailed for having been too 'liberal' at

---

99 *High Tide and After Memoirs 1945–60* by Hugh Dalton, Frederick Muller, 1962, p. 157
100 Gaddis, op. cit., p. 264

the London conference. Molotov, all too familiar with the hideous dangers of falling into the leader's displeasure, wrote a cringing letter of self-criticism and contrition. And he took care that he would avoid any suspicion in future of striking out on any 'liberal' line without full authorisation from the leader himself. This fear was obviously a factor in the problems the West had in dealing with him on other occasions.[101]

Harriman Offers Stalin an Olive Branch

After the London breakdown Harriman attempted some fence mending. He visited Stalin at his holiday home with a letter from the President summarising his views on the foreign ministers' talks. As Harriman feared, Stalin immediately noticed that Truman had omitted any mention of the thorny issue of Japan. The Ambassador did his best to smooth things over. With the disarmament of Japan now completed, it should be possible for a limited number of Soviet, Chinese and British troops to be stationed there.

Stalin called for a Control Commission on the German model. Harriman's reply was that the USA wanted a Control Council with an advisory not an executive role. Both agreed that final decisions would have to rest with the Supreme Commander, MacArthur. It seemed like progress and the mood of the talks was friendly. It was very different the next day. It seemed that Stalin had been persuaded by colleagues that he was not being sufficiently tough. He had a number of complaints about Japan, centred mainly on MacArthur's personal rule and the lack of any consultation with Russia. Perhaps, concluded the Soviet leader testily, it would be better for Russia to quit Japan altogether 'rather than remain there as a piece of furniture'. There followed what seemed a remarkable suggestion. Harriman recorded Stalin's suggestion:

> The Soviet Union would not interfere. For a long time the isolationists had been in power in the United States. He had never favoured a policy of isolation but perhaps the Soviet Union should adopt such a policy. Perhaps, in fact, there is nothing wrong with it.[102]

An isolationist Soviet Union! It would seem the answer to all the fears about aggressive Communist expansion. Harriman was cautious about that obvious interpretation. He did not think Stalin could possibly mean isolationism in the classic sense. Rather that he meant unilateral action. It would mean the Soviets ceasing to rely on the Western powers for economic assistance or trade or on military cooperation. It would mean the Soviet Union maintaining its hold on Eastern Europe while relying on the Communist parties of Western Europe to promote Russian influence. It was some sort of 'self reliance' that Stalin must mean.

---

101 See CWIHP
102 Harriman and Abel, op. cit., p. 514

But there was still the issue of the loan which was making little progress. The original request had, remarkably, been physically mislaid in the State Department's bureaucratic machine. Stalin said he was prepared to negotiate on this matter but not if 'offensive' conditions were attached. He instanced the conditions urged by a group from the House Select Committee on Post-war Economic Planning. It had visited Moscow in September. One of its many conditions for a loan was the withdrawal of Soviet occupation forces in Eastern Europe. On top of that Moscow must supply details of its budgets with the opportunity for them to be verified. As if that was not enough, there must be a guarantee for freedom of religion and of the press with the right of free distribution for American newspapers and films.[103]

Stalin did not raise objections when Harriman suggested that Eastern Europe should be settled at a major peace conference to include all countries which had provided troops to the Allied effort. Brazil, for instance, should be included because it had sent troops to fight in Italy. When he got back to Moscow, Harriman used his considerable powers of persuasion on Molotov to get the foreign ministers' conference back on the rails. The two men argued fruitlessly over the terms Control Commission and Control Council. The Ambassador reported back to Washington that Russian fears about Japan had to be understood. 'Japan has for two generations been a constant menace to Russian security in the Far East and the Soviets now wish to be secure from that threat.'[104]

Harriman also found Byrnes helpful in the sense that he was now ready to discuss settling Eastern Europe without France and China being involved. This 'delighted' Molotov. On the other hand Harriman found Byrnes 'stupid' in wanting to hear from the Soviet government what its plans were for the next foreign ministers' conference before he talked to other departments in Washington. Were the internal politics of Washington to take precedence over diplomacy?

When the foreign ministers reconvened in Moscow, the Ambassador found Byrnes 'difficult' as well as stupid. However, the Secretary of State was prepared to agree on an Allied Council in Tokyo with an automatic right to be consulted about occupation policy. MacArthur would still retain final authority.

Eastern Europe remained a running sore. The Russians accepted the very recent Hungarian election which had seen the Communists routed. But there was no movement on Bulgaria and Romania – both of more military significance for Russia than Hungary. Byrnes appealed to Stalin who conceded that the governments in Romania and Bulgaria could include some non-Communists. A tripartite mission would go to Bucharest to observe and report. The USA was now ready to recognise the Bulgarian government. With these face-saving concessions on both sides, the conference ended. Byrnes was sufficiently pleased with his achievements to make a broadcast to the American public. He had characteristically failed to consult

103   Congressional Record, 2 August 1946
104   Harriman and Abel, op. cit., p. 517

Truman about this publicity exercise. But the President's displeasure ran deeper than this and he was supported in his reaction by Leahy who complained that the concessions did not fit in with the President's calls in his Navy Day speech in October for a 'righteous' foreign policy. 'It appears now that Russia has been granted every request that wrecked the London conference,' wrote Leahy.[105] Truman wrote a stiff comment about Byrnes, complaining that the White House had not been notified of the proposed change of line on Bulgaria and Romania. He recorded in his memoirs:

> Byrnes was forcing policy in a direction which I could not and would not agree ... There is no doubt in my mind that Russia intends an invasion of Turkey and the seizure of the Black Sea straits to the Mediterranean. Unless Russia is faced with an iron fist and strong language another war is in the making ... I am tired of babying the Soviets.[106]

A more emollient view of the Soviet position had been advanced between the two conferences by Eden in the Commons, though of course from the opposition front bench. The breakdown of the London talks prompted him to declare:

> Nobody here will deny that there has been an increase of suspicion and mistrust between the Soviet Union and the other two parties in victory. We all deplore that ... We want the fullest Russian participation in world affairs on equal terms. Many times Russian statesmen have spoken to me of their need for security and the necessity as they feel for friendly relations with their neighbours ... Against whom are all these Russian arrangements made? I know the answer; they have given it many times. They are aimed against the possible resurgence of German plans for the domination of Europe ... We know that Russian arrangements are not made against us. We can surely ask her to believe that our arrangements are not made against her either.[107]

Eden's words might have held good for Britain, but with the man in the White House believing that he had to deal with a would-be world conqueror, this interpretation of Soviet motives would find few echoes. Besides, Truman had already decided that it was time to spell out in public the righteousness of the USA and the 'evil' embodied by its great rival.

---

105   Donovan, op. cit., p. 359
106   Truman memoirs Vol. 1, pp. 540–542
107   *Anthony Eden*, op. cit., p. 261

CHAPTER 13
TRUMAN'S NAVY DAY SPEECH

Truman warns Russia – enunciates the principles of US foreign policy – main points clearly aimed at Soviets – Harriman writes cautioning note – Stalin calls on Soviet people for vigilance and sacrifice – Washington alarmed – US Embassy sees no belligerence in the speech

This was a key moment in the development of the Cold War, little as the President's October 1945 speech at the Naval College figures in most history books, and little as it aroused domestic opinion at the time. It was the opening shot in the Cold War. After all the pugnacious rhetoric of the Cold War, its sentiments may now seem almost commonplace in its juxtaposition of American values against the forces of 'evil'. The speech was delivered in late October, just after one foreign ministers' conference and not long before another. The USSR was plainly enough the target and the Kremlin, if not others, was listening carefully. The speech implied that the two sides were so far apart in all respects that trying to compromise could be construed as morally wrong. After revelling in a description of US military might, he laid down twelve points for American foreign policy.

> The foreign policy of the United States is based firmly on fundamental principles of righteousness and justice. In carrying out those principles we shall firmly adhere to what we believe to be right; and we shall not give our approval to any compromise with evil. Outside of the right to establish the necessary bases for our own protection we look for nothing that belongs to another power. But we know that we cannot attain perfection in this world overnight. We shall not let our search for perfection obstruct our steady progress toward international cooperation. We must be prepared to fulfil our responsibilities as best we can, within the framework of our fundamental principles, even though we recognise that we have to operate in an imperfect world…

Let me restate the fundamentals of that foreign policy of the United States:

1. We seek no territorial expansion or selfish advantage. We have no plans for aggression against any other state, large or small. We have no objective which need clash with the peaceful aims of any other nation.

2. We believe in the eventual return of sovereign rights and self-government to all peoples who have been deprived of them by force.

3. We shall approve no territorial changes in any friendly part of the world unless they accord with the freely expressed wishes of the people concerned.

4. We believe that all peoples who are prepared for self-government should be permitted to choose their own form of government by their own freely expressed choice, without interference from any foreign source. That is true in Europe, in Asia, in Africa, as well as in the Western Hemisphere.

5. By the combined and cooperative action of our war allies, we shall help the defeated enemy states establish peaceful democratic governments of their own free choice. And we shall try to attain a world in which Nazism, Fascism, and military aggression cannot exist.

6. We shall refuse to recognise any government imposed upon any nation by the force of any foreign power. In some cases it may be impossible to prevent forceful imposition of such a government. But the United States will not recognise any such government.

7. We believe that all nations should have the freedom of the seas and equal rights to the navigation of boundary rivers and waterways and of rivers and waterways which pass through more than one country.

8. We believe that all states which are accepted in the society of nations should have access on equal terms to the trade and the raw materials of the world.

9. We believe that the sovereign states of the Western Hemisphere, without interference from outside the Western Hemisphere, must work together as good neighbours in the solution of their common problems.

10. We believe that full economic collaboration between all nations, great and small, is essential to the improvement of living conditions all over the world, and to the establishment of freedom from fear and freedom from want.

11. We shall continue to strive to promote freedom of expression and freedom of religion throughout the peace-loving areas of the world.

12. We are convinced that the preservation of peace between nations requires a United Nations Organization composed of all the peace-loving nations of the world who are willing jointly to use force if necessary to ensure peace.[108]

Of the twelve points, seven were clearly aimed at Russia, including the general point about not compromising with 'evil'. Point 2 obviously related to the Soviet role in

---

Eastern Europe. There were no other areas where the USA was complaining about the loss of freedom and self government, though there were candidates enough. The high-mindedness of Point 2 was to be seized on by the ever opportunistic Ho Chi Minh who telegraphed the President from Vietnam to invite his help in liberating Indo-China from French rule. He was ignored. In due course, the USA was to provide aid to the French forces fighting him.

Point 4 was an extension of Point 3 with the added warning, repeated in Point 9, that no attempt to interfere in the affairs of Latin America would be tolerated. From the point of view of Russia, this was humbug. The USA was determined to play a major role in Eastern Europe. No attempt by the Soviet Union to play a role in Latin America would of course be tolerated.

In Point 6, Truman was saying that the Soviet-dominated governments of Eastern Europe would not be recognised. It was, leaving aside any issue of Soviet security, an odd claim, but at least a piece of diplomatic hypocrisy which the Russians could appreciate. The Polish government had already been recognised by the USA in the summer. And despite all, work continued on the Romanian and Bulgarian peace treaties, the two (non democratic) governments being eventually recognised in 1947.

Points 7 and 8 signalled renewed economic demands. While freedom of the high seas was not controversial, the call for the internationalisation of rivers passing through more than one country was a revival of Truman's pet scheme for opening up trade along the Danube, as he had proposed at Potsdam. In Point 8 he implies that it should be a condition of being accepted into 'the society of nations' that the Soviet Union open up itself and its satellite states to equal trading rights – the very point that the Russians could not accept. Point 11 and the call for religious freedom were of course aimed at officially atheist Russia.

But perhaps the most remarkable point was in the preamble about bases. The USA would regard the opportunity to establish (or retain) bases in another country as a 'right'. Such bases would clearly be thousands of miles away and close to the Soviet Union. Yet any 'rights' by Russia to have bases in Eastern Europe to guard against a resurgent Germany would not be recognised.

In the circumstances, Moscow would have to discard the aspirations for peaceful cooperation formulated in the Maisky/Gromyko/Litvinov memoranda. Dealings with business left over from the war would have to continue but in an atmosphere of growing confrontation, at any rate so far as Truman was concerned.

Yet wiser counsel was available to the State Department from Harriman. And it may have played some part in the more amenable attitude of Byrnes at the second of the foreign ministers' conferences. The message, from the retirement memorandum which Harriman sent to Byrnes on leaving Moscow as Ambassador, deserves quotation. Harriman wrote in late November:

One must bear in mind that high Soviet governmental and party leaders have lived throughout their lives in an almost constant state of fear and tension, beginning with the days when they were conspirators in a revolutionary movement ... They feared capitalistic encirclement and dissension within the ranks of the party, leading to two ruthless purges.

... The German invasion all but destroyed them. There must have been a feeling of tremendous relief when the tide of war turned. With victory came confidence in the power of the Red Army and in their control at home, giving them for the first time a sense of security for themselves personally and for the revolution such as they had never had before. In September 1941, it will be recalled, Stalin told me that he was under no illusions, the Russian people were fighting as they always had 'for their homeland, not for us', meaning the Communist Party. He would never make such a statement today. The war has assisted in the consolidation of the revolution in Russia. They determined that the Red Army should be kept strong, and industry developed to support it, so that no power on earth could threaten the Soviet Union again. Political steps were taken to obtain defence in depth, disregarding the desire and interests of other peoples...

Then suddenly the atomic bomb appeared and they recognised it as an offset to the power of the Red Army. This must have revived their old feeling of insecurity. They could no longer be absolutely sure they could obtain their objectives without interference ... This attitude partly explains Molotov's aggressiveness in London ... The Russian people have been aroused to feel that they must again face an antagonistic world. American imperialism is included in the threat to Russia.

It is in no sense that this message should suggest any course; it is only as a partial explanation of the strange psychological effect of the atomic bomb on the Soviet leaders' behaviour.[109]

We do not know if Truman ever read this message. He certainly showed no understanding of the Ambassador's shrewd analysis. In a telling private note in late 1946 the President wrote: 'A totalitarian state is no different, whether you call it Nazi, Fascist, Communist, or Franco's Spain.'[110]

In early 1948, in a long letter to his daughter, he summarised not just his feelings about totalitarian states but also his difficulties on becoming president. The tale is a mixture of innocence but no doubt partly to set the record straight for future biographies – one of them a notably intimate picture by Margaret Truman herself. There is a remarkable picture of him as a novice in the White House:

As you now I was Vice President from 20 January to 12 April 1945. I was at Cabinet meetings and saw Roosevelt once or twice in those months. But he

109   Harriman and Abel, op. cit., p. 521
110   *Harry S Truman* by Margaret Truman, op. cit., p. 359

never did talk to me confidentially about the war, or about foreign affairs or what he had in mind for peace after the war...

Then I had to start (arriving at the Presidency) reading memorandums, briefs and volumes of correspondence on the World situation. Too bad I hadn't been on the Foreign Affairs Committee or that FDR hadn't informed me on the situation. I had to find out about the Atlantic Charter – which by the way does not exist on paper – the Casablanca meeting. The Montreal meeting, Tehran meeting, Yalta Hull trip to Moscow, Bretton Woods...

Well, many agreements were made at Potsdam ... none of which Russia has kept. So that now we are faced with exactly the same situation with which Britain and France were faced in 1938–9 with Hitler...

The oligarchy in Russia is not different from the Czars, Louis XIV, Charles I, and Cromwell.[III]

The latter comments are remarkably naive comments being written against the background of his Navy Day speech and its formulation of the US approach to the world. It implied that there was only one foreign policy suited to Tsarist Russia, Nazi Germany, Communist Russia and Franco's Spain. These countries may have been deplorably totalitarian. The one thing they were not was 'all alike'. Any foreign policy based on this belief was bound to produce confusion and disorder.

Stalin Rings Alarm Bells

It was Stalin's turn in early 1946 to raise the temperature. In an address to what was called a voters meeting of the 'Stalin Electoral District Moscow', he described how capitalism had made the Second World War 'inevitable' as it had the First. He went on to announce the dismaying news that more five-year plans would be needed to increase steel output. The official report records 'prolonged applause' from the cowed audience. The programme would be needed to 'boost heavy industry to ensure the Motherland against all contingencies' (loud applause).

The worst was promptly assumed in Washington, not least by Byrnes and Dean Acheson, the Assistant Secretary of State. In a note of hysteria, the speech was described as tantamount to a 'declaration of World War III' by William O. Douglas, the famously 'liberal' supreme court judge. He was the confidant of the mentally unstable Defence Secretary James Forrestal. Admiral Leahy, no doubt with satisfaction, recorded that the President was now becoming strongly critical of recent 'appeasement' and spoke of taking a strong line without delay.

The excitement in Washington was overdone. What Stalin said was that, as Marxists believed, war between capitalist states was 'usual' because it came from an imbalance when raw materials and markets were unevenly distributed. He went on in his speech to pay tribute to the United States and Britain as 'freedom

---

III   Margaret Truman, op. cit., p. 358–360

loving countries' who had joined with the Soviet Union in the war to destroy the Fascist states. He declared that a major lesson of the war was the success of the Soviet social system, so denigrated by outsiders; the economic wisdom of the previous five-year plans had been shown by the ability to use heavy industry to equip the Red Army. According to Robert Tucker in the US Embassy, it was not a belligerent speech. It was 'long and boring'.[112]

If one started off from an assumption that Stalin had the sort of global ambitions Truman attributed to him, then the Moscow speech was a signal that the industrial backing for it was being put in place. But only if such ambitions existed. A saner interpretation was that the new industrial programme, insofar as it was military, was driven by the Soviets' fear for their own security. If wars were natural between capitalist nations, then the Soviet Union had to be militarily prepared for their consequences. In any case, there was certainly a need to rebuild the country's devastated heavy industry and harsh five-year plans were the only means according to Communist economics. Within the Soviet Union the prospect of more grinding years of toil was widely regarded with dismay.

There were dissenting voices in Washington. Henry Wallace, Truman's troublesome Secretary of Commerce – dismissed later for his views about Russia – offered his own view. He argued that it appeared obvious to Stalin that the American military was preparing for war and that it was setting up bases all the way from Greenland, Iceland, Northern Canada and Alaska with Russia in mind. 'I said that Stalin obviously knew what these bases meant.'

In the circumstances of the time, it is certainly hard to see why Stalin's speech should have been regarded as being any more aggressive than Truman's Navy Day speech. Rather the opposite. Yet General Lucius Clay, Military Governor of the American zone in Germany, reacted with the comment that Stalin's speech had caused him to revise his view that the Russians did not want war. If it came, he was to warn, it would be with great suddenness. Fuel was added to the flames when the first Soviet atomic spy ring was revealed. But again, it was no great surprise that this existed. Both sides were energetically spying on each other.

Not long after Stalin's speech a further row was to flare up over Iran which Truman said in his memoirs 'threatened the peace of the world'.[113] This grotesque claim underlines a difficulty about the man himself. So simple in his tastes and so affable in manner, he could yet reach paranoid judgements.

The confrontation over Iran turned on the simple issue of oil needs. The Russians' oil sources in Baku had been strained to the limit by the demands of war. Maintenance had been abandoned in the interests of draining every last drop of oil. The entire machinery of the oil centre was in need of repair and overhaul.

---

112   Interview with Prof. R. Tucker, www.gwu.edu/~/nsaarchiv/interviews
113   Truman Memoirs, Vol. ii, op. cit., p. 93

The rich and well-maintained Iranian fields were wholly controlled by the Anglo-Persian Oil Company, then entirely under British control. The Russians wanted a concession too. During the war both British and Soviet troops occupied the country which was a useful supply route by rail for Lend-Lease material to Russia. The Russian troops predominated in the northern Azerbaijanian province, on the Soviet border. Moscow agreed to remove its troops by early 1946. But, unsurprisingly, it was negotiating hard for an oil concession in that area.

Attempts by Byrnes and Bevin to get the issue cleared up at the London conference had failed. Both men suspected, correctly, that the Soviets would not meet the withdrawal timetable. Molotov hoped that he could use a delay as a means of exacting an oil concession. At first it seemed as if it would. An agreement was signed. The Russian troops were eventually withdrawn six weeks after the early March deadline following a complaint from Iran to the UN Security Council that there was a danger under the heading of the Charter: 'threats to world peace'.

The oil concession which the Russians had obtained was subject to ratification by the Iranian parliament, after the troops had gone. It was rejected. Consequently Britain, now with the USA, became once more the controllers of all of Iran's oil. Given the relentlessness with which the USA and Britain exacted oil concessions wherever and whenever they could, there was a lot of the pot calling the kettle black in this entire episode. All the Russians wanted was an oil concession, not territory.

The battle in the Security Council had been bitter. When Iran raised the matter of the Russian presence, the Soviet delegation retaliated by raising the issue of Greece and the presence of British troops. Bevin defended Britain's role fiercely. The Iran business had been a bruising encounter and the first in which East and West had played the 'you too' issue in the Security Council itself. If the dispute over the slow withdrawal of the Soviets from Iran had been settled peacefully, it still left the Russians envious of the foreign oil concessions which the British and the Americans enjoyed. The USA had raised its own domestic output sharply and enjoyed a very lucrative monopoly of Saudi oil. Britain had its vast concession in Iran. Yet again the Russians felt a sense of isolation.

If Stalin's speech caused a great stir in Washington, it did not cause the same alarm in the US Embassy in Moscow. Robert Tucker, an official in Moscow at the time, later said of it: 'it didn't use any phrase like Cold War, it was not a belligerent speech.' Tucker's interpretation was 'that if you look carefully, while it was not a declaration of Cold War, it foresaw what would come to be called the Cold War.'[114]

Elsewhere in the Embassy, but begun well before the Stalin speech and not related to it, Kennan was preparing his grim telegram for the State Department. And Churchill was preparing to fling his thunderbolt at Fulton.

---

114 Interview with Prof. R. Tucker, www.gwu.edu/~/nsaarchiv/interviews

CHAPTER 14
CHURCHILL WARNS OF THE IRON CURTAIN

Churchill's momentous speech at Fulton – a threatening sentence included – British government disassociates itself – Eden humiliated – Truman waits to assess public opinion – Acheson snubs Churchill – Moscow's bitter reaction

Of all the speeches made during the onset of the Cold War, Churchill's 'Iron Curtain' speech at Fulton in March 1946 is the best remembered, and it had the greatest impact on public opinion at large. He had been out of office since mid-1945 and was chafing at his decline from world statesman to mere Leader of the Opposition in the Commons. He wanted the ears of the world again. The invitation to accept an honorary degree from Westminster College and speak to an admiring American audience in the presence of the President was a chance not to be missed.

There never was such an acceptance speech. The fact that Truman had brought him on the presidential train and was part of the wildly applauding audience magnified the importance of the occasion. Other speeches hostile to Soviet Russia, like Truman's on Navy Day, kept to the diplomatic convention of indicating but not naming a foe. Churchill did not hold back.

The great oration had been worked on since Churchill arrived in Florida for a holiday and various drafts had travelled to and fro along the lines to the White House where he would stay with the President before the address. Truman was however careful to claim, unconvincingly, in the early and uncertain days of the speech's national reception, that he had played no part in the speech's contents.

The language was as usual magnificent. After a long introduction, including his stress on the belief that all countries have the right to free elections, Churchill came to the point:

A shadow has fallen upon the scenes so lately lighted by the Allied victory. Nobody knows what Soviet Russia and its Communist international organisation intends to do in the immediate future, or what are the limits, if any, to their expansive and proselytising tendencies…

… From Stettin in the Baltic to Trieste in the Adriatic, an iron curtain[115] has descended across the Continent. Behind that line lie all the capitals of the ancient states of Central and Eastern Europe. Warsaw, Berlin, Prague, Vienna, Budapest, Belgrade, Bucharest and Sofia, all these famous cities and the populations around them lie in what I must call the Soviet sphere and all are subject in one form or another, not only to Soviet influence but to a very high degree and in many cases, increasing measures of control from Moscow. Athens alone, Greece with its immortal glories, is free to decide its future at an election under British, American and French observation.

The Russian-dominated Polish government has been encouraged to make enormous and wrongful inroads upon Germany, and mass expulsions of millions of Germans on a scale grievous and undreamed of are now taking place. The Communist parties which were very small in all these Eastern states of Europe, have been raised to pre-eminence and power far beyond their numbers and are seeking everywhere to obtain totalitarian control. Police governments are prevailing in nearly every case. And so far except in Czechoslovakia, there is no true democracy.

Turkey and Persia [Iran] are both profoundly alarmed and disturbed at the claims which are being made upon them and at the pressure being exerted by the Moscow government.

Churchill warned about the position in Germany:

If now the Soviet Government tried by separate action to build up a pro-Communist Germany in their areas this will cause new serious difficulties in the British and American zones … Whatever conclusions may be drawn from these facts – and facts they are – this is certainly not the liberated Europe we fought to build up. Nor is it one which contains the essentials of permanent peace.

About Italy and France he had forebodings. But it was not just there that he had fears for non-Communist states:

Communist fifth columns are established and worked in complete unity and absolute obedience to the directions they receive from the Communist centre. [They] constitute a growing challenge and peril to Christian civilisation.

---

115 Churchill had used this memorable phrase before in the Commons and in his correspondence with Truman, sometimes as 'an iron fence'. The phrase can in fact be traced back to Doctor Goebells, said in turn to have read it in a newspaper leader warning of the division of Europe threatened by this Soviet advance.

However he dismissed the idea that a new war was 'inevitable or imminent':

> I do not believe that Soviet Russia desires war. What they desire is the fruits of war and the *indefinite* [author's italics] expansion of their powers and doctrines.

He went on to attack the idea of 'appeasement', declaring that the Russians respected nothing more than strength. Appeasement was not a workable policy, he declared, citing his own experience of and warnings about Hitler and Munich. In a particularly significant passage he referred to the perils of life behind the Iron Curtain and added:

> It is not our duty *at this time* [author's italics] when difficulties are so numerous to interfere forcibly in the internal affairs of countries we have not conquered in war.[116]

These words, so carefully chosen, together with the insistence that all countries have the 'right to free unfettered elections' was bound to be seen from Moscow as straightforward threat. They carried the obvious implication that there might be a time when difficulties were less 'numerous' to undertake the duty to 'interfere forcibly'.

The intimations of dismay, disillusionment and disappointment which run through the speech remain unconvincing. The element of retrospective self justification in the speech is strong. His fear, like Eden's, that history would regard him as the author of an eastern Munich was playing on his mind. The Polish government, with its obvious role as a Soviet cat's paw, had been recognised by Britain while Churchill was still Prime Minister. He had had to bow to the inevitable but it still rankled.

In the case of some Eastern European states, he had offered Stalin effective control in the 'naughty document'. Only under American pressure had he accepted the idea that this was a temporary arrangement for 'war conditions'. His concern about the displacement of Germans to provide territory for Poland was sincere enough. But it paled into insignificance alongside the depredations of Hitler's Germany in that country.

Reactions to Fulton
Reactions to the speech in the USA and Britain were very mixed. Truman, who could (just about) excuse his personal role and applause at Fulton as a tribute

---

116 There is some mystery about this important passage. It appeared in various versions of the American press but not in others. Some of the reports were from transcripts made available to reporters. The possibilities remain that it was either an interpolation or that Churchill, considering at the last moment that it was too provocative, left it out. The archives are unhelpful. Either way, the fact that it was widely reported was quite enough to rouse Soviet anger.

to the world's most revered statesman, waited to see which way the cat would jump. Even some of the hawkish figures in the State Department were worried by Churchill's aggressive tone. Byrnes privately complained that he had not been consulted about the speech and told a press conference that its contents were nothing to do with him. Dean Acheson, US Secretary of State, delivered a snub to Churchill by cancelling his own attendance as the speaker at a New York dinner to honour the former Prime Minister. However, given the state of public opinion about Communism as shown in opinion polls (see chapter below) the man in the street was not going to be a problem for the President.

At home, Churchill was belaboured by *The Times*, describing the speech as a counsel of despair in seeing the two world's differences as 'irreconcilable' and 'doomed to a fatal conflict'.[117] The British Government was also unenthusiastic. Bevin wanted an official dissociation from Churchill's views; Attlee produced a bland compromise in the Commons: 'The Government is not called on to comment on a speech by a private individual.' Government policy, he said, would be as laid down by the Foreign Secretary.

Eden was taken aback by Fulton, not least because Churchill had declined the most elementary courtesy of consulting him about its contents or even telling him that the speech would be about East–West relations. Poor Eden was humiliated. He had even denied in the Commons some Labour MPs' claims, on the eve of the event, that Churchill was about to make a speech fiercely critical of the Soviet government.

> I have not heard anything of the kind from my Right Honourable friend and, may I add, I do not believe it for one single moment … There is nothing in which my Right Honourable friend is more sincere – and I think I can claim to know him in these matters – than in his regard for good relations with the Soviet Union.[118]

Evidently, Eden knew him – and his erratic ways – less than he thought. It could well be that Churchill's' motives in this discourteous treatment of his deputy was a concern that Eden would strongly demur from his warlike approach. It was a reasonable fear given that Eden had delivered a sympathetic analysis of Soviet motives in the Commons in late February. He went on:

> It has been said many times in this debate – and I think with truth – that it is difficult for us to understand the profound impression that has been made on the minds of the Soviet Government and the Soviet people by the wide and deep invasion of their land by the German armies. I am convinced that

---

117　Carlton, op. cit., p. 264
118　Ibid., p. 265

it is the scourge of invasion – and not the only one in that country – which is the dominant feature in Soviet foreign policy. The determination not to allow Germany to be in the position to do this again resulted in the determination to have as friendly neighbours as they can.[119]

But he was not too starry-eyed. He went on to complain that the current problem was that Russia wanted collaboration only 'on her own terms'. This, he said, would not work. 'Sooner or later this must land us all in difficulties. As a summary of the position, it would be hard to fault Eden's speech and it is the more intriguing because he was swerving away from the tougher approach to the Soviets which he had been taking at Potsdam. It seemed that a period of reflection left Eden able to see the wood rather than the trees.

The reaction in Moscow to the Fulton speech was predictably bitter. In an interview with the newspaper *Pravda*, Stalin denounced Churchill for every sin from discourtesy and tactlessness to warmongering and enunciating a racial theory 'worthy of Hitler'. Other matters apart, he pointed out that to include Berlin and Vienna in the list of cities under Russian control was obviously inaccurate. Each was ruled by a four-nation Control Commission in which Russia had only a quarter of the vote. The comment about the 'indefinite expansionist tendencies' of the Soviet Union was a slander which spoke for itself.

The circumstances of the war, Stalin continued, should not be forgotten. The Soviet Union had been invaded through Finland, Poland, Romania, Bulgaria and Hungary. This was possible because all these countries had governments which had been hostile to the Soviet Union. Russia had lost millions during the war, a figure many times greater than that of Britain and the USA put together.

> And so what can there be surprising about the fact that the Soviet Union, anxious for its future safety, is trying to see that governments loyal in their attitude to the Soviet Union should exist in these countries? And how can anyone who has not taken leave of his wits describe the peaceful aspiration of the Soviet Union as expansionist tendencies on the part of our state?

Stalin also took a racial angle, turning on the claim that Churchill was now taking the view that 'only the English-speaking nations are superior nations who are called on to decide the destinies of the entire world'.[120]

The mixture of reactions in the USA and Britain to Churchill's speech give a fair picture of the state of the East–West relations in early 1946. More moderate voices could still be heard in the State Department. Kennan's secret Long Telegram was at that time not yet received doctrine but it was making the rounds. In London,

119   Carlton, op. cit., p. 262
120   Fleming, op. cit., Vol. I, p. 353

there was still a widespread feeling that peaceful coexistence was possible and even, despite difficulties, probable. The big problem as seen from the Europeans' angle was not Russia but economic recovery. Aid from the USA was badly needed. This was to be provided in varying forms, culminating in the Marshall Plan. But it had conditions. And these, sensible and straightforward as many of them seemed to be, were in due course to heighten tension between East and West disastrously.

Truman Deals With His Dissidents

In the months following the Churchill speech, Truman asked Clark Clifford, Special Counsel to the President, to draw up a list of the Soviet violations of agreements. With the zealous assistance of Truman's assistant naval aide, George Elsey, Clifford produced a Kennan-like polemic about the aims of Soviet policy. Supposedly secret, the document appeared in full in *Memoirs* by Arthur Krock, the *New York Times* Washington Correspondent.[121] The White House authors' alarmist views represented a cross section of opinion in the Washington establishment which they consulted carefully. Their conclusions were straightforward.

The Russians were putting off the peace treaties simply to enable them to keep their troops in Eastern Europe. The Soviets' wider aims included turning Turkey into a satellite, setting up a 'friendly' government in Greece and gaining oil fields in the Middle East. Moscow was also, he claimed, supporting Mao in China:

> Development of atomic weapons, guided missiles, materials for biological war, a strategic air force, submarines of great range, naval mines … were designed to extend Soviet authority … well into the areas which the US regards as vital to its security.

Airfields were being developed in eastern Siberia which would put the North American continent within striking distance. US policy must obstruct further Russian aggression. The USA 'must be prepared to wage atomic and biological warfare' as a deterrent. This analysis was a fascinating mirror image of Russia's view of the world, though with the important exception that the USA could easily afford a massive military programme and the Soviet Union was ill-placed to do so. Yet it was now the USA which was seen as having to fear encirclement by Russia.

Truman was delighted with the report. It bore out his own instinctive views. But he resisted the suggestion that the document should be shown to Henry Wallace, the Cabinet's dove – who had recorded his own view to the President that there were military thinkers who 'advocate a preventive war with Russia' before it acquired the A-bomb.

Wallace had his own form of preventive war to wage against the rest of the Washington establishment. He could speak with the authority of a former vice

---

121   Published by Cassell, London, 1968

president and hoped that, by doing so, he could rally others to resist what he saw as a headlong rush into confrontation. He chose a speech at a Democratic rally in New York, declaring: 'The tougher we get, the tougher the Russians get. We must not let our policy be guided or influenced by those inside or outside the United States who want war with Russia.[122]'

He called for a recognition by Americans that:

> We have no more business in the political affairs of eastern Europe than Russia has in the political affairs of Latin America, Western Europe and the United States ... Whether we like it or not the Russians will try to socialise their sphere of influence just as we are trying to democratise our sphere of influence.[123]

Wallace's speech was endorsed by his fellow speaker, Senator Claude Pepper, who asked what could be expected of a foreign policy which met with the approval of Senator Vandenberg and Foster Dulles. Wallace also published a letter he had sent the President in July which criticised the scale of the new defence budget and offered these thoughts:

> How would it look to us if Russia had the Atomic Bomb and we did not, if Russia had 10,000-mile bombers and air bases within 1,000 miles of our coastlines and we did not? ... Most of us are firmly convinced of the rightness of internationalisation and defortification of the Danube or the Dardanelles but we would be horrified and angered by any Russian counter-proposal that would involve also the internationalising and defortification of Suez and Panama.[124]

Truman handled the subsequent upset indecisively. He wanted to avoid a row during a mid-term election campaign. He hesitated. The White House formally denied that there was any military school of thought urging a pre-emptive war with Russia. Finally, a week after the speech, and faced with the possibility of resignation by the protesting Byrnes, he dismissed Wallace.

The election itself went badly for Truman. The Republicans gained control of both houses of Congress. They had made great play of the dangers of Communism. The sinister J. Edgar Hoover, head of the F. B. I. helped with a speech in November warning of the threat from American Communists and their army of 'fellow travellers and phony liberal allies'. Playing the Red Card had certainly helped the Republicans. The administration was not slow to take the lesson on board.

---

122 Fleming, op. cit., Vol. I p. 419
123 Fleming, op. cit., Vol. I p. 420
124 Fleming, op. cit., p. 421

Yet, in the last weeks of 1946, there was actually some improvement in East–West relations. There was final agreement on the shape of the peace treaties which the previous foreign ministers' conference had been debating for months. The Russians accepted the idea of some sort of internationalisation of the Danube, though only in principle – never in practice. There was also progress on the exclusive American trusteeship and control of the formerly Japanese-occupied islands in the western Pacific. But this modest improvement did not last long.

CHAPTER 15
THE TRUMAN DOCTRINE AND THE MARSHALL PLAN

Truman commissions an analysis from a hardliner – military aid for Greece and Turkey basis of new doctrine – early preparations for economic assistance to Europe includes Soviet Union – domino theory advanced

Nineteen-forty-seven was a key year in East–West relations, the time when the battle lines for the Cold War seemed to be finally drawn. The USA launched two major initiatives, the Truman Doctrine and the proposals which culminated in the Marshall Plan. Neither was quite what it seemed. The Truman plan was set out as a measure primarily to stop Soviet expansion in Greece and Turkey. Yet it was not Russia but Yugoslavia which was aiding the Greek rebels against the instructions of Moscow. This finer point went unmentioned in Washington where the idea of Communism as monolithic was firmly entrenched. There was no serious threat to Turkey.

The Marshall Plan to aid European recovery has always been presented as a fine act of altruism – or at the least an act of economic assistance to save Western Europe from Communism. It came in the wake of the Truman doctrine but did even more harm to East–West relations because of the conditions it imposed on assistance to the USSR.

Both plans had bipartisan support in the USA. Dulles, as a spokesman for the Republicans, called for Western European economic unification as a barrier to Communist expansion. The Republican Senator Vandenberg had called for a UN inquiry into blatantly unfair elections in Poland. Acheson had warned a receptive Congressional Committee that 'Russian policy is an aggressive and expanding one' which provoked a formal complaint from Moscow.

Truman's first major speech that year at Baylor, Texas, added to Kremlin fears. It was another impassioned call for free trade throughout the world. His exposition of the problems of the interwar years was in fact faultless. As he also said, protectionism and economic counter-measures by nations could lead to economic warfare. Though he stopped short of saying that it could lead to anything worse, he emphasised that politics and economics, were inevitably interdependent and that only the free enterprise system, properly operated internationally, ensured peace.

In the foreign ministers' meeting at Moscow that spring there was stalemate. The main issue was devising a peace treaty with Germany where cooperation between the powers was breaking down. The Americans and the British had merged their two occupation zones into 'Bizonia'. Byrnes was calling for a provisional German government. He opposed any idea that the industrial Ruhr and the Rhineland should be separated from the rest of the country. But he found the French and the Russians united in a desire to keep Germany weak. In the Control Council, France had embarked on a series of obstructive tactics, vetoing proposals for a central administration of services ranging from finance to the electrical grid.

For the Russians, rather more than the French, the creation of a German government provoked serious concern. Moreover, the Soviets still could not get the West to agree to the level of reparations which they regarded as their due. It was in this atmosphere, two days after the Moscow talks started, that the President stood before Congress to launch his ground-breaking 'Truman Doctrine'.

The spur for this new policy – military and economic intervention to help friendly nations under threat – was British economic weakness. The President's speech went through a period of careful gestation. Intervention in the Eastern Mediterranean was a novelty and it could bring the USA into collision with the Soviet Union. Clark Clifford suggested an addition to say that pressure which led to the disappearance of free enterprise would threaten the USA's economy, indeed her very democracy. Acheson rejected this passage, not least because it might go down badly in London where the free enterprise system was getting a rough handling from the nationalisation-prone Labour government.

Clifford was not to be discouraged. He hoped there would be a reference to the need to safeguard 'the natural resources of the Middle East'. This concern was certainly in the administration's mind but, openly declared, it could sound too much like a crude play for oil. The President's speech was supposed to be couched in more high-minded terms than that.

There was one important alteration by Acheson to the draft of the speech. He substituted 'must' for 'should' when it came to the policy of the USA intervening to support free peoples.

On 12 March Truman delivered the address. Nations had to choose between 'alternative ways of life … the choice is often not a free one'. He went on:

> One way of life is based on the will of the majority and is distinguished by free institutions, representative governments, free elections, guarantees of individual liberty, freedom of speech and freedom from political oppression. The second way of life was based upon the will of the minority forcibly imposed upon the majority. It relied upon terror and oppression of controlled press and radio; fixed elections and the suppression of personal freedom.

I believe it must be the policy of the United States to support free people who are resisting attempted subjugation by armed minorities or by outside pressure ... The very existence of Greece is today threatened by the terrorist activities of several thousand armed men led by Communists.[125]

The Athens government had asked for aid and the USA would provide it, in the form of economic, political and military assistance. The disappearance of Greece as an independent state, the President went on, would have a profound effect upon those countries in Europe: '... who are struggling against great difficulties to maintain their freedom and their independence while they repaired the damages of war.'

The President acknowledged that the Greek government was 'not perfect'. It had made 'mistakes'. The aid programme did not mean that the USA condoned everything that had been done there. This was something of an understatement. The 'mistakes' had included mass arrests and widespread brutality which shocked British and American newspaper correspondents.

Turkey, the President claimed, was no less important to the freedom-loving peoples of the world. Her government had asked for American aid and it would be provided. Failure to maintain the independence of these two countries, Truman said, would mean that 'confusion and disorder would spread throughout the Middle East'. He once more attacked Soviet policy in Eastern Europe. Poland, Romania and Bulgaria were singled out as the victims of coercion and intimidation about which the USA had made 'frequent protests'. The President concluded: 'If we falter in our leadership, we may endanger the peace of the world – and we shall surely endanger the welfare of our own nation.'[126]

The warning about the effect 'throughout the Middle East' was another exposition of the domino theory. The same false analysis had been made in even more sweeping and over-excited terms before the Truman speech by George Marshall, seen normally as a sobering influence in matters of state. Succumbing to the general excitement, he declared that if Greece fell, Turkey would be 'surrounded' and even France and Italy would be in peril:

Soviet domination might thus extend over the entire Middle East to the border of India. The effect of this upon Hungary, Austria, Italy and France cannot be overestimated. It is not too alarmist to say that we are faced with the first crisis of a series which might extend Soviet domination to Europe, the Middle East and Asia.

Truman's speech provoked some dismay, not just in the USA but also in Europe where there was limited sympathy for the existing Greek regime; and Turkey

---

125 Fleming, op. cit., p. 421
126 See CWIHP

was not seen as seriously in danger from Russia. The new line suggested that peaceful negotiations would be replaced by military action. At home, even some Republicans were alarmed at the nature and the cost of this open-ended commitment to assist any nation which the administration deemed to be in danger of revolutions 'by small armed minorities' – a normal pattern for revolutions, critics might comment. But in general the Republicans were favourably impressed. And Truman had certainly tried to meet Vandenberg's urging that he should 'scare the hell' out of the country to stiffen the anti-Communist line and increase the military budget.

Truman's simplistic view of the world was well captured when he unburdened himself in a letter to his daughter after the speech:

> The attempt of Lenin, Trotsky, Stalin et al, to fool the world and the American Crackpots Association represented by Joe Davies, Henry Wallace, [Senator] Claude Pepper and the actors in immoral Greenwich Village, is just like Hitler's and Mussolini's so-called socialist states. Your pop had to tell the world just that in polite language.[127]

The world did not view the language as polite. One of the critics had been Kennan, now back in Washington as the designated head of the new planning staff. He said at the drafting stage that he thought the plan wrong and the language objectionable. Turkey should get no aid. His grumbles were ignored. Acheson was quizzed at a Congressional hearing about negotiations with the Soviets following the Truman Doctrine.[128] 'You cannot sit down with them' he brusquely replied.

It was inevitable, after the President's speech, that the foreign ministers' conference made limited progress. But even at that stage, Stalin offered a note of hope. He was not sorry to see the Yugoslavs' programme of aid to the Greek rebels run up against a brick wall. In a conciliatory mood he told a visitor, the prominent Republican Harold Stassen, that cooperation between East and West was of course possible. It did not matter that the two systems were different. After all, the Germans and the Americans had had the same economic system but they had still fought each other. The Americans and the Russians had different economic systems but had cooperated during the war. Why not in peace – so long as the desire to cooperate was there?

But a further form of transatlantic cooperation was being devised in the State Department which, without intention, was to end hopes of any improvement in East–West relations.

---

127   Margaret Truman, op. cit., p. 343
128   Donovan, op. cit., p. 286

LAUNCH OF THE MARSHALL PLAN FINALISES THE EAST-WEST SPLIT

The apparent altruism of the US proposal – British and French foreign ministers agree ways to keep Russia from participation – initial high hopes voiced that plan would improve East-West relations – satellites keen but conditions unacceptable to Moscow – Iron Curtain more firmly in place than ever

Tough as the Truman Doctrine seemed to be with its military emphasis, it was the Marshall Plan which provided the final split in East–West relations. The President's Council of Economic Advisers had been warning him that Western Europe was running out of money to purchase America's substantial and valuable exports. Europe's capacity to pay would last only for a year or so. Western Europe must be put back on to its feet; massive American aid was the only way. Otherwise the USA faced lost markets and the nightmare of an international relapse into protectionist policies.

Care was taken to disguise the plan's political dimension. Senior State Department officials welcomed the possibilities of it luring east European nations into the capitalist camp. However, the department also warned that excluding Russia would be seen in a bad light. It would be regarded as an attempt to divide Europe still further as well as being harsh towards a country that had suffered so much. It would serve best if Russia was invited to join the other prospective beneficiaries and could then be manoeuvred into refusing to cooperate. In any case it might present difficulties in Congress if it was asked to provide funds to help the Soviets.

The mechanism for launching the plan was carefully devised. Marshall himself enunciated the general principles which included, significantly, that all the European governments should confer on what they would need. Bevin, suitably warned, greeted Marshall's speech with enthusiasm, as did his French counterpart. Less publicly, the two men fell in with the idea that Russia should be both invited and discouraged.

In London, the two foreign ministers had already met Will Clayton, Assistant Secretary of State, to discussed ways of preventing Soviet participation without being too obvious. Bevin was particularly keen on the prospects that American aid might lure the satellites from the Soviet orbit. Given the number of Soviet sympathisers in the Foreign Office, this would not have been a secret from Moscow.

At first, proposed Marshall, the nations of Europe should confer to agree output targets for industries on a Europe-wide basis (an odd approach from believers in free markets). He wanted to encourage west European economic integration along the lines later emerging as the Iron and Steel Community and the Common

Market. This would also discourage Moscow since economic integration with the rest of Europe, or the imposition by any outsiders of targets for its own industries, would obviously be unacceptable.

At the same time, Marshall stressed the familiar call for more open trading and access to raw materials. This, again, could be relied on not to appeal to the Kremlin. Nevertheless, there was a readiness in Moscow to see if it might win benefits from the overall plan. The satellite states were keen and, at first, encouraged by Moscow. But as preliminary talks between Britain, France and Russia progressed, the Kremlin had second thoughts. Suspicion of political motives behind the aid were added to by a warning from Novikov in the Washington Embassy:

> The Marshall Plan in place of the previous disorganised actions directed at the economic and political subordination of the European countries to American capital and the creation of anti-Soviet groupings, envisions a broader frame of action, aiming to solve this problem more effectively.[129]

Nevertheless, Novikov thought that participation in the Paris conference would give the Soviet camp an opportunity on the one hand to propose measures to help the most war-damaged states and at the same time hinder attempts to create 'an anti-Soviet bloc'. Attendance would enable the Soviets to press their wish for country-by-country aid rather than a broader plan.

When Molotov appeared at the preliminary Paris conference with a veritable army of advisers and economists, it seemed that Russian participation might be productive. However, Soviet archives show that the operating instructions for the delegation were very cautious.

> In the discussions of any concrete proposal dealing with American aid to Europe, [the] Soviet delegation should object to any conditions of such aid which would carry with them the infringement of the sovereignty of the European countries or their economic enslavement. In the process of discussion of this question, the Soviet delegation should make clear the negative attitude of the Soviet Union to such conditions of aid as were put into place in Greece and Turkey.[130]

The Soviet team was also instructed to take a strong line on Germany. They were to stand firm against involving Germany in the Marshall Plan unless reparations were allowed from current German production, not just from the removal of industrial plant. They should also object to any attempt to transfer the German question out of the hands of the four-power Allied Control Council where Russia had a veto.

---

129   See CWIHP
130   See CWIHP

Molotov made a stand against what he called 'Dollar Democracy' and 'Equal Opportunity', raising the issue of international waterways to illustrate his point. The internationalisation of the Danube and free trade around it had been an obsession with Truman. The US had accumulated great wealth, Molotov said, adding:

> It is surely not too difficult to understand that if American capital were given a free hand in the small states ruined and enfeebled by the war … American capital would buy up the local industries, appropriate the more attractive Romanian and Yugoslav and all other enterprises and would become the masters in these small states. Given such a situation we would probably live to see the day when in your own country, on switching on the radio you would be hearing not so much your own language as one American gramophone record after another.[131]

After a few days, Molotov summarised the Marshall Plan as involving an intolerable degree of intervention in the affairs of other states and left in a huff, or apparent huff. The satellite states then withdrew their acceptance to attend the later full conference on the plan, though they only did so under pressure from Moscow and only after some protests. At this stage, there was sufficient independence among the east European nations for it to be safe – but not for long – to show some individuality.

The walkout, combined with the satellites' reluctant withdrawal, handed the Western side a massive propaganda opportunity – eagerly seized upon. Molotov had been abrupt and dismissive. The Soviet Union and the east European states were in desperate need but they were forced to reject the generosity of the United States. Could intransigence go further?

This propaganda victory was not however followed by harmony among the Western European nations. The Americans indicated their strong desire for an integrated economic (and political) community in Europe, not unlike the USA itself, a forerunner of decades of support for the cause of the Common Market and European Union. Some nations wanted to see greater European economic integration as Washington hoped. Some argued that one type of integration would be better than another, with the French proving almost as difficult as Molotov, though less abrupt. They were opposed to an American wish that Germany's steel, chemical and heavy industries be restored to nearly pre-war levels. Some countries argued for a nation-by-nation approach without the burden of multinational targets. The British did not want to participate in a proposed customs union which would endanger their Commonwealth trade. The Scandinavians objected to the plan not being launched under United Nations auspices.

---

131 http://www.highered.mcgrraw-hill.com/olc/dl/35266

It was a wearisome process but in the end an agreement was reached. The USA donated funds through the European Recovery Programme which eventually totalled $13billion by 1952. It provided the spur and Western Europe was soon on the road to economic health.

The Political Consequences of the Marshall Plan

In economic terms the plan may have been a major success. Politically, it also succeeded in providing the USA with great leverage in the affairs of Western Europe. But in the widest political terms the consequences proved grim. The involvement of Eastern European nations into the wider free world economy was now out of the question. Soviet suspicions could not be allayed.

The Iron Curtain was now to be wrung down with a terrible finality. Western Europe was more dependent than ever on the USA. The eastern nations were in turn more dependent than ever on the Soviet Union which concluded a rapid series of trade agreements across the bloc. Conscious of the widespread criticism of the Soviet attitude to the plan, Andreii Vishinsky played hard for sympathy at the United Nations:

> The so-called Truman Doctrine and the Marshall Plan are particularly glaring examples of the manner in which the principles of the United Nations are violated … The United States government … [is] using the economic resources distributed as relief to individual needy nations as an instrument of political pressure. This is clearly proved by the measures taken by the United States government with regard to Greece and Turkey which ignore and bypass the United Nations, as well as by the measures proposed under the so-called Marshall Plan in Europe. This policy conflicts sharply with the principle expressed by the General Assembly … that relief supplies to other countries 'should at no time be used as a political weapon.'[132]

Dubbing the Marshall Plan merely a variant of the Truman Doctrine he denounced the proposal as interfering with:

> The inalienable right of European countries to dispose of their economic resources and plan their national economies in their own way … The United States also counted on making all these countries directly dependent on the interest of American monopolies which are striving to avert the approaching depression by an accelerated export of commodities and capital to Europe … It is becoming more and more evident to everyone that the implementation of the Marshall Plan will mean placing European countries under the economic and political control of the United States and direct interference by the latter

132   See CWIHP

in the internal affairs of those countries. Moreover this plan is an attempt to split Europe into two camps …

An important feature of this plan is an attempt to confront the countries of Eastern Europe with a bloc of Western States including Western Germany. The intention is to make use of Western Germany and German heavy industry as one of the most important bases for American expansion in Europe, in disregard of the national interests of the countries which suffered from German aggression.[133]

This was of course a case of the kettle calling the pot black, given Soviet interference in the internal affairs of East European countries. On the other hand, it was true that the United States did regard the Marshall Plan as providing it with vital political levers. Economic power, in the form of aid and trade terms, enabled the United States to exercise its power over great distances and into any chosen corner of the globe. If this was, at least partially, inspired by hostility to the Soviet Union – as we have seen it was – then the Kremlin had cause for alarm.

Moscow proceeded to tighten its grip on the satellites and to safeguard its own military bases there. Coalition governments had been accepted until then, with varying levels of non-Communist participation. The non-Communist elements were now purged. In Hungary Ferenc Nagy, who had been Prime Minister as leader of one of the minority parties, was removed and later fled to Switzerland. The Czech government was already heavily Communised following the party's strong successes in genuinely free elections. It was to be all but entirely Communised with the appointment of a new government. Only Foreign Minister Jan Masaryk, son of the former Prime Minister, remained among the non-Communists. He later killed himself by jumping from a window. In the West it was doubted if this was genuine suicide.

At an international level, and before the purges of 'reactionary elements' in the satellites, Moscow set up the Cominform, seen in the West as a simple successor to the Comintern, once the Soviet weapon for spreading revolution, which had been disbanded when Russia became an ally of the West in 1943. The Cominform was born out of a desire to respond to the Marshall Plan and all its allegedly sinister motives.

The satellites fell into line with whatever the Cominform decreed. But there was some trouble with the French and Italian Communist parties. They were ordered to involve themselves with direct action – meaning protests, demonstrations and strikes – in opposition to the Marshall Plan. The result was to be a sharp fall in the Communist vote in each country.

Andreii Zhdanov, who organised the Cominform, conceded that Socialism and Capitalism would both survive together for a long time. But the Marshall Plan and American imperialism were the danger that parties were ordered to expose and resist. Drafts of Zhdanov's final speech contained an explicit declaration

---

that the world was now 'finally' divided into two camps. This did not reach the final form, the CWIHP archives show. But the message seemed plain enough in any case.

CHAPTER 16
THE BERLIN AIRLIFT

Moscow alarmed over new German currency – Washington nearly misses a message – Soviets attempt to cut off Berlin – the Airlift works – US and USSR try to sway Italian elections – Hollywood enrolled – CIA cuts its teeth – Communists vanquished

Unsurprisingly, 1948 proved a very tense year. Berlin became the focus of East–West hostility. Moscow had found it hard to make up its mind about the way forward on Germany. There were three possible courses. The Soviets could play a full and friendly part in the four-power Control Commission agreed at Potsdam, to include France. This would end, in theory, with a four-power agreement on Germany and a peace treaty which would, again in theory, leave the country neutralised. Or Moscow could neutralise eastern Germany as part of its cordon sanitaire. Or it could retain its military presence and control there.

The nominally shared objective of the four powers was a reunited but pacified Germany. Truman constantly stressed the importance of putting the vanquished nation back on its feet. Russia and France, which had actually been invaded by Germany, were less high-minded. They disliked the idea of a revitalised traditional foe. The USA had additional motives anyway. If Germany did not revive, it further drained American finances. Moreover, it was accepted by Britain and the USA that there would be no serious economic revival in Western Europe unless Germany was part of it. The French came round to that view, though reluctantly. As recipients of Marshall Aid they did not have much choice. If the Russians had no faith in the idea of a reunited Germany, restrained by treaty from remilitarisation, it was hardly surprising. The Versailles Treaty was supposed to keep Germany pacified. But it had not worked.

The Control Commission's plans were regularly vetoed by the Russians or the French – often supporting each other in their hostility towards a too swiftly revived Germany. But the turning point in the disagreement which ended in the confrontation over Berlin was triggered by the currency question. The three

Western powers not only merged their zones but also pressed ahead in 1948 with plans to re-establish a West German government which would also have its own currency. The existing all-Germany currency was being undermined by the Russians' readiness to print money freely which led to inflation and undermined the chances of a German economic recovery. Attempts to hold down inflation by price controls and rationing were inevitably unsuccessful.

The prospect of a revitalised Germany, buoyed up by Marshall Aid, was just what the Russians feared. How long before the new state became independent and even armed? The Russians had a weapon at their disposal: Berlin. The arrangement for four-power control of the city was extraordinarily inept from the start. To reach Berlin in the centre of the Soviet zone, the Allies had to pass through a Russian-controlled corridor. Fears had been voiced during wartime negotiations in both London and Washington. It would have a serious potential for trouble. But the critics were little heeded. Stalin had insisted that there would be no trouble.

In March the Russians walked out of the Allied Control Commission. The Soviets subsequently announced that Allied personnel would be checked as they passed through the corridor which the other three refused to accept. With the formal announcement that the new German government would be issuing its own new currency, the Russians became increasingly intractable. They offered to drop all hindrances if the plan was abandoned. This was refused and the Soviets gradually tightened all control of the corridor. By mid-summer, the threat of collision was real. The three powers tried negotiation but they found the Russians at their most intransigent. The ambassadors had two interviews in Moscow with Stalin who appeared reasonably helpful. Then in each case they found it impossible to negotiate with Molotov over a firm arrangement.

The Russians seemed determined to force the Allies out of Berlin. Armed convoys were considered by the Western powers but the idea was abandoned. The risk of a shooting war was too great. In the end the Allies launched the Berlin Airlift to supply their zones in the city. It lasted for a year and was an impressive demonstration of unity and air power. The blockade was eventually ended, though after a rather curious episode, recalled in the Truman memoirs. In late January Stalin answered questions from an American correspondent and in his replies about Berlin omitted all reference to the Soviet demands about the currency.

The point was noticed in Washington but it was only a month later that the American representative at the UN asked his Soviet counterpart in an informal moment whether the omission was accidental. In due course the Russian reply came that it was not. Truman wrote: 'This is an example of how difficult it was to do business with the Russians on a straightforward basis.'[134]

---

134   Truman memoirs, Vol. II, p. 131

Yet dropping hints through newspaper interviews was an old-established diplomatic manoeuvre. So it was that some fourteen months after the first restrictions had been attempted and a year after the Air Lift began the two sides called a truce. The Soviets had not only failed to win their objective; they had also been badly worsted in propaganda terms.

To the West, the episode was the clearest proof that firmness paid. In Russian minds, the lesson seemed to be that attempts to hinder Western plans needed more thought to prevent humiliation. Meanwhile there was a political battle to be fought out in Italy.

Washington Massages the Italian Elections

In the State Department fear was growing that the Communists would do well in the Italian elections of 1948 – even an excitable fear that they might stage an armed coup in the north of the country where their base was strong. There were also worries about the Communist vote in France, though not so serious. It was thought too dangerous to French susceptibilities to interfere too obviously in elections there. Italy was another matter.

The outright opposition of the Communist parties in both countries to the Marshall Plan was losing them votes. Washington would not take any chances in Italy. The party there had received some financial support from the Soviet Union. The Americans set out to counter that with a larger and more ambitious campaign. The Truman Doctrine may have declared American hostility to 'outside pressure' being exerted on countries and governments. Molotov may have denounced the Marshall Plan as an attempt to interfere with the internal affairs of other nations. But neither side showed any compunction about aiding their chosen friends abroad.

The various agencies of Washington, particularly the CIA, set to with a will. Cash was handed out to selected politicians to cover their campaigning costs. Using pamphlets, broadcasts from the USA and an elaborate letter-writing campaign among Americans of Italian origin to their relatives, voters were warned not just of the peril of Communism but that aid from the USA, conveniently stepped up during the election campaign itself, could be in immediate jeopardy.

There had also been a remarkable threat by the Attorney General, Tom Clark. Those who voted Communist would be deemed ineligible for entry into the USA, let alone for citizenship. How these votes would be unearthed was never explained. William Donovan, the wartime head of the Office of Strategic Services, saw to it that Italians were warned through short-wave broadcasts that a Communist victory could see them transported to Russia for forced labour. Among prominent figures called in to help with the propaganda were Frank Sinatra and Gary Cooper. Others, including two former Secretaries of State and Mrs Eleanor Roosevelt, signed a manifesto to 'freedom loving Italians'.

In the weeks before the vote itself, Washington conveniently announced extra food aid, well publicised by the American Ambassador himself at the port of unloading. Among the items of American assistance to Italy was the provision of gold to replace what Germany had stolen, the return of merchant ships seized during the war and the forgiving of $1bn of accumulated debt.

The Russians could hardly compete with the propaganda skills of the Americans, let along the sums disbursed directly and indirectly. How well the Communists would have fared without the American intervention cannot be known. The results were certainly a delight to Washington. The Christian Democrats won 48 per cent of the vote and the Socialist–Communist alliance polled only 31 per cent. The Liberals and Republicans, also targets for CIA largesse, won more votes than they expected.

The CIA campaign appeared to be a brilliant success. And it was to lead to a rapid rise in the agency's budget and powers of intervention overseas which were used to the full, not least in Vietnam.

Hysteria

In the months before the Cold War took a violent turn and the Korean conflict broke out, the National Security Council had prepared a report for Truman on the East–West conflict. NSC-68 became the basis for the administration's strategic thinking. It unhesitatingly saw everything that the Soviet Union stood for as bad and everything that the USA championed as good. In a moment of optimism, the document comments that so resilient was 'freedom in the USA, that the country could tolerate those within it, who would wish to use their freedom to destroy it'. This would have come as a surprise to those Americans on the receiving end of the persecutions culminating in the campaign launched by Senator McCarthy.

The authors of the report, primarily Dean Acheson and Paul Nitze, also from the State Department – formerly a Wall Street banker and a novice in international affairs – appeared at no stage beset by doubts. Acheson himself admitted later that the primary purpose of the report was 'to bludgeon the mass mind of top government'. This was to be achieved by NSC-68 warning that the free world was in great danger and the USA, and only the USA, could save it. Of the American system, the authors observed:

> From this idea of freedom with responsibility derives the marvellous diversity, the deep tolerance, the lawfulness of the free society. This is the explanation of the strength of free men ... The free society does not fear, it welcomes diversity. It derives its strength from its hospitality even to antipathetic ideas.[135]

Yet NSC-68, for all its protestations about American moral superiority, proffered the green light to any tactic which might be advantageously used against the Soviet Union:

---

135   www.state/gov/r/pa/ho/time/cwr

The integrity of our system will not be jeopardised by any measures, covert or overt, violent or non-violent, which serve the purposes of frustrating the Kremlin design, nor does the necessity of conducting ourselves so as to affirm our values in action as well as words forbid such measures, providing only they are appropriately calculated to that end and are not so excessive or misdirected as to make us enemies of the people instead of the evil men who enslaved them.

In short, the end would justify the means, so long as they did not make new enemies, so long as they frustrated the Kremlin's wicked aims. NSC-68's ambitions were not small. It was of little use to try to negotiate with Moscow because the USA did not have sufficient power to impose its will. There needed to be an attempt to change the world situation by means, short of war, in such a way as to frustrate the Kremlin and hasten the Soviets' decay. This and other suggestions about taking the initiative in bringing about the fall of the Communist system were to meet strong objections from Kennan, back in the State Department. But his changing view of the Soviet threat was losing him his influence in Washington. After claiming that the sheer size of the existing Soviet forces must indicate the Kremlin's desire for world domination – something which might also be applied to the USA at that point – NSC-68 leads up to the predictable call for a larger military budget, more nuclear weapons and the means to deliver them.

Admiral Sir Eric Longley-Cook, the deputy head of British naval intelligence, gives an indication of the near hysteria which existed in Washington when NSC-68 was being drawn up. He recorded that he had had conversations with 'many responsible and influential Americans who are obviously convinced that war with Russia is inevitable'. And he had reached the 'alarming conclusion' that they had fixed a date for that in mid or late 1952. He doubted whether 'the US will be able to control the Frankenstein monster which they are creating'.[136]

Soviet policy was in fact driven by fear not aggressiveness. After the Cold War had ended a colloquium was held in Oslo in which Georgi Kornienko, first Soviet vice foreign minister in the late 1970s and early 1980s took part. He commented:

All of our leaders whom I knew from the late 1940s and early 1950s, all of them feared war and were willing to go to great lengths for peace … Yes, ideology was ideology and pronouncements of their faith in the Communist future of the world – everything was there; but there was as you know no master plan for conquering Europe, for conquering the Third World.[137]

A further comment was offered by Karen Brutents, former deputy head of the International Department of the Communist Party of the Soviet Union:

---

136   www.guardian.co.uk/uk/2001/jun/16

137   CWIHP

This generation coming in from the war – it was a terrible war – I think they had decided there would never be a repetition … any price which is necessary to pay for security will be paid – and finally it was that price which destroyed the country. For security, not for conquering the world.[138]

NSC-68 had drawn a Manichaean picture of the world where the ruthless enemy was faced by a United States empowered by freedom and tolerance. Yet this was at a time when blacks were still shorn of basic civil rights in the South and could get little justice before the law. They faced intolerance throughout the USA, despite having had a much longer residence in America than so many of those who treated them badly.

The Path to McCarthyism

Anti-Communist paranoia had been building ever since the Congressional elections of 1946 when both Democrats and Republicans had started to play the Red Card and compete in their assertions of their total hostility to Communism or anything associated with it. Truman's Attorney General, Tom Clark, set a tough standard by declaring: 'Those who do not believe in the ideology of the United States shall not be allowed to stay in the United States.'[139]

He was also to order the arrest of Gerhart Eisler, a prominent Communist, on the highly undemocratic grounds that he had been 'making speeches round the country that were derogatory to our way of life'. During the summer, a dozen Communists were tried and convicted under the Smith Act of 1940 which made it illegal to advocate the overthrow of the US government. Being a Communist, it was argued, was sufficient proof of that intention.

During the 1948 presidential election Clark was to complain that Congress had refused him a law which would have allowed him to take some 2,000 alien Communists into custody because of their beliefs. The uncovering of two genuine spy rings stirred public alarm – eagerly fanned by the Republicans. Truman promised a tough review of government employee loyalty and appointed a commission to decide procedures. Torn between claiming that the Truman administration was beyond suspicion and his ferocious hostility to Communism, Clark told the commission that that there was no serious problem yet. But Truman was carried away on the anti-Communist tide, declaring that 'the fact is that one disloyal person is one too many'.[140] Given that there were over 2,300,000 government civilian employees, this was an alarming claim.

Within a week of the promulgation of the Truman Doctrine in 1947, the President signed an executive order initiating the Employee Loyalty Programme.

---

138   See CWIHP including Odd Arne Westad transcript from a workshop at Lysebu
139   *The Great Fear* by David Caute, Simon and Schuster, 1978, p. 15
140   Donovan, op. cit., p. 293

This established, so it seemed, his sound anti-Communism on both foreign and domestic fronts. But the loyalty programme was to get out of hand, as Truman later complained in his memoirs, undermining the very civil liberties so vaunted as a contrast to what prevailed under the Soviet system.

All government departments had to establish loyalty boards. There was a system of appeals but only to a body with advisory powers. The Federal Loyalty Review Board had its own list of subversive organisations which ranged from the National Negro Congress to the Walt Whitman School of Social Sciences. Despite the President's misgivings, the fanatically anti-Communist and paranoid J. Edgar Hoover and his FBI were given the investigative role. Hoover himself threatened to resign if his bureau was not chosen for the job. It was not long before a vast system of files and records was being set up to cover the activities of government employees. To make matters worse, accusers were to have their names withheld if it was thought essential to the programme's 'effectiveness', which it often was.

The FBI was also ordered to take into account the views and findings of Congress's House Un-American Activities Committee (HUAC), which was already acquiring its unsavoury reputation for the zealous pursuit of many well-known figures, including film stars, broadcasters and script writers. The loyalty programme meant that, for the first time, the doctrines of guilt by association and guilt for disloyal thoughts – as opposed to disloyal deeds – were to become public policy. The HUAC eagerly supported the principle. Its hearings became a major media circus when those who pleaded the Fifth Amendment under examination were effectively labelled as guilty without proof. Truman was later to describe this as a complete violation of the Bill of Rights: 'Whenever we come to the point where we are spying on each other, as was done under Hitler and Mussolini and as is now done in Russia ... we cease to be the Republic we were set up to be.'[141]

Specifying the excesses of the McCarthy period which ran from 1950–54, Truman also wrote:

I recall the periods of mass hysteria in this country which led to witch hunts. Demagogues and unprincipled individuals have always seized upon crises to incite emotional and irrational fears. Racial, religious and class animosities are stirred up. Charges and accusations are directed at many innocent people in the name of false patriotism and hatred of things foreign.[142]

Truman directed his fire at the obvious and vulnerable McCarthyite phase. However, this had ended in the downfall of the rabid Senator from Wisconsin – an unsuccessful lawyer and one-time Democrat in local politics whose career had

---

141   Truman memoirs, Vol. II, p. 271
142   Truman memoirs, Vol. II, p. 272

always been followed by charges of corruption and dishonesty. Searching for a cause to boost his unimpressive career in the Senate, the rambling Joe McCarthy was to take up the anti-Communist cause in 1950, tapping into a rich vein of public paranoia with his lists of secret 'Reds' within government departments. Yet it was the President's own employee loyalty programme which set the hysteria in train. Various states brought in measures of their own to ensure that their own employees were sound. They ranged from demanding oaths of loyalty for university teachers – and even students – to the remarkable case of Indiana where even professional wrestlers were required to acclaim their loyalty.

The State Department was to be a particular target for the investigators, especially on the grounds that it could only be the subversive activities of individuals which had 'lost China'. Despite the contempt for Chiang Kai-shek's Nationalist government voiced by successive American envoys, the success of the Communists was seen as inexplicable except by some conspiracy in high places. Matters got worse under Dulles, Secretary of State after 1952. Zealous Red hunters even sought to question the appointment of Charles Bohlen as Ambassador in Moscow. Bohlen had been Roosevelt's interpreter at Yalta – and thus, presumably, privy to the 'betrayal' of Eastern Europe. Three senior department officials who had been antagonistic to Chiang Kai-shek were sacked.

This was not an atmosphere in which foreign policy could be sensibly evolved. But since Dulles himself was subjecting every aspect of policy to his own particular brand of evangelical anti-Communism, perhaps the investigations made little difference.

McCarthy was to raise the anti-Communist hysteria to new heights with the State Department one of his favoured targets. Elected in 1946, the ambitious new senator made little impact in Washington. The widespread belief was later established that he adopted his anti-Communist crusade only after a friend suggested it to him as a means of attracting headlines. The advice proved correct.

He caused his first sensation in a speech to a Republican Women's Club, claiming to have a list of 205 government employees who were 'card carrying Communists' or sympathisers. The number was pared in his next speech to fifty-seven – which provoked jokes that he found the number from a Heinz label. In the Senate, the number recovered to eighty-one.[143] His speeches there, like the numbers, were a model of confusion.

It is a comment on the times and the country that such a demagogue could be taken seriously. With the backing of the HUAC, he became a widely approved national figure. It must of course be remembered that this was when the USA had become involved in Korea under the UN flag. Nevertheless, the sheer wildness and inconsistency of his claim should have made him widely derided. A poll at the time showed that about half of the population approved of him. But intolerance

---

143   Congressional Record 11 Feb, 1950, 81st Congress

was not new. In mid-1946 a Gallup Poll showed 44 per cent favoured outlawing the Communist Party and making membership illegal.

By 1949, the figure had risen to 68 per cent. In 1954, a survey conducted by a Harvard professor found just over half the population in favour of imprisoning all Communists. Other surveys found similar or higher figures. The intolerance extended to 45 per cent who would not allow 'socialists' to publish their own newspaper. A startling 42 per cent wanted to deny the press the right to criticise 'the American form of Government'.[144]

McCarthy had picked up a trend. He did not create it but merely exploited it. He was however to overreach himself in a series of confrontations with the army, where he claimed there was considerable subversion. Eisenhower had been cautious about dealing with such a popular figure until then. But the attack on the army was too much and the President went on the offensive. In late 1954, McCarthy was censured in a special session of the Senate. Yet his approval ratings, right up to the time of his death in 1957, did not fall to less than 35 per cent.

Eisenhower was no slouch himself in rooting out supposed security risks. In his State of the Union speech in 1954 he claimed to have dismissed over 2,000 security risks from federal employment. This was a major exaggeration and potentially misleading. The real number was a fraction of the figure claimed. And it included such people as alcoholics, homosexuals and serial debtors.

To understand McCarthy's brief but remarkable success we need to recall how regularly paranoia found a home in the USA. The US historian Richard Hofstadter in *The Paranoid Style in American Politics* analysed the appeal thus:

> The distinguishing thing about the paranoid style is not that its exponents see conspiracies here and there in history but that they regard a vast or gigantic conspiracy as the motive force in historical events. History is a conspiracy, set in motion by demonic forces of almost transcendent power, and what is felt to be needed to defeat it is not the usual methods of political give-and-take but an all-out crusade. The paranoid spokesman ... is always manning the barricades of civilisation. He constantly lives at a turning point; it is now or never in organising resistance to conspiracy. Time is forever running out.[145]

Dulles, with his own apocalyptic vision of the world and the moral struggle, was himself a later symptom of the paranoid tendency in American politics. For him, time was always running out, the power of Communism was demonic and if not fought at the barricades would overwhelm the world. He was also no friend to the freedom of the press. The desire of newspapers to report on China – still not recognised by the USA – was normal enough. But the State Department put every

---

144   *The Great Fear* by David Caute, Simon and Schuster, 1978, p. 215
145   Hofstadter, op. cit., pp. 29–30

obstacle in the way of reporters and in the way of cultural exchanges in general. The latter, Dulles explained, would in the case of China's Asian neighbours 'add to their peril'.

He used the power of the State Department to grant or renew passports as a weapon to bully newspapers. In the face of bitter complaints from the press, Dulles half retreated from his position in 1957. But he still tried to exercise press censorship by selecting the correspondents who would be allowed to travel to Red China.

CHAPTER 17
THE COLD WAR HOTS UP: KOREA AND CHINA

US relations with China - Stalin's nervous of his ally - persuaded by Acheson speech it was safe to support Korean attack - US forces on retreat - MacArthur rebellious - Truman hints at use of A-bomb - alarmed Attlee flies to Washington - sacked MacArthur becomes US hero

By the time that NSC-68 had been fully digested as it circulated through the major departments in Washington, the Korean war had broken out. The authors of the report immediately saw this as a clear vindication of their warnings. The reality was more complex.

In 1949, the Americans had come to face a new problem as Mao Zedong's armies swept into the remaining areas held by Chiang Kai-shek's Nationalists. The People's Republic of China was proclaimed. In the USA, which had been aiding Chiang's forces, this was seen as a shattering defeat for the free world. In the eyes of people like the increasingly vocal Dulles, who saw everything in ideological terms, it had been another triumph for the 'monolith of Communism', adding 500m people to the 300m already under Soviet control.

In fact the Kremlin eyed the Chinese triumph warily. Throughout the long history of the Chinese civil war, which dated back to the 1920s, Soviet assistance to Mao had been erratic at best. Moscow was ready to support Chiang Kai-shek as the man with whom it could do business. The State Department, though always backing military and financial aid to Chiang in one way or another – most strongly when he was fighting Japan, especially after Pearl Harbor – was regularly plagued with doubts about him. General Joe Stilwell, who had been sent to him as his chief military adviser, compared the Nationalist regime with the Nazis, adding: 'To reform such a system, it must be torn down.'

'Vinegar Joe' was eventually recalled at Chiang's request. General Patrick Hurley was made Ambassador in the hope of finding a way to inject some effectiveness into the Nationalist regime. It was to prove beyond saving, despite Hurley's call for all-out support. In 1947 Marshall had paid a visit to Chiang but then publicly condemned the regime. He was to come under fire in the USA after Mao's triumph when Congress launched an investigation into who was responsible for 'losing China'.

Truman decided in his own mind after the proclamation of the People's Republic that there should be a firm line of US defence in Asia; but it excluded Taiwan (then Formosa) to which Chiang had retreated, and – ominously – Korea. Acheson was rash enough to specify these new limits publicly. There were few American forces in Korea, having been gradually withdrawn from the south as the Russians withdrew from the north. Two hostile regimes eyed each other across the thirty-eighth parallel: the Communist North under Kim Il Sung and the South under President Syngman Rhee who, Americans noted reassuringly, was a Christian. The South had a democratic constitution but a murderous brute in Rhee. His party won fewer than 25 per cent of the seats in the last elections before the outbreak of war. In the chaos which followed the North Korean advance, Rhee had thousands of his opponents murdered.[146]

The outbreak of war in June 1950 has generated intense debate among historians about who started it. The Soviet delegate at the UN had walked out on another issue. He was not present when the Security Council backed an American demand for a UN force to rescue the South, which Russia could have vetoed. This stirred claims that Moscow could not have been privy to the North's decision. But archive material reveals that it certainly was. The decision was Kim's but only taken after the Kremlin had been consulted. Writing under the pseudonym 'Comrade Filipov' a hesitant Stalin finally agreed to the invasion, provided it was sanctioned by Mao. It was. Stalin himself did not believe the Americans would come to the rescue of South Korea given Acheson's rash speech.

The invasion from the north began in mid-1950, initially providing immense successes for the North. The war was to last two years, bringing with it the first military clash between China and the USA and its allies. Washington had been nervous about any attempt by the UN force, controlled by General MacArthur, to carry the war north of the thirty-eighth parallel. It carried the obvious danger that China might get involved and Peking issued several warnings to this effect. But the gung-ho MacArthur assured Truman that the Chinese were too weak to fight. In any case, he was another Manichaean with a mission. In his own words: 'There can be no compromise with atheistic Communism

---

146   For details of Rhee's methods see *The Hidden Hand* by Richard Aldrich, The Overlook Press, 2002, pp. 267–287. This also relates that American commanders were ready to ignore what happened to those it handed over to Rhee's forces. There were some protests from British officials and considerable hostile coverage from the British press, which London tried to suppress as unhelpful to the war effort.

– no halfway in the preservation of freedom and religion. It must be all or nothing.'[147]

He drove his forces close to the border with China, still assuring his Washington masters that it was safe to do so. Then the Chinese struck and threw the UN forces back in headlong retreat. Truman was appalled. He wanted the war stopped – as it could have been when the North's forces were thrown back past the thirty-eighth parallel. He agreed reluctantly to let MacArthur continue despite the General's increasingly open defiance of Washington which included an appeal to Chiang Kai-shek to join in the war, definitely not State Department policy. Truman himself was not however averse to extreme measures. In November he called for a worldwide mobilisation against Communism – including the possibility of using the A-bomb.

The USA's allies were horrified. Attlee hastened to Washington for a reassurance that talk of using the weapon was not serious. Truman, under heavy fire on all sides, retreated. When MacArthur again demanded in effect that China should be forced to surrender and proposed the use of the A-bomb, Truman had had enough of this political general and dismissed him in 1951 But MacArthur returned to a quite spectacular welcome in the USA and an ecstatic ovation when he addressed Congress. In this he called for 'every available means' to be used to secure victory in Korea. This was received with enthusiasm.

The extremist credentials of this American hero are worth noting, even in domestic matters. In his autobiography, he referred to the Federal Income Tax law of 1914 as a 'Marxist inspired device'. His autobiography proved a number one best-seller. The MacArthur reception at all levels put new heart into the Republicans and helped prepare the way for Eisenhower's presidential victory in 1952, bringing Dulles' elevation to the role of Secretary of State.

An unorthodox analysis of the war's causes came later from Kennan. He suggested that the Soviets were keen to control Korea because the USA was concluding a treaty with Japan. That would allow American troops to remain there indefinitely, rearming Russia's old eastern enemy.

As a conflict the war offered a serious lesson to all the participants. It had involved one miscalculation after another. The Americans had banked on there being no attack on the South by the North. Stalin had banked on no American intervention. The Chinese were sure the Americans would not intervene or, when they did, that they would bring their forces only up to the borders of the People's Republic. MacArthur worked on the assumption that the Chinese forces were too weak to make an impact even if Beijing wanted to fight.

The danger of miscalculations on this scale in a nuclear age spoke for themselves.

---

147   *The Devil and John Foster Dulles* by Townsend Hoopes, André Deutsch, 1974, p. 122

PRELUDE TO VIETNAM

French fight to retain Indo-China – Dien Bien Phu – Geneva talks partition Vietnam – Dulles injects new note of belligerence – Eden critical – US attempts to coerce Europe on defence – French resentment builds

While the fighting continued in the Korean war, the State Department was entangling the USA in the grimmest miscalculation of the Cold War: Vietnam. Washington decided to provide aid to the French army fighting the insurgency led by Ho Chi Minh. It had its paradoxical side since, during the war, Ho and his guerrillas facing the Japanese had received assistance through the OSS. At that time, State Department staff viewed him as primarily a nationalist rather than a Communist. But the red tag was what mattered to Acheson as Secretary of State. His decision to aid the French in this battle in a small and relatively unimportant faraway country of which he certainly knew next to nothing was a radical move. It extended the Truman Doctrine from Europe to Asia. It was also the first demonstration of the global policy called for in NSC-68.

It was assumed that the French, with American aid, would hold the line. But with the military disaster of Dien Bien Phu in 1954, the French were in full retreat. A new government in Paris, elected on a promise to negotiate, was ominous for Washington. Talks were arranged in Geneva in 1954 between France, Britain, the USA and China. Dulles started badly – though not by his standards – insulting Zhou by refusing to shake his proffered hand and, later, walked out of the conference. It was at these talks that Eden was overheard to say to Dulles: 'The trouble with you is that you want World War Three.'

The outcome of Geneva was an armistice which partitioned Vietnam at the seventeenth parallel with elections throughout the country promised within two years. The Americans baulked at this prospect of the populace being allowed a vote. The new ruler of the South, Ngo Dinh Diem, was an American nominee (another of the Christians in whom the State Department placed such faith). He cancelled the election plan in 1956. Washington did not complain which was unsurprising. Eisenhower had taken the view in 1954 that: 'Had elections been held at the time of the fighting, possibly eighty per cent of the population would have voted for the Communist Ho Chi Minh as their leader rather than Chief of State Bao Dai.'[148]

Here then was a remarkable about-turn in American policy. From the Atlantic Charter to the Truman Doctrine, the emphasis had been on the rights of people to choose their own government. This was only acceptable, apparently, so long as they

---

148   *Mandate for Change* by Dwight D. Eisenhower, Doubleday, 1963, p. 372

did not choose Communists. It was the mirror image of Russian policy in Eastern Europe: elections were tolerable but only if they led to governments which were Communist, or at least very friendly to the Soviet Union.

It was in the run-up to the Geneva agreement that Dulles was later to say that the world had been brought 'to the brink' by American readiness to use the atomic bomb to ensure that the Chinese limited their assistance to North Vietnam. American foreign policy, under his leadership, was acquiring its most belligerent tone yet.

The Politics of John Foster Dulles

Eisenhower's succession to the Presidency in 1952 saw Dulles accepted as Secretary of State, the post he had so long coveted. He was a rich Wall Street lawyer, staunch Presbyterian and violent opponent of all aspects of Communism and most of Socialism. He proved the most powerful – and dangerous – Secretary of State in the entire history of the Cold War. He was the perfect example of the uncompromising ideologue. He believed the same of Stalin. He kept three books on his desk at the State Department: the Bible, *The Federalist Papers*, and Stalin's *The Problems of Leninism*. The first was apparently to provide the solution to the problems arising from the third. As Townsend Hoopes, a former Defense Department official, commented in his authoritative biography of Dulles: 'By transforming every difference with the Soviet Union into a moral issue, he would make every compromise settlement seem immoral and thus politically unacceptable.'[149]

Dulles had been given a role in foreign policy since the early days of the Truman administration, to underline its bipartisan nature. A distinct coolness set in between him and Truman after the 1948 presidential contest which the Republicans had expected to win easily. Dulles' robust Republican rhetoric on domestic issues looked like spoiling his prospects. But eventually, after strong pressure from leading Republicans, Truman agreed that he play a part in advising the State Department. This bipartisanship was a much vaunted aspect of American policy but in reality it diminished the prospects, such as they were, of useful criticism of the administration's policy.

Dulles' views were propounded in book form: *War or Peace*, published in 1950. Religion, as always, played a prominent part in his views. In the book he wrote: 'Soviet Communism starts with an atheistic Godless premise. Everything else flows from that premise.'[150]

Certainly everything that Dulles did flowed from his own premise that he was called on to lead a Christian crusade. When Eisenhower was touted as Republican candidate for the 1952 presidential election, Dulles hastened to the General's NATO headquarters in Paris, to impress him with his qualifications as a potential Secretary

---

149   Townsend Hoopes, *The Devil and John Foster Dulles*, Little, Brown, 1973, p. 84
150   Ibid., p. 83

of State. He was soon making the most belligerent noises – to Congress at his ratification hearing in January 1953 and elsewhere. The situation was simply outlined:

> We have enemies who are plotting our destruction. Any American who isn't awake to that is like a sentry asleep at his post ... 800 million people are being forged into a vast weapon of fighting power backed by industrial production and modern weapons that include atomic bombs.[151]

Characteristically he refused to distinguish any differences between the Russian and Chinese regimes. The Communist camp was monolithic and united in the single aim of world domination.

His tenure, which was to last until 1959, was marked by a steadily hardening line in all dealings with Communist governments. The policy of mere 'containment' was no longer enough. The Soviet empire was to be forced into retreat. All chances had to be seized to weaken the authority of Communist governments in the pursuit of 'liberation'. This was to be accomplished by propaganda, particularly by radio.

The Soviets were not the only victims of Dulles' inclination to bully and threaten. His dealings with allies were clumsy and often counter-productive. At an early stage, the French were told that if they did not agree to the American plan for a unified European Defence Force, the USA would have to go through 'an agonising reappraisal' of its policy towards Europe.[152] The French were decidedly reluctant to see a revival of a German army even if they could share control of it. They deeply resented the American pressure and insisted on major amendments to the plan which eventually ran into the ground anyway.

In Germany's 1953 elections, Dulles openly backed Konrad Adenauer's Christian Democrats, declaring that if they lost it would damage the cause of freedom. This interference in the internal affairs of another country was a massive breach of diplomatic manners. It caused anger abroad and alarm among State Department officials. As Eden was to say of Dulles, he was the only bull who carried his own china shop around with him.

His clumsiness in handling foreign governments was echoed in his dealing within the State Department, now swollen to 32,000 employees. Eisenhower agreed reluctantly to the appointment of a second Under Secretary of State who would run the department's bureaucracy. Don Lourie, President of the Quaker Oats Company, was no doubt a talented businessman. But he was an innocent in politics. Charged with ensuring security within the department, Lourie casually asked one of his Chicago neighbours if he knew of a suitable man. The neighbour, who seemed even more innocent than Lourie, suggested two names. The one chosen was Walter McLeod, a one-time journalist who later had a brief spell in the FBI.

---

151   Townsend Hoopes, op. cit., p. 161
152   Ibid., p. 189

McLeod was a McCarthyite. He tried to purge the department, detecting subversion in the fact that many officials received the Communist *Daily Worker* and others the liberal periodical *The Reporter*. It would have been odd had these publications not enjoyed any readership within the department. Only protests to the senior Under Secretary, Walter Bedell Smith, stopped this publications witch hunt.

But McLeod was not finished. He sought to interfere with the appointment of Charles Bohlen as Ambassador to Moscow. His attempt to take his belief in the unsoundness of Bohlen to the White House itself misfired because the proposed Ambassador was an old friend of the President. Dulles considered firing McLeod but was dissuaded by Bedell Smith. It was too early in the life of the new administration to start sacking officials. However, McLeod had helped reinforce the McCarthyites on Capitol Hill.

CHAPTER 18
DEATH OF STALIN: AN OPPORTUNITY IGNORED

Stalin dies – Malenkov suggests 'peaceful coexistence' – British receptive – Dulles presses Eisenhower to resist – Churchill's call for East-West meeting rejected – East Berlin riots – Dulles calls to 'crowd the enemy' – hints at use of nuclear weapons even in small conflicts – Moscow decides to boost armaments

In 1953 there was a sudden possibility of defusing if not ending the Cold War. Stalin died on 1 March. The remaining Kremlin leaders heaved a sigh of relief. They were safe now, safe at any rate once they had executed Lavrenti Beria, the dreaded head of the KGB (MGB then). Georgii Malenkov succeeded as Premier, soon to be supplanted at the top by Khrushchev in his role as party leader, though the general arrangement was described as 'collective leadership'. The new leaders swiftly sought an improvement in East–West relations.

In speeches and newspaper articles, the new Soviet line was articulated. 'Peaceful coexistence and cooperation' were possible. The whole world must take steps to avert the menace of a global conflict. Fewer resources were to be allocated in the Soviet Union to heavy industry, needed for war production. As for the only 'hot spot', Korea, the Council of Ministers despatched letters to Mao and Kim Il Sung in less than three weeks, calling for the 'soonest possible' conclusion of the war. Proposals from General Mark Clark on the exchange of sick and wounded prisoners should be treated urgently and the Soviet delegation at the UN should initiate the new peaceful line.

Washington's very new administration was taken off guard by this change of approach. Eisenhower blew hot and cold, initially taking a very suspicious line. The influence of Dulles could be discerned. By contrast Churchill, now re-elected as Prime Minister and with Eden once more in the Foreign Office, was highly receptive. In his own speeches, Dulles was utterly dismissive of peace feelers. Insofar as these Russian speeches and articles were not just a propaganda exercise designed to undermine the West, they showed him that the Russians were cracking. The Soviets were running scared. Trying to curb the President's welcome for the new Soviet attitude, Dulles told him: 'What they are doing is because of outside pressures and I don't know of anything better we can do than keep up those pressures right now.'[153]

But Eisenhower came to the view that there must be a more positive response. During the drafting of a Presidential speech within a month of the new Soviet initiative, Dulles made unavailing attempts to turn it into a list of impossible demands before any agreement to East–West détente. These included, among other things, a clear move to self-determination in Soviet satellite states. That would strike at the very roots of what the Soviet Union regarded as its essential security. The episode underlined Dulles' lack of serious interest in détente of any sort. He only wanted to raise the temperature and the prospects of regular conflicts with the implacable foe until it acknowledged defeat.

The speech Eisenhower delivered in response to the Soviet initiative was replete with what Dulles regarded as dangerously friendly overtones. The USA wanted peace everywhere, the President declared. The cost of armaments threatened living standards for everyone as humanity 'hung from a cross of iron' under the peril of war. The only acceptable total war was upon 'poverty and need'. In the search for peace in Asia an 'honourable armistice in Korea' should be the first step.

In the wake of the Soviet initiative, the Chinese Premier had already agreed to a mutual exchange of prisoners in Korea. Nor was this all. State Department officials listed the Soviet gestures which had been made in the wake of the dictator's death. There was Zhou's initiative which also included proposals for a resumption of the Korean negotiations. There was a Soviet suggestion of talks with Britain to deal with air incidents in Germany. General Chuikov said that a peace treaty with Germany, including reunification, would be acceptable to Russia. A group of American correspondents seeking admission to the Soviet Union were allowed in. And, most important, the Kremlin had suggested through a Norwegian diplomat that Eisenhower and Malenkov should meet to discuss a range of topics.

If Dulles could not amend the President's speech – in effect turn it through 180 degrees – he could at least torpedo a British initiative for a new round of 'Big Three' talks. Churchill, like Eisenhower, thought there was a real chance of securing agreements. At least the possibilities must be explored. He suggested talks without any agenda. The French supported the idea.

A date was set for an initial conference in Bermuda between the President, Churchill and the French Premier Joseph Laniel on the right approach. But Churchill had a heart attack and the meeting had to be cancelled. In its place there was a three-nation conference of foreign ministers or their deputies. Dulles was determined to fend off Churchill's proposal. Instead there was to be a further foreign ministers' conference including Russia in the autumn with only Germany

---

Townsend Hoopes, op. cit., p. 171

and Austria as topics for discussion. This was no more than a means of placing obstacles in the way of major progress. The problem of Germany was immensely complicated and at times looked intractable, given the way that the country had been divided up.

Churchill remained keen on an East–West summit at least as a means of personal contact. When Dulles visited London in the autumn Churchill aired the idea of meeting with Malenkov alone. The Secretary of State responded harshly that this would reduce Britain to the status of intermediary, not ally. Churchill, for whom the Anglo-American alliance was sacred, did not press his idea.

The Russians were in favour of the Churchill plan. But with the prospects of a reduction of tension still in the air, Dulles chose this moment to make his speech in Germany which not only endorsed Adenauer for the forthcoming elections, but also described the division of the country by the Russians as a 'scandal' and 'a menace to peace'.

In June, riots broke out in East Berlin, followed by disturbances in other East German cities. Tanks, notably in Berlin, swiftly repressed the dissent. It started with protests against working conditions, even though there had been some slackening of the harsher aspects of Soviet rule since Stalin's death. The riots were to deliver a blow to the prestige of the Soviet Union and, less obviously, that of the USA.

The disturbances emphasised the poverty of claims that a serene workforce enjoyed great benefits under Communist rule. The veteran Communist playwright Bertold Brecht commented that the government was clearly disappointed in the people and had decided to elect a new one. But any hopes that the West might speed to the assistance of the repressed workers were dashed. It was judged too dangerous to take any military action. All that Dulles was authorised by the President to do was to offer $15m worth of food aid which Molotov dismissed as a provocation.

This was a blow to Dulles' plan to exploit the change in the Soviet leadership by stepping up the pressure. 'This is the time to crowd the enemy' he told a Cabinet meeting 'and maybe finish him once and for all'. The inability to go beyond words and East Germany's rejection of the food offer weighed heavily on Dulles and other hardliners. The National Security Council tried to set out clear objectives in a remarkable new memorandum. The tone was certainly aggressive but the thinking was muddled, indeed dangerously so. Washington understood the danger of being sucked into revolts in Eastern Europe. Its new policy outline seemed a good example of being willing to strike but afraid to wound.

NSC-158 was headed 'United States Objective and Actions to Exploit the Unrest in the Satellites'.[154] The aims included the encouragement of 'resistance', the undermining of satellite puppet authority, and the establishment of 'secure

---

154   For full NSC-158 text see CWHIT

resistance nuclei capable of further large-scale expansion'. Yet it spells out twice that 'mass rebellion in areas under Soviet military control' was to be avoided. Quite how resistance was to be safely compartmentalised was not clear.

Among measures to be taken within sixty days, Phase I, was to 'covertly stimulate acts and attitudes of resistance … aimed at putting pressure on Communist authority for specific reforms, discrediting such authority and *provoking open Soviet intervention*' (author's italics). There should also be 'black radio' broadcasts to encourage defectors. And trade unions in the free world alongside religious organisation should be urged to demand inquiries into economic and working conditions in the satellites. More alarmingly one aim would be to 'encourage elimination of key puppet officials'. This is an interesting ambiguity. How is elimination, which sounds very like assassination, to be 'encouraged'? Was this a not-so-gentle hint for the CIA?

Phase II, which had no timetable, calls for the organisation, training and equipping of 'underground organisations capable of launching large-scale raids or sustained warfare when directed'. This should accompany 'simulating Soviet officer conspiracy to establish honourable peace with the West'. The document was a muddled compromise between hawks and doves. The repetition of the condition that 'mass rebellion' was to be avoided, suggests nervous interpolations. But the overall message was clear. The overthrow of the Soviet government was the official policy. Any search for peace by Moscow would be a waste of time.

Dulles turned up the heat several notches in early 1954 with a new policy of 'massive retaliation'. Until then, the American approach to local conflicts had been to keep them local. All this was to change. He delivered a speech complaining that 'emergency policies are costly, they are superficial and they imply that the enemy has the initiative.' From now on collective security would be made less costly and more effective 'by placing more reliance on deterrent power and less dependence on local defensive power'. Local defence must be reinforced by 'the further deterrent of massive retaliatory power':

> So long as our basic policy concepts were unclear, our military leaders could not be selective in building our military power If an enemy could pick his time and place and method of warfare – and if our policy was to remain the traditional one of meeting aggression by direct and local opposition – then we need to be ready to fight in Asia, the Near East and in Europe; by sea, by land and by air; with old weapons and new weapons … The basic decision (is) to depend primarily upon a great capacity to retaliate instantly by means and at places of our own choosing.[155]

This alarming idea might seem tolerable from a purely American point of view. Though both sides now had nuclear devices, American superiority remained

---

155 Townsend Hoopes, op. cit., p. 198

massive because of its air force and its extensive bases, many of them near the Soviet border. In a resort to nuclear weapons, the USA might hope to remain unscathed while it destroyed, among other things, the Soviet military's power to retaliate. But what of the countries in the front line or faced with 'local defence' problems? For them, the increased danger inherent in Dulles' doctrine of having a nuclear war waged across or near their own soil was deeply disturbing. The policy also failed to give any clue as to what local 'defence' problem would trigger massive retaliation. Might some small Communist nation (Korea was a good example) manage to entangle its masters in some clash because of a border dispute? Might not the Soviet Union itself get into a direct dispute through a whole variety of misunderstandings or errors?

The new Dulles doctrine, by raising the possibility of nuclear attack, also spurred the Soviets on to develop their missile and long-range bomber programme. He had not cowed the Kremlin. And he seemed to be towing the President along in his wake. In 1955, at a press conference Eisenhower observed: 'I see no reason why they [nuclear weapons] shouldn't be used just exactly as you would use a bullet.'

Washington was giving new impetus to the arms race. The protests from within the government and the outside world forced Dulles to publish an article two months later in which he hastened to explain that massive retaliation was not the sort of power 'which could most usefully be evoked under all circumstances'. His policy, he said, did not mean that: 'In the event of some Communist attack somewhere in Asia, atom or hydrogen bombs will necessarily be dropped on the great industrial centres of China or Russia.'[156]

But in a magazine interview in January 1956 he made it alarmingly clear that massive retaliation went along with 'brinkmanship'. He claimed, speciously, that 'going to the brink' had worked in the case of Korea because it had been transmitted to the Chinese that if there was no break in the Korean stalemate the USA would 'lift its self-imposed restrictions on its actions and hold back no effort or weapon to win'.[157] This was the policy which Truman had disavowed under pressure from Attlee. Dulles also claimed a success in stopping Red China from a possible attack in Vietnam because the 7th fleet had weapons for 'instant retaliation', i.e. nuclear weapons.

The interview aroused a storm of protest. There were calls for his resignation by some Congressmen. In foreign capitals opinion was alarmed. But he was unmoved, wholly convinced of the righteousness not just of his cause but also of the shrewdness of his strategy.

---

156 'Policy for Security and Peace', *Foreign Affairs*, April 1954
157 Townsend Hoopes, op. cit., p. 310

CHAPTER 19
1956: THE YEAR OF SHATTERED ILLUSIONS

Khrushchev denounces Stalin – London and Paris conspire with Israelis – Suez attack launched – global anger aroused – Dulles accused of betraying Britain – Moscow represses the Hungarian uprising – Russia prepares its 'Sputnik' shock

Nineteen-fifty-six was to be a year of savage disillusionment across the globe. The new Soviet leadership's denunciation of Stalin left Communists the world over aghast and ordinary Russians bewildered. The Soviet repression of the Hungarian revolution in October spelt an end to belief on the Left everywhere that Communism spoke for the masses. The conspiratorially-hatched and disastrous Anglo-French intervention in Suez following the Canal's nationalisation left deep divisions within both countries. It also produced a wave of hostility in Asia and Africa which lasted a generation. The success of the Israeli armed forces aroused a sense of humiliation among Arab nations which never went away. American policy, which had included plenty of harsh words about President Nasser's 'seizure' of the Canal, ended with Washington's refusal to support the pound. The intervention collapsed. It provoked charges in Britain of betrayal by its chief ally. The failure of the American administration, in the case of Hungary, to go beyond denunciation made the Dulles moralistic policy seem mere bluster.

Yet 1956 had had a promising start. The Soviet leadership, after a brief power struggle, was now in the hands of Nikita Khrushchev and Nikolai Bulganin, seen as symbols of commitment to liberalisation. The pair set out on a world tour in 1955 which included Britain. Though Khrushchev had denounced Britain's imperial past on his trip to India, the pair were genially received as the 'K and B' show. There was even a visit to the Queen. Moscow also established diplomatic relations with the German Federal Republic. At home, the new leadership had set in hand agricultural reforms which allowed farmers to get proper prices for their produce.

In February 1956 there had been the dramatic shift when, in a secret session of the party, Khrushchev denounced Stalin, the cult of personality and the years of his brutal purges of the party. It soon leaked. It was not, as many noted, a wholesale denunciation of the brutalities of the regime – in which Khrushchev himself had been involved – but of the fake trials and casual murders of innocent party members. Nonetheless, this was a hopeful sign that the old regime was dead and buried.

But the year which had opened so promisingly was to close in disorder and mutual vituperation with the twin Suez and Hungarian crises, affecting both sides of the Cold War. President Nasser had been looking forward to American aid in building the huge Aswan High Dam which promised a leap in the country's power supplies. However, when he made an arms deal with Czechoslovakia Dulles was outraged. Washington withdrew the US offer to finance the dam, regarded by Cairo as vital. Nasser responded by nationalising the Suez Canal, then owned and operated jointly by an Anglo-French company. Both London and Paris regarded Nasser and his vigorous leadership of Arab nationalism as a general menace to their Middle East and North African interests. They regarded the takeover of the Canal as an act of piracy. Yet it might provide a chance to bring down the Egyptian leader. Eden, who had succeeded Churchill (at last) and won a general election in May 1955, denounced Nasser as a threat to Britain's oil supplies, which could bring British industry 'grinding to a halt'. The US administration warned that it could not support drastic counter-measures.

Despite Washington, Eden responded with his elaborately contrived military expedition to Egypt. The Israelis were secretly invited to attack Egypt to enable Britain and France to 'intervene' on the grounds that the waterway must be preserved for international use. The fighting, which began in October, had only lasted a few days before pressure on the pound in the foreign exchange markets threatened the British position. With the USA firmly refusing to support the British currency, London had no choice but to abort the operation. Eden's resignation followed in early 1957. Whether Dulles felt satisfaction about this is hard to tell. Eden was in his view a weak link in the struggle against the dark forces of Communism. But the US move angered British opinion where the term 'John Twister Dulles' found some circulation. And in the Third World, the withdrawal of the Aswan finance offer was regarded as an act of bullying. Russia said it was prepared to finance the Aswan Dam. The net result was that both Britain and the USA lost face in the Third World and Russia, ready to replace American finance for the project, had made an apparent strategic gain.

Hungary
But this was almost immediately lost in the drama of the Hungarian uprising. There had already been a smaller revolt in Poland during the summer. Dissidents and demonstrators were swiftly dealt with by the Polish army. But Moscow also

set out to appease the rebellious mood by a change of power in Warsaw. The imprisoned Wladislaw Gomulka, who had been removed from office in the late 1940s as a potential Tito, was released and made head of the party. The Poles were also allowed more control over their own economic policy. Thus far, Moscow seemed able to hold satellite revolts in check.

But Hungary proved a tougher proposition. Moscow had made Imre Nagy Prime Minister, seen during Stalin's time as a dangerous liberal. The new leader set about reforms which included slowing the pace of industrialisation, so damaging to the agricultural sector. Khrushchev sensed trouble and replaced Nagy with the hardliner Matyas Rakosi. A revolt exploded. At first, the Kremlin was inclined to believe that a softer line would curb the rebellion. After four days, Soviet troops pulled out of the country and Nagy was returned to power.

Within days he had gone too far for Moscow. He had decided that the one-party system was to go – clearly a dangerously contagious policy. Soviet forces returned and Nagy threatened to pull Hungary out of the Warsaw Pact. Soviet troops and tanks now set about putting down the revolt in earnest, calling in Janos Kadar as the new Premier. Rebel leaders appealed for help from the West. Western leaders could only look on with horror as Soviet tanks fired on the populace. But they moved no further than fierce denunciations plus a personal letter of strongest protest from Eisenhower to Bulganin. The USA had peered over the abyss and decided with little hesitation that the risk of intervention leading to war was far too great.

This of course left the Dulles doctrine of 'liberation' exposed as bombast and Voice of America propaganda, encouraging 'liberation', as irresponsible. Paul-Henri Spaak, the Secretary General of NATO, had already warned Dulles in 1955 that his constant talk of liberation implied a readiness to help any rebellious movements in Eastern Europe – help which the alliance had neither the means nor the will to provide. It had taken less than a year for the Dulles programme of brinkmanship and attempts to face down foes with 'massive retaliation' look like hollow threats.

The repression of the revolution destroyed all notion of contentment in the satellite states. There was a paper blizzard of torn up party cards in the West. In the Third World, Soviet prestige took a severe knock. In a report to the party, the Soviet Foreign Ministry reported that Russia's reputation had plummeted:

Recently many political figures, organs of the press and a range of figures of the Colombo countries (India, Pakistan, Indonesia, Burma, Sri Lanka) have begun to speak very critically of the foreign policy of the Soviet Union, pointing out that in this regard the events in Eastern Europe bear witness to the 'insincerity of the Soviet Union' and about its unwillingness to consistently adhere to the five principles of peaceful coexistence.[158]

This was particularly annoying to the Kremlin since it had expended great diplomatic efforts to woo these former colonies which now represented such a combination of power in the region.

Russian prestige was to recover in one unexpected area in 1957 when an astonished world learnt that the Soviet Union had put the world's first satellite, the Sputnik, into orbit. There was incredulity and anger in the USA. How could the country have let itself get behind the Soviet Union? A triumphant Khrushchev upgraded the Soviet policy from 'peaceful coexistence' to 'competitive coexistence'. Put together these meant a shift in the struggle – or 'competition' – into the neutral areas of the Third World. The demarcation lines in Europe were tightly drawn except, significantly, in Berlin. In the Far East the thirty-eighth parallel was the plain demarcation line in Korea; and neither side wished to get embroiled again in a war there. The line between mainland China and Formosa was patrolled by the US 7th Fleet.

This left plenty of territory for active rivalry. Both sides dissipated immense efforts and large sums of money in their pursuit of allies or at least countries which would decline to fall within the other's orbit. The highly moralistic tone of American policy was not to stop it in subsequent years backing repellent regimes, notably in Latin America, because they faced (supposedly) Communist rebels. This was to arouse dismay in the USA where the moral cause of anti-Communism was becoming suspect. Dulles advanced the view that neutrality was 'immoral'. Resentment in the Third World forced Eisenhower to change his line. But Dulles ignored his chief's feelings.

In the struggle for Third World favours, the USA had one clear advantage and one clear disadvantage. The USA had the most money. It could provide more 'aid' of all types. And with more highly developed intelligence agencies than those of the Soviet Union it was better placed to bribe and cajole Third World regimes into support. On the other hand, the USA was the key nation in the Western Alliance which included countries like Britain and France which had been the world's leading colonial powers. They were still viewed as powers from whom independence had had to be fiercely wrested and whose motives, following Suez, were deeply suspected.

Most of the new leaders in the Third World had strong left-wing credentials. After all it was from the Left in such countries as Britain and France that so much impetus for colonial freedom had come. Indeed it was only a resentment of colonialism in its classic form that united so many disparate groupings in the Third World. They were not seriously interested in most cases in democratic institutions – or if they were at first their enthusiasm soon waned. The idea of state-directed and/or state-owned industries had a natural appeal for them. They believed that the Russian model of rapid industrialisation naturally suited them. All this made them inclined to warm to the Soviet Union. The absolute determination of the Americans not to let 'international Communism' chalk up a victory in Vietnam led the USA into the longest war and the worst defeat in its history.

THE INDUSTRIAL-MILITARY COMPLEX: EISENHOWER'S WARNING

Second World War establishes the power of the armaments industry – boosted by Cold War – Eisenhower issues grim warning – pork barrel politics – Congressional influence – CIA as a vested interest – financial power of the industry – role in prolonging Cold War – support from the church militant

It is easy to forget the influence played in the prolongation of the Cold War by the vested interests of the armaments manufacturers. By 1945, the rise and rise of this industry had provided a rip-roaring boost to the American economy. The onset of the Cold War provided a new demand for armaments which continued to boost the US economy and the fortunes of individual industrialists. It also provoked concern about the vested interest this was creating, though the complaints were mainly from the Left. The powerful public relations machine established by the manufacturers brushed these aside as un-American.

But in 1961 this menace was taken up by a disillusioned Eisenhower in the most memorable speech of his career. But being made on his departure from office it could only have a limited impact on defence policy itself. It also raised an obvious question. If the influences he spoke of were so malign, why had he not done something about them?

In his final address to Congress in January 1961 he delivered his stern warning and coined the ringing phrase: 'the industrial-military complex.' He commented 'We must never let the weight of this combination endanger our liberties or democratic processes.' In the key passage, he warned:

> This conjunction of an immense military establishment and a large arms industry is new in American experience. The total influence – economic, political, even spiritual – is felt in every city, every statehouse, every office of the federal government. We must not fail to comprehend its grave implications. Our toil, resources and livelihood are all involved; so is the very structure of our society. In the councils of government we must guard against the acquisition of unwarranted influence, whether sought or unsought by the industrial-military complex. The potential for the rise of misplaced power exists and will persist.[159]

It did indeed persist. The Defense Department blossomed. When Eisenhower uttered his warning, there were over 750 retired senior officers, colonel or above, who

---

159   *America, Russia and the Cold War 1945–1966* by Walter LaFeeber, John Wiley & Sons, 1967, p. 219

were on the payroll of the hundred largest defence contractors. By the early 1970s, the total had risen to nearly 3,000. Lockheed alone employed 200 such retired officers – and won the largest total of military contracts. Any defence project could muster a lobby of ex-serving officers, as well as established commercial lobbyists, to explain to Congressmen its essential nature.

However, the total masks the crucial local issue. Key figures in Congress could be bought by steering Pentagon spending to their districts. Defence contractors were munificent employers and the defence budget was enormous. The urge to see such employers, or indeed military establishments, established and retained locally became a driving force among Congressmen of both parties. It was pork barrel politics at its most relentless. In an extreme case, a *Time* article revealed that in 1973 the South Carolina district of Congressman Mendel Rivers included an air force base, any army depot, a naval shipyard, a marine air station, a recruit training centre, two navy hospitals, a naval station, a ballistic missile submarine training centre, a Polaris missile factory, an Avco corporation plant, a Lockheed plant, a General Electric plant and a large site just purchased by the Sikorksy Aircraft division.

Rivers also happened to be the Democrat chairman of the House Armed Services Committee. His enthusiasm for defence spending was not surprising. He told his electors that he and his party had been responsible for bringing 90 per cent of the defence projects to the area. Voting Democrat would keep these installations in the area. And naturally, since defence spending had to be represented as essential to the nation's safety, the Communist threat was represented as still immense and all pervasive.

The Cold War did not just mean a perpetuation of orders for the established wartime suppliers of military equipment. It also established whole new industries specialising in the new advanced technology of missiles. The defence industry had two political channels for the profitable use of all these business's funds. One was, most obviously, in backing for the more hawkish presidential candidates at election time. This could be a Democrat almost as easily as it was a Republican. Another was to assist in funding various think tanks and publications of a similarly hawkish disposition.

On the military side, it was plain enough that the prospect of successful careers in the forces' hierarchy would be enhanced by large military budgets. The high-ranking officer who doubted the importance of the Cold War's campaign against Communism was a very rare bird indeed. The CIA, which also blossomed during the Cold War, had its own vested interest in East–West tension. Without the Cold War the agency would have been very modest in size. It did not of course dispose of funds for covert political purposes in the USA itself. But overseas it was a channel for formidable spending in bribery and assistance to politicians. It had earned its spurs in helping to corrupt the Italian election of 1948.

The CIA laid out cash to overthrow Left-leaning governments in Latin America in the 1950s: Guatemala, Costa Rica and British Guiana. Thereafter the agency ramped up its activity throughout the Third World, though Latin America remained its most expensive operation. Because the agency was paid to resist Communism, careers depended on the continuation of the Cold War.

The confrontation produced another vested interest: the self-acclaimed strategists whose expertise lay in the conduct of Cold War policy. They had usually studied politics at university and gone on through various think tanks. Any decline in East–West tension decreased their value. They had little inclination or incentive to strive for détente. Besides, a career as a Cold War expert could offer glittering prizes in government. It was not just a rising career in the CIA or the National Security Council or the bureaucracy of the State Department that might crown their work, but an appointment in government itself. The Committee for the Present Danger which was set up in the early 1950s to agitate for larger military budgets was revived in the 1970s and went on to provide more than thirty officials in the Ronald Reagan administration. They flourished no less under President George W. Bush. The civilian and military hawks shared a further advantage. They could move seamlessly into the world of the defence industries and draw substantial payments as company directors or at least as informed and well-connected lobbyists.

One further group which added to the perpetuation of the Cold War, though it could hardly be called a normal vested interest, was made up of the churches with their immense influence. The cry that the USA had to confront 'atheistic Communism' could always be relied on to find a favourable echo there. The Roman Catholics had of course always been bitter and active opponents of Communism.

However, it was in the other numerous churches, particularly in the so-called Bible Belt, that the warnings about the menace of the Soviet Union were particularly virulent. These sentiments were certainly sincere, though they were often combined in the South with discreditable warnings that the full emancipation of the negroes would be a symbol of Communist success.[160]

The combination of the military-industrial complex plus the churches was a formidable one. The fear of Russia was real enough. But stoking that up sat all too comfortably with the financial and career-vested interests of the first group and of the Cold War civilian professionals. The fact that General Eisenhower, no less, was to utter the first warnings about the industrial-military nexus is significant. He knew the military machine as well as anyone. The industrial machine was for him a novelty whose pressures he only felt when he became president. As weaponry increased the size and wealth of the industrial lobby was also to increase. No president during the long years of the Cold War ever shook it off. Any aspiring

---

160   Truman was accounted a progressive on the racial issue. However, it is worth quoting from his speech to the National Colored Democratic Convention in which he declared, with immeasurable condescension: 'Let me make it clear, I am not calling for the social equality of the negro ... The highest types of negro say frankly that they prefer the company of their own people.'

president who offered a programme of reduced armaments would know that funds
were liable to flow from this wealthy sector into the campaign funds of his rivals.

These political, military and industrial forces combined to promote a cycle in
American politics, as historian Alan Wolfe diagnosed so presciently:

> Anti-Soviet perceptions will rise when there is no rough balance between the
> military services in terms of their relative share of the budget and one service
> or another service seeks to enhance its position as a result. Equilibrium tends to
> break down when a new political party enters the White House. Traditionally the
> Democrats favour the Army while Republicans incline towards the Air Force.
> The Navy has advocates in both parties but, historically, has been associated
> with the 'moderate' wing of the Republican Party, now almost obliterated. The
> most time-honoured way of re-establishing an equilibrium among the service
> branches is to expand the overall military budget. Thus a recurrent pattern
> emerges: a new political party comes to power; that party then shifts money
> towards its favourite service; those branches that stand to lose will 'discover'
> the Soviet threat and issue harrowing warnings about America's future; at this
> point presidents back off from confrontation, not wanting to appear weak in
> the face of the external threat; as they back off the budget begins to climb, a
> new equilibrium is established and the most negative perceptions of the Soviet
> Union appear to taper off.[161]

Thus the Soviet threat was emphasised and the defence budget climbed, whichever
party was in office. In this process the power of the heavily financed lobbies in
influencing the press was very important. It is clear that the power of the military-
industrial complex is little diminished – and even enhanced – today, despite the
end of the Cold War.

---

161   *The Rise and Fall of the Soviet Threat* by Alan Wolfe, South End Press, 1984, pp. 76–77

CHAPTER 20
AMERICAN RELATIONS WITH CHINA

Prolonged US-China quarrels - the finger on the nuclear button - US allies alarmed - Washington backs exiled Chiang against Mao - the offshore island dispute - signs of a Moscow break with Beijing

The history of US–Chinese relations during the Cold War is a sorry and unbusinesslike affair. The Americans came close to triggering potentially nuclear combats with China on four occasions. Though this clearly demonstrated the urgency of having full diplomatic relations with Beijing, the USA insisted that the only legal government of China was in Taiwan (Formosa). It was not until 1971 that Washington withdrew its veto and allowed the People's Republic into the UN. Thus the world's most powerful nation had very limited contact with the world's most populous nation during various crises despite the constant urgings of the USA's allies to normalise relations.

There were of course contacts of a sort, including those at two meetings at Geneva on Indo-China and the first Formosa crisis in 1955. But Dulles' behaviour was so hostile at Geneva that relations were soured rather than improved. The Secretary of State's attitude was widely supported at home. China was Communist. Little more needed to be said. And since Communism was seen as monolithic for most of that period, the State and Defense Departments treated Chinese aims as merely those of the Soviet Union operating in a more fluid and thus more dangerous environment than Europe. The top priority in Asia was the means for containing China. It included the possible use of atomic weapons in Korea, Vietnam and (twice) over Taiwan.

How far the American desire to isolate China fuelled the assertiveness of Beijing is one of those questions which cannot be answered with certainty. But the refusal to recognise any regime is a diplomatic snub which is always resented. Arguments that China was a brutal dictatorship, though wholly correct and loudly voiced in the US, were hardly a reason to refuse to conduct business with

Beijing. The world could boast a substantial array of dictatorships which had to be recognised, some warmly backed by the USA itself.

Even relative pinpricks produced foolish reactions in Washington. A dozen American flyers shot down when patrolling over China in open breach of international law had been sentenced to prison for espionage. The UN Secretary General Dag Hammarskjold returned from Beijing in early 1955 with Zhou's promise that these men would be released once their relatives had visited them and seen the conditions in which they were held. Dulles refused to issue the relatives with passports.

This issue faded into insignificance against other and mightier matters around the same time. Beijing had always claimed that Taiwan was a historical part of China. After the start of the Korean war, Truman drew a new line of areas the USA would defend, including Formosa, to be protected by the US 7th Fleet. This still left open to doubt the status of the two islands of Quemoy of Matsu, just a few miles from the Chinese mainland. They were not just a problem for Chinese prestige. They were also threats to shipping at the ports of Amoy and Foochow.

In 1955, the Chinese seized some very small offshore islands and proceeded to bombard Quemoy. In return for which the Chinese Nationalists made some bombing runs over the mainland. President Eisenhower gained easy Congressional authorisation not just to defend Formosa but also to attack any 'concentration of troops' on the mainland which were aimed at this objective. Warily, however, Eisenhower reminded the Commander on the spot, the aggressive Admiral Radford, that he needed clearance for any launch of his own atomic weapons.

Whether Quemoy and Matsu were included under the American umbrella was not clear at the time. The dangerously ambiguous position was left that if the islands were seized as part of a general attack on Formosa, US guarantees would operate. Otherwise not. Concern mounted in the USA and in Europe when Dulles threatened to use what he called new and powerful precision weapons on military targets. By this he meant atomic weapons. And given the inclusion of troop concentrations as a signal for conflict, this meant the use of these weapons on the mainland itself. Matters were not helped when Eisenhower was quizzed on the Dulles speech and said he did not see why such weapons should not be used on military targets.[162]

There was consternation among the USA's allies. The Australian Prime Minister, Robert Menzies, insisted that his country could not support a war over Taiwan or the islands. Canada followed suit. Japan declared that it would not allow its territory to be used for such a conflict. Eden criticised American policy openly. This led to complaints from Eisenhower to Churchill that Britain and its allies were not seeing the Communist threat correctly.

---

162   Fleming, op. cit., p. 714

Indeed he went on to argue that failing to defend Formosa would lose an ally, and make neutrals think the USA did not mean what it said when it pledged its support for those who wanted to remain free. It would sap the morale of America's friends.

This was stern stuff. The implication was that Formosa had to be defended at all costs and that this could include the use of atomic weapons. The warlike attitude in the USA was not abating. The head of the Navy, Admiral Carney, revealed to reporters that the military was calling on the President to destroy China's military potential in order to curb the country's aggressive instincts and this would include the use of atomic weapons. Eisenhower was swiftly forced to disavow Carney, though stopping short of dismissing him from his post.

Washington had gone too far. If there was a war over Formosa it would certainly be without allies. Britain's former Ambassador in Washington, Sir Oliver Franks, warned that the urge to crush Communism on all fronts contributed to 'a widespread fear that the Americans would get the United Kingdom and others into a third world war'.[163] 'Eisenhower realised that matters were getting out of hand. He revealed that he had been receiving letters from Marshall Zhukov, speaking as one old soldier to another. A new tone crept into the President's comments. In the hope of finding a peaceful settlement, it was proposed that there should be a meeting between the two sides. Dulles was for finding a settlement through diplomatic notes. Zhou was for each side's diplomats to meet in person. He got his way; and the crisis subsided.

The second Formosan crisis came in the summer of 1958. Again the big guns opened on Quemoy as Mao set out to test continuing US determination. It was undiminished. Two extra aircraft carriers were sent out, each armed with a nuclear bomb. Dulles had procured from Eisenhower the promise that the USA would definitely use force if the Chinese invaded Quemoy. An alarmed Dean Acheson fired off a warning from the sidelines, accusing the administration of: 'Drifting either dazed or indifferent toward war with China, a war without friends or allies, and over issues which the Administration has not presented to the people and are not worth a single American life.'[164]

In October, China declared a unilateral ceasefire, followed by the theatrical gesture from Mao that it was prepared to bombard Quemoy on alternative days, if that was suitable. Whether Mao had any intention of seizing the island or attacking Taiwan is highly dubious, as the Soviet archives show. He confided to Khrushchev in August 1958 that China was not intending to capture Quemoy or to indulge in any large-scale operations in the area of Taiwan. He had only made threats 'to create complications for the United States' which was at the time tied down with problems in the Lebanon. 'Although we fire at

163   Fleming, op. cit., p. 739
164   Ibid., p. 934

the offshore islands, we will not make attempts to liberate them ... not only will we not touch Taiwan but also the offshore islands for ten, twenty perhaps thirty years.'[165]

Khrushchev seemed surprised at this news. He could not see the point of firing at the islands if there was no intention of capturing them. He said: 'Between us in a confidential way we say that we will not fight over Taiwan but for outside consumption, so to say, we state the contrary that, in the case of an aggravation of the solution because of Taiwan the USSR will defend the Peoples' Republic of China.'[166]

But that could lead too easily to a 'kind of pre-war situation', he believed. He thought the Chinese should seek to ease East–West tensions on this issue. The Soviet Union wanted a relaxation of tensions and for people to understand that the Communist world stood for peace – 'It is not worth shelling the islands in order to tease cats.'[167]

These passages were part of some often ill-tempered discussions between Soviet and Chinese leaders. Mao accused the Russians of wanting to dominate China. He disliked the 'Big Brother' attitude of the Soviet Union towards its new partner which he regarded as patronising to a truly revolutionary power. Khrushchev himself regarded the Beijing leadership as headstrong and was highly critical of the way that the brief war between India and China (breaking out in August 1959) had been allowed to develop, not least because the Soviet Union had not been kept adequately informed.

There must have been times during these low points in Sino-Soviet relations that Khrushchev regretted having provided the technical assistance which helped make China an atomic power. The exchanges also provide an interesting indication of the mixture of threat and conciliation which marked Khrushchev's approach. He was prepared to make open threats about supporting China militarily over Taiwan, dubious as the cause or his threat might be. But he was at the same time determined to press China to do something to reduce East–West tension.

As far as the USA was concerned the Formosa issue was left unresolved. But the death of Dulles in May 1959 meant a lowering of the temperature. His successor was Christian Herter who proved reassuringly colourless and sought no disputes with China. But by the late 1950s in any case it was the more formidable problem of Vietnam that was beginning to cause serious headaches for US policy makers.

---

165   CWIHP
166   CWIHP
167   CWIHP

THE U-2 INCIDENT AND THE BERLIN WALL

Tensions ease – Khrushchev visits USA – American spy plane shot down – Kennedy becomes President – Bay of Pigs – defence budget spirals – Berlin Wall built – USA stands firm on Berlin's status

East–West tension seemed to relax by the end of the 1950s, not least because of the death of Dulles. Personal contacts showed some signs of warmth. Khrushchev visited the USA in 1959 and established a rapport with Eisenhower – and his 'wonderful' grandchildren. The main points of difference between the two countries remained though they immediately turned on continuing arguments about nuclear tests, their detection and the possibilities of a ban. Hopes rose when an East–West summit was arranged for 1960, to take place in Paris.

A sharp reverse took place when the Russians shot down a U-2 spy plane flying at great height. The Soviets knew that such flights were taking place. Soviet fighter planes could not fly high enough to attack the U-2s but the military had been working hard on a new missile. The Russians launched bitter criticism on the flights as an unquestionable breach of international law – which of course they were – and demanded an apology. As Kennan commented, if Russian spy planes had been detected flying over the USA 'all hell would have broken loose'.

Eisenhower fell into the trap laid for him by the Russians by first denying that such flights took place. But the Soviets had in fact captured the pilot. When they produced him, Washington still refused to apologise. This led to the collapse of the Paris summit where Khrushchev revealed details of the flight with his usual sense of theatre. The Russian leader was emerging as a volatile and emotional figure. Following a 1954 meeting between Soviet and British Labour Party leaders, Ambassador Sir William Hayter described Khrushchev as 'rumbustious, impetuous, loquacious, free-wheeling, alarmingly ignorant of foreign affairs'. The Soviet leader had undoubtedly acquired some finesse since then. But there was no doubt that the cold, hard calculation of the Stalin-era was being replaced by a disturbing element of unpredictability. The diplomatic quadrille was, however, resumed after the failed summit with proposals to discuss how effective tests of any disarmament measures might be achieved.

The arrival of John Kennedy as the new President in 1961 appeared to offer some progress in these matters. Khrushchev told his colleagues that, while he had some respect for the new young leader, he feared that American public opinion was more aggressively anti-Communist than the President. 'He can neither stand up to the American public, nor can he lead them.' Kennedy justified the Soviet leader's doubts within three months of his taking office in the notorious 'Bay of Pigs' episode.

Cuba had been a source of alarm to the USA after the success of Fidel Castro's revolt in 1958. Ironically the State Department had contributed to his triumph by withdrawing all forms of assistance and cooperation with the famously corrupt Batista regime. It had become an embarrassment to an administration which preached the virtues of democracy. The view of the State Department about Castro was that he was more a nationalist than a Communist.

He soon proved that wrong, turning to Moscow for support and preaching revolution to other Latin American countries, where he became a left-wing hero. Washington was determined to get rid of him. The Eisenhower administration had worked up a hare-brained scheme in which some 1,500 CIA-trained Cuban exiles would invade their homeland. Preceded by a couple of air raids to soften up Castro's military, the exiles would land at a point known locally as 'The Bay of Pigs'. They would brush aside resistance and advance amid popular acclaim, gathering strength as they went. This scheme was presented in detail to Kennedy shortly after he came to office. He was extremely hesitant, especially after the warning that the exiles were relying on direct US military support in the (unlikely) event of the expedition's failure.

Dean Acheson, as a former Secretary of State, was invited from outside Kennedy's close circle, to offer his advice on the plan. Astonished, he asked, 'Are you serious?' When the President told him that the Cuban force that would resist the exiles would probably amount to 25,000, Acheson commented on the odds: 'It doesn't take Price Waterhouse to figure out that 1,500 are not as good as 25,000.'

Nevertheless, Kennedy endorsed the plan after further consultations with his top twenty advisers. Senator Fulbright was the only one who dissented – a grim comment on the quality of advice on which the President relied. The Chiefs of Staff all endorsed the plan, an equally alarming portent for the quality of information and thinking the military would provide over Vietnam.

The invasion was a gross failure. The exiles were soon defeated and rounded up by Castro's army. Any air operations were a breach of both national and international law since attacks on foreign countries required Congressional authorisation. And of course any air raids would appear to commit the US to formal military intervention if the rebels failed. One was carried out; a second raid was cancelled by Kennedy at the last minute in a loss of nerve. But the single raid inevitably served to alert the Cuban forces.

There was however a second unofficial raid. Four members of the Alabama Air National Guard, training exiles in Nicaragua, launched their own second strike in two B-26s. They were both shot down and none of the crew survived – to the relief of the White House.[168] The administration had assured the world that no Americans, only Cuban exiles, were involved in the entire operation.

---

168   *The Dark Side of Camelot* by Seymour Hersh, Little, Brown, 1997, p. 215

Washington did not abandon its plans to remove Castro. The Church Committee, set up to study the work of the intelligence agencies, reported in 1975 that the CIA had devised a variety of plans to kill the Cuban leader, including poisoned cigars and poisoned pills. Leading Mafia figures were drawn into the plot for their presumed technical knowledge about assassinations. The President did not appear to have directly authorised these efforts. However, a series of nods and winks from the White House – but no written messages – left the CIA confident that it had the authorisation to continue its assassination efforts.[169] Two plans were formulated by the Agency, JMWAVE and Operation Mongoose. Neither succeeded in getting rid of Castro, though there were such activities as demolishing a railway bridge and burning sugar cane fields. Despite the abject failure of the Bay of Pigs, the President's public approval ratings rose sharply. It seemed that any anti-Communist activity, however futile, enhanced the administration's standing.

Once the invasion of Cuba was out of the way, normal diplomatic activity managed to survive. A summit was arranged for June. The Democrats had won the election on the sort of claims that oppositions habitually make about governments. American prestige had 'declined' under the Eisenhower administration. The USA was not the world power it ought to be. In support of his election pledge the Kennedy administration was to raise the defence budget by more than a third. The arms race was entering a new and costly phase as the USA acquired an overwhelming lead in Intercontinental Ballistic Missiles. The new Defence Secretary Robert McNamara was to concede some years later that the position of 1960, where the Americans had superiority but not enough to launch a successful first strike – a balance of sorts – might have persisted without a new surge in the arms race. He blamed inaccurate information about the strength of the Soviet arsenal for the build up of an unnecessary and, to the Kremlin, a provocative lead.

The President promised to call for arms limitation at the talks. But he warned the Soviets in advance against any step to alter the balance of power, either in Europe or the Far East – where in fact the Russians had little power – or anywhere else in the developing world. The last point marked an increase in the American readiness to intervene in Latin American countries.

The summit talks were marred by Khrushchev's announcement that he would sign a peace treaty agreement with the East German government of the GDR, still unfinished business left over from Potsdam. That would mean turning over control of the access roads to Berlin to the East Germans. Kennedy did not waver. If the use of force was necessary, that was what the West would use.

Khrushchev dropped his plan, for the moment. But within weeks, he authorised the GDR government to launch into what was to be prove, from the propaganda point of view, a disaster for the Soviets. East Germans had been fleeing to the

---

169   For the extensive role of the President's brother, Attorney General Robert Kennedy, see Seymour Hersh, op. cit.

Western sector in growing numbers. The GDR was losing its most skilled workers; and the flights were bad in any case for Communist prestige. Under pressure from GDR leader Walter Ulbricht, Khrushchev agreed to the building of the Berlin Wall in August 1961. The Wall was to have several conflicting consequences. At one level, it reduced tension because it, literally, seemed to set in stone the division of the city. Russia was accepting that West Berlin had a firm and defined status; it also implied acceptance of the partition of Germany along existing lines. From the West's point of view, having East Berlin shut off from the Allied sector should, at least in theory, provide less chance of incidents that could lead to major collisions.

However, the Wall involved blows to US as well as Soviet prestige. In the USA the inability of the Western powers to prevent the building of this brutal barrier was seen as a failure. More important, from the Kremlin's point of view, the Wall was a blow to its claims about the attractions of Socialism. Dramatic pictures of easterners trying to flee across the wall and in some cases being shot by border guards further eroded Communist prestige.

Further alarm was provided in Ulbricht's subsequent announcement – at Moscow's behest, of course – that he was ready to sign a peace treaty with the Soviet Union after which he would be largely free to decide the status of Berlin. Kennedy reacted with his own excitable version of the domino theory, declaring that if Berlin fell, all of Germany then Western Europe would fall to the Soviets. Both sides now waited to see who would blink first.

Khrushchev himself, as we now know from archives, was prepared to take a massive risk.[170] The Soviets should consider closing the air corridor to the city, even to the point of shooting down Western planes if necessary. This proposal came to nothing. Either he had second thoughts or, more probably, his colleagues blanched at their hotheaded leader's suggestion. The Americans held firm in Berlin, insisting on their established rights to send armed patrols into East Berlin, most famously through 'Checkpoint Charlie'. The Soviets had to recognise defeat. But Khrushchev was plotting his retaliation.

CHAPTER 21
THE CUBAN MISSILE CRISIS: ARMAGEDDON NARROWLY AVERTED

Khrushchev targets Cuba to humiliate the USA – installation of missiles begins – Kennedy offers promise not to invade – Soviet military hotheads ignore orders – Kremlin backs down in response to secret Turkish missiles deal – US warship nearly sets off nuclear exchange[171]

M oscow had two reasons for the secret despatch of missiles to Cuba. One was a genuine belief that it had to deter the USA from a full-scale invasion of the island. In fact, Kennedy had decided against such an adventure, though he had not entirely ruled out such a possibility at some future date. US naval manoeuvres might be seen as a rehearsal for such an attack. The other motive was the desire to make the Americans know what it felt like to have nuclear missiles sitting on its own doorstep.

Khrushchev said in his memoirs that the decision to send the missiles was hurried because the Kremlin concluded that 'there was not much time before the American invaded the island'.[172] The first secret steps in establishing the missile system were spotted by a US spy plane, provoking outrage and fear throughout America and the Western alliance. Khrushchev claims[173] that Dean Rusk, Secretary of State, told Gromyko, the Soviet Ambassador, allegedly after drinking 'a lot': 'You are accustomed to living with our missiles encircling you but this is the first time we have had to face such a threat. That is why we are in such a state of shock.'[174]

---

171   For full material on the conflict and exchanges between US and Soviet leaders, see CWIHP and/or State Department for 'Kennedy-Khrushchev exchanges' at www.state.org.

172   *Khrushchev Remembers*, Little, Brown and Co., p. 171

173   Ibid., p. 174

174   Ibid., p. 175

The reality of US policy was described by former Defense Secretary, Robert McNamara, in his brutally frank and self-critical book *In Retrospect*:

> Before Soviet missiles were introduced into Cuba in the summer of 1962, the Soviet Union believed the United States intended to invade the island in order to overthrow Castro. We had no such intention. The United States believed the Soviets would never base nuclear warheads outside the Soviet Union but they did. In Moscow we learned that by October 1962, although the CIA was reporting no nuclear weapons on the island, Soviet nuclear missile warheads had indeed been delivered to Cuba and were to be targeted on US cities.[175]

Kennedy was urged by some of his advisers to destroy the missiles by an air attack, with further suggestions of an amphibious invasion. They were almost certainly mistaken in their belief that the Soviets would not respond militarily. At that time the CIA reported 10,000 Soviet troops in Cuba. At a Moscow conference after the Cold War, US participants learnt there were in fact 43,000 Soviet troops on the island along with 70,000 well-armed Cuban troops. Both forces, in the words of their commanders, were said to be determined to 'fight to the death'. The Soviets, including the cautious Gromyko, expressed utter disbelief that the Soviet Union, in the face of a catastrophic defeat, would not have responded militarily somewhere in the world. Very probably the result would have been 'uncontrollable escalation', McNamara wrote in retrospect.

The crisis unfolded swiftly. Under the pretence of supplying Cuba with anti-aircraft missiles for self defence against another American invasion, the Soviets had in fact sent in missiles with ranges of up to 2,000 miles. Cuba was only ninety miles from the US coastline. Here in Moscow's eyes was the perfect riposte to encirclement by the USA. Here was the ideal quid pro quo for the American missile sites in Turkey – so close to the Russian border that, as Khrushchev pointed out, the sentries ranged within sight of each other. Kennedy did not in fact think that military advantage was likely to be Russia's motive.

Kennedy himself found it hard to understand Khrushchev's motives. He was dismissive of the idea that it was to prevent what the Soviets supposed was an American plan for an early invasion. Was Khrushchev's plan to put the USSR in as strong a position as possible in other areas of dispute, the most obvious being Berlin, maybe elsewhere? Whatever the motive the Soviet leader must learn that he would face a completely resolute USA.

The President had very belligerent advisers during the crisis, especially General Maxwell Taylor, later a key figure in the disasters of the Vietnam war. They seemed to be predominating. Khrushchev wrote that Robert Kennedy, the president's younger brother and Attorney General, said to the Soviet Ambassador at one

---

stage: 'If you do not meet us halfway on this, the military will force President Kennedy to take an action that he himself would not like to take.'

Given that there were already Russian military personnel on the island, an invasion would have raised the clear risk of war – more than was understood in Washington as McNamara's retrospect bears out. But the President was prepared to give the Russians an open declaration that the USA would never invade Cuba. In the Kremlin this was regarded as not enough, though Khrushchev regarded Kennedy himself, following their meeting in Vienna in 1961, as a man he could trust. But of course Kennedy could only commit himself, not future administrations.

The President opted to quarantine the island and prevent any further shipments of missile components from the Soviet Union. The tension rose during the flurry of messages between the two leaders. A U-2 reconnaissance plane was shot down by Soviet SAM missiles and its pilot killed. This was assumed in Washington, reasonably enough, to be on the orders of the Kremlin. As we now know, the decision to fire was made by two local commanders without the authorisation of the overall commanders of the Soviet forces on the island.

At sea, warships and merchant vessels circled each other warily. Khrushchev's letters displayed his volatile nature, Kennedy's his steadiness and resolution. As the crisis continued, Khrushchev made an emotional appeal to Kennedy:

> Mr President, Mr Kennedy, you and I are like two men pulling on a rope with a knot in the middle, the harder we pull the tighter the knot until it will have to be cut with a sword. Now why don't we let up the pressure and maybe we can untie the knot?

Eventually it was Khrushchev who untied the knot after suggesting that the bases in Cuba could be traded for those in Turkey. The President publicly declined the offer but sent a message through his brother Robert Kennedy, the Attorney General, that the Turkish bases would be dismantled so long as the promise was not made public. The Soviet ships were turned back and the missiles in Cuba were removed. In the end, Khrushchev emerged as the loser in this battle, but not by a large margin. He had been shown to be duplicitous and to be the one who blinked first. He had at least resolved the issue of the Turkish bases but this was a secret.

Ambassador Dobrynin later commented:

> The whole world was under the impression that Khrushchev had lost because he gave in to the pressure of a strong president. He had taken everything out of Cuba but got nothing in return. No one knew at the time about the agreement of the missiles in Turkey. If you ask who won and who lost, I'd say neither Kennedy nor Khrushchev.

How close the two sides came to nuclear conflict is even further underlined by a chilling McNamara passage. When the majority of Kennedy's advisers were favouring an invasion of the island if the missiles were not removed, there were – contrary to the CIA's assessment, says McNamara –approximately 160 nuclear warheads there. These included scores in the tactical range. An American invasion, he commented, would almost surely have led to a nuclear exchange with 'devastating consequences'. We now also know that certain Russian commanders had ignored orders from Moscow which insisted that the nuclear warheads be kept at a certain distance from the missiles to prevent premature action. In fact they had been brought up to the rocket sites themselves.

The brush with Armageddon had been even closer at one point. Four Soviet submarines were operating at the limit of the US blockade. They were armed, unknown to the Pentagon, with both conventional and nuclear-tipped torpedoes. To block the progress of one of these vessels, an American destroyer dropped depth charges to force it to the surface. Though unlikely to cause lethal damage, these charges caused very unpleasant shocks within the submarine. The bombardment went on for hours, oxygen ran low and the temperature soared unbearably.

The captain feared that war had already broken out and that he was being forced to surface to surrender. In an emotional and vengeful frame of mind, he seriously considered using his nuclear-tipped torpedo to scatter and destroy the American ships. That would have been likely to trigger the uncontrollable nuclear exchange which McNamara feared. Three officers had in fact fainted in the extreme heat. Restraint only prevailed when one of the three officers needed to authorise the use of the weapons refused his support. When the submarine did surface, it found no war in progress and the American ships content to leave the submarine alone. It had been a very near thing.

The rashness of the venture also spelt doom for Khrushchev. His colleagues tired of his volatile attitude. Moreover, the agricultural policy on which he had been so insistent had failed to produce results. He was removed in 1964 and succeeded by the joint and cautious leadership of Leonid Brezhnev and Alexei Kosygin.[76]

---

176   Notes of Vladimir Malin, Soviet Archives, Miller Centre, University of Virginia

CHAPTER 22
DEBACLE IN VIETNAM

The US involvement – estimates of resulting deaths – the 'losing China' syndrome – McNamara's assessment – escalation by Kennedy – flaws in US policy – de Gaulle's advice rejected – President Diem forcibly removed

The Vietnam war was, at the time, the longest armed conflict in American history, leading to the deaths of some 58,000 American servicemen and an eventual, ignominious retreat. Estimates inevitably vary for the deaths among the populations of Vietnam, Cambodia and Laos. But a figure of around three million is widely accepted, including deaths from subsequent starvation and the 600,000 or so murders by the Pol Pot regime in Cambodia, a hideous by-product of the conflict. In its early and even its middle stages, the war was warmly backed by American public opinion, though support dropped off sharply later. Most of the USA's allies had urged caution from the start but had been ignored. America at large accepted the domino theory advanced by both Eisenhower and Dulles without reserve. If Vietnam fell, the rest of South East Asia would follow.

At first sight, the failure of the men who entangled the country in this morass and kept escalating this unwinnable war is bewildering. They were far from stupid, even those who made the worst judgements. But they were hopelessly enslaved by ideology, supposed only a Soviet problem. Dulles, who set the involvement in train, is the most easily explained because of his famous fanaticism. The problem becomes more challenging with the new team assembled by President Kennedy. The White House acquired a new intellectual tone and none of the top advisers was tainted by the sanctimonious self-righteousness of Dulles – or his natural clumsiness in diplomacy. They continued in important posts when Lyndon Johnson replaced the assassinated Kennedy and went on to achieve a massive majority in the 1964 presidential election.

The failure of Washington to understand the driving force of nationalism in Asia in all its various forms has been widely and ruefully acknowledged. The belief was that, under the skin, all Asians regardless of their divergent cultures, were longing to be Americans in all but colour. The notion that the American way of life and its culture must be everyone's goal was ineradicably set in the Washington mind. Hence, every effort to bring that about was – surely? – bound to appeal to the people that the USA was determined to protect. The idea that populations might prefer a dictatorial nationalist leadership to a democratic leadership under the control of the USA was too much to swallow.

There was another blind spot in Washington, rarely analysed in the debates about the errors of that time. The Vietnamese understood that the USA was not, and never could be, the sovereign power in the country. One day, the Americans would go away. Faced with that, it made sense to the Vietnamese, even those with no enthusiasm for Ho Chi Minh, to come to terms with the ultimately successful side if possible.

James Thomson, Jnr, a former State Department official, has offered some valuable insights into the weaknesses behind American policy. There was, he said, the legacy of the State Department, still addicted to the doctrine that China had been 'lost' by the weakness of the Truman administration. As usual, a horror of 'weakness' was the driving force in Washington. Kennedy had been elected by a thin majority and the fact that McCarthyism had been so popular had to make the White House nervous of being attacked as feeble towards Communism – still regarded as a monolithic menace, despite the evidence of growing splits between Moscow and Peking.

The State Department had also been the victim of a Dulles purge and those with expertise in Asia, regarded as being a cause of 'losing China', were removed. Adequate substitutes were not installed. This led to confusion as the new advisers struggled to understand whether they were fighting Ho Chi Minh's Vietminh revolutionaries, Asian nationalism, China, Russia or just 'Communism'. This last label made things easier (and more misleading) and meant that the war was just part of a world crusade. Sending ever increasing forces to Vietnam was one aspect of a grand strategy played out in other areas like disarmament negotiations and the deployment of new missiles across the globe. The domino theory itself involved the patronising and even insulting assumption that any one Asian was much like another.

The risks of Vietnam leading to a greater and perilous East–West conflict was always a shadow behind the conflict itself. In 1965, ex-President Eisenhower was consulted about the war and said that more troops might well be needed. A Communist takeover had to be avoided. If the Soviets and China threatened to intervene, they should be warned that a nuclear strike might follow.[177] In his memoirs Robert McNamara also wrote about the advice of the serving Chiefs of Staff: 'The President and I were shocked by the cavalier way the Chiefs of

177 McNamara, op. cit., p. 173

Staff and their associates referred to, and accepted the risk of, the possible use of nuclear weapons.'[178]

He might also have added to his sense of dismay the superficiality of the analyses made by supposed experts on Vietnam. Daniel Ellsberg was employed by the Rand Corporation which acted as consultants to the government. Disillusioned by war, he leaked 7,000 documents to the press covering the conflict's progress which greatly assisted public concern. (Nixon's 'plumbers' tried to discredit Ellsberg by breaking into his psychiatrist's office, hoping for damaging material.) Subsequently Ellsberg revealed that a Vietnamese friend told him that his fellow countrymen regarded 1945 as the time they regained their independence and French efforts were seen as an attempt to reconquer the country. Ellsberg adds: 'I scarcely knew then what he was talking about; nor would, I suspect, almost any US official I had worked with.'[179]

The process of escalation in the war provides an instructive insight into policy-making in Washington. Indirect American intervention began as early as 1950 with aid to France as it was being forced to give up its colony. France succeeded in making agreements with Cambodia and Laos. Vietnam proved a much harder nut to crack. Dulles fiercely resisted an attempt by the French in 1953 to come to terms with the Communist Vietminh. After the Dien Bien Phu shock in 1954, American intervention was increased, mainly through the provision of 'advisers' from the military and the CIA, plus immense amounts of equipment. It was hoped to stiffen resistance by Saigon which was expected to provide immense amounts of manpower.

The conference of the main powers' foreign ministers held at Geneva with the two Vietnams left Dulles in a belligerent mood and wanting to move directly into military intervention. The National Security Council urged Eisenhower that 'nothing short of military victory in Indo-China be accepted'. Geneva produced the agreement that Vietnam would be divided at the seventeenth parallel with elections promised. The Vietminh were recognised as a group entitled to operate as a political group in the south. Eden was to comment, referring to the mood of the USA, that if the talks had broken down 'we would be in World War III by now'.[180]

But the American delegation refused to sign the accords themselves, accepted by the Vietnamese delegates. It left Washington free to pursue its own policy. The number of US military advisers sent to South Vietnam was increased. Its leader, Ngo Dinh Diem, began a campaign against the Vietminh who changed their name in the south to the Vietcong.

Kennedy, succeeding Eisenhower in 1960, soon stepped up the pace, with the number of 'military advisers' planned to increase to 16,000. They were, so the plan

---

178   McNamara, op. cit., p. 160
179   *The Cold Warriors* by John Donovan, DC Heath and Co., 1974, p. 168
180   Carlton, op. cit., p. 347

ran, to complete their task of training the South Vietnam forces by 1965 and then withdraw. More and more South Vietnamese were recruited into the army. Indeed, by the end of the conflict almost half the eligible males in the country were to be serving in the armed forces or the police alongside more than half a million US troops. At no time was victory genuinely in sight, though the commanders on the spot were constantly to maintain that, with one more push, one more increase in US troop numbers, the Vietcong and later the North Vietnamese regulars would be defeated.

1963 was 'the fateful year', according to McNamara. He finally resigned in 1968, confessing – though not yet publicly – that the war had been a monumental mistake and the USA was doomed to lose it. His memoirs, published first in 1992, must rank as the most searing confession of error ever made by a senior politician.

The year of his departure found Washington struggling with two problems. The Vietcong forces launched its massive Tet (Vietnamese New Year) offensive, taking the Americans entirely by surprise, seizing major cities and blasting their way into the US Embassy compound. It should have been warning enough in both the military and political sense. The scale of the attack was beyond what the American high command thought possible. Moreover, though the US authorities gave generous rewards to informers, none had come forward to reveal the elaborate preparations for the attack.

The other problem was that the puppet Saigon regime carried little authority in the country. It was held in low esteem by its own armed forces. Worse, it was in conflict with the Buddhists, a national majority. By midsummer there was open warfare with hundreds of monks seized and imprisoned. Kennedy's advisers were divided. Apparently the war could not be won if power was left in the hands of Diem – whose Catholic Christian credentials had once seemed so reassuring. His troops killed nine when they opened fire on a Buddhist demonstration. A protesting monk burnt himself to death within sight of the presidential palace.

Washington agonised over whether Diem, along with his widely unpopular brother Nhu, should be replaced. It would be a grave step to force the replacement of a government in an allied country. And from a practical point of view there could be no certainty that the generals who were likely to replace him would be significantly more effective or more popular. A further worry was that Diem appeared to have established secret contact with Hanoi.

From Paris, General de Gaulle was calling for the reunification and neutralisation of Vietnam. He had already warned Kennedy that the Americans would sink 'step by step into a bottomless quagmire'. Washington did not believe him and was highly dubious about warnings from a French President who was so anti-American. However, the USA was reluctant to get into an open conflict with France since the country was seen as essential to the effectiveness of NATO. The possibility that Vietnam could be unified and neutralised – as Laos had been – was realistic, McNamara thought in retrospect. But Washington did not take the proposition very seriously. In any case, the hawks in Washington were still holding to the domino theory.

After a month of indecision, the White House decided against a coup. Diem was to be instructed to change policies. And, in a gesture designed to show confidence in the war's progress alongside a desire to avoid deep entanglement, the President announced that 1,000 advisers would be withdrawn by the end of the year. But by October the Embassy in Saigon was protesting that the generals' plan for a coup was so far advanced that it should not be thwarted. So, assured that the move would be swift and successful, the President gave it his reluctant blessing. Diem surrendered to his generals and, along with his brother Nhu, was murdered. General Taylor, Kennedy's chief military adviser, was to say later that the killings had not been part of the plan but were 'not a surprise'.

A NEW PRESIDENT PUMPS UP THE WAR

Lyndon Johnson in the White House – further escalation – Tonkin Gulf incident manufactured to win support from Congress – Goldwater beaten in presidential election – troop numbers soar – bombing fails to break the North – McNamara quits – his analysis of errors

Lyndon Johnson, catapulted into the White House by the assassination of the President in November 1963, proved even more willing to listen to the hawks on the issue of Vietnam. Kennedy, the sophisticated East Coaster, was naturally cautious about this expert advice. The experience of the Bay of Pigs was burnt on Kennedy's mind. Johnson, the burly and assertive Texan, found the military mind agreeable and believed the USA must come out on top in any and every struggle.

The year 1964 saw serious escalation. As early as March, the State Department secretly drew up a resolution for Congress to give the President support in any way he chose to increase American efforts in Vietnam. The chance to use it came with the Gulf of Tonkin incident. What actually happened on those two nights in August 1964 is now little disputed. As presented by a shocked President to an outraged American public, the destroyer *Maddox* was on a peaceful 'routine patrol' in international waters near North Vietnam when it was wantonly attacked by patrol boats. On the grounds that this may have been an attack at the initiative of a local commander only, Washington confined itself to sending a stiff note of protest to Hanoi. Meanwhile the US Naval commander sent the destroyer *Turner Joy* to patrol with the *Maddox*. Two nights later, both were attacked, according to the official report.

Were the American vessels on an innocent patrol – and if so what were they patrolling against? South Vietnamese vessels were already involved in covert actions against the North in response to the aid from Hanoi to the Vietcong. This activity, code named Plan 34A, involved launching high-speed hit-and-run attacks on shore installations and landing agents to send back intelligence. We now know that the American destroyers were involved in electronic intelligence gathering. The second attack led to the President authorising retaliatory attacks by planes from the carrier *Ticonderaga* on North Vietnamese patrol boats and oil installations.

The evidence is that the second attack on the US destroyers did not take place. But the episode as reported presented Johnson and his fellow hawks with their chance. The President was said to have been walking around with the draft resolution to Congress in his pocket for months. Now it could be presented. Congress passed the resolution unanimously. Only two voices dissented in the Senate. It empowered the president to take any further measures he thought necessary to prevent 'further aggression'. It was a blank cheque.

But Johnson waited to cash it. He was facing election in the autumn. His opponent Barry Goldwater, the Republican Senator from Arizona, wanted to escalate the war, even speaking casually about the possible use of nuclear weapons. The Senator went on to declare about East–West relations:

Our strategy must be primarily offensive in nature ... (we should) declare the Communist movement an outlaw in the community of civilised nations. Accordingly we should withdraw diplomatic recognition from all Communist governments including that of the Soviet Union ... we must, ourselves, be prepared to undertake military operations against vulnerable Communist regimes.[181]

All this provided Johnson with the ideal opportunity to portray himself as the only Commander-in-Chief who could be trusted to prevent the war getting out of hand. The Chiefs of Staff had in fact prepared a plan early in 1964 for bombing North Vietnam. Johnson held it over until after the election which he won by a landslide, assisted to some extent by the alarm his belligerent opponent had provoked. However, Goldwater's domestic policies were more probably the main reason for his failure.

In February 1965, the re-installed President decided to embark on bombing North Vietnam and the Ho Chi Minh trail through Laos and Cambodia which supplied the Vietcong. He hoped to bomb Hanoi to the conference table. As part of the internal debate about this and further steps, ex-President Eisenhower was asked to talk to senior officials. When asked about how far the USA should be committed, Eisenhower replied that if many more troops were required, then the burden should be accepted. And if China or Russia were to threaten to intervene, they should be warned that 'dire consequences' could follow.

Johnson kept it a secret that he had embarked on the bombing which aroused intense indignation. It was to be far from the last covert move by Washington. The President hoped, vainly, that the bombing campaign would prevent him having to

---

181   *The Conscience of a Conservative* by Barry Goldwater, Bottom of the Hill, 2010, p. 116

send more troops. But Hanoi responded to the bombs by sending regular forces into the south. The American counter-response was to raise the level of US forces from 33,000 to 82,000. But again the White House was less than candid. The scale of the planned escalation was not to be spelt out to the public. Instead, 'individual deployments would be announced at appropriate times'. In the hope that Hanoi would respond to American suggestions of talks, the bombing was briefly suspended in May. Hanoi was unmoved. Which was not surprising since it was winning the war.

General Westmoreland, the commander in Vietnam, was soon calling for more troops, indicating that he wanted to raise the total to 175,000. Washington was now deeply divided, more so than the public at large which did not have access to the gloomier estimates of likely success. The President doubted if the appetite of the military would be satisfied by anything less than an open-ended commitment. The situation in the South was deteriorating. The hearts and minds of the Vietnamese were not being won as planned. McNamara feared – and he was to be proved right – that the presence of large numbers of American troops would provoke not soothe the population in the South. The fact that, between 1965 and 1967, the US Air Force dropped one million tons of bombs in South Vietnam, as well as the half million on the north, did not help.

The terms of Johnson's broadcast to the nation after the Gulf of Tonkin incident marked a key point in the conflict. This was a struggle against 'the deepening shadow of Communist China'. South Vietnam would be assisted to resist assault from the North. Hanoi must understand that in this mission, essential to the backbone and morale of the USA's allies everywhere: 'We will not be defeated; we will not grow tired; we will not withdraw, either openly or under the cloak of a meaningless agreement.'

In this display of bravado, Washington had put the credibility of American foreign policy firmly on the line. Misgivings within the administration were brushed aside. The USA had never been militarily defeated in its history. American power was at its zenith. Moreover, its military technology made it unthinkable that a backward nation of Asiatics could win against the determined resistance of the USA. Helpfully, Washington also knew that Moscow was none too keen on a conflict which was liable to increase the power and influence of China in Asia. Johnson insisted that winning the battle was essential because it involved 'our own security'.

The number of troops was raised to 300,000. But by 1967 General Westmoreland, the commander in the conflict, was calling for another 200,000 as the North and the Vietcong guerrillas continued to notch up victories. American public opinion was dividing sharply. An extension of conscription aroused deep misgivings. Johnson's policy had raised the stakes enormously in both political and physical terms. It would take a brave or desperate administration to retreat from Vietnam after this.

Poor morale was to prove a vital factor in the subsequent conflict, especially as reluctant American conscripts, often trigger happy, became increasingly involved in the brutal tactics of guerrilla warfare against the Vietcong and the infiltrated regular forces of North Vietnam. As the Americans sent more forces to Vietnam, the North produced and trained even more.

In early 1967, General Westmoreland requested 200,000 extra troops, which would have brought the total to 670,000 (in fact the number peaked at 550,000). McNamara asked him for an estimate of the outturn. If the forces were raised by 200,000, 100,000, or kept at 470,000, how long would it take to 'wind down our involvement'? The General's answer was two, three and five years respectively.

The war was spinning out of control. This was to be the breaking point for McNamara. The Chiefs of Staff recommended yet heavier attacks on the North by land, sea and air. They added that the invasion of the North and Laos and Cambodia might have to be considered. The USA was on a treadmill. The quality of military advice was deplorable. The faith in advanced weapon technologies was naive (as it still was some forty year later). Military intelligence lived up to the jibe that it is a contradiction in terms. Casualty figures among the Vietcong were constantly exaggerated and included all too many innocent civilians in the body count. The ability to break the spirit of the North by military ferocity showed a complete inability to understand what a driving force lies in the hatred of the foreign invader (see also Iraq and Afghanistan).

McNamara saw the cause as hopeless and made enemies by explaining his views in internal memoranda. In February 1968, he resigned to become President of the World Bank, a post he was supposed to covet. Whether he really resigned or was fired was not clear – even to him, he said.

In his memoirs he explains some of the errors behind the war:

1. We misjudged then – as we have since – the geopolitical intentions of our adversaries (in this case Vietnam and the Vietcong) supported by China and the Soviet Union and we exaggerated the dangers to the United States of their actions.

2. We viewed the people and leaders of South Vietnam in terms of our own experience. We saw in them a thirst – and a determination to fight for freedom and democracy. We totally misjudged the political forces within the country.

3. We underestimated the power of nationalism to motivate a people (in this case the North Vietnamese and the Vietcong) to fight and die for their beliefs and values – and we continue to do so in many parts of the world.

4. Our misjudgements of friends and foes alike reflected our profound ignorance of the history, culture and politics of the people in the area and the personalities and the habits of their leaders.[182]

Though McNamara was to say, perhaps out of tact, that these misjudgements did not apply to American policy towards Russia, many will argue that it was precisely

182   McNamara, op. cit., pp. 321–323

Woodrow Wilson: thought
he could do better than
Jesus Christ

Franklin D. Roosevelt:
always suspicious
of British imperialism

John Foster Dulles, stern Presbyterian: determined 'to crowd the enemy'

President Harry S. Truman: had not been told about the Bomb ... no experience of foreign affairs

ABOVE The Big Three at the Yalta conference: giving away Poland?
BELOW The Big Three at Potsdam: the end of East–West cooperation

ABOVE LEFT Stalin: more
ruthless than Hitler
ABOVE RIGHT Anthony
Eden: found Stalin a realist
BELOW Churchill: sure that
Stalin would keep his word
OPPOSITE President
Eisenhower: warned the
USA of the industrial-
military complex

ABOVE McNamara, US Defense Secretary:
disillusioned by Vietnam
BELOW President De Gaulle: resolute
to avoid US entanglements
OPPOSITE ABOVE Reagan: determined
to end the Soviet 'evil empire'
BELOW LEFT Gorbachev: found Reagan
'a primitive'

ABOVE LEFT   President George H. Bush: launched the first Iraq War
ABOVE RIGHT   President George W. Bush: launched the second Iraq War
BELOW   The Twin Towers: the peak of Arab/Muslim revenge

the sort of failures he outlined which had helped give rise to the Cold War in the first place. The need to disentangle the US from Vietnam was now becoming desperate. Lyndon Johnson refused to fight another election. It was to be left to Richard Nixon – one of the nation's more notable and habitual hawks – to decide that enough was enough.

CHAPTER 23
AMERICAN IDEALISM COLLAPSES: THE CIA 'ROGUE ELEPHANT'

The American claim to be the champion of democracy as leader of NATO was put to the test in 1967 in Greece. The Truman Doctrine of 1947 involved the supply of economic and military aid to the country, which had become a vital part of NATO's defence perimeter. The US aid was always conditional. The country's voting system of proportional representation was having the effect of providing leverage to small and left-wing parties in the regular formation of governments by coalition.

The Greeks were told to change to the American system of simple majority vote, otherwise aid would be at risk. The change was made but this did little to establish lasting stability. The Communist Party was firmly suppressed but left-wing groups continued to be very evident. Washington's view that Athens could be ordered around was exemplified at the time Greece and Turkey were in fierce conflict over the future of Cyprus. The Americans had a plan for settling the dispute which was not acceptable to the Greeks. In 1964, President Lyndon Johnson called in the Ambassador for an astonishing lecture, (detailed by the *Observer*'s Washington correspondent):

> Fuck your parliament and constitution. America is an elephant, Cyprus is a flea. Greece is a flea. If those two fleas continue irritating the elephant they may just get whacked. We pay a lot of money to the Greeks, Mr Ambassador. If your Prime Minister gives me talk about democracy, parliament and the constitution he, his parliament and the constitution may not last long.[183]

It was unsurprising in such conditions that a strong anti-US and anti-NATO line developed in Greece. Its main exponent was Andreas Papandreou, on the Left but certainly not a Communist. The administration by 1967 was an interim government appointed by King Constantine. Elections were promised in that year and Papandreou was expected to be the main beneficiary. In anticipation, a junta

---

183 *I should have died* by Philip Deane, Atheneum, New York, 1977

of four colonels carried out a coup. The head of the army was one of the first arrested but soon set free after a promise to back his colonels.

The King was not complicit in the coup. But he did swear in the new regime when the colonels demanded it. Within a week, the new regime was recognised by the USA but with some show of sorrow. Washington had known of the colonel's secret plan but had chosen not to pass the information on either to the King or the interim administration. It was tantamount to participation, dubious as the Americans were about the military's credentials.

The rule of the colonels followed a familiar pattern. Some 8,000 deemed political opponents were arrested. Torture was allowed in certain cases. The international reaction was confused. In most NATO countries they followed the US lead. Less pliant were Denmark and Norway, as well as Sweden, not a NATO member. They laid a complaint before the Commission of Human Rights in the Council of Europe. When the CHR proved critical, the Greek Junta terminated the country's membership of the organisation. America was urged to intervene but did nothing.

The junta lasted in power for seven years during which the King contemplated a counter coup. The colonels' forced him out and declared a republic. The colonels proved deeply unpopular and, by 1974, had fallen out with each other. The junta fell apart. Democracy was recovered. Several of the military officers put on trial were found guilty of treason and sentenced to death, though this was later commuted to imprisonment. Others were tried on torture charges and received long sentences.

It had been a grim episode. The idea that the issue of NATO membership could topple a country put the American role in Europe in a new and unflattering light, as did the reputation of other NATO countries prepared to recognise the junta. The one power which could have prevented the coup at an early stage was the USA. But it regarded its military priorities as more important.

The USA, with its claim to be fighting the Cold War from a clear moral superiority, was under increasing challenge in the 1960s. The sheer spectacle of the world's greatest military superpower remorselessly pounding a small, underdeveloped country could only provoke sympathy for the David who would not give in to Goliath. The truth about the course of events in Vietnam was not the only thing held back from public opinion in vain.

An insight into the mood (and standards) which came to prevail in the USA during the war was provided by reactions to the massacre in My Lai, when a platoon ran amok in a Vietnamese village, killing 500 civilians. The court martial of William Calley, the young platoon commander, found him guilty of twenty-two murders. For this he was sentenced to life imprisonment with hard labour. There was widespread indignation about the harshness of the verdict. The White House soon moved Calley from prison to house arrest in a military base. Finally he was pardoned by President Nixon. For many he became a national hero.

Just as Johnson lied to Congress about the Gulf of Tonkin incident, Nixon tried to keep secret the rise in the bombing of Cambodia. He also lied about Watergate, which finally brought him down. Deceit was becoming a habit. President Ford and his Secretary of State Henry Kissinger certainly avoided an honest account of their friendly talks with President Suharto of Indonesia in 1975. They were followed by a massacre of Suharto's political opponents of all shades of opinion. It is widely believed that Suharto was assured that he would keep receiving US aid regardless of controversial domestic intentions.

Whether, much later, President Reagan deliberately lied over his role in the Iran-Contra arms programme, let alone allowed its illegal initiation, has been long debated. But the almost unavoidable conclusion is that he did. He pleaded memory loss to the Senate investigation. However, the authorisation of that highly controversial and illegal action could hardly have come from anywhere lower than the Oval Office. The same standards were to be revived when President George W. Bush lied over Iraq's Weapons of Mass Destruction.

Nor is there any need to wonder why Washington's standards fell so low during the Cold War. The argument that the end justified the means was widely accepted. The Doolittle Committee which Eisenhower appointed to investigate the CIA in 1955 reported:

> It is now clear that we are facing an implacable enemy whose avowed objective is world domination, by whatever means and at whatever cost. There are no rules in such a game, hitherto accepted norms of human conduct do not apply.[184]

The CIA had the green light. If the KGB could infiltrate, lie, cheat and murder, the Agency was not going to be left behind. An outcry over the revelation that the CIA was regularly intercepting the public's mail – the agency was legally confined to overseas work – led to two committees of investigation. Congressman Church's committee described the CIA as 'a rogue elephant out of control'.

A record of covert actions by the USA between 1945 and 1983, excluding those in the Indo-China region, ranges from funding tyrannical rallies to outright assassination. Countries affected, sometimes more than once, ranged from Greece to Bolivia. Latin America remained the chief focus where there were twenty-three interventions, a US tradition from long before the Cold War, despite long-standing declarations about non-interference. This was ultimately blessed in a Congressional resolution in 1965 which called for the use of force by any 'American' nation if necessary to prevent a Communist takeover within the American hemisphere. The vote was a resounding 312–52.

---

184   *Rise to Globalism* by Stephen Ambrose, Penguin, 1985, p. 132

There were very few countries in which the CIA was not given permission for interference, always in the name of saving democracy, despite the governments it supported so often being undemocratic and brutally repressive.

Yet the Church Committee was not fully informed of all CIA training methods. A CIA manual of 1954 – released under the Freedom of Information legislation in 1997 – contained chilling items:

> For secret assassinations, the contrived accident is the most effective technique. When successfully executed it causes little excitement and is only casually investigated. The most effective accident is a fall of seventy-five feet or more onto a hard surface ... the act may be executed by sudden vigorous grabbing of the ankles, tipping the subject over the edge...[185]

The manual goes on to point out that drugs can be very effective if the assassin is trained as a doctor or nurse. An overdose of morphine 'will cause death without disturbance and is difficult to detect'.

Of 'edged weapons' the manual says that they are easy to obtain legitimately but 'a certain minimum of anatomical knowledge is needed for reliability'. For Vietnam, the CIA suggests that interrogation techniques of value include 'arrest, detention, deprivation of sensory stimuli through solitary confinement or similar methods, threats and fear, debility, pain, heightened suggestibility and hypnosis, narcosis and induced regression'. These techniques were to resurface later in the notorious prison camp at Guantanamo Bay. And in perhaps the only endorsement of torture ever uttered by a Western head of government, Bush declared that 'waterboarding' – simulated drowning – was an acceptable interrogation technique.

A notorious example of CIA action was the intervention in Chile. When the Communist Salvador Allende won the 1973 election, the army wanted to intervene. It was held back by the chief of staff, General Rene Schneider, who took the view that the will of the people must be respected. He was assassinated, though the Americans held that this had been a bungled operation by its locally recruited allies. The aim had been to remove him, not kill him. Nevertheless, the assassins were paid $35,000 for their bungle.

Schneider's successor General Pinochet was no such problem. He carried out a military coup, made himself head of state and presided over a vicious programme of torture and murder. Subsequently released CIA documents show that the head of the Chilean secret police, General Manuel Contraras, was being paid by the Agency. The FBI also became involved, providing information to the so-called Operation Condor in which the governments of Chile, Paraguay, Brazil, Uruguay and Argentina located and assassinated exiles, even in the USA itself. After democracy was reasserted in Chile, Contraras was jailed.

---

185   For findings of the Church committee see http://www.aarclibrary.org/church

The offsetting conclusion of the Church Committee in its 1975 report was that:

> The Committee does not believe that the acts (of assassination) which it has examined represent the real American character. They do not reflect the ideals which have given the people of this country and the world hope for a better, fuller, fairer life. We regard the assassination plots as an aberration.[186]

If the Committee had known of all the assassinations, not to say other covert activities in which the CIA was involved it might have reached a harsher verdict. The rogue elephant's continued practices led to Ford issuing a presidential order that no US government employee should 'engage in or conspire to engage in political assassination'. In 1978 Carter reiterated the message, as did Reagan in 1984 – but cancelled the order in 1985 as he stoked up the fires against 'the Evil Empire' of the Soviet Union.

The *New York Times* in 1984 published a further CIA manual specifically designed for the Nicaraguan Contras fighting the left-wing Sandanista government. It suggests riots in which conflict with the police may usefully provide martyrs. Sweepingly it adds:

> It is possible to neutralise carefully selected and planned targets such as court judges, mesta judges (magistrates), police and State Security officials, CDS chiefs (members of the Sandanista Defence Committee) etc.

The category 'etc.' would seem remarkably broad.

NIXON: FROM RETREAT TO DÉTENTE

Nixon takes over – extends the war to pressurise North Vietnam – bombing supply trails through Laos and Cambodia ineffective – domestic opinion angered by efforts to keep raids secret – public uproar over deaths at Kent University – US army attacks Cambodian areas – Washington accepts Hanoi's stern terms – Nixon wins massive majority

Nixon's first four years, starting in 1969, were a remarkable mixture of triumph and disaster. Though he succeeded in achieving a real measure of détente with Russia and China, his efforts to bomb Hanoi to the conference table left America more deeply divided than ever. But by the end of his first presidency

---

he could offer – or seem to offer – the prospect of a swift settlement in Vietnam combined with the greatest improvement in East–West relations seen in all the years of the Cold War. It was to prove enough, despite the hate figure that he had become to so many Americans, to secure a landslide victory in 1972.

His promise in the presidential contest was a determined search for 'peace with honour' in Vietnam. Dr Kissinger, who became his National Security Adviser – effectively relocating foreign policy to the White House – claimed that a settlement could be reached within six months. He knew this was wildly unlikely. It was to take all of the new presidency and a constant alternation of bombing and bargaining to achieve an agreement which nevertheless remained a surrender to Hanoi.

There was Cold War weariness in both Moscow and Washington, driven by the constant sense of danger and the cost of the arms race as sophisticated weaponry became increasingly expensive. This apart, Washington hoped that a more friendly Kremlin would put pressure on the North Vietnamese, to whom they were important arms suppliers. Moscow was willing to help up to a point. But given the state of Sino-Soviet rivalry, it was reluctant to push Hanoi into dependence on China. The mirror image of this was that Beijing, because of that rivalry, was keen on a more amicable relationship with Washington.

As inducements, Nixon was prepared to offer Moscow disarmament talks, grain sales, a trade agreement, an easing of tension in Berlin. But all this would depend on the Russians helping over Vietnam. Moscow tried but found it difficult to restrain the North Vietnamese. They were flushed with military success and the prospects of more, given Nixon's election promise to work for the removal of American forces from the South. He had already promised voters early reductions in the number of troops on the ground. The fig leaf of respectability for withdrawal was the promise to 'Vietnamese' the conflict by giving the South a larger role and, of course, the military aid required. In reality, no one expected the South to be able to hold out against the North on its own.

When negotiations in Paris, involving North and South Vietnam and the USA, showed no signs of progress, Nixon resorted to heavy bombing raids on the North's supply lines which ran through Cambodia along the border with the South and through Laos, further to the north. Starting in March, over 100,000 tons of high explosive were dropped on the Cambodian sector by B-52 bombers in 3,600 sorties. Laos, further to the north and squeezed between Thailand and North Vietnam had already been subjected to air raids because of the Communists' supply trails. Some two million tons of bombs were dropped in total between 1965 and 1973. The US was well on its way to dropping more bombs in Indo-China than on Germany in World War II, many of them of a particularly unpleasant nature. In a remarkable display of simple-mindedness, the White House believed that the surge in raids on Cambodia could be kept secret. They became public knowledge through the press in May.

Meanwhile talks continued in Paris. The stick-and-carrot process was taken a further stage by Nixon announcing that 25,000 troops would be withdrawn by

August. But this did little to assuage public outrage about the bombing or its attempted secrecy. Cambodia was a neutral country and this act of war, without Congressional authorisation, was illegal. Even if the bombing was having an effect on the North Vietnamese forces, for which there was limited evidence, Hanoi could see that Nixon was likely in the end to run out of domestic support for the war. Nixon and Kissinger had underrated the willingness of the North Vietnamese to incur heavy casualties and overrated its readiness to seek even a short-term settlement which, of course, would still leave its final objective in place.

Nixon made his famous appeal to the 'silent majority'. He felt sure of enough support to maintain his stick-and-carrot tactics. But there was a limit to what American public opinion would endure in the way of sticks. In early 1970, a pro-American coup was contrived in the Cambodian capital of Pnomh Penh which ousted Prince Sihanouk, the agile leader who had managed to maintain Cambodian neutrality, ignoring the Vietnamese supply trails and the American bomber raids on them. In May Nixon went on to announce the withdrawal of a further 150,000 troops, to be completed within twelve months. But at the same time, he authorised a joint attack by American and South Vietnamese army units on the strategic area in Cambodia, believing that this would also help the new leader in Pnomh Penh, Lon Nol. It was in fact to start the process of break-up in Cambodia which culminated with the triumph of the Khmer Rouge and the arrival in power of Pol Pot.

Protests at home about the escalation of the assault on Cambodia reached new heights. At Kent State University, National Guardsmen opened fire on student demonstrators, killing four and wounding eleven others. Congress was in uproar. On the other side of the world, the luckless Lon Nol was entitled to his own outrage since he was not notified of the assault on his own country until it was already under way. The row on Capitol Hill led to a Congressional resolution, passed by a large majority, forbidding further military action against Cambodia. The illegality of Nixon's policy might well have been the grounds for a later impeachment had not the Watergate scandal provided the diversion.

The military action did not last long and was declared, like almost every other US action in Indo-China a 'success'. But the North Vietnamese were still intransigent. So Washington resorted again to bombing, this time making Hanoi itself the target. By the time the next presidential elections were under way, the White House decided it had better accept the tough terms which Hanoi was laying down. Moscow's influence had helped in reaching this settlement. But the North Vietnamese position was so strong that Hanoi could dictate its own terms. Instead of the original insistence that both North Vietnamese and American forces should be withdrawn from the South at the same time, Washington accepted that the North's forces should remain in many of the areas they had conquered. But the agreement proved just enough for Nixon to claim as the pace of the Paris talks accelerated that 'peace is at hand'. It proved enough for the war-weary American voters. The President won his massive majority.

South Vietnam had been thrown to the wolves. But no one seriously expected it to survive in any case. Saigon surrendered in 1975 and was renamed Ho Chi Minh City. No dominoes fell. But at least the end of the fighting left the way open for the process of détente between the major powers to continue.

CHAPTER 24
THE PRAGUE SPRING AND BREZHNEV DOCTRINE

Restlessness in the satellites – Czech liberalisation alarms Kremlin – Prague leaders hold out – Moscow confers with hardliners – Dubček offers to resign – Warsaw Pact forces invade – Polish party ousts leader who suppressed shipyard workers – Brezhnev Doctrine enunciated

If the Vietnam war was going horribly wrong for the USA, at least there was the consolation for Washington that the Soviets were facing daunting problems on their own European doorstep. These threatened the concept of the satellite states as a buffer against the West. At the same time, the supposed unity of the global Communist world – never very strong at the best of times – was coming apart at the seams.

Tension between Russia and China had been rising visibly since 1961. By the end of the decade, Moscow had increased its forces from a nominal presence on the Sino-Soviet border to fifteen full strength divisions. According to Henry Kissinger's memoirs, there had been a discreet inquiry from the Russians about possible American reaction if the Soviet Union attacked China's newly established nuclear bases.

Among the satellites, Czechoslovakia and Poland were becoming very restless. In the former, gradual reforms had been taking place in political and artistic freedom which came to a head in the so-called Prague Spring of 1968. The new party secretary, Alexander Dubček, declared his desire for 'socialism with a human face', stressing the value of human rights and freedom from political persecution. The mood was eagerly transmitted throughout the party and the country. The new-found freedom of the press resulted in regular attacks on the old regime and its ways and, of course, on the Soviet model. It was not just Brezhnev in the Kremlin who was alarmed. Fear was at least as strong among the hardliners in East Germany and Poland.

Nor was it just the danger of other satellites following the Czech example which worried the Kremlin. There was the basic military issue. There were no Soviet forces on Czech soil. Several requests to accept such a presence had been rejected by Czech leaders who warned that the presence of such troops would be liable to promote public hostility. But by 1965 an agreement had been reached to allow the stationing of surface-to-surface nuclear weapons on Czech soil, which the Russian military saw as essential for the continuity of the Warsaw Pact defence strategy. And the weapons would, it was agreed, be guarded by Soviet units. The rockets and the sites were not ready in 1968, though it was envisaged that they would be in the following year. The new reformist trends in Prague threatened to discontinue the preparations.

Matters came to a head in August. After a four-day conference between Czech and Soviet leaders in early August, Brezhnev believed that the reformist tendencies would be halted. Part of the deal was that anti-Soviet sentiments emanating from the Czech media would be halted. But they continued. In mid-August, the Soviet archives record Brezhnev and Dubček having prolonged and turbulent telephone conversations. The Soviet leader alternated between hints of threats and pleas for action on the press and on the continued growth in the Czech hierarchy of figures hostile to Moscow. Dubček evaded, pleaded for time and at two points said he would prefer to step down from his job. At this point, it was far from clear that Moscow was set on an invasion.

A conference of satellite leaders was convened in the Kremlin which had before it not just the facts but also pleas from hardliners in the Czech Communist Party for action. There were many in that party, so it was claimed, who were anxious for Soviet intervention. Whether the Kremlin decision to intervene was unanimous remains far from clear. The length of the talks suggests it was not. The fact that the East German leader, Walter Ulbricht, and the Polish leader, Wladislaw Gomulka – but especially Ulbricht – were pressing for action helped sway the decision.

Warsaw Pact forces, including a large number of tanks, were ordered into Czechoslovakia in late August, only Romania declining to take part in the operation – not out of any squeamishness but because it was forming its own policy of independence of Moscow. The Czech insurgency was crushed. Tens of thousands fled to the West. The spectacle of Czechs defying Russian tanks was a propaganda disaster for Moscow. Western Communist parties suffered another surge of resignations. At least on this occasion Moscow dealt with the dissidents less harshly than it had in Hungary, no doubt part through fear of more damage to the Communist image. The death toll of Czechs was assessed by the Prague authorities in a secret report at 100. Dubček himself was removed but left to live on as a humble worker in the forestry service.

The West reacted with predictable indignation but only in words: 'reaffirming the inviolability of the principle … that any intervention by one state in the affairs of another is unlawful'. Given the infinitely more bloody intervention by the USA in Vietnam, this was a shaky doctrine. The nearest NATO came to action was to say that it was 're-assessing the alliance's defences'.

It is still not clear whether the Soviet Union regarded its action as in danger of leading to any conflict beyond Czechoslovakia. An American intelligence report claimed that Soviet forces were put on nuclear alert at the time. But General Ivan Ershov, deputy commander of the Czech invasion, declared in a radio interview in

arsenal which could provide deterrence but which would not be large enough to allow a pre-emptive capability to knock out the other side's weapons. Further encouragement came when Harriman, acting once again as a personal envoy of the White House, sent a message to Moscow through the Soviet Ambassador in Washington just after the election saying that Carter wanted to get the talks based on Vladivostock moving again. The President favoured a summit. Indeed summits might with advantage become an annual event. The omens seemed good – except for one part of the Carter message, carefully noted by the pessimists in Moscow – which said that he 'could not of course be bound by previous negotiations on strategic weapons'. Why not?

Nevertheless the way seemed clear for progress when Carter wrote to Brezhnev in late January, shortly after his inauguration, to express his satisfaction with a speech the Russian leader had made declaring that the Soviet Union did not seek armaments which would give it a first strike capability. All it wanted was a deterrent power. In his letter Carter added that a SALT II Treaty should be achieved 'without delay'.

But three weeks later Carter sent a letter which confirmed the suspicions of the Kremlin pessimists. He called for a whole new set of negotiations, leaving out the Vladivostock agreement on curbing long-range cruise missiles, an area where the USA was ahead of the Soviet Union. In short, the SALT talks should restart on a different basis. Five years of negotiations seemed to be going down the drain. Brezhnev particularly resented this blow to his efforts since he had worked hard to win over his own hardliners about Vladivostock (Ford had had the same experience). Matters were made worse by the President adding in his letter that he intended to take a strong line on human rights. The new phase of détente was over before it had started.

The problem behind the swings from détente to Cold War and back again was Carter's character. After Nixon, the voters were hungry for honesty. Carter seemed to meet the need. But he was also an innocent. Having come from being a Governor, he was relatively unfamiliar with the workings of Washington. He enrolled two powerful but often contradictory voices in foreign policy – Cyrus Vance as Secretary of State and Zbigniew Brzezinski as National Security Adviser. The latter was viscerally anti-Communist and anti-Russian, no doubt due to his Polish roots. When Vance was listened to, détente proceeded. When Brzezinski had the upper hand, it was confrontation.

The new American proposals which followed the breakdown of the Vladivostock programme were ill-received in Moscow. They appeared to favour the USA's position in terms of weapons. There was also resentment that the proposals had been leaked in Washington before being put to Moscow. The whole episode smacked of a propaganda exercise. In fact, Carter had run up against the hardliners in and around the new administration. One of the more baleful influences in Washington was the Committee for the Present Danger. Originally established in 1950 to encourage a tough line against Moscow, the Committee was revived as soon as Carter was elected and included an impressive array of figures – impressive at any rate in the sense that they had held a variety of government posts from the time of Dulles onwards.

The Committee fostered the belief that Carter's original approach was dangerous appeasement. It called for the abandonment of the SALT II talks. The hawks won some support in Europe. The German government was expressing alarm at developments in Soviet missile technology which, it said, made it easier for the Russians to select and knock out essential strategic targets in Europe. The original Carter policy of détente was set back but not brought to a complete halt. In 1979, at summit talks in Vienna, Carter and Brezhnev signed the SALT II Treaty. But there still remained major differences between the two leaders on activity in the Third World. The American assumption remained that the Soviets' progress in Ethiopia, Angola and Mozambique represented serious victories for Communism. A more realistic approach would have been to regard them as further burdens which were a drain on the resources of the ramshackle Soviet economy. But this did not fit in with fashionable thought at the time when there was a horror of the other side gaining a new client state. Soviet strength continued to be overrated.

But at least the two leaders established some sort of rapport. Though neither could understand the other politically, there were signs that they found each other personally agreeable. There was none of the fierce animus which was to be a mark of the subsequent Reagan administration. Carter also established good relations with the Chinese leader Deng Xiaoping who visited Washington. The President wrote in his diary that his guest was alarmed about the Russians. The Chinese leader thought Russia would attack his country 'eventually', though that could be not until the end of the century. Meanwhile, the USA, China and India (Moscow had backed Pakistan in its war with India) ought to co-ordinate their activities to restrain Russia.

Restraint however was to prove unnecessary. It was in 1979 that the Russians began their slide into the deep morass of Afghanistan. As it progressed it was treated in the West with outrage and alarm. In reality it was the final Third World drain on Russian resources, military, financial and moral, which was to be the eventual undoing of Communism. By the end of the decade military budgets on both sides had risen, despite Carter's dove-like image. The USA could afford the increase better than the USSR.

The Senate declined to ratify SALT II. The Soviets baulked at the idea of a SALT III. In 1980, Carter signed Presidential Directive 59 which accepted that the use of nuclear weapons, below that of an all-out nuclear exchange, was permissable. The hawks regarded this as a warning which would curb the dangers of war with the Soviet Union. But clearly it made a conflict, should it occur, much more dangerous.

The Helsinki Accords

In the non-military field, the spirit of détente led to success in the European Security conference of 1975. This involved three major developments, alongside the declaration that détente must be the policy of all concerned. The first was the acceptance of the existing boundaries throughout Europe – denounced by American hawks as a second Yalta. The next was the acceptance that none of the signatories would take any aggressive steps towards its neighbouring countries – in short no repeats of the Hungarian or Czechoslovakian episodes on the Soviet side and, in theory, none in Latin America by the USA. The third point was an agreement that all parties should protect and advance 'human rights'. This was a remarkable decision by the Soviets, given the certainty that Moscow would do no more than inch towards freer conditions for its citizens. Both sides agreed also on the importance of increased cultural and scientific exchanges.

Who got the better of the Accords? The West had no intention of disturbing the status quo in Eastern Europe, for East Germany or any other country. The hardliners in the West claimed that acceptance of this was a display of weakness. On the other hand to have the Soviets proclaim the importance of human rights seemed a moral victory. And, inevitably, the predictable failure of the Soviet Union to implement the accords could be turned to propaganda advantage as progress was monitored. The open and sincere declaration that détente must be the policy of both sides was obviously reasonable, though even that was also to upset some of the West's hardliners.

As expected the Russians were regularly berated from Washington for not keeping to human rights clauses. It was good propaganda material though bound to hinder détente. On the other hand, Washington was to plunge further into Latin American problems which its critics at home and abroad denounced. It provided formidable anti-American propaganda.

The Soviets' Afghan Disaster Begins

The end of the 1970s saw the start of the ultimately fatal war in Afghanistan, not to reach its conclusion for ten years. The decision of Moscow to embark on the war was controversial within the Kremlin from the start. The Soviet archives relate the agonising of the Politburo from the time that requests for assistance came from the Communist-led government in Kabul to the final withdraw of all personnel in 1989.

The Kabul government made repeated requests for military assistance in 1979, faced with the common enough Afghan problem of a rebellious populace which was split along tribal lines. Some Soviet advisers were shot after an uprising in the city of Herat that year. But the Kremlin kept to its limitation of only providing military hardware. It was when President Hafizulla Amin – who had been prominent in these requests – ousted the Premier, Mohammad Taraki, that the Politburo changed its mind. It feared that Amin would reorientate the country towards the USA. The CIA had in fact just been authorised by Carter to provide aid to the rebels. The Kremlin was also concerned that the secular regime in Kabul would be replaced by Islamic fundamentalists who would – crucially – stimulate opposition to Moscow among the Muslim-dominated regions in Russia.

The Soviet military protested when the Politburo decided on armed intervention, pointing to the American experience in Vietnam. But the decision to send troops was made in December. As in the American case, the first moves were modest, aimed at the protection of the towns. But the need to guard the troops themselves led to a further escalation. Then, with the inability of the troops to deal with the rebels who retired in traditional form to their mountain strongholds, still further escalation took place.

The Kremlin found itself fighting for an unpopular government against rebels who were both hostile to all foreigners and to what they regarded as an unforgivably secular regime in Kabul. Ironically, the CIA was giving assistance to, among others, those who emerged later as the Taliban regime which the Americans and their allies were later to fight. It appears from the archives that the Kremlin had second thoughts as early as 1980. But the doubts were finally brushed aside. The scale of the involvement of Soviet troops in Afghanistan, mainly conscripts, and the casualties which resulted led to the nearest thing we know as a revolt among Soviet citizens.

In 1986, with a decision to end the war now under discussion, the Politburo had to take into account grim warnings from the military about the prospects. The new General Secretary Mikhail Gorbachev was now making his authority felt in these discussions with stern warnings about the unpopularity of the war at home. Yet it was not until 1989 that the last vestiges of Soviet intervention were removed.

To outward appearances, the Carter administration was no more than an onlooker in the Afghan invasion – though of course a moralising one. In fact stirring up a Soviet invasion, perhaps remembering some real lessons from Vietnam, became official though secret policy. Within months of Carter coming to power Brzezinski had set up the Nationalities Working Group. Under this harmless title, the organisation was designed to exploit ethnic problems in the Soviet Union, in particular by encouraging Islamic militancy in the Muslim regions.

Brezezinski commented in 1998:

> According to the official version of history, CIA aid to the Mujaheddin began ... after the Soviet army invaded Afghanistan ... But the reality, secretly guarded until now, is completely otherwise. It was in July 1979 that President Carter signed the first directive for secret aid to the opponents of the pro-Soviet regime in Kabul ... We didn't push the Russians to intervene but we knowingly increased the probability that they would.

Brzezinski was not only cunning, he was also versatile enough to contemplate an alliance with the new clerical regime in Iran which displaced the Shah. But when Carter agreed to the cancer-stricken Shah coming to the USA, the outraged Ayatollah Khomeini authorised students to take over the US Embassy and seize the hostages. They were held for over a year. Carter's scheme for a daring rescue by helicopter forces foundered in a sandstorm. The blow to the prestige of the President and the US itself was a gift to Republican opponents.

If the Afghan war and the creaking and groaning of the Soviet system served to bring the arch-reformer Gorbachev to power, the picture was very different in the USA where Ronald Reagan swept into office in 1980 in what seemed a reversion to the worst years of the Cold War.

CHAPTER 25
THE REAGAN ERA: GORBACHEV TAKES OVER IN MOSCOW

New belligerence in foreign policy – Reagan's eccentricities – nuclear war narrowly avoided – the vital double agent in London – a new and nervous leader in Moscow – the Iran-Contra affair – the President's memory conveniently short – Gorbachev brings hope

Ronald Reagan, the first professional actor to become President, brought with him both the glitter and the moral simplicities of old Hollywood. As in all cowboy films, there were the good guys and the bad guys. In between there were often the waverers who, through weakness, would not stand up to the villains. The final drama would invariably end with the triumph of the men in the white hats distinguished by their steadfastness and representing the values of a great pioneering nation. Brute force would finally be repaid in kind as the drama moved to its inevitable climax and happy ending.

Reagan reflected this simplicity. Policy under him became more Manichaean than ever. His views on the danger of Communists and their sympathisers taking over in Hollywood in the McCarthy days were well known. As president of the Actors' Guild he constantly stressed the danger of Communists. He was also to maintain against all the evidence that there had been no 'blacklist' of left-wingers in the industry. Despite this disquieting background, he was to prove the most charming president of the USA in modern times, able to radiate warmth, good humour and friendliness before any audience. This served to cover a very limited intellect. His inability to debate with Carter during the election contest on any points of policy – his standard riposte was 'there he goes again' – became famous but uttered with a geniality that audiences warmed to.

His chief of staff during his second term, Donald Regan, formerly Treasury Secretary, related that it was often difficult to know what the President had actually decided when confronted with issues of any complexity. He seemed to leave it to his staff to interpret what the President wanted – or would have wanted if he had fully understood the question in hand. The President's Cabinet colleagues sometimes encountered the same problem. This periodic vagueness was not helped by his reliance on his wife and her reliance in turn on her astrologer in San Francisco. It was impossible at times, Regan relates, to understand the President's reluctance to do certain things on certain dates without appreciating the 'Nancy factor'.[187]

The new Soviet leader Mikhail Gorbachev was to say of Reagan that he was 'a primitive'. The President could certainly lay few claims to sophistication. He told one audience that he wanted to strengthen the position of his arms negotiation groups 'two of which are in Geneva and one, I believe, still in Switzerland'. He had also voiced the view of the graduated income tax, when campaigning for the governorship of California, that 'the entire structure was created by Karl Marx'. Nor did he seem to demand knowledge of foreign affairs of his advisers. Judge Clark who was installed in the State Department before being appointed National Security Adviser was roughly handled at his confirmation hearings when he was unable to name the South African Prime Minister or define the Third World.

Reagan could also cause something of a stir by his inattention to foreign affairs beyond the Soviet Union and Latin America. When he visited China he fell asleep during the welcoming banquet. More worryingly he dozed off at a private meeting with Deng Xiaoping, the Prime Minister, who was explaining the People's Republic's attitude towards Taiwan. The worried Premier asked of a colleague whether Reagan had 'understood anything I said'.

The two Reagan presidencies (1981–1989) were to conclude with the end to the Cold War, which myth attributes to his aggresive stance. It was in fact a period of dangerously heightened tension and a brush with all out nuclear conflict, with the most dangerous episode since Cuba. His election theme was a harsh and simplistic anti-Communist message, promising a rise in defence spending and a restoration of American 'prestige' – a normal cry with presidential candidates. There was to be no more talk of a nuclear freeze, as favoured by the outgoing Carter regime and many European governments. There was to be no more détente with those he described in his first press conference as reserving to themselves 'the right to commit any crime, to lie, to cheat'. He proposed to see Communism consigned to ' the ash heap of history'. The Communists, he insisted, wanted to dominate 'every square mile of the globe'.

In his most famous phrase he dubbed the Soviet Union 'the evil empire'. This label alarmed the professionals in the State Department who had watched the wane of détente with alarm. The President had planned to use the phrase in a speech in London. The State Department saw it and cut it out. However it was to emerge later when he made a speech to Church leaders – not something in which the State Department was expected to play a role. To his text Reagan added that the Soviet Union was 'the focus of evil in the modern world'. In the subsequent hubbub of

---

187 *For the Record* by Donald Regan, Harcourt Brace, 1998, pp. 66–75

reaction, *New York Times* columnist Tom Wicker sagely observed: 'The holy war mentality on either side tends to evoke it on the other; and holy wars are both the hardest to avoid and the least likely to be settled short of one side's annihilation'.[188]

The State Department and the President's less aggressively-minded advisers might have known what they were in for from the time he won the Republican nomination. The team that Reagan brought to the White House seemed to have escaped from the film *Dr Strangelove* (subtitled 'Or how I learned to stop worrying and love the Bomb'). The alarming idea was advanced even during the campaign itself that a nuclear war was winnable. When Reagan's running mate, George Bush Snr, claimed this was so in an interview, there was a public outcry. Bush swiftly backtracked, claiming that he was only voicing Soviet thoughts.

Among those recruited from the Committee for the Present Danger was Thomas Jones as Assistant Under Secretary of Defence. He made the remarkable claim that, after a nuclear war, the US could recover in two to four years. It was a matter of civil defence: 'If there are enough shovels to go round, everybody is going to make it.' Holes covered with two doors and three feet of dirt, would enable the populace to emerge after a while and resume life.[189] He was asked more than once by a Senate subcommittee to appear and justify this extraordinary claim. He managed to avoid an appearance.

Reagan also voiced some curious ideas about nuclear warfare. During the campaign he told *Los Angeles Times* reporter, Robert Scheer: 'They [the Soviets] have gone very largely into a great civil defense programme, providing shelters, some of their industry is underground and all of it hardened to the point of being able to withstand nuclear blast.'[190]

This picture of Soviet industry was sheer fantasy and, incidentally, made nonsense of the various claims by administration officials that a nuclear war was winnable. Another absurdity was his claim that there was no word for 'freedom' in the Russian language. (The word is *svoboda*.)

Other Reagan gaffes included the warning that a 'window of vulnerability was opening up because the Soviets had a superiority at sea'. Again wholly untrue – as were many claims advanced by the CIA and the NSC about the size of the Soviet nuclear arsenal. He also claimed that the Soviet Union had for some time been preparing a pre-emptive war. In an address to cadets at West Point he drew their attention to a book 'Survival and Peace in the Nuclear War' which included the comment that 'a nuclear war is likely sooner or later'. The claim which he also made that the Soviets had a first strike capability – the power to destroy American retaliatory power – was to be dismissed by ex-Defense Secretary Robert

188   *President Reagan* by Richard Reeves, Simon and Schuster, 2005, p. 141
189   *With Enough Shovels: Reagan, Bush and Nuclear War* by Robert Scheer, Random House, 1982, p. 18
190   Ibid., p. 105

McNamara as 'absurd'. In 1983, as the next presidential election loomed, Reagan described the nuclear position between East and West with a series of statistics which showed a Soviet military superiority which, of course, necessitated an expanding US military budget. Whether he was deliberately misleading the public is hard to say. But the salient point was that he had excluded from the figures for American strength the 572 Pershing and Cruise missiles due for deployment in Europe within months and the new missiles being allocated to the strategic bomber force. The nuclear armaments of Britain were also excluded.[191]

The danger in warlike rhetoric was to be illustrated shortly after the aged Yuri Andropov had succeeded the ailing Brezhnev in 1982. The new leader became convinced that the Reagan administration's declarations meant that the USA was preparing to launch a pre-emptive nuclear attack and told his senior colleagues so. Two events in 1983 raised the tension as the time for autumn manoeuvres. or war games, approached. The Strategic Defence Initiative(SDI), or 'Star Wars', plan had already been announced in March 1983 and been condemned by the Soviets as a breach of the existing Anti-Ballistic Missile (ABM) Treaty. The plan, literally starry-eyed, was for US missiles based in space to intercept Soviet missiles.

The other event which alarmed Andropov was the American invasion of the small British dependency of Grenada on the grounds that it was becoming Marxist. This was a relatively trivial matter in the global context but it made a strong impression on the Kremlin. It suggested that the administration was trigger happy and unconcerned about outraging even its own allies.

Reagan's bellicose attitude from the start had brought the world nearer to nuclear Armageddon. Soon after his arrival at the White House, the USA's sea and air forces were authorised to test the existing prevailing level of Soviet military readiness by a combination of flights on the edge of Warsaw Pact territories and submarine operations up to the coastal waters of Russia. The official line was that no boundaries were to be crossed, no sea or air spaces actually invaded. The purpose was to test the level of Soviet alerts in response to each of these measures which were carefully analysed in Washington. The process set the Kremlin's nerves on edge. Combined with Reagan's rhetoric, real fears of a sudden onslaught were not surprising.

The American tests, named Operation PSYOPs, led the Kremlin to respond with Operation Ryan, a major intelligence gathering from all NATO countries to detect any signs of preparations for war, such as food stockpiling or exceptional hospital arrangements for large civilian casualties. Little was found to buttress Soviet fears but the intelligence operation was maintained, not least because there was never any let-up in Reagan's rhetoric.

In 1983, tension was heightened by Reagan's announcement of his 'Star Wars' project which would in Russian eyes leave the USA with a monopoly of missile power. The programme was announced with drama appropriate to Hollywood.

---

191   Reeves, op. cit., p. 137

The idea of rocket-destroying vehicles in outer space greatly excited the public – as of course it was intended to do. The practicality was another matter. Many scientists doubted if it could work at all. At any rate the cost would be uncertain but prodigious and the system could not be developed for many years.

The myth that SDI could and even did bring the Soviet economy to its knees because of the cost of the necessary counter-measures has proved remarkably resilient, right up to the present day. The matter is put in perspective by a CIA review when the scheme was announced.

It appears there will be a large variety of possible counter measures the Soviets can choose from to preserve the viability of their ballistic missile force. Intercontinental ballistic missiles and submarine-launched missiles can be upgraded with new boosters, decoys, penetration aids and multiple warheads. The signatures of these systems can be reduced and new launching techniques can be devised which make them less vulnerable to US missiles warning and defensive weapons systems. These systems can also be hardened or modified to reduce their vulnerability to direct energy weapons…

We believe it is highly unlikely that the Soviets will undertake a 'crash' programme in reaction to US BMD developments but will rather seek to counter them by steadily paced efforts over the *decades* [italics added]. The United States will need to develop and deploy its overall defence.[192]

And this was supposing that such a SDI system could be built.

Congress took the trouble of actually passed a law requiring the Defense Department to answer a variety of searching questions on SDI within two years. No answers came despite this legal demand. Congress did however get an estimate from the National Laboratory that in the event of its use, SDI would stop no more than 20 per cent of enemy missiles getting through.

East–West relations were to deteriorate further with the shooting down of Korean Airlines flight 007 when it strayed into Soviet air space. It was a grim error but a consequence of intelligence gathering by similar Boeings of the American Air Force testing Russian defence readiness. They flew up to and sometimes across the legal boundary. It was plain enough why there had been an over-zealous reaction from a Soviet fighter pilot. There had already been one American intelligence gathering flight that day in the area. But it provided another chance for Reagan to denounce the Soviet Union as barbaric. Its airline Aeroflot was banned from flights to the USA.

Two other events served to demonstrate the danger of a conflict. In late September, with nerves already taut, the Soviet colonel on night duty at the early warning station near Moscow was confronted with an automatic signal from his

---

radar proclaiming 'Launch, Launch'. It signalled that the USA had fired off a missile at Russia. But spy-satellite pictures of USA missile sites showed no firing. Then the system declared that a second missile had been fired. Colonel Petrov was both alarmed and baffled. If the USA was going to attack the USSR it would be a massive attack not just the use of first one, then two and finally five missiles, least of all given the continuing lack of evidence from the satellites. Refusing to press the panic button, he detected after some minutes that the system had been alerted by cloud formations. The world was lucky that Petrov kept his nerve when the Soviet defence system had already been brought to a high level of alert by the Korean episode.

But this incident was just a moment in a more protracted crisis. The planned Operation Able Archer involved the USA and other NATO powers in manoeuvres to test the readiness to counter a Soviet attack. This was, it was explained at length, only a war game. The drills were practice not the real thing. But the Kremlin noted, among other things, that the operation was designed to take account for the first time of the effectiveness of the new Pershing missiles being deployed in Europe in response to the deployment by Warsaw Pact countries of the mobile SSRs, one of the Pact's most effective weapons.

The Kremlin put Operation Ryan into top gear. Every sign of military and political activity in the West was watched for exceptional activity. The number of lights staying on well into the night at the American Embassy and at the Ministry of Defence in Whitehall were scanned. A special watch was kept in case the American Ambassador drove into Downing street, seen as almost inevitable should war be launched. At the same time, Soviet missile bases, warships and bomber aircraft were put into the highest state of alert short of war itself – preparation for a nuclear attack.

Fortunately for the world, there was a double agent in the Soviet Embassy in London. Oleg Gordievsky, who headed the KGB in London. He not only assured the Kremlin that there were no signs of proper preparations for war, he also warned Britain how panic-ridden and dangerous the Kremlin had become. There was also assurance from an East German spy who had infiltrated NATO at a high level that a shooting war was not in prospect, only a war game. The aged Andropov, conducting the response to Able Archer from his sick bed, accepted that no attack was planned. But a high alert for Soviet forces was kept. He remained, naturally enough, deeply suspicious of Washington.

As part of his Hollywood-style showdown with the Soviets, Reagan also disowned the SALT II Treaty which had taken six years to negotiate and been supported by three former presidents. As for the scale of US commitments needed to prosecute the President's version of the Cold War, the official list for troop deployments gives an idea of his global ambitions:

> Overseas basing of United States forces will continue in Europe, the Western Pacific, Latin America and when circumstances permit in Southwest Asia.

Naval and air forces will provide a continuous presence of combatant forces in the north Atlantic, Caribbean, Mediterranean, Western Pacific and Indian Ocean/Southwest Asia regions. Selective deployments of significant forces will be made in South America, Africa, south-east Asia and the south-west Pacific. Ground and air deployments will periodically be made to Southwest Asia as political considerations permit.[193]

The Reagan presidency – until he was persuaded to become less belligerent – marked a reversion to the stone age of the Cold War. Moscow was effectively told that attempts at peaceful coexistence would cut no ice with Washington. The President was exceptionally fortunate, as was the whole world, in the arrival of Mikhail Gorbachev in 1986 as his opposite number. Andropov had only lasted fifteen months, replaced by the elderly Konstantin Chernenko who did not live long either. Gorbachev was over a generation younger than his predecessors and a natural reformer, painfully aware of the shortcomings of the Soviet system. Both his grandfathers had been arrested on trivial charges of not meeting work targets.

The Washington administration was by this time pursuing policies which, in Latin America in particular, made the Reagan claim to moral superiority sound very hollow. The President and top advisers were to be engulfed in massive scandals when the White House itself was discovered lying and cheating over illegal arms sales to Iran and to the Nicaraguan Contras. The 'Iran-Contra' scandal involved one of the most tangled webs of lies, half-truths and evasions ever to surround the White House. The Watergate scandal which brought down Nixon looked relatively straightforward since it did not start with a policy of defying the will of Congress.

Reagan had decided that aid should be given to Nicaraguan exiles seeking to overthrow the country's left-wing government, seen in Washington, at any rate by his advisers, as pure agents of Communism. The CIA organised and equipped a force of some 10,000 Nicaraguan 'freedom fighter' exiles in Honduras and Costa Rica. Congress, with the fiasco of Vietnam still in its mind, insisted in 1982 on a halt in this aid for a year. But the CIA continued it in secret. When this became apparent, Congress, as holder of the purse strings, demanded a halt. However, the CIA went ahead with a scheme for mining Nicaraguan harbours, despite warnings that this was illegal. Reagan also tried to sidestep Congress by soliciting funds for the Contras from the governments of Saudi Arabia, Brunei and from private individuals. He was also warned that this was illegal.

Most importantly the White House arranged a novel source of funds through Colonel Oliver North of the National Security Council. He arranged the sale of arms to Iran, still the great foe of the USA since the seizure of American hostages. In return Iran was supposed to help free US hostages held by terrorists

---

in the Lebanon. The help for Iran was the more paradoxical since Washington had also been sending aid to President Saddam of Iraq, no friend of Tehran. Israel cooperated as the conduit for the sale of missiles and other equipment to Iran. The scheme boiled down to one enemy of the USA, Iran, financing an insurgency against another enemy of the USA, Nicaragua.

The subsequent inquiry set up by an enraged Congress led to no fewer than fourteen individuals, mainly from the White House, being charged with, or pleading guilty to, serious offences ranging from perjury to withholding information from Congress. Among the senior figures were the Defense Secretary Caspar Weinberger and the National Security Adviser Robert McFarlane – who attempted suicide when due to take the stand. Reagan pardoned five of them as he left office. He never testified. However he had to say something publicly and this was to the committee he set up to study the work of the NSC. It was chaired by an old friend, Republican Senator John Tower. Reagan said he could not remember the specific decisions that were now being investigated.

This absence of mind was accepted, at any rate by Tower, but the senator said in producing his report: 'It is a chilling story of deceit and duplicity and the arrogant disregard of the rule of law. It is a story of how a great nation betrayed the principles which made it great.'[194]

Reagan and Gorbachev Summits

Rescue from domestic embarrassments was at hand for Reagan. The new Russian leadership wanted a summit. It also had its own problems at home. The war in Afghanistan was hugely unpopular. The Soviet role in the satellites was under pressure. Romania had set off on an independent role of its own. The Polish shipyard workers in Gdansk were leading a public revolt. Communist agriculture was, as usual, failing to provide. The absence of consumer goods was lamented everywhere. The arms burden was immense. The whole system was failing. Gorbachev advanced his new doctrine of *Glasnost* and *Perestroika* – openness and freedom – as his solution for both domestic and foreign problems. The two sides clearly had to talk at top level.

The first of three summits was held in Geneva in November 1985. This was in essence a preliminary to serious negotiations – talks about talks, as well as a chance for the two leaders to get acquainted. General positions were outlined on the crucial issues of arms reduction The aim on both sides was for cuts which would avoid giving one side or the other a superiority.

The start of the talks found Reagan clumsily undiplomatic. After opening with a lecture on the importance of human rights, he raised the issue – surely unnecessary at this stage – of the Soviet responsibility for the start of the Cold War. To which he added how he remembered that in the Second World War Moscow

---

194   Tower committee report

had refused even to allow US bombers to land and refuel in Soviet territory. This was untrue, though it was the case that negotiations for such a deal had been slow and acrimonious. This provided an insight into the President's mind.

Secretary of State George Shultz lamented: 'Sometimes President Reagan did not care much about the facts and the details. On occasions I would try to correct the inaccurate detail of a favourite story … He nodded in agreement and kept right on telling the same story.'[195]

Reagan also ignored a Gorbachev hint that he might withdraw from Afghanistan. He chose to allude to Afghanistan as just one of several ways that the Soviets were undermining peace. When he raised human rights for a second time, Gorbachev queried the right of Americans to lecture since these rights were being ignored in the USA. He instanced rights for blacks, the inequality for women and the levels of unemployment.

When they got down to the more serious issue of arms limitation, Gorbachev called for an end to the SDI project. Reagan became passionate about the scheme, insisting it could end the dangers of nuclear attack. The two exchanged stern words. At the end of which Gorbachev politely conceded that at least one need not doubt his opponent's sincerity (much as he was to question it later).

The conference ended with an anodyne press release. Shultz thought that serious progress had been made. The two men appeared to get on well. Precedents were being established for the mechanism of further summits – including discussions on a fifty per cent arms reduction plan and progress on an interim Intermediate-Range Nuclear Forces (INF) agreement. Also valued was the news blackout for two days which had left the participants free from outside pressures.

The Reykjavik summit in Iceland followed a year later. It allowed for more carefully detailed agendas on both sides. Meetings of officials in Moscow and Washington had clarified a number of arms control issues. At the same time, the Democrat-controlled House of Representatives was calling for less nuclear testing and challenging Reagan's decision to abandon Phase II of the Strategic Arms Limitation talks. The Russians' firm belief that SDI was a breach of the ABM Treaty was to be a constant bone of contention. But they accepted the American definition of strategic weapons, which equated missiles by their range rather than by their presumed targets. These apparent niceties were of great importance. Somehow, in any arms limitation agreement, some equation between long range bombers and missiles had to be achieved.

Once the talks got under way, it became clear that the Soviets were making many concessions – 'more movement from the Soviets than anyone had thought possible', according to Shultz, and without any concessions from the Americans. It looked promising. But the President proved immovable on SDI which had become his pet project. The Russians called for a ban on the testing in space of all space components

---

195   'Remembering Reagan', George Shultz, see http://reagan2020.us/remembering/shultz.asp

of anti-ballistic missiles defence – in accordance, they said, with the ABM Treaty. Meanwhile there should be a progressive elimination of strategic offensive arms on both sides over a ten-year period. Reagan would not budge on SDI.

Gorbachev summed up the problem:

> I am a convinced opponent of a situation where there is a winner and loser in our meeting. If that is the case, then after agreement and ratification the loser would take steps to undermine the agreement. So that cannot be the basis. There has to be equal footing. Otherwise you can say that the agreement is in keeping with the US position and I can't say it is in the interests of the USSR. So the documents should be ratified in the interests of both sides.[196]

Reagan would still not be moved. He took to quoting Marx and Lenin on the situation which caused Gorbachev some amusement. The summit broke up on missile issues and was widely deemed to have been a flop. Yet the Russians had made many concessions about arms talks, had even shown a readiness to keep the human rights issue on the table. Outer space was the big problem. But as observers kept pointing out, the two men seemed to get along.

In fact, Gorbachev had formed a low opinion of Reagan. It was spelt out at a gloomy Politburo meeting on his return. Success had been very close, he told his colleagues. But in Reagan he had encountered 'not only a class enemy but also such a representative of our class enemy who exhibited extreme primitivism, a caveman outlook and intellectually impotent'.[197] If the US thought that the Soviet Union was coming to the conference from weakness, they would soon realise otherwise, he insisted.

As for the specifics, he though it must be attractive to Europe that the Soviet Union proposed to destroy short-range nuclear weapons. This opportunity to exploit the differences in the alliance should be seized. Reactions in the US and throughout the world to the failure of Reykjavik were a help to the Soviet position. But the propaganda effort remained inadequate. Much had to be learnt there. In an emotive passage which underlined how his high hopes had been disappointed, Gorbachev told his colleague: 'Representatives of the American administration are people without conscience, without morals. Their line is one of pressure, deceit, of greedy mercantilism.'[198]

His colleagues were warm in their response. One referred to Reykjavik as 'ripping off the mask of the United States'. Another reported how the French Ambassador had acknowledged that the responsibility for the failure of the

---

196   CWIHP
197   CWIHP
198   Soviet archives source: The Volkogonov Collection, Library of Congress

summit lay with the Americans. Another complained how Reagan's broadcast after the meeting had involved an anti-Soviet attack.

But the Politburo agreed that further negotiations should still proceed. But next time, Soviet propaganda should match that of the Americans.[199]

Resentment at Reagan's intransigence at the Summit was compounded by a row over diplomatic expulsions which the Politburo discussed two weeks later. It had started after two arrests in August. The FBI had charged a Soviet spy and the Soviet Union had retaliated by arresting an American journalist, also for espionage. This was run of the mill stuff, though highly insensitive during such important negotiations. The dispute escalated in September with Washington expelling fifty-five Soviet diplomats on the familiar charge. It also ordered another 105 Soviet personnel from non-diplomatic posts to be sent home. The establishment in Soviet embassies and consulates was always large because the Russians did not trust locally recruited staff in humble positions such as drivers or cleaners or cooks. Moscow responded with a curb on locally recruited staff at the US embassy. It was a foolish episode, initiated by the US which seemed determined to show that its diplomatic missiles were the biggest. Soviet archives provide an intriguing guide to the Kremlin's mood in the wake of the failed summit.

> GORBACHEV: We need to exchange opinions concerning measures in connection with the new hostile action by the USA administration. The development of events after Reykjavik show that our 'friends' in the USA don't have any constructive programme and are doing everything to inflame the atmosphere. In addition they are acting very rudely and are behaving like bandits.
> SOLOMONTSEV: Yes they are acting like highway bandits.[200]

Gorbachev goes on to complain that US customs were delaying materials for publicising his speech at Reykjavik. He adds:

> Lately Reagan and his staff haven't found anything better to do than commit another hostile act – deport fifty-five Soviet diplomats … We cannot let this hostile action go unanswered. We should not exclude the most decisive measures. Americans are making threats and claiming that if we take retaliatory measures then they will take further steps towards our diplomatic personnel in the United States.[201]

Among Gorbachev's suggestions were a curb on US businessmen and those classified as visitors to the US Ambassador. Eduard Shevardnadze, the foreign

---

199   Volkogonov, op. cit.
200   CWIHP
201   CWIHP

minister, suggested that the US administration was driven by the need for a 'new aggressive action prior to the elections' (Congressional elections were then due).

'The inability of Reagan to handle his gang' was demonstrated by the post-Reykjavik events, suggests Gorbachev. Gromyko proposes that any announcements should be in a form which 'does not fence off Reagan himself'.

GORBACHEV: Yes, Reagan appears as a liar. The appropriate formulation should be devised.[202]

The 'appropriate' term used in a broadcast by Gorbachev was to speak of 'distortions' by the American administration.

Low as Gorbachev's opinions were of Reagan, negotiation had to go on. Moscow was feeling the pinch, politically and economically. Reagan was under pressure too – from Congress, now firmly Democrat controlled. There had been some progress in the summer on START (Strategic Arms Reduction Theory). And SDI was no longer a stumbling block for Gorbachev because his scientists were assuring him that the project was most unlikely to work. And somewhat along the lines of the CIA analysis made when the project was first mooted, they calculated that a retaliatory system to SDI would only cost 10 per cent of the costs of setting it up.[203]

In late 1987 Gorbachev travelled to Washington for the long-planned summit. Negotations were smooth, though the Russians made a considerable show of their reluctance to accept the US position on SDI. The INF Treaty was signed. There were still some grey areas, notably the interpretation of the ABM Treaty's conditions as they affected SDI. A limit on ballistic missiles was informally agreed after the Treaty signing. Gorbachev told Reagan that he would announce a withdrawal plan for Afghanistan if the Americans would stop supplying the Mujahidin. Each side should also stop supplying rivals in Nicaragua. These points were put into the hands of officials to work on.

The two leaders were in affable form, though Reagan at the subsequent joint press conference made a joke in bad taste about the Soviet system. The President related how a professor asked a young student what he proposed to do for a living and found he had not made up his mind. The same professor asked a Russian student what he proposed to do and got the reply, 'They haven't told me yet'. Gorbachev ignored it and confined himself to glorifying a day that would go down in history as a watershed for mankind. With the conference over and the world mesmerised by the event, Shultz set off for Brussels to tell NATO members what the US had agreed to – on their behalf. They had no complaints.

In 1988, in his last year as President, Reagan repaid with a visit to Moscow where he was warmly received though his decision to hold an embassy dinner for dissidents was regarded as highly tactless.

---

202   CWIHP
203   Richard Reeves, op. cit.

Events now moved at great speed in Russia. In 1989, Gorbachev announced the first nationwide free elections for the Presidency. Safely elected he announced a further programme of democratisation. In Berlin the hated wall was at last demolished. Two years later Gorbachev announced the dissolution of the Soviet Union.

The Cold War was finally over. Reagan was widely hailed as the man who had brought the Soviet Union to its knees. The Soviet Union was in fact dying on its feet, economically and politically. A major catalyst in the final stage was the Russian public's strong objection to the Afghan war and its death toll of some 12,000 in the conscript army. Credit for making the Kremlin's task even more hopeless in Afghanistan should go in the first instance to the Carter regime which initiated a policy of military and financial aid to the Afghans. It continued until the withdrawal of Russian troops after a decade of failure. There were lessons to be learnt from the doomed nature of the Soviet intervention but they were not learnt in Washington.

The wheel of history in Russia had turned. Public reaction to the incompetence and military posture of a despotism had produced the revolutions of 1917. With less bloodshed – but in some degree for the same reasons – popular opinion had now forced a change in the Kremlin. Communism was as discredited as Tsarism. Russia had its new revolution. It did not run smoothly but at least it offered hope.

CHAPTER 26
IN RETROSPECT

'The great enemy of the truth is very often not the lie – deliberate, contrived and dishonest – but the myth. Too often we hold to the clichés of our forebears. We subject all facts to a predetermined set of impressions. We enjoy the comfort of opinion without the discomfort of thought.' President Kennedy at Yale, 1962.

The Cold War, all too clearly, was as unnecessary on the part of the West as it was potentially fatal to mankind. It is also plain that its start was predominantly the fault of the Americans not the Soviets – though the latter remain, in most eyes, the villains of the piece. Since history is largely a series of myths, reiterated according to their acceptability, this view has been inadequately unchallenged, despite some impressive 'revisionist' history available in the USA itself.

The myth of Soviet blame remains readily, even eagerly, swallowed. The alternative is the disconcerting thought for the West that forty years of very high risk could have been were averted and that forty years of heavy expenditure was unnecessary. Pride in having 'won' the Cold War would have to be replaced by shame that it had ever been allowed to develop. It would also follow that the USA, the world's dominant power for over half a century, was incapable of intelligently pursuing the primary aim of foreign policy: peace. It implies something fundamentally wrong with the American approach to the rest of the world, that it is capable of seeing states which are not a real threat as enemies. Any state which is treated as an enemy is always liable to become one. American foreign policy is at least as likely to conjure up foes as it is to maintain friends.

The desire to police the world, where a superpower has the resources and the wisdom to do so, is no bad thing where the goal is no more than peace itself. But a highly moralised and moralising policy which seeks to impose particular types of government on other nations is doomed to provoke resentment and even hatred, especially where accompanied by a failure to appreciate the motivations and attitudes of other cultures. In the United States there is a sincere belief, which remains strong to this day, that the country owes it to the world to impose its own type of government and even its own type of economy on others. It may be a bully but it is a well-meaning bully.

The USA's periodical lapse into a so-called ethical foreign policy is guaranteed to provoke resentment without securing results. Foreign governments resent being told, with appropriate use of the media for maximum publicity, how they must have more regard to 'human rights'. Lecturing them will not lead to a major change in their ways, change though they may according to the circumstances of their own development. And those who are not greatly challenged in their own individual lives by the issue of, for example, political freedom, will resent their country being effectively labelled backward. An implication of racial superiority by the lecturing country is readily assumed.

To the average, law-abiding, hard working, famously hospitable American the resentment of the outside world he encounters when travelling abroad or which he discovers through the media is bewildering. He means the rest of the world well. He has contributed substantially through his taxes to any number of policies designed to assist, revive or defend other countries. Yet this seems to provoke a widespread unpopularity. As he sees it, the USA has saved the world three times – in two world wars and then in the Cold War. Yet the world shows no gratitude. He is not alone in feeling this, his leaders see matters in a similar light. Despite the fact that Americans pride themselves on being quick learners there is little if any inclination to rethink foreign policy. Mistakes are repeated. Previous errors are quickly forgotten. It is that 'charm' of the Americans referred to by Zhou Enlai of having no historical memory – or at least of being able to blot it out.

We have dealt with the reasons why the Cold War got under way. We have also to ponder why it was never called off. Opportunities existed. The weapons negotiations could have made much greater progress than they did. But suspicion had become ingrained. It was always liable to be assumed on both sides that any proposal by one party was driven not so much by the urge for peace as a desire to gain a weapons lead or a propaganda victory.

The most obvious moment for winding down the Cold War was the death of Stalin in 1953 and the peaceful gestures of Malenkov and his colleagues. This was chosen by Dulles as a moment of weakness in which to 'crowd the enemy'. The Secretary of State had become a crusader who wanted nothing less than surrender. To say he positively enjoyed the Cold War might be an exaggeration. But there is no question that the contest provided him with a sense of political and religious fulfilment and made him one of the world's most powerful men.

Much of this was owed to the economic hegemony of the USA. Did countries want loans? The USA had to be approached. Dulles final approval was always necessary. Did other countries want an assurance that if their currencies came under pressure then it was essential to keep on the right side of the Americans and the International Monetary Fund, itself dominated by Americans. Washington's power in this respect was exemplified by the Suez crisis and the threat to let the pound tumble unless Eden called of his ill-fated venture. Dulles had at his disposal a weapon even more powerful than Palmerston's gunboats.

Alongside the stimulant of power, there was the undeniable lure of fame and flattery to which no politician is immune and in which a crusader like Dulles would revel. Everywhere the Secretary of State went, the press would gather. Every editor wanted to know his views. All politicians wanted to meet the American Secretary of State, whether Dulles or his successors. It was rare that Dulles himself was subjected to seriously difficult or hostile questioning though Eden in 1955 dared to tell him in privately that his trouble was that he wanted World War Three. What Dulles wanted in fact was not war but for the 'crowded' enemy to admit defeat. This would have involved a withdrawal from Eastern Europe which was never on the cards, though he seemed to think it was.

The failure of Washington to respond to the Malenkov initiative had some unexpected longer-term results. The new Soviet leader did not last long, being replaced by the erratic Khrushchev who was to prove a greater danger than Stalin. It was supposed that the brutal dictator represented the worst that the West had to confront. But Stalin was very conservative and, much of the time, decidedly cautious. He would never have been as adventurous as Khrushchev in placing nuclear missiles in Cuba in his dangerous game of tit-for-tat.

The Quality of US Diplomacy

Dulles was rated an experienced diplomat, at any rate by American standards. Truman's Secretaries of State had been James Byrnes, who had been a judge, and George Marshall who had been a great soldier but was a novice in foreign affairs. The tradition of appointing outsiders – lawyers, bankers and particularly the military – to senior political posts in Washington persists to this day. Reagan chose General Alexander Haig as Secretary of State. George W. Bush selected General Colin Powell. The post of National Security Adviser, effectively a rival to the Secretary of State, was filled under President Ford by General Brent Scowcroft. Reagan chose Admiral Poindexter. Admiral Leahy of course had been a key figure under Roosevelt and then under Truman – himself so ill-informed about foreign affairs.

This pattern would be almost unthinkable in a European democracy. The essence of diplomacy is negotiation. Generals are more experienced in the task of subjugation. However admirable may be the qualities of military men, they are liable to be excessively conservative by nature and training. Two men provide some exceptions to the general rule: Generals Eisenhower and de Gaulle. The latter proved a wily politician and a radical president.

It was Eisenhower who underlined a vital reason why the Cold War was so difficult to call off: the military-industrial complex. Had that phrase and that warning been uttered by anyone on the Left it would have been seen as just part of a traditional phobia about 'vested interests'. From Eisenhower it was a very serious warning. The interest of the military in large military budgets (and more generals) was all too plain. If generals were appointed to top government posts, they would by instinct promote higher defence spending. And if they were recruited, as they regularly were, to lucrative positions in the defence industries, then the power of the complex was complete. This trend was to become even more marked after the end of the Cold War when it seemed at first as if defence budgets might be endangered.

The stakes were enormous, the fortunes made were vast. The money available for promoting the cause of the industrial complex was almost unlimited. And since the cause of national defence was being promoted, the extent of the Communist threat had to be promoted. Those of the right political persuasion who wanted to stress the Soviet menace in print or by any other means could always rely on the support of the complex. Insofar as there was any urge to call off the Cold War, it would always be countered by the pressures, direct and indirect from this machine. Some important figures in the State Department were to have their doubts about their former roles. Kennan regretted his Long Telegram. The once hawkish Acheson openly wondered if the doves may not have been right. Both were much better qualified in foreign affairs than those who came to dominate the department.

As for the novice quality of presidents themselves, there is a telling episode related by Theodore White in his *The Making of the President*, an account of the 1960 Kennedy campaign. On an aircraft flight, White described – more with admiration than concern – how Kennedy asked his campaign advisers what they thought about summit conferences, whether they actually helped, whether China had been 'lost' and if so by whom. It is hard to imagine a European politician on the verge of becoming the head of government asking his campaigning entourage such questions. He would already have decided views on these grave matters. They would have been part and parcel of his political life. He would no doubt discuss foreign policy with the very top advisers when he gained power. But these matters would not be strangers to his thinking. The fact that Kennedy at that point had been a Senator for thirteen years is significant. Despite this position, he had not got deeply into foreign affairs.

Robert McNamara's memoirs provide an insight into the amateurish nature of Washington appointments, including his own as Defense Secretary. He had previously been head of Ford, the motor giant, and was without any political experience whatsoever. The President asked him for his choice as Secretary for the Navy, suggesting a name himself. McNamara described the man as a playboy and unqualified. Kennedy pressed his case, observing that the individual had played an important role in his campaign to become the Democratic candidate. McNamara would not be moved. He learnt later that this important role involved spreading an unpleasant rumour about Kennedy's rival Hubert Humphrey.

American diplomacy also suffered from the powerful urge for publicity. The Kremlin could conduct its affairs without the urge to tell the Russian people what it was doing or why; and the military were kept severely in the background, unlike Washington. Sometimes a change of policy would be signalled by nothing more than a discreet paragraph in Pravda. This had the distinct advantage that changes could easily be made. In the USA foreign policy was conducted in the full glare of publicity, aptly termed megaphone diplomacy. If the government did not reveal its thinking in a press conference, there was always the certainty of leaks, both from those who wished a policy well and those who did not. There was always jockeying for media approval. Besides, there always seemed to be an election on hand, of not for the presidency, for Congress; if not for an election itself then for the run up to the nomination of the next presidential candidate.

While the need to carry national opinion is proper enough, diplomacy itself is particularly unsuited to extensive publicity. Once an attitude is struck it is hard to go back on it without the charge of weakness or indecision. Once a policy is adopted, abandoning it for whatever reason is liable to mean humiliation. This condition, though it is now growing in European countries, was never as serious an impediment to steady diplomatic negotiation as it was in the United States. The American position became even more serious if a policy was adopted, as it often was, to the accompaniment of high sounding moral justification. To go back, however sensible it might be, then sounded immoral. Thus it was that rigidity, thought to be a special fault of the Kremlin, was in fact a more serious problem with the USA.

Though the Cold War proffered so many lessons in foreign affairs there is little evidence that the United States learnt anything or indeed that its allies have learnt much. Americans remain in thrall to the myth that it 'won' a conflict started by the Soviet Union, an enemy of mankind, plotting the downfall of the West. The failure of imagination after the Cold War has been much the same as in its beginning. To understand a country like Russia which was obsessed by fears of invasion required a certain amount of vision. But Washington only observed the behaviour of the Soviet Union and not the motives behind it. A knowledge of Russian history or of the complex diplomacy of the interwar years and the fears it inevitably generated is not acquired overnight, least of all by a nation to whom invasion is a mere curiosity. On the other hand, a straightforward categorisation of countries as democratic or non-democratic, of rulers as enlightened or brutal, of economic systems as liberating or repressive – these had the attraction of simplicity and moral superiority. As was the grim reminder that the Soviet Union was avowedly atheistic, a persecutor of the church and thus a representative of the forces of darkness.

There was also the map of the world, which American leaders from Dulles to Reagan were fond of using in an absurdly simplistic way. 'Communism' could be shown to have taken over a huge area of the world. Further advances would be inevitable unless firm action was taken. It was the domino theory on a global scale. The fact that the two major Communist powers were bitter rivals was regularly dismissed as untrue or of no relevance. As for Eastern Europe, many Americans seemed to believe that the states there had been democratic before the arrival of the Russians. Only Czechoslovakia filled that bill. Hungary, Romania, Bulgaria – even Poland in the later 1930s – had little to show that was democratic. When it came to anti-Semitism, chosen so often as the litmus test for national shame, Poland and Hungary scored badly.

The West European nations, by and large, had a more sceptical and realistic view of the world. Britain, though still so anxious to preserve its 'special relationship' with the USA – in part a substitute for the decline of the British Empire – had the benefit of Eden's wiser and more experienced views about the tensions between East and West. But as the Cold War developed he too put great emphasis on the need for military preparedness. Once the possibility of a Soviet resort to force became a reality, he saw no alternative. France never bought the full USA-as-saviour-power package. At one point, NATO was told by President de Gaulle that it must remove the organisations headquarters from Paris. And American pressure for the European Defence Union, a merger of French and German armed forces, ran up against French hostility. De Gaulle feared that a close alliance with the USA would lead to entanglements harmful to French interests. Few would now dispute his foresight.

Vietnam provided what should have been the most obvious lesson. As McNamara emphasised, the great failure of the United States was that it confused nationalism with Communism. The Vietnamese people allied themselves with the Communist north – or at least were prepared to make their peace with it – because it was the only force that would rid the country of the foreigners. It was a presence which soon came to look like an outright invasion. South Vietnam was turned into an American satellite. When Washington decided that Ngo Dinh Diem was an unsatisfactory leader, it engineered the coup which replaced him, though not with any great gain.

The inability of the Americans to understand nationalism in others must always be a puzzle. Nationalism is a powerful sentiment in the USA, involving flag worship at all levels. But understanding has always been limited because the USA has never suffered the trauma of invasion. There has been no understanding of the passions that are provoked by the foreign invader or even the well-intended and helpful – and supposedly temporary – occupier. America has been invaded too little, Russia too much.

Insofar as any lessons from Vietnam were learnt in Washington, they were soon forgotten. The war had admittedly been a mistake. But it had been undertaken with the best of intentions. The idea was to save the Vietnamese. The blame for failure was sometimes placed on the military, sometimes on Washington politicians for failing to provide enough troops. The reluctance of the Vietnamese themselves to be saved was a puzzle. Perhaps, it was argued, the 'hearts and minds' policy had not been pursued strongly enough or early enough. But this programme missed the point that what stirred the Vietnamese was nationalism rather than political ideology.

Moreover the doctrine that the end justified the means had been taken a very long way, for instance, in the bombing of Cambodia and Laos as well as North Vietnam. The spectacle of millions being killed so that they, or at any rate, their countries could be 'saved' shocked the world and enraged Washington's own critics. Unkind historians searching for a parallel might well look back to the time when Stalin ruthlessly starved millions in the name of agricultural revolution and economic progress. They had to suffer to allow the system to work, he maintained to Churchill.

Yet the feeling lingered that the war could have been won if waged more skilfully; and that the sacrifice of so many civilians was due to a momentary lapse of commonsense and humanity. Thus it was that Washington continued to pursue an interventionist policy, despite its defeat in Vietnam. Americans still found it hard to believe that they were not welcome. In the longer history of the USA, it had swung from isolationism to intervention. It seemed unable to find a mid course.

There are echoes of the gross over-simplicities of the Cold War in the attitude of the USA to later problems in the Middle East. It should have learnt that it is dangerous to provoke the power of nationalism. When the force runs alongside religious fervour the risk is multiplied. If the Arab world, alongside its Muslim co-religionists, suffers decades of military defeat and humiliation, the dangers of serious conflict are inevitable. But again, as in the Cold War, efforts to understand the underlying grievances and motivation of an enemy and to appease it – dreaded word – are seen as displays of weakness unfitted to the American character. A knowledge of the grievances which derived nearly a century ago from the Palestine settlement following the First World War is very rare in America. This is not to say that an effective settlement was easily available. The British grappled with it between the wars and could not find a solution to the problem they had helped create. But at least the origins were ruefully understood.

Serious debate was also a casualty of the Cold War, despite the American conviction that it was a country almost uniquely devoted to free speech. Discussions was constantly stifled by the Manichaean approach. Minds were closed. Bad motives were constantly imputed. It was widely held throughout the conflict that those who criticised American policy and sympathised with the Russian position must be supporters in some degree of Communism. And correspondingly that true supporters of democratic values would naturally support the USA in its declared intention of implanting 'democratic' values worldwide.

The Soviet Union had indeed been a failure, economically, politically and socially. The regime was wickedly repressive. But it was a naive jump to conclude that the principles of Soviet foreign policy were necessarily wicked or even misguided; or indeed fundamentally different from the foreign policies of other countries for whom security must always be the primary consideration.

The formation of an entire Western alliance against 'Communism', involving most of the nations of Europe, seemed a natural development as tension rose during the early stages of the Cold War. Once formed of course, and with its requirement of high spending and the perpetuation of large conscript armies, it had to be constantly justified. Though no government in Europe quite followed Senator Vandenberg's advice to Truman to 'scare the hell' out of the public, warnings about the Soviet threat became commonplace and self-reinforcing. European analyses of the threat from the Soviet Union were readily quoted in the USA – and vice versa. Politicians, as in the 1930s, became prisoners of their own propaganda. With the danger from the Soviet Union apparently established, it was never difficult to reinforce fears by pointing to the repressive nature of the Soviet regime and its attendant horrors. And once more in an echo of the 1930s, Socialist governments were often anxious to show that they were not 'soft' on Communism. There was little effort for the most part to differentiate between the wickedness of Russian domestic policy and Russian foreign policy. The legacy of the 1930s and the Second World War suggested to susceptible minds that cruel dictators were naturally menacing to other nations and anything that smacked of 'appeasement' was morally wrong and politically naive. Beguiling parallels were always easy to draw between Hitler and Stalin. Which was the greater monster? Who was responsible for the most deaths?

Both Churchill and Eden fretted that they might be called appeasers when they reluctantly yielded to the Russian position in Poland, the reality being that they had no choice. *Realpolitik* was necessary but it was not the moral stance which Western politicians were keen to strike. The Second World War had been noisily characterised as a moral crusade. In this way, *realpolitik* could be stigmatised as immoral. Old fashioned diplomats might murmur that few causes are more important to mankind than the pursuit of peace, regardless of the nature of any regime. But that did not chime with the atmosphere of the Cold War.

On the Russian side, the legacy of the interwar years was always powerful. If the Americans had 'absolutely no political memory' the Russians had it in superabundance. Britain and France had not only sought to prevent the Bolshevik revolution, they had hoped to turn Hitler's ambitions eastwards. They had been prepared, apparently, to fight the Russians over Finland while lying doggo on the Western front. Such things were not forgotten. Russian memories are long. The USA itself can be acquitted of any attempt to turn Hitler eastwards. However the Americans' horror during the interwar years of what they called Socialism, let alone Communism, would not be ignored in the Kremlin.

It has long been a loose habit of Western commentators to argue that the Berlin blockade, the Korean war and even the Hungarian repression of 1956 'proved' that the Russians were primarily responsible for the Cold War. But to argue that from these events is like trying to locate the causes of the Second World War in the battle of El Alamein. The war was already on. Its causes could not be divined from the battles to which it led.

What would Russian policy have been in Eastern Europe if the Kremlin had not been Communist but democratic? Clearly it would have been determined, as Stalin was, to dominate Eastern Europe, the path of two horrific invasions – he said three, throwing in Poland. A democratic Russia would also have resisted the reunification of Germany. Some sort of democratic model might have been allowed in Eastern Europe. Perhaps some more benevolent version of the Warsaw Pact might have been formed. But Poland was an old enemy. Romania and Hungary had sided with Germany. Russia would probably have insisted on stationing large forces in these countries. The basic principle would be the same. The east European nations would be used as buffers between Russia and Germany. Attempts to break away from this obligation would not have been tolerated. Traditional pro-German sentiment in Hungary and Romania would have been sternly frowned on.

There is also little doubt that a democratic Russia would have wanted to develop atomic weapons, the ultimate deterrent to invasion. As we have seen since the fall of Communism, the USA and Russia have often been at odds. The attempt by the West to bring NATO up to the very borders of the newly democratic (and much smaller) Russian state is a reminder of how old suspicions linger, however foolish they may be shown to be in retrospect.

During the Cold War, ideology as opposed to mere rivalry was eagerly embraced by both sides. It was a while before this word crept into the American political vocabulary. Washington at first did not at first regard itself as a prey to such a thing. It merely stood for the democratic decencies of life – freedom, universal suffrage and the rule of law – which it wished for others. Ideology was the problem of the Soviets. They acted in accordance with the sacred texts of Marxism or Marxism–Leninism.

It was a wildly exaggerated view of course. There was nothing in these writings which advocated the ruthless elimination of internal rivals or mass murder. Yet Stalin was regarded as a sincere Marxist rather than, as he was, a tyrant who found his path to power through Marxism. But since Marxism proclaimed the world proletarian revolution, some people found little difficulty in believing that the Soviet Union wanted to take over the world. It was to find an echo in those who preached fear that Islam has set out on world conquest.

In terms of ideology, the USA was to prove as vigorous as the Marxists. A combined belief in democracy, 'freedom', Christianity and liberal capitalism proved a heady brew for American idealists. From Dulles to Reagan, the religious angle was constantly stressed. Marxism or at any rate Marxism–Leninism was berated for claiming that the end justified the means. But this became Washington's view of its own purpose. NSC-68 spelt it out clearly as did the Doolittle report produced for President Eisenhower. Its most potent application was in the use of the CIA for various, unscrupulous activities.

Later in the Cold War, 'human rights' became a rallying cry under President Carter. He declared that US foreign policy would be dictated by this cause. Many other countries, sadly, have taken up this naive ideal. It was always arguable that the CIA and by extension Washington showed little concern for these rights and was thus open to the charge of humbug. But hypocrisy is as a common enough feature of government. More dangerous in this case was that arraigning foreign governments on charges about human rights could destroy the very first purpose of foreign policy, the maintenance of peaceful relations, doubly important in a nuclear age.

At the end of the Second World War, each nation had its own version of its own unique contribution to victory. Britain had stood alone. Russia had simple numbers to quote: it had finished off over three quarters of the German army. The USA could rightly claim to have defeated Japan almost single-handedly. More than that it had provided the arms with which both Britain and the Russians were enabled to carry on the war. American casualties were relatively small and its mainland was untouched. Its sense of strength was overwhelming and its much enhanced economic power was unchallenged.

However much we analyse events of the Cold War, the motives behind particular courses of action and the attitudes they provoked, we keep coming back to very opening stages of the Cold War and the effect of the change from Roosevelt to Truman. Roosevelt may have often have been naive and clumsy. But at least he set out to understand the Soviet attitude. He had no difficulty understanding Churchill. Stalin was more of a puzzle; and he attempted to get close to the man, sometimes to the point of upsetting his British ally.

Truman was a very different matter. We know something of his attitude to Russia, though not much because he showed so little interest in foreign affairs. We do know his hope, as soon as Germany invaded Russia, that the USA would support whoever was losing in the hope that as many Nazis and Communists would be killed off as possible. It remains an unsolved puzzle that Truman showed so little interest in the Big Three meetings which involved Roosevelt, despite the decline in the president's health, so apparent to others. He was likely to have to shoulder the burden before long but did not think it necessary to keep up with these historic meetings. Curiosity alone, one would have thought, would have propelled him to find out more. Not only was he not interested in foreign affairs, he resented the time and trouble they demanded. Domestic issues had brought him into politics and that was the field he enjoyed. Abruptly finding himself in the White House he had immediately to find out about the major issues in foreign affairs. His attempt to learn was simple and unsophisticated. It did not involve any serious study. He simply invited the staff he took over from Roosevelt to brief him. It went no further than that. Molotov's rough treatment by Truman at the White House was just the first result. Truman did not look much further for advice. His comment that the Russians 'could go to hell' if they did not accept US views on the United Nations suggests that he did not think the Soviet Union mattered much in the post-war settlement. There is here some echo of President Wilson's earlier attitudes, before the USA was dragged into the First World War. He seemed to glory in ignorance in his memorable declaration that he was not concerned with the objects and causes of the war, or its 'obscure foundations'. It was an odd attitude in an academic figure.

If Truman found foreign affairs a distraction, that was no doubt partly due to the overwhelmingly strong position of the USA. Its much enhanced economic power was unchallenged. It alone had the A-bomb. It was the ultimate victor. Its leader expected recognition as the greatest power the world had ever seen. In its triumphal mood it was in no mood to be thwarted. To find Russia, economically so backward and the epitome of brute force, standing in its way was a serious irritant. Given the more aggressive line which set in when Truman succeeded Roosevelt, we have to ponder the role of personality in policy. The broad sweep historian lays his emphasis on the changes that occur as the creeds and ideologies of mankind make themselves felt on the policies their leaders pursue, both at home and abroad. These changes matter, of course. They can at times be irresistible and convulsive.

Yet we have also to consider the role of chance, as so often a key factor in national behaviour. There was a high element of chance in the fact that Truman became President. Henry Wallace had been Roosevelt's Vice President from 1940–44. The reason why he was ousted as Roosevelt's running mate in 1944 was that he had made enemies. He had written an article at a magazine's request on whether Fascism was possible in the United States. He saw that as possible though not in the sense that Germany or Mussolini had embraced it. The danger lay in the great power accumulated in few hands, notably the press barons of the day. This made him powerful –indeed mortal – enemies. At the Democratic Convention in 1944, his critics managed to have him replaced by the affable but not particularly distinguished Senator from Missouri. Wallace was Commerce Secretary after the Democrat's victory. It was not a position of any power.

His views about East–West relations were to gain him fame, or notoriety, in 1946. Observing the decline in relations with the Soviet Union he protested that the USA had no more right to interfere in the affairs of Eastern Europe than the Soviets and to interfere in the affairs of Latin America. And how would it look to Americans, the later asked, if Russia alone had the atom bomb and was establishing air bases within range of the USA. This was the speech for which Truman sacked him.

The world might have been very different if Roosevelt had lived or Wallace been his successor. These are among the spectacular 'ifs' of history.

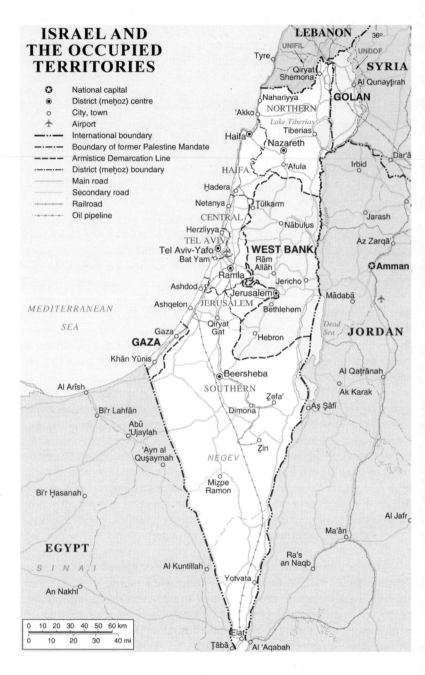

ISRAEL AND THE OCCUPIED TERRITORIES

✪	National capital
◉	District (mehoz) centre
○	City, town
✈	Airport
—··—··—	International boundary
—·—·—·—	Boundary of former Palestine Mandate
——————	Armistice Demarcation Line
—···—···—	District (mehoz) boundary
————	Main road
————	Secondary road
+—+—+	Railroad
•—•—•	Oil pipeline

LEBANON   36°
UNIFIL   UNDOF
Tyre
Qiryat   SYRIA
Shemona
Al Qunayţirah
Nahariyya   GOLAN
NORTHERN
'Akko
Lake Tiberias
Haifa   Tiberias
Nazareth
HAIFA   'Afula   Irbid   Dar'ā
Ḥadera
Netanya   Ṭūlkarm
CENTRAL   Jarash
Herzliyya   Nābulus
TEL AVIV   Az Zarqā'
Tel Aviv-Yafo   WEST BANK
Bat Yam   Rām   ✪Amman
Allāh
Ramla   Jericho
Ashdod   Jerusalem   Mādabā
Ashqelon   JERUSALEM
Bethlehem
MEDITERRANEAN   Qiryat   Dead   JORDAN
SEA   Gaza   Gat   Sea
GAZA   Hebron
Khān Yūnis
Al Qaṭrānah
Al Arīsh   Beersheba   Ak Karak
SOUTHERN   Zefa'
Bi'r Lahfān   Dimona   Aş Şāfī
Abū
'Ujaylah
'Ayn al   Zin
Quşaymah
NEGEV
Bi'r Ḥasanah   Mizpe   Al Jafr
Ramon
EGYPT   Ma'ān
SINAI   Ra's
an Naqb
An Nakhl   Al Kuntillah   Yotvata

0	10	20	30	40	50	60 km
0		10	20	30		40 mi

Elat
Ṭābā   Al 'Aqabah

Israel dominates its Arab neighbours

CHAPTER 27
MAINTAINING THE MILITARY MACHINE

US Cold War machine struggles for survival – intelligence maintains strength – finding a role in the Balkans – Saddam the perfect target – global bases remain – oil always a spur – military budgets survive

It would have been a bold spirit who dared to forecast at the end of the Cold War that the world was set for a prolonged period of dangerous instability. There were no longer two hostile superpowers dominating the world stage. There was no longer a fear of a global holocaust. There was no longer the menace of a slide into major conflict as the two major powers' proxies – in the Middle East, the far East, Africa and Latin America – confronted one another. What had been seen as the grand global struggle was over. The Americans, as they supposed, had defeated the Evil Empire whose adherents and supporters could no longer look to the Kremlin for ideological inspiration, military assistance or financial aid.

By rights, certainly according to the fundamental principles on which the Cold War had been fought, the end of the global struggle should have ushered in an era of peace. Massive spending on defence would no longer be necessary. The US bases surrounding the Soviet Union could be dismantled. The huge network of intelligence agencies expressly created to detect and counter Communist – or potentially Communist – infiltration in every continent was surplus to requirements.

The great machine, which represented the USA at its zenith of power, no longer had its grand strategic purpose or indeed its principal moral mission. The world no longer needed saving, except in the sense that it still had so much to learn, so it was supposed, from the American way of life and its institutions. Taxpayers, not surprisingly, looked forward to the peace dividend.

But great bureaucracies, whether military, civil, political or commercial, never take kindly to contraction, let alone disbandment. They believe in the inherent importance of their existence. They acquire the usual bureaucratic habit of pressing not just for their continuance but for expansion. In some instances – certainly in the case of Washington's Cold War machine – the staff had been trained for little else. Their laboriously acquired expertise, often at university level, was suddenly in danger of being deemed pointless.

However, it is never beyond the power of such machines to unearth cogent reasons for prolonging their life. There is always so much left to do. As seen in Washington after the Cold War, there were trade routes to be safeguarded, sources of raw materials needing to be watched, allies who might need the reassurance of a powerful US presence, aid to be distributed to the deserving. The agencies were determined not to become Cold War surplus.

And there were still some hot spots in the world. There was the constant problem of Israel and its hostile neighbours. Alongside this was the recurrent concern about Middle East oil. That needed to be safeguarded even though Russia could no longer threaten this supply – might indeed be seen as a reliable provider itself. China needed to be watched since it laid claim to Taiwan, traditionally Chinese territory. And it threatened to become a world power. India and Pakistan were regularly at loggerheads and might need American weight to be thrown on one side or the other. There might be brush fires involving as yet unidentified nations. There was no longer a Soviet threat to Latin America; but pressure on certain unfriendly regimes needed to be kept up. The region was inherently unstable. It needed constant American surveillance and guidance, it was argued.

Two conflicts proved life-savers to the Washington machine: the Balkans and Saddam's invasion of Kuwait. They could hardly compare with the threat of annihilation and the consequent need to maintain vast, global forces. But they would do. There were, as could hardly be prevented, cuts in the military budget. Taxpayer pressure saw to that. But the retrenchment was not large. By the end of the century – and before the Republicans under the second George Bush took power – the military budget had only been reduced by removing the increases on which Reagan had insisted. In real terms, allowing for inflation, expenditure on the military was by the year 2000 more or less the same as it had been in 1980 or even in 1965 when the Vietnam war was being waged.

So far as the intelligence services were concerned, there were some cuts since their predominant role had been to tackle actual or threatened Communist infiltration and the propaganda of Moscow. The reductions proved remarkably modest. The personnel employed by the CIA by the end of the century – and before the advent of the 'war on terror' – had fallen from a Cold War peak of 21,000 to around 16,000. The larger National Security Agency saw a fall of one fifth in its staff, down to 20,000 by the year 2000. The Defense Intelligence Agency survived the economisers' onslaught, marginally increasing its numbers from 7,000 to 8,000 during this period.

There were substantial dangers in maintaining large and regularly rival agencies of this sort – and the agencies were to grow under the George W. Bush presidency. This had the effect that the politicians could pick and choose between different assessments to suit their own book, This was particularly noticeable in the run-up to the second war with Iraq. Another danger was that if their purpose was to monitor threats, they had a vested interest in claiming to have detected them and of magnifying their potential importance where the evidence was slight. For example, warnings of what Saddam might do, rather than what he had done, figured significantly in analyses by the different agencies. He was said to 'wish' to equip himself with Weapons of Mass Destruction (WMDs), to be weighed against evidence that he no longer had any.

When it came to bases, it was as if the Cold War had never ended. Existing bases were maintained and with Bush's 'war on terror' the network was expanded. By the early years of his administration, the only countries which prevented a contiguous ring round the globe were Iran and Syria. And it was in the turbulent Middle East, with its deep-rooted problems, that the Americans found an unfortunate opportunity to demonstrate their military power.

In Europe, the State Department's strategy aimed at ensuring that Russia could never reassert itself as a major hostile force, or, better still, as even a major power. Washington went on a recruiting drive and by the end of the century the Czech Republic, Poland and Hungary had been wooed into NATO membership. In 2004, Estonia, Lithuania and Latvia were also adopted as NATO members. The alliance was marching steadily towards the Russian border which was itself an area of instability. The new states of Georgia and Ukraine were as keen to get out of Moscow's orbit as Moscow was to keep them in. NATO offered membership of the alliance to both Georgia and Ukraine. Both hesitated for fear of incurring Moscow's wrath.

At the end of 1995, NATO – which could be read as simply the USA – organised IFOR, the multinational implementation force operating under a UN mandate, to deal with a disorderly break-up of the former Yugoslavia. Its operations lasted eleven weeks and seemed to demonstrate that Russia and the US could cooperate militarily. However, the danger in the operation was graphically illustrated when the American overall commander gave an alarming order to General Sir Mike Jackson: it was to swiftly seize an important airport before it was taken over by the Russians – as had been already agreed. Jackson declined the order with the comment that he did not intend to 'start World War III'.

The Americans clearly regarded Russia as a successor enemy to the Soviet Union. The Americans were to conclude agreements with Poland and Romania for the establishment of missile sites and with Turkey to build a radar station. Moscow's protests were met by American assurances that these were needed by the ongoing dispute with Iran and its advance towards nuclear status. In the light of this serious danger, Moscow offered to integrate the Russian and NATO missile systems, a clear olive branch. The suggestion was immediately rejected.

A new Cold War with the Russians was being established. Relations between the two nations deteriorated. It was unsurprising that Moscow proved uncooperative in the United Nations. The US Secretary of State, the aggressive Hillary Clinton, kept up the tension by denouncing the Russian electoral system as corrupt during the 2012 presidential elections. Vladimir Putin, the hard man in Russia, was the target. However, Putin won by such a wide majority that surely victory would have been assured no matter how the voting system was rigged. The noisy and substantial protests during and after the election were, the Putin camp claimed, assisted by Washington.

PALESTINE - THE NEW 100 YEARS WAR

Conflicts in US policy - oil needs - the Balfour Declaration - Palestine in turmoil - Truman's backing for Israel - State Department's reservations - fuel for the Cold War - Israel's wars - refugees - the growth of anti-American terrorism

American policy in the Middle East from 1947 onwards was confused by two contradictory aims: the desire to ensure oil supplies and the determination to safeguard Israel. The pursuit of the second incurred enmity among Arab states which would otherwise have had no quarrel with the USA. This conflict of aims gave rise to accusations of duplicity and hypocrisy. It inevitably made it difficult for Washington to play a successful role as an honest broker in Palestine. Moreover, as the Arabs complained, the domestic pressures in the USA were all one way. President Truman observed that in 1947 he had been inundated with letters from hundreds of thousands supporting Zionism but could not find even thousands of Arabs as voters. The domestic pressure from the Jewish community in the USA has never diminished, at any rate from the staunch Zionists. Some of the sternest critics of both Israel and US policy towards it have in fact been Jews.

The Arab–Israeli conflict is nearly a century old. All the newly created Arab states after the First World War were opposed to the 'national home' for the Jews promised in the Balfour Declaration of 1917 with its carefully crafted ambiguities. They were to become bitterly hostile over the following decades. Britain had sought and been given the League of Nations mandate for Palestine at the peace talks in Paris. The Eastern Mediterranean was regarded by Britain as a vital link with India and other parts of its eastern empire. But Palestine proved a poisoned chalice. Britain had to rule a country where the vast majority were Arabs but where Jewish immigration was rising inexorably. There were also voices among the immigrants calling for an eventual Jewish state comparable to the Israel of Biblical times. The Jewish National Fund had ample money with which it bought land farmed by Arabs to help form the core of the new state.

The Balfour Declaration of the British government on behalf of a 'national home' for the Jews, with its likelihood of creating irresolvable disputes, has to be seen in context. Britain was fighting for its life. The war was going badly in 1917. The support of Jewish interests everywhere was sought, particularly in the USA. Though the Americans were in the war by then, it was plainly vital to keep up their resolve, to encourage electoral and financial support for Wilson and to ensure US support in whatever peace terms might be negotiated. Reports that Germany was itself making overtures to the Zionist movement, had made the Balfour letter a matter of urgency. Arthur Balfour, the British Foreign Secretary, declared in his letter to Lord Rothschild that the British government would use its best endeavours to achieve the Jewish national home – 'it being clearly understood that nothing shall be done which may prejudice the civil and religious rights' of the existing inhabitants. But given the ambitions, the energy and wealth of the Jewish people, it was plain enough that the local inhabitants were liable to be progressively displaced as the 'home' became crowded.

Britain was soon to face the consequences. In 1929, in the wake of steadily rising Jewish immigration and steadily rising Arab dissent, a dispute over access to the Wailing Wall led to riots in which over 200 Arabs and Jews died. In 1936 the Arabs proclaimed a general strike, demanding an end to immigration and a halt to the transfer of land to Jewish owners. But, by this time, the persecution of Jews in Germany was well under way. The obvious refuge of the United States was virtually closed by Washington's refusal to admit more than 5,000 Jews a year. The Jewish population of Palestine inevitably continued to rise, from 13 per cent in 1922 to 30 per cent in 1939. The regular outbreaks of violence only died down when the Second World War began as most Jews recognised that Britain was an ally in need. A hard core of terrorists remained active in the form of Irgun and the Stern Gang which assassinated Britain's Deputy Minister of State for the Middle East. The group's leader was Menachem Begin, who became Israel's Prime Minister in 1977.

Troubles multiplied after the war. In the wake of the Holocaust, large numbers of Jews were determined to enter an increasingly unstable Palestine though forbidden to do so by the British authorities. An ugly insurgency followed with frequent terrorist acts against the British forces trying to maintain the status quo. When Britain declared in 1947 that it would no longer operate the mandate, the USA took the lead in supporting the creation of the new state of Israel. President Truman was sternly warned by George Marshall at the State Department that this would endanger access to Arab oil, a view echoed by Forrestal at the Department of Defense. Marshall went so far as to send the President his resignation. It was with difficulty that Marshall was persuaded to withdraw it. Loy Henderson, in charge of Near Eastern Affairs in the State Department, argued that the decision violated the UN principles regarding self-determination. The recognition of the state would make many enemies in the region and, he suggested, it would require US troops to make any division of Palestine stick. No troops were sent.

Truman later wrote about the pressure on him to back the creation of Israel: 'The White House was subjected to a constant barrage. I do not think I ever had as much pressure and propaganda aimed at the White House. The persistence of a few of the extreme Zionist leaders – actuated by political motives and engaging in political threats – disturbed and annoyed me.'[204]

This has a certain air of innocence. Jews constituted a sizeable vote and could be decisive in New York state with its lead in the electoral college. They were usually Democrat supporters and they were also important in the party hierarchy. With Truman facing a presidential election in 1948, which looked like being tight, he needed little prompting to cultivate the Jewish cause and his rival, Thomas Dewey, was racing him on the issue of recognition. He needed the vote. The *New York Times*' Arthur Krock recorded in his memoirs that George Marshall sought his counsel. Truman wanted his Secretary of State to provide a public assurance that there was no security problem in recognising Israel. Did Krock, think the President was using him and his prestige for electoral gain? Krock thought he was. Marshall, thought so too.

Access to the world's most abundant and cheap oil had seemed assured at the end of the Second World War. The USA promised it would support the Saudi Arabian regime and the Saudis would guarantee the position of Aramco, the American giant which had the lucrative oil concession. The situation was not without its ironies since, while Truman was calling loudly for democracy in Eastern Europe, he was also supporting one of the most authoritarian regimes in the Middle East. This was also to be a later problem for Britain which, with some reservations, was supporting the American stand on Eastern Europe but soon found itself in trouble with a government in Iran which could actually lay some claims to popular choice.

The UN in November 1947, decreed that the land of Palestine should be divided by population but remain an economic union. The land was to be divided, with more than half going to the Jews, who made up less than half of the total population. The proportions were to be 55 per cent and 45 per cent. The UN was to take over the key areas of Jerusalem and Bethlehem.

A vicious civil war followed with atrocities on both sides. The Jews soon gained the upper hand, expelling large numbers of Arabs. In May 1948 the Jewish leader David Ben Gurion, declared the existence of the State of Israel, which was promptly recognised by the USA. The new state was immediately attacked by the forces of Egypt, Syria, Iraq, Jordan and Lebanon. In population the Israelis were clearly outnumbered. But they were fighting for their existence and with a huge proportion of the population under arms, the balance of strength lay with Israel. It soon turned the balance of weaponry in its own favour as arms poured in from abroad. The attackers also lacked coordination but the myth of gallant little Israel

---

as David vs Goliath gained considerable strength.

Israel emerged a clear victor after just over a year of warfare, now in control of 80 per cent of the original land of Palestine. The number of Arab refugees this created is much disputed. About 750,000 is a widely accepted figure. This was a grim portent of a great running sore throughout the Middle East. Israel complained that its actions were not the cause of these flights. They were encouraged by the attacking Arab states which issued lurid warnings about the brutality of the Israeli military, alongside assurance that those who had to flee would be returning to an Arab Palestine once the war had been won. But personal diary and official minutes make it clear that driving out the Arabs was Ben Gurion's policy.[205] After the Israeli victory, the enmity festered and the threats continued. The Americans gave constant economic and military assistance to Israel. The Arab nations turned increasingly to the Soviet bloc for support, fulfilling the fears originally expressed by Loy Henderson.

Warfare was to follow intermittently between Israel and various of her Arab neighbours. In 1956, the doomed Anglo-French response to the nationalisation by Egypt of the Suez Canal – an attack made in collusion with Israel – allowed the new state and its young army another victory. This conflict might have been avoided had not Dulles abandoned his promise to President Nasser to finance the enormous project of the Aswan High Dam. The nationalisation of the Canal – though it would have come about anyway at some point – was Nasser's swift response, alongside a request to the Soviet Union to finance the Dam to which Moscow agreed.

Though Israel occupied large swathes of Egyptian territory it subsequently withdrew under international pressure. The campaign had badly damaged the Egyptian army and demonstrated the superiority of the newly formed Israel Defence Force (IDF) despite its heavy dependence on reservists. No Arab state seemed likely to launch a major attack – not at any rate for some years – and not without the risk of a humiliating defeat. Nasser continued to threaten to destroy Israel but his words carried little weight. Border fights with Syria continued but they were intermittent clashes. They were sparked off by disputes over the water sources of the Sea of Galilee, important to Israeli agriculture together with the periodic assistance Syria gave to paramilitary groups crossing into Israeli territory.

The 1967 war, which massively increased the boundaries of Israeli control, has long been described as that country's pre-emptive war. In fact there seemed to be considerable elements of pre-emption on both sides, but with the Israelis getting in their pre-emption first. Relations with Egypt were tolerably peaceful. With Syria they were usually bad, occasionally involving serious border clashes. With Jordan – which had long been ready to establish some modus vivendi with Israel – relations had sharply deteriorated following an incident in late 1966 when three IDF soldiers were killed. Israel launched a major operation against an

---

205 *Israel's Wars* by Ahron Bregman, Routledge, 2000, pp. 21–22

area of Jordan containing many PLO (Palestine Liberation Organization) fighters. With between 3,000 and 4,000 troops deployed, plus armoured vehicles, the IDF achieved a swift victory, destroyed many buildings and put bands of refugees on the road. A counter-attack by Jordanian troops was easily defeated.

Washington wavered in its usually warm support for Israel. Walt Rostow at the State Department described the Israeli attack as 'disproportionate' – a term we shall hear many times – and a serious setback to the forces for peace in Jordan. King Hussein ordered mobilisation. The UN Security Council unanimously condemned Israel and warned that in the event of a repetition, it would have to consider 'further and more effective steps'. In May 1967, Hussein offered the American Ambassador in Amman his gloomy conclusion that long-range military and economic requirements would mean that an Israeli attempt to occupy the West Bank was inevitable.

The trigger for the war was provided by Moscow. In May, the speaker of the Egyptian parliament, Anwar Sadat, paid an official visit to Moscow and was told as he departed in an almost casual aside that Israel was concentrating ten brigades on the border of Syria. That country was then, along with Egypt part of the new United Arab Republic, though a union more theoretical than real. From then on, both sides prepared for battle. Nasser put two divisions into Sinai, sent away the UN peace-keeping force and closed the straits of Tiran, essential to the port of Eilat, Israel's only outlet to the Indian Ocean. The Israeli government decided it would act militarily if the Straits were not reopened.

What did the Soviet Union hope to gain from encouraging a war? The head of the Egyptian department of the Soviet Foreign Ministry has since explained that a war would show how the Arabs could fight provided they had the advantage of military and political support from Moscow. It also seems likely that what was in the mind of the Soviet government was the urge to maximise the USA's weakness. The Vietnam war was going very badly for the Americans.

But a mood of caution descended on the Kremlin as the tension grew. An Egyptian team went to Moscow, explaining its desire to launch an attack. It wanted assurances that it would get the necessary military material to replenish what would be used up in the war. The Russian Premier, Alexei Kosygin, proved unhelpful. Moscow would not support a pre-emptive strike. It would make Egypt the aggressor and 'we are against aggression'. Direct support would only be forthcoming if the Americans came in on Israel's side. But the USA had no intention of direct involvement. One Vietnam was enough.

It was the more curious that Nasser should have swiftly adopted such a bellicose mood. He could easily have ascertained through his own intelligence service – as perhaps he did – that there were no new forces massed against Syria. It seems likely that he was simply relying on the Arab side's apparent superiority to win the war. Syria and Jordan were both primed to join the battle. In the event, Israel struck with devastating effect. Nearly 300 Egyptian planes were destroyed in the first week. In six days Israel captured the Golan Heights from Syria, the

West Bank from Jordan and the Gaza Strip from Egypt, reaching the east bank of the Suez Canal. The state tripled in area, though much of the conquered territory was later handed back to its one and a half million Palestinians.

After the victory, Israel embarked on a policy of building civilian settlements on the West Bank and the more distant Gaza strip, seized from Egypt, but later abandoned to its inhabitants. The civilian settlements have always been illegal under International Law. But there has been no let-up in the process, a constant provocation in Israel's relations with Arab countries. Except for one moment under the first President Bush, whose patience had been tried too far, the Israeli government has continued to approve the building of one settlement after another. Little more than faint noises of disapproval have been heard from the White House. This steady expansion has also increased the power of the extreme parties in the Knesset. The inhabitants are their warmest supporters.

Matters were made worse by the mischievous chance that Israel adopted for its elections the single transferable vote system. It led to minority and extremist parties gaining the power to decide who would rule, coalitions being normal in Israeli politics. Washington could have stopped the settlement process but did not choose to do so, merely acknowledging that the process was unfortunate and undesirable. The settlements continued to be built under successive Israeli governments well into the Presidency of Barack Obama.

In October 1973, it was Egypt's turn to take Israel by surprise in the so-called Yom Kippur war. Anwar Sadat had succeeded as Egypt's leader on the death of Nasser. He was later to prove one of the most courageous forces for an Arab–Israeli peace settlement. But scores had to be settled first. Egyptian pride must be restored. The Arab world would not back any settlement unless it could be shown that it could fight on equal terms with Israel.

Seeking support from the USA in 1972, Sadat had expelled the 15,000 Soviet 'advisers' who were supporting and training the Egyptian forces. He wanted Washington to put pressure on Israel to withdraw from at least some of the territories it had won in 1967. But the Americans, in part of a persistent pattern, would not pressurise Israel. Sadat proceeded to reach an agreement with Syria to launch a limited war, to recover the territories lost by both countries – to show Israel its vulnerability. It was a parallel to the American policy of that time which believed that North Vietnam could be 'bombed to the conference table'. The missing country in this alliance was Jordan, hoping to recover the West Bank, wanting to keep Palestinian guerrillas out of its territory and reach a settlement with Israel. Indeed, King Hussein secretly warned Golda Meir, then Prime Minister, that an attack was to be expected.

Initially, the Egyptian-Syrian forces made substantial progress. But Israel, hastily mobilising all its reservists, swung the war the other way. It was another defeat for the Arabs, with considerable losses of men and material. Under intense international pressure, the two sides ended the conflict in October. Egypt argued for public consumption that the war had shown that Israel was not invincible, that it had been forced at the start of the war to retreat, that the Arab forces could fight the common enemy on terms of some sort of equality. In the Israeli political crisis which followed the war, Menachem Begin, the former terrorist, took over as Prime Minister. His record made the pursuit of a possible peace easier in practice – since no one was likely to accuse him of being soft on the Arabs. Sadat talked directly to Begin and signed a peace agreement in 1979, Israel agreeing to hand back Sinai.

It was, however, well before the Yom Kippur war that serious divisions had started to emerge between the USA and the European nations, principally Britain and France, about the Middle East. When Golda Meir visited London in 1970, she found the atmosphere unfriendly. UN resolution 242 called for the withdrawal of Israel from its territories 'conquered in recent conflicts' – i.e., not any conquests in the 1948 war. In exchange for this there should be recognition by the Arabs and for security within the boundaries which existed before 1967. Though the USA had formally agreed with Resolution 242, it declined to use its unique relationship with Israel to see the resolution implemented. When the Yom Kippur war broke out, the gap between the USA and its European allies grew larger. Britain, France and Germany refused the USA permission to use air bases in their countries or indeed to overfly their territories in supplying military aid to Israel.

Trouble was brewing from another quarter. The PLO in Jordan, led by Yasser Arafat, claimed a membership of 20,000. When King Hussein continued his campaign for a peaceful settlement by effectively recognising Israel, the PLO planned a coup. The Jordanian army went into action and expelled the PLO – most of which was accepted by Lebanon – in one of history's most rash displays of hospitality. The PLO sought to set up a state within a state periodically launching attacks on civilian sites in Northern Israel, though not heavy ones. The response of Israel, as we shall see, was a series of counter-attacks which culminated in the political disaster of the 1982 invasion and the briefer assault of 2006. In both cases the blow to Israel's international moral reputation was devastating and Washington's stand also took a battering.

There was another major problem, the price of oil – once seen as reliably low – had become an unexpectedly powerful weapon in the hands of Israel's neighbours. It started with the oil suppliers decision to create and enlarge the Organization of Petroleum Exporting Countries in the early 1960s.

CHAPTER 28
OIL BECOMES A POLITICAL WEAPON

Cheap energy – suppliers need buyers – the growth of OPEC – erratic prices – oil not in shortage – the military obsession – USA establishes the Strategic Petroleum Reserve

Abundant oil supplies are the lifeblood of the industrialised Western World. Two thirds of the oil which can be extracted at a reasonable price lies in the Middle East, the principal states being Saudi Arabia, Iraq, Iran, Kuwait and the United Arab Emirates. Other nations, like those of the former Soviet Union, have become oil and gas exporters. The figure for known reserves is the key – meaning fields from which oil can be profitably extracted, given the existing level of technology. This can mean that the level of 'known' reserves rises as the world price rises because geologically difficult fields become worth operating.

The need to maintain good relations with the producers is self-evident though it is equally self-evident that the suppliers need to sell anyway. Without ample oil there would be an economic crisis in the West. But without large and continuing sales, the oil states would face economic and thus political crises.

Clearly, it is always in the interests of the Middle East suppliers to get as high a price as possible for their sales. It is also clearly in the interests of the buyers to keep prices low. The only qualification for the pursuit of a high price by the producers is that they will not want to see a financial crisis among their customers such as would lead to a falling demand. This is the background to the creation of the Organization of Petroleum Exporting Countries, or OPEC. It is an interesting shadow of the cartel of oil companies, principally American, which tried and usually succeeded in keeping oil production down in the earlier years after the Second World War to ensure that the price did not drop too far.

The formation of OPEC in the early 1960s and the determination of those countries' governments to exploit their strength brought politics and, in particular, relations with the USA to the forefront. The OPEC members' aim was to sell less oil but at a significantly higher price in order to boost net revenues. There was always the problem that some member nations would cheat by producing and exporting to world markets more than the quota allotted to them after OPEC bargaining – and many of them did – but the economic and thus the political power of the organisation became formidable. A measure of this was the OPEC decision after the 1973 Middle East war to cut back production. Israel's triumph over Egypt and Syria had been possible because of US economic and military aid. The oil price, which had been as cheap as $2 a barrel – and even $1.20 at one stage – rocketed. At the same time, OPEC declared an embargo on sales to the USA (and to the Netherlands which had allowed its airfields to be used by American supply planes during the conflict.) Though the embargo was soon lifted, oil went to $11 a barrel and an alarmed USA imposed petrol rationing, a lower speed limit on cars and froze the selling price of its own producers – though it allowed an increase for any newly discovered oil. The world suffered an economic recession. There was also a genuine fear in the 1970s that oil was simply going to run out – which was entirely false.

Washington, sensibly, set up a Strategic Petroleum Reserve (SPR) from which supplies could be released in times of shortage. Other countries followed suit. The SPR could be enlarged when the oil price was low, allowing a possible release when the price rose.

In this way, provided the reserve was large enough, oil shocks could be avoided or at least mitigated. However it was some time before the USA built up stocks to a genuinely effective level. There was also a belief, certainly a hope, that OPEC might well prove ineffective in the end. New sources of oil were being discovered – for example in the North Sea by Britain. The technology for offshore drilling was being constantly improved. Differences of opinion within OPEC, plus the regular 'cheating' by member states, were liable to weaken the power to hold prices high for a substantial period.

However, a major boost to OPEC came from Iran in 1979 with the abrupt downfall and removal of the Shah, 'America's Policeman on the Gulf'. Washington could no longer rely on his help in curbing the zeal of other OPEC members. The immediate impact of the Iranian revolution was dramatic. Western oil personnel left hurriedly and the USA imposed a series of sanctions on Iran – never entirely lifted – to secure the release of American hostages seized by the Revolutionary Guard. Iranian exports tumbled, the world price soared to $40 a barrel. Saudi Arabia and Iraq stepped in to make up some of the losses, but using their extra power to demand higher royalties.

Over the years since OPEC was founded the price oscillated wildly but only partly due to the organisation itself. The price ranged from $40 in the early 1980s to between $10 and $20 in the latter years of that decade. The first Gulf War in which Kuwait was liberated from Iraq saw the price jump to over $30, leading to a release from the USA's SPR which brought it down again to $20. By the mid-1990s it was down to $15 rising to $23, then falling below $10 when a rise in world output coincided with two warm winters and an Asian economic crisis. Prices tripled in the eighteen months after January 1999 due to generally strong demand and adverse weather conditions in the USA, given an added push by another production cut agreed by OPEC members. A further fall in price took place when world demand fell but then took off again when Hurricane Ivan caused lasting damaged to the facilities in the Gulf of Mexico, a major source for the USA. Political disruption in Iraq and more tropical storms in the Gulf of Mexico led to a release of further supplies from the SPR to stabilise prices.

The oil world remains a complex mixture of politics, business and meteorology, plus technological advances in extraction and prospecting which can substantially alter the level of known reserves. From the political point of view, Saudi Arabia is vital. It is the oil superpower, not only sitting on by far the largest reserves of any country but also technically capable of increasing output reasonably swiftly. Fear of what might happen if the Western-friendly Saudi regime were to fall always worried Washington. CIA and CIA-trained operatives safeguard the Royal Family in Riyadh. But nobody thinks this is a sure-fire guarantee against a revolution.

The Longer Term

Fear has been a regular driver of the oil price. The West, principally, the USA worries about the instability of the governments in the supplying states, where anti-American feeling runs so strong. The fear is that the Arab states plus Iran will use their power to cause the West deliberate damage. This is possible though the prospect is limited. There is a natural stability built into the world's oil market through the anxiety of both sellers and buyers to do business with each other. Cutting supplies to the West can cause it an economic recession, perhaps a grave one. But failing to sell oil would reduce many of the suppliers to penury. They have nothing else to sell.

Forecasts that the world will soon run short of oil have been commonplace for some time. They have helped to bolster the popular belief among fearful American voters and among many Washington politicians that the USA must pursue an active and even aggressive policy in the Middle East to ensure that sources of oil are kept open and exploration pursued. The fear of looming shortage is not confined to the USA. The catastrophist school of thought has long enjoyed the belief that the world is running out of all sorts of commodities. In fact the world has massive known sources of oil with the certainty that many more will be opened up in the future. It is only the temporary disruption of existing supplies for whatever reason that are a proper cause for concern. For the long-term future, the newly developed process of 'fracking' – boring into rock and shale – promises a vast supply of gas.

American policy has been conspicuously unsuccessful in making oil supplies from the Middle East safe or cheap. The US role in the 1973 Arab–Israel war is one example. Another is the prolonged struggle with Iraq which has the second largest reserves in the Arab world after Saudi Arabia. Two wars with the US-led alliance, plus the period of sanctions in between, saw a halving of Iraqi output. In the normal course of events it would have been producing considerably more than before the first Gulf War.

The steady rise in the world price into the $60 range started at about the same time as the Second Gulf War though this was affected by various factors unrelated to Iraqi output. The 2003 invasion and the subsequent chaos in the country certainly added a risk premium to the world price. The steady rise, despite another release from the SPR, was due to various factors ranging from Mexican Gulf storms to attacks by militants on Nigerian oil installations.

The high and often volatile price served to convince the Americans that there had to be an active policy towards all the major oil producers, even if it was not very clear in the minds of Washington's leaders what exactly the form for that should be.[206]

---

206   For fuller background see Appendix

CHAPTER 29
THE SHAH OF IRAN: AMERICA'S POLICEMAN IN THE GULF

Iran's history as oil supplier – demands for better terms – Britain and USA oust Mossadegh – Shah helpful to West – Iran's revolution – rule by clerics – US hostages seized – the era of sanctions begins

Despite the grandeur of his full title – 'King of Kings' – the Shah of Iran was an upstart. The Pahlevi dynasty had only been established in 1925. Reza Shah was deposed by the Allies during the Second World War as a supporter of Germany. He was replaced by his 22-year-old son, Mohammed Reza Pahlevi who proved highly malleable. Britain and the Soviet Union had invaded Iran in 1941 to secure the country's oil and also to maintain a link for military supplies to Russia. The new Shah commanded little instinctive loyalty among the Iranian people and was widely resented as an American imposition. His other and less formal title – 'America's Policeman in the Gulf' – was what came to matter to the West but it also helped to undermine him at home.

Iran's oil production had been in the hands of the Anglo-Iranian Oil Company, later renamed British Petroleum, now BP. In the early days of the concession it had been easy for AIOC with the powerful backing of the British government to extract advantageous terms. In the 1950s, the British government was gaining more in company tax on BP's profits than the Tehran government was paid for the entire concession. The Russians, who eyed this oil source with envy, had been seen off in 1946 when they showed considerable reluctance to vacate the north west of Iran occupied with Allied agreement to facilitate Lend-Lease supplies. Russia's own internal supplies were suffering from the disruption of its own Baku oil fields during the war. The Soviets left Iran in 1946 after being granted a concession by Tehran which was swiftly withdrawn once the troops had gone.

The generous terms which the AIOC enjoyed clearly could not last and were to become a constant issue in Iranian politics. In 1951, the veteran politician Mohammed Mossadegh came to power, his position as Premier was approved by free votes in the Tehran parliament. After failing to secure the better terms he demanded, he announced the nationalisation of AIOC. In London there was alarm and even outrage, though since the then Labour government had been indulging in its own extensive programme of nationalising British industry, this attitude proved awkward to sustain. When Churchill returned to power in late 1951, London could make a more convincing stand. Mossadegh was branded a Communist, which he was not, though he inclined towards Russia as the lesser threat to Iranian interests. The CIA and British Intelligence set about the business of removing Mossadegh from power and reinstalling the Shah who had left the country. Funds and arms were smuggled in to Mossadegh's rivals.

The exercise was successfully completed in 1953 and the Shah regained his power. A better deal for Iran in the matter of oil revenue was conceded. The Americans demanded and obtained a substantial slice of the oil concession in return, having played a leading role in the coup and being seen as co-guardian of the continuing British interest.

The Shah remained in power for twenty-five years. He was, it might be argued, no worse than many of the world's other despots. And at least his regime was largely secular and he introduced land reforms as well as improving the lot of women. But his secret police, SAVAK, was notoriously brutal and all-pervasive. A report by the International Red Cross in 1977 was particularly damning. However, for Britain and the USA especially, the Shah had two advantages. He was a useful client who saw stability in the region as essential. He was also, unlike his neighbours, friendly to Israel, some of whose leaders were received in Tehran. There were even exchanges of information between the military in both countries. Not being an Arab nation, Iran did not feel so strongly about the loss of Arab lands, though as an Islamic state it proved fatally susceptible to the growth of religious militancy which later put it firmly into the anti-Israel camp.

The Shah's much-praised secularism was to play a major part in his downfall. He disregarded the strongly religious element in the country which increasingly resented his reforms. Opposition coalesced around the fundamentalist Ayatollahs who were harder to repress than other dissidents. The most effective of them was Ayatollah Ruhollah Khomeini who made repeated attacks on the government. He was arrested at one point but released, only to make more vigorous attacks, not least on a new law which allowed Americans charged with any crime to be tried only in their own country. The protests were now on a scale which threatened civil war. The Ayatollah was exiled to Turkey. Later he moved to Iraq but kept up his barrage of criticism. Under pressure from Tehran, he was ordered out, settling in a Paris suburb which became the centre of Iranian dissidence.

When the Shah left Iran in 1979 amid widespread unrest, ostensibly for medical treatment, Khomeini returned to an ecstatic welcome. The monarchy ended and the rule of the clerics began. A mob, mainly of students, attacked the US Embassy and seventy hostages were seized. More than fifty of them were kept in captivity for over 400 days. President Carter attempted his dramatic military rescue using helicopters and special forces but in the face of a sandstorm. Eight servicemen were lost. The failure of the mission, which was personally controlled by Carter from the White House at every stage, undoubtedly helped Reagan to power in the subsequent election. The hostages were eventually released after a freeze on Iranian assets abroad was lifted.

Now began three decades of US-Iranian hostility. Sanctions of one sort of another remained in place. The power of Tehran as a supporter of the extremist Hezbollah in Lebanon offered scope for bargaining, or so it seemed, in the grim business of kidnapping Westerners in Beirut. But if it was not clear how far Tehran's could control Hezbollah, neither was if clear at times who was the government in Iran. The armed Revolutionary Guard which emerged from the instigators of the 1979 coup owed little loyalty to anyone but the Ayatollah. He also had to approve candidates for political office.

But Washington was determined to exact a price for its humiliation. The opportunity was to be seized later when war broke out between Iraq and Iran.

REFUGEES: TRAGEDY AND MENACE

The steady rise in refugee numbers – the effect on recipient countries – American attempts to secure peace settlements – negotiation failures – a breakthrough by Begin and Sadat – the murder of Sadat

Overshadowing all efforts for peace in the Middle East and relentlessly stimulating Islamic militancy has been the sixty-year-old problem of Arab refugees. The scale has only to be stated to see the massive problems facing the search for settlement. Palestinian refugee numbers grew from some 750,000 in 1950 to over four million by 2002 with another two million fleeing Iraq after the invasion of 2003 – to say nothing of the 'internal refugees' in that country who moved to different homes and towns in an effort to escape the violence. The definition used by the UN in reaching the figure for Palestinian refugees is not straightforward. Such a refugee is a person whose normal place of residence was Palestine between June 1946 and May 1948 who lost both home and means of livelihood as a result of the 1948 Arab–Israeli conflict plus their descendants regardless of whether they reside in areas designated as 'refugee camps' or in established permanent communities. The camps themselves are generally poorly built settlements but with schooling and basic medical care provided by UN funds.

A further complication of the definition of refugees is that the UN term excludes those who leave for countries other than Jordan, Lebanon, Syria, the West

Bank or the Gaza strip. The inclusion of 'descendants' is inevitably controversial. And the definition did not include the three-quarters of a million or so Jews who fled from Arab countries in the Middle East and North Africa during the decade after 1948. The scale of this movement led to some claims that what had really taken place was really 'a population exchange'. The most notable of the Arab leaders who used this more peaceful formula was the Iraqi Prime Minister, Nuri es-Said, murdered in a military coup.

The original exodus involved about two-thirds of the Arab population of Palestine. There is a later self-excoriating description of the event by the former Israeli Foreign Minister, Shlomo Ben-Ami, who was in office briefly, appointed in late 2000 and only lasting into early 2001, when he refused to serve the militant Premier Ariel Sharon:

> The reality on the ground was that of an Arab community in a state of terror facing a ruthless Israeli army whose path to victory was paved not only by the exploits against the regular Arab armies but also by the intimidation and at times atrocities and massacres perpetrated against the civilian Arab community.[207]

The fears were multiplied by the propaganda of the Arab states warning of impending horrors. There were also those assurances from Arab sources that when the war was brought to a successful conclusion, the refugees would be able to return to a country from which Israel would have been expelled and on whose territory they could exercise old claims. To flee was in certain cases extolled as a patriotic duty, leaving the invading armies to fight against Israel with few territorial impediments. Israel passed a law to prevent the refugees returning, despite which it is estimated that tens of thousands did so.

Every war between Israel and its neighbours led to more displacements and the ugly growth of the camps. The treatment of refugees varied from country to country. Jordan was a model of hospitality, with the ready grant of citizenship, offered until the activities of the Palestine Liberation Organization (PLO) led to outright warfare. Half a million settled in Saudi Arabia but were rarely allowed to become citizens. Lebanon refused them the right to own property or work in certain professions.

To many in the West, it seemed a simple case of Arabs extending or failing to extend a reasonable welcome to fellow Arabs. But that failed to understand the complexity of Arab society with its extensive tribal, religious and sectarian differences. Moreover, few countries readily extend a warm welcome to great numbers of refugees of uncertain loyalties or lacking a close identity with their hosts. Alongside these difficulties was the utilisation of refugees as a political weapon.

---

207   http://www.democracynow.org/2006/6/28/fmr_israeli_foreign_minister_shlomo_ben

Israel had legally barred refugees from returning because their sheer numbers would overwhelm the Jewish state. The Arab governments campaigned for their return precisely because this would be the result. Maintaining Palestinian refugees as an ethnic entity was seen as an essential part of this policy. In 1957, the Arab League instructed member states not to allow citizenship to Palestinian Arabs since that would diminish and even destroy the exiles chance to overwhelm Israel once they returned. Granting citizenship, in the words of the League's grim message, would be 'an act of treason'.

This moved Ralph Galloway, the former director of UNRWA to complain: 'The Arab states do not want to solve the refugee problem. They want to keep it open as a running sore, as an affront to the United Nations and as a weapon against Israel. Arab leaders do not give a damn whether Arab refugees live or die.'[208]

The Arab attitude was a boon to Israel's sympathisers in the West. Here was an example of the inhumanity of the Arab states and their leaders. Who could be surprised that Israel's call for peace and the recognition of its right to exist could find no solution. The plight of the refugees was recognised in a searing comment from Khalid al-Azm, six times Prime Minister of Syria until ousted in 1963. He wrote ten years later:

> Since 1948 it is we who demanded the return of the refugees, while it is we who made them leave. We brought disaster on Arab refugees by inviting them and bringing pressure to bear upon them to leave. We have rendered them dispossessed. We have accustomed them to begging. We have participated in lowering their moral and social level.[209]

He added that these refugees had been exploited in encouraging them to commit crimes against Israel or murder, arson and bombing – 'all this in the service of political purposes'.

The problem of numbering the refugees ran alongside the problem of the lost territories. The Arabs who found themselves under Israeli rule were not defined as refugees though they were often displaced by security measures imposed by the IDF and by the establishment of Israeli settlements. Both were factors in the recruitment of militants. The USA hoped for an Israel at peace with its neighbours and made regular efforts to achieve it. The initiatives came one after another. Ralph Bunche, an American diplomat seconded to the UN, negotiated the armistice after the 1948 war. President Eisenhower made two proposals – sensibly in secret – in which Israel would trade some of its less attractive territories for a peace treaty with its neighbours. Neither side would agree to this.

President Kennedy tried a variation of the Eisenhower proposals but again without success. After the 1967 Six Day War, President Johnson backed the

---

208   http://www.freerepublic.com/focus/news/817157/posts
209   http://www.eretzyisroel.org

scheme embodied in UN Resolution 242 calling for the return of territories which had been occupied by Israel and a recognition of established states. It meant that the Arab states would have to recognise Israel. They refused. But in any case, Israel was very reluctant to give up its conquests.

There was however the memorable breakthrough in 1977 by President Sadat who changed the entire pattern by travelling to Israel to expound his plan before the Knesset. Talks at Camp David, presided over by President Carter in 1978 led to a peace settlement in 1979 between Sadat and Begin. The two men appeared together on the White House lawn. Israel agreed to the formal return of Sinai to Egypt which had been the first piece of territory that any Arab state had regained (in the 1973 war). It looked as if real peace was at hand. But Sadat was to be murdered by extremists in 1981. Despite this, Egypt remained at the forefront of Arab attempts to secure a settlement. But other tensions on Israel's borders threatened attempts to find peace. Overshadowing the hope for a long-term peaceful solution was the conflict in neighbouring Lebanon involving several factions within the country.

CHAPTER 30
THE LEBANESE COCKPIT

Lebanon's role in the Cold War – increasing conflicts with refugees – as base for guerrillas – civil war – Israel's intervention – US pressure for settlement – refugee camp massacre – civil war – Syrian involvement – Israel withdraws

Once seen as an oasis of calm, Lebanon became a savage battleground between Israelis and Arabs. The country, carved out of a resentful Syria at Versailles at the request of France, was split between (Maronite) Christians and (mainly Shia) Arabs. They lived in a reasonable but fragile equilibrium until the establishment of Israel and the arrival of 100,000 Arab refugees. The number was later to rise to around 400,000. This was driven by the 1967 war and Jordan's expulsion of its own Palestinian refugees when Arafat's PLO plotted to overthrow King Hussein.

The USA's first plunge into the complex politics of Lebanon came in 1957 under the so-called Eisenhower Doctrine, though it was chiefly driven by Dulles and written in familiarly simplistic language. The doctrine was enunciated following the Hungarian uprising and its repression. But it also included warnings about the Middle East: Russian interest in the Middle East, said the President, was for 'her announced purpose of Communising the world'. He had hoped that with the death of Stalin matters would improve. 'But we have just seen the subjugation of Hungary by naked armed force.' International Communism wanted a recognisable success for its overall strategy. This had to be countered.

Hence the USA would help any nation threatened by armed aggression from any country 'controlled by International Communism'. He had Egypt and Syria in mind, hard as it was to see these two countries as other than more friendly to Russia than America. Their support for an Arab uprising in Lebanon against the Maronite President Camille Chamoun was sufficient evidence for the USA to despatch a force of 15,000 marines to support the existing government. The insurgents stepped back and the troops were soon withdrawn. There had not been a single US casualty. Washington leapt as so often to the misleading conclusion that a show of force could secure American interests at little or no cost.

The 1960s were a period of relative peace for Lebanon, with Beirut resuming its reputation as the Paris of the Middle East with tourist and commercial trades flourishing. This lasted until the 1967 war stirred Arab nationalism as well as producing a further flood of refugees. At their head, the PLO used areas it controlled for occasional guerrilla attacks on Israel. Newly formed militant groups also murdered Israelis overseas and attacked Israeli airliners which drew retaliatory attacks on Beirut airport itself. The Lebanese government was warned that it must control the PLO. In an increasingly unstable country a peace was patched up in which the PLO recognised Lebanon's own sovereignty but with the Lebanese government recognising PLO authority within the refugee camps. There remained a sense of festering outrage in the Christian Maronite community.

By the mid-1970s, the country was plunged into open civil war. Syria intervened with the backing of Washington. Damascus's policy towards Lebanon during the subsequent thirty years or so caused considerable confusion. Syria was opposed to the existence of Israel and in particular to the continued occupation of the Golan Heights. On the other hand it had an interest in peace on its own borders. And while it would help militant groups, it did not want them to get out of hand and draw in external intervention.

Israel invaded Lebanon in 1976 to support the newly formed but unofficial South Lebanon Army and again in 1978 in response to further attacks from the PLO which culminated in two bus bombs, killing thirty-seven passengers. The Israeli aim was to clear out PLO bases in South Lebanon. But the operation had very limited success. The United Nations passed a resolution calling for a withdrawal. The Israelis agreed to depart but left a security zone controlled by the SLA. The United Nations despatched the force which was to oversee the withdrawal.

However, the rising incidence of clashes between Syria and increasingly militant Christian factions, notably the Phalange, led to Israel supplying the latter with arms and support. As the violence set in, President Reagan called a senior US diplomat out of retirement as a mediator. Philip Habib, supported by the Saudi government, secured what seemed a reasonable enough settlement in 1981 though incidents still occurred.

It was the decision by Begin, re-elected Prime Minister in 1981, to appoint the former military hero Ariel Sharon as defence minister which set off a disastrous chain of events. Sharon and the army chiefs plotted an attack which would, as they saw it, eliminate the PLO and its infrastructure in West Beirut, in particular the ability of the Palestinians to shell northern Israel. It would at the same time drive out the Syrians whose anti-aircraft missile system in the Bekaa valley was eyed with concern. It was hoped that the defeat of the PLO would lead to the choice of a pro-Israeli government in Lebanon. A probable bonus would be that Arafat, after his defeat, would lose his standing in the West Bank.

The planning for this campaign began in mid-1981, shortly after Habib's ceasefire had come into force. The plan, Operation Oranim, was presented to the Cabinet which demurred precisely because it could drag in the Syrians – Sharon and the military chiefs' hope and the civilians' fear. Even Begin was uneasy about this danger. Sharon played it down.

The IDF (Israel Defence Force) was supposed to take control of Beirut within four days. The plan was secretly discussed with representatives of the various Christian militias. When, in February, a group of terrorists infiltrated into Israel from Jordan, the Chief of Staff sought authorisation for air strikes against the PLO in Lebanon and to move the army up to the Lebanese border. Washington made a firm protest and the moves were abandoned.

Keeping the Americans Onside

It was essential, as ever, for Israel to secure approval from Washington for its major actions. The USA was not only Israel's chief political ally, it was also a provider. Between 1949 and 1997, it was estimated economic and military aid came to $113bn. This was despite Israel being among the top twenty nations when measured by income per head.[210]

Given the flow of aid, whichever party was in power in the US, any ambitious military plan had to be cleared with Washington. Sharon as defence minister did not share with all his Cabinet colleagues the size of the onslaught he was planning. He held talks about the outline of his plan with the American Ambassador and Habib in Tel-Aviv. He was furiously rebuked by Habib who insisted that the scale of PLO activity, relative to Israel's responses, was too modest to justify any invasion. The plan was postponed.

But when an Israeli officer was killed by a landmine in South Lebanon, the Israeli Air Force struck back, killing twenty-three. The PLO's response was to shell the areas around Israeli settlements but not the settlements themselves. The implication was plain enough. The Palestinians were not looking for a major conflict. Indeed Arafat sent a message to Begin through a UN intermediary saying, with a hint of flattery, that he, Begin, would know better than anybody that guerrillas could not be defeated on a battlefield. He should not try it.

In May a frustrated Sharon flew to Washington to try again for US support. At the State Department he confronted Secretary of State General Alexander Haig. The US reaction was ambiguous. Haig knew only too well Reagan's strong pro-Israeli feelings. He recorded that after the talks, which alarmed officials, he decided to see Sharon alone.

---

210   Stephen Zunes of San Francisco University also calculated that Israel received $1.5bn from tax-deductible contributions from private citizens through charity-listed bodies. The proportion spent on arms was described by Matti Peled, a former Israeli general, as 'little more than an American subsidy to US arms manufacturers' – see http://www.jewishvoiceforpeace.org.

I told him privately in the plainest possible language, what I had repeated to him and Begin and their colleagues many times before: unless there was an internationally recognised provocation, and unless Israeli retaliation was proportionate to any such provocation, an attack by Israel into Lebanon would have a devastating effect in the US.[211]

But this was hardly the plainest possible language. Terms like 'internationally recognised provocation' and 'proportionate response' were dangerously vague. Then, in June, the Israeli Ambassador to Britain was shot, though not killed. The fact that the gunman was from Abu Nidal, a group opposed to the PLO, was not allowed to stand in the way of Begin and Sharon, whose army chiefs were now straining at the leash. The Israeli Air Force attacked nine PLO centres. When Israeli and Syrian planes clashed – conveniently for Sharon's personal strategy – all out attacks on the latter's positions were launched. The Syrian Air Force was devastated with no Israeli losses. Damascus sued for a ceasefire after four days.

But the attacks on the PLO continued. Begin declared publicly that this was a limited operation, limited to pushing back Israel's northern border by forty kilometres to prevent terrorist shelling. This geographical limit was exceeded almost at once. The army's high command – which had always planned to move much further – set about the siege of Beirut, first cutting off the road to Damascus. A brief truce was achieved one week after the assault through American mediation. But Sharon was soon declaring that Israel could have no truce with terrorists and the siege of the capital resumed with 400 tanks arrayed against the defenders who, from their alliance with Syria, could themselves muster 100 Russian tanks within its considerable defences. As Begin and Sharon knew, the war was bound was bound to be prolonged and bloody. Their talk in Washington about a four-day operation had been deliberately misleading.

The main Israeli force closed in on West Beirut, causing countless civilian casualties by direct bombardment and others by cutting off the water and power supplies. The PLO fought back from underground bunkers. The scale of the devastation in the city and the attacks on the refugee camps, all so plainly portrayed on television, shocked the world. The US government declared itself deeply shocked. Nevertheless, the USA vetoed a UN resolution calling for sanctions against Israel if the IDF did not withdraw. This was just the first of six resolutions critical of Israel's invasion of Lebanon which the USA vetoed. When Begin flew to Washington to see the US President, the reception was frosty. Hostilities had to be ended quickly, ran the American message. The invasion was causing a serious deterioration in American influence on the Arab world. But Begin dug his heels in. The US press had little difficulty interpreting the meeting: the President, whatever his reservations, was 'backing Israel'.

---

211   Bregman, op. cit., pp. 157–158

The fighting continued, the devastation grew worse, civilian casualties mounted. It was a curious episode which finally stirred Reagan into meaningful action. Pleas for a firmer line with Israel came from George Shultz (who had replaced Haig as Secretary of State after a Washington turf war), from King Fahd of Saudi Arabia, Habib and William Clark the National Security Adviser. Yet the key figure turned out to be Michael Deaver, the PR man. He had been the burnisher of the President's image for twenty years and one of the most powerful figures in the White House inner circle. In August, after a fourteen-hour and particularly savage bombardment of Beirut, Deaver told Reagan he intended to resign. The US could halt this carnage. 'All you have to do is tell Begin you want it stopped.'

The President recoiled at the prospect of the resignation. He called Begin and warned him that 'our entire future relationship' was at stake. Begin called off the attack. Reagan told Deaver: 'I didn't know I had that kind of power.' Displays of genial innocence were one of Reagan's tactics. He knew perfectly well that his power to influence Israel was overwhelming. It was only necessary to follow the money.

American aid to Israel, predominantly military, had risen in the previous decade from $481m a year to $2,268m. Nor was dissatisfaction with Israeli policy to curb this massive inflow. By the end of the century, the level of this aid was up by 50 per cent – alongside fifteen further vetoes of US Security Council resolutions criticising Israel. Thereafter the purely economic assistance so obviously unnecessary, was to tail off but not the all-important military support.

On 19 August, the Israelis and the PLO accepted a plan from Habib for the PLO to leave Lebanon under UN protection. Some 10,000 with their dependants would disperse and resettle in Syria, Jordan, Iraq, Tunisia and South Yemen. The American contribution to the UN's Multi-National Force (MNF) was to be 800 marines who were quickly despatched. Other contributors to the MNF included France and Italy.

'In no case will our troops stay longer than thirty days,' the President declared. It was now time for Reagan to launch the Middle East peace plan which had been nurtured in the State Department. It turned on Israel giving up the greater if not the whole part of the lands occupied in 1967. Begin's cheeky response was to announce that he was increasing the size of Israeli settlements in the occupied lands, their populations to rise to 34,000 without delay and with plans for 100,000 by 1987 – and eventually to hit some 500,000. These moves were condemned in a joint magazine article by former Presidents Carter and Ford who described the settlements policy of the Israeli government as one of the chief obstacles to peace in the region. No doubt it was but it continued.

The MNF left having fulfilled its mandate of securing the planned PLO departure.

But further horrors were to come. Bashir Gemayel, as arranged in talks between him, Begin and Sharon, had been elected President by the predominantly Christian

Lebanese parliament. He was assassinated in a massive bomb blast within days. The IDF was ordered back into West Beirut. The US President was not inclined to exercise that power he claimed he did not know he had. This time he was justifying Israel's policy as being a reaction to 'Leftist militias'. The State Department pointed out, unhelpfully for the chief, that no one had fired on the IDF itself.

The Israelis swiftly established total control of Beirut and, crucially, surrounded the refugee camps of Sabra and Shatila. The Israeli Cabinet gave permission to the IDF to enter the two camps and search for any of the PLO which were still hiding there. What took place was not a search but a massacre by Phalangist militias – eager to settle old scores and deliberately let loose by the IDF which even supplied transport to the camps. For three days, they rampaged through the two camps, killing men, women and children. The number of deaths was put at nearly 2,000 in an official Lebanese government report. Other estimates ranged from 600 to 3,500.

The feelings of outrage and shock not only ran through the outside world, but through Israel itself. There had been angry mass protests since July. Now 400,000 demonstrators gathered in Tel Aviv to demand the heads of Begin and Sharon. The government's response was to set up a commission of inquiry. The American response to the massacre was led by Reagan who declared that 'all people of decency must share our outrage and revulsion.' Distancing himself from the Israeli government, he insisted that Washington had in fact strongly opposed Israel's move into West Beirut, which was highly questionable.

The new Lebanese President, Amin Gemayal, brother of the assassinated President, called on both Israel and Syria to withdraw their forces and called for the MNF to return to the country. It did and for the first time there were some clashes, though minor, between Americans and the IDF which withdrew but in no great haste. In February 1983 the commission reported. It condemned Sharon directly and Begin indirectly. The defence minister had made a 'grave mistake' in ignoring the likelihood of bloodshed and acts of revenge 'when he decided to move the Phalangists into the camps'. The commission effectively called for Sharon's resignation. He resigned as defence minister but was allowed to remain in the Cabinet as a minister without portfolio.

Arab hostility to Israel was now entering a new and increasingly dangerous phase. The PLO had been defeated but various of the Shia militant groups were coalescing into the more extreme group Hezbollah, 'the party of God'. The movement gained assistance from Tehran in the form of men and money. Syria backed it too, mainly with money. In the large areas which it came to control it also set up schools and hospitals – to prove fatal targets in a yet another Israel invasion, much later. Hezbollah also gained international notoriety and the familiar 'oxygen' of publicity by kidnapping Europeans as hostages.

In late 1982, Israel withdrew once more from all but a security zone and a UN peace-keeping force was sent in including American and French contingents. At first the Americans sent in 800 troops. Then they raised the number by a further 1,000. There was little if any hope that the Americans would be seen as neutral peacekeepers. Anti-American feeling in the region had become pervasive. The Americans supplied arms to Israel who were in turn suppliers to the Lebanese Christian (Maronite) forces. The USA had also sought to demonstrate its sheer power through the use of a battleship to bombard certain hostile positions still holding out against the truce.

It had an impact on Arab opinion but not the one desired. Driving a lorry packed with explosives into the American camp, a suicide bomber killed 241 American marines. The French suffered fifty-eight deaths in a further suicide bombing. Both countries withdrew their troops. The prestige of the militants surged and that of the Americans tumbled. The lesson had some parallels with Vietnam. A determined local enemy relying on terror tactics is very hard to defeat whatever the firepower or size of an American force. Shultz drew the conclusion that the Defense Department was at fault because it had not supplied enough marines or with a clear enough mandate to fight. It is doubtful in practice if an enlarged force would have meant any more than the provision of more targets. A vastly increased force in Vietnam had been criticised along Shultz's line as too little too late. The later problems in Iraq were also to be blamed on an inadequate military presence – the easiest of excuses.

The Lebanese army was now in a state of collapse and fighting continued from 1985–1989 in a conflict which the outside world found too complex to understand. The country became divided between a Christian government in East Beirut and a Muslim government in West Beirut. In 1989, the Christians launched an attack on Syrian forces. In the 1990s the Syrians, supported by the USA, counter-attacked and sent the then controversial Prime Minister into exile.

The civil war sputtered to an end, with Syria recognised for its role in bringing about a ceasefire. In 1991, all militias were disarmed except, ominously, Hezbollah, which was seen as the only force that could fight to regain the quarter of the country occupied by Israel. In the late 1990s the newly reconstructed government took action against Sunni extremists in the North, as they formed a particularly violent group with links with al Qaeda. The disarming of militias – except Hezbollah – went on as the Lebanese army was rebuilt but assassinations and violence persisted.

Peace of a sort seemed to beckon when parliamentary elections were held for the first time in twenty years. But Syria remained a problem. The presence of its armed forces had been legitimised by the Lebanese parliament and the Arab League. Damascus had also been given credit for ending the civil war. Damascus and Beirut justified the presence of these forces because the regular army was as yet too weak to deal with internal and external tension. Both had agreed that Hezbollah would eventually be dismantled and Syrian forces would leave.

But Syria was in no hurry to go. It still had some 15,000 troops in the country. Israel withdrew in 2000 but Syria stayed with Shia support. The Maronites called for withdrawal. In 2005, the UN in resolution 1583 called on the Lebanese government to extend and exercise its authority. In the same year, a series of mass demonstrations and counter-demonstrations were staged by Hezbollah supporters and its opponents, the latter mustering by far the largest number, on the issue of the Syrian presence. On this occasion Sunnis were united with the Maronites.

The Arab league set a date for Syrian withdrawal. In 2005 they left. But over the previous decade, Hezbollah had become a formidable force both militarily and politically. With its allies it gained some 20 per cent of the seats in the Lebanese parliament. They had been strengthened by Israel's actions.

Mossad, Israel's famously powerful secret service, was also to feel around this time the eventual consequences of a clumsy attempt at assassination. When it came to tracking down and despatching the country's most militant enemies, Mossad had a remarkable record. It seemed able to strike anywhere. And its relations with the Americans through the CIA were close.

In 1997, in a move authorised by the then Israeli Prime Minister Benyamin Netanhayu, it attempted to murder Khalid Bashir in Jordan. He was a senior figure in Hamas which, at that time, was very much a lesser force than Fatah, part of the bitterly strained coalition of groups under the Palestine Liberation Organization whose leadership was actively looking for a peace settlement with Israel.

The details of this attempt read like a James Bond novel. [212]

Three agents travelled to Aman, posing as Canadian tourists, and sprayed Bashir's ear with a fatal poison. He was to survive in the end but only after a spectacular confrontation between Jordan and Israel which threatened to derail all attempts at a peace settlement.

King Hussein, one of the most remarkable of all Arab leaders, had managed to balance his small country between Arab extremism and Israel with great skill. Israel was allowed an embassy in Aman. But hardline Arab activists were also allowed to live in the country, notably Bashir.

An attempt to murder him on Jordanian soil outraged the Jordanian government – and Washington too which could hardly believe that anything so diplomatically dangerous would be tried by Mossad, least of all with Netanyahu's sanction. The King made fierce demands. The Israelis must provide the secret antidote for the dying Bashir. Netanyahu and the hated defence minister, Ariel Sharon, were forced to make secret trips to Amman to face the furious monarch in an effort to scale down his demands for visible compensation. President Clinton, who saw the prospects of any peace settlement recede, backed the King. This time the American intervention was wise. But it had also involved an element of

212 *Kill Khalid* by Paul McGeough, Quartet Books, 2009

humiliation since Hamas had earlier been declared a terrorist organisation by the President and its bank accounts frozen.

The price Israel paid was the release from prison of the elderly and crippled Sheikh Ahmad Yassin together with a group of both Fatah and Hamas fighters. Later hundreds of Hamas members held by Fatah as prisoners in Gaza were also set free. There was to follow a prolonged civil war between Fatah and Hamas, which the latter won.

In 2006 it went on to win 74 of the 132 seats in the West Bank and Gaza elections. Washington, despite all the Bush rhetoric about the need for democracy in the Middle East, had threatened to end its aid package if anyone from Hamas secured a ministry in the West Bank administration. As so often with Washington's threats, they strengthened rather than weakened its opponents. In the event, no ministry was granted but the rule of Gaza and the West Bank became separated because of Hamas's support in the strip. The lesson from Lebanon appeared to be stubbornly resisted in a later episode when Israel launched its 2006 month-long invasion. The lesson was there but apparently not understood by either Israel or Washington.

CHAPTER 31
SADDAM: FROM AMERICAN ALLY TO 'MOST WANTED'

Iraq and Iran go to war – Saddam favoured by Washington – chemical warfare – a war to exhaustion – invasion of Kuwait unwittingly helped by US – First Gulf War – a swift victory – sanctions on Iraq

During the prolonged Lebanon conflict, a great deal more blood was being spilt by a war between Iran and Iraq, leading eventually to the two Gulf Wars and the ousting of Saddam Hussein. Washington's policy towards Iraq over the medium and long term could hardly have been more inconsistent – or more duplicitous, according to one's standpoint. In 1980, the USA was smarting badly from its humiliation at the hands of a vengeful Iran. When war broke out between Iraq and Iran ostensibly over a long-standing border dispute, Washington did not hesitate to side with Saddam, the principal instigator. This was despite Iraq being on a list drawn up by the Carter White House of countries that supported terrorism (against Israel). Since Iran was also on that list, perhaps it was felt that one cancelled out the other.

The Iranian armed forces, once so generously supplied by the USA, were in a sorry condition. Many of its senior officers had been removed. Maintenance of aircraft and tanks, dependent on US-made components, was poor. Iraq's military equipment had come mainly from China and Russia and the Krelim remained a helpful source since they wanted to divert Tehran's support for the Afghans resisting the 1979 Soviet invasion. Later the Russians changed sides as Communism crumbled. Ironically, the Americans were to sell some weapons to Iran in the late stages of the conflict but this was never a properly authorised policy. It was part of the illegal deal backed by President Reagan, or at any rate his staff, to provide illicit funds to assist the pro-American Contras in Nicaragua – without the authorisation of Congress.

When Iranian fanaticism proved too much for the Iraqis who had expected a relatively easy victory, Reagan stepped up the programme of US aid to Baghdad.

In 1982, policy was set in a secret National Security Directive of June 1982. This stated that though the USA was officially neutral, it would do everything it could to prevent Iraq losing the war. Direct arms sales would have needed Congressional authorisation. But items with a military potential could be supplied under other headings. The direct sale of helicopters was allowed on the grounds that they were for 'crop dusting'. Other items came through transfers of weapons from some Arab countries who were promised replacements from the USA.

Most notoriously, there was a supply of the ingredients for chemical weapons which were used in poison gas attacks by Saddam after military reverses in 1982; and were to be used later against rebellious Iraqis. This excited international indignation but the White House was not deterred. At the end of 1983, Reagan sent a personal emissary to Baghdad to assure Saddam of his continuing support, which was followed by later-celebrated pictures of high-level handshakes with the Iraqi dictator. The man chosen was a former Defense Secretary from President Ford's brief regime – Donald Rumsfeld, subsequently the leading hawk for the 2003 invasion of Iraq. He later insisted under media questioning that in this embarrassing episode the talk had been about the Lebanon – a claim challenged under oath by one of the authors of the National Security Decision Directives (NSDD).[213]

The Reagan administration approved the shipment to Iraq on seventy occasions of various cultures which act as precursors to such chemical weapons as botulism and anthrax. There were also exports from the US of items which assisted in the development of Iraq's SCUD missiles. When the Senate sought to pass a resolution for sanctions on Iraq following its use of poison gas, Reagan intervened to prevent it. Iraq was also allowed a loan guarantee under a further NSDD directive. The USA succeeded in preventing what it feared, an Iranian victory. But its involvement in providing important weapons to Iran under the illegal Iran-Contra deal as well as material to Iraq remains a truly remarkable case of double dealing.

A UN-backed peace initiative eventually brought about a ceasefire in 1988, by which time both combatants were exhausted. It had been a bloody war and is thought to have cost one and a half million lives all told. Saddam, for whom the war had been so expensive, now began to eye the small but immensely rich territory of Kuwait. It had once been part of Iraq. There at any rate he would face no great military challenge. He had a dispute with the state's rulers about its level of oil production, believed to exceed its OPEC quota. He also alleged more seriously that the Kuwaitis were extracting oil from a field which ran under Iraqi territory.

But could he rely on the USA not intervening? Of course it would protest, as was required by the standard diplomatic decencies. But would it do any more than that? Saddam consulted the US Ambassador to Baghdad, April Glaspie. Her

---

213   Teicher affidavit of 1/31/95, US District Court, Southern District of Florida

comments were remarkable. She asked for an explanation for the concentration of troops near the Kuwait border, given the hostile remarks which Baghdad was making about that state. '[We] ask you in the spirit of friendship, not confrontation, regarding your intentions.' She went on: 'We have no opinion on Arab–Arab conflicts, like your border disagreement with Kuwait.' She had been in the US Embassy in Kuwait during the late 1960s, she pointed out. The instruction then was 'that we should express no opinion on this issue … James Baker [Secretary of State] has directed our official spokesman to emphasis this instruction.' She added that it was the US hope that any problem could be solved through the Arab League or through Egypt's President Mubarak.

She went on with the fatal words: 'All that we hope is that these issues are solved quickly.'[214]

All too plainly, a solution through the assistance of the notoriously slow mechanism of the Arab League was most unlikely to bring a rapid result, only protracted discussions. There was only one genuinely 'quick' solution, apart from abandoning the dispute: invasion. Saddam went ahead and swiftly occupied Kuwait.

Both Glaspie and Baker had blundered. It was no doubt true that Baker did not want the USA to get involved in disputes between Arab states. There were twenty members of the Arab League, including North African nations, often in disagreement. Any attempt to arbitrate or throw US support on one party or another could be a diplomatic nightmare. But what was unsaid in Baker's comment, so literally interpreted by Glaspie, was that if a vital ally were at risk then it must be a wholly different matter. There could be no question of Washington standing aside. And there was no more vital ally than Saudi Arabia, shocked by the invasion and the increasing proximity of Saddam that this entailed.

The Saudis had assumed that the USA, as Iraq's ally, would not allow Saddam to invade Kuwait. The USA now found itself called on not just by Saudi Arabia but by the smaller Arab states in the Gulf to force Iraq's retreat. Besides which there was the general sense of outrage in the international community at large. Within a few days the UN imposed economic sanctions. When they had made no impression, the Security Council authorised the use of force. This provided the Americans with a welcome chance to show the Middle East and everyone else what the military power of the USA could achieve, even at a vast distance. Iraq was sure to be defeated. The war was legal given the UN sanction. Swift and effective military action could go some way to atone for the humiliation of Vietnam. Operation Desert Storm was launched. The US-led force, which included a considerable Saudi contingent as well as traditional European allies, drove the invaders out of Kuwait. Iraq suffered huge losses, though not before it had fired some forty SCUD missiles at Israel with little effect. In the ceasefire

---

214 For the text of the Glaspie messages see the Bush Library and the Margaret Thatcher Foundation.

terms, Saddam agreed to abandon any claims to Kuwait, to accept responsibility for the immense damage that had been caused and, crucially, to get rid of his Weapons of Mass Destruction – both chemical and bacteriological.

Sanctions Fail to Unseat Saddam

The USA reaped benefits in the Middle East from the First Gulf War in terms of its military reputation and its readiness to assist an invaded Arab state. But increasing doubts about the sense and humanity of American policy set in when Washington led a policy of sanctions to remove Saddam. It would have been easy for the coalition force to drive on into Baghdad after its triumph in the First Gulf War. However, this would have counted as regime change in contravention of the UN charter – though it was later to become an openly declared policy under President Clinton, who arrived in office in 1993. A final drive in 1991 was unnecessary in any case, according to a crucial analysis by the CIA. Soon after the victory it gave an assurance that Saddam was so weakened that his toppling by some rival was sure to follow swiftly.

The agency had underrated him and misunderstood the power a military despot can wield. He was to stay in power for over a decade. There now began a prolonged cat-and-mouse game between the US (leading the sanctions) and Baghdad (determined to obstruct the UN-authorised WMD inspection process). The pressure on Iraq was intensified by a no-fly zone policed by the Americans with assistance from Britain and France and intended to provide safe havens for Kurds in the north who had revolted against Baghdad. France later withdrew, doubting the legality of the operation. The Russians expressed similar doubts. So far as the Kurds were concerned, and to some extent rebellious Shias in the south, this appeared at first to be helpful. Later the Shias complained that they were being encouraged to rise up against Saddam but were denied help which would prevent Saddam's ground forces from repressing any signs of revolt.

The American belief, provided by Washington's intelligence services, was that Saddam would never allow the WMD inspections and thus, regardless of whether he retained any such weapons, an excuse for finishing the job would be provided. The sanctions, which could have serious humanitarian implications, would not be needed for too long. This proved another miscalculation. The protracted Iraqi resistance to the intrusion of the inspectors derived from pride, resentment, a typical reluctance of an authoritarian regime to allow foreign scrutiny and a growing suspicion that the USA was using the process to spy on Iraq's conventional military resources. This last suspicion proved all too well founded.

Scott Ritter, a US Marine officer, was a senior inspector who had been involved in weapons investigations in the former Soviet Union as part of the scrutiny under the Intermediate Nuclear Forces Treaty. He was tiresomely honest and was to prove a thorn in the side of Washington where the CIA and the State Department had their own agendas for ousting Saddam. After the Iraq war of 2003, he produced his candid memoir *Iraq Confidential – the Untold Story of America's Intelligence Conspiracy* in which he wrote of 'the USA … manipulating, suppressing and undermining … the inspection process in support of a different agenda – regime change'.[215]

The oddity of this entire process was that the Iraqis had in fact done what was asked of them. They were systematically disarming their WMD capability from 1991 onwards. Soon there was nothing substantial remaining, only US claims that it was an Iraqi 'desire' to restart the programmes one day. The periodic obstruction of inspections was, on the face of it, extremely foolish. But they were part of a still unsettled conflict in which the Americans periodically attacked Iraqi air missile sites and radar bases and at one point the intelligence HQ in Baghdad. That was in retaliation for an alleged plot to assassinate President Bush when visiting Kuwait. Saddam was to tell an interrogator after the war that he allowed an impression to survive that he *might* have WMDs to convince Iran that it dare not attack Iraq.

A significant moment came in 1998, as the usual protracted negotiations to inspect particular sites was proceeding. The Iraqis were being obstructive but the inspectors thought they were achieving a breakthrough. Washington became alarmed rather than pleased. It wanted a fight. It even had provisional dates set for a bombing campaign. When Ritter became aware of the plan and protested, Madeleine Albright, Secretary of State, tried to have him removed from the UN inspection team. His protesting deputies refused to provide an alternative.

Despite the team gaining admission to the Ministry of Defence in Baghdad, the jewel in the crown for the inspectors – and finding nothing – the USA declared that the inspection process had been hopelessly obstructed. It embarked with British support on Operation Desert Fox. In the four-day bombing offensive approximately 100 targets were attacked. They were said by Washington to include WMD sites, Baghdad's military command and control system and the Republican Guard intelligence headquarters. It was subsequently concluded by the US Chiefs of Staff that 1,400 Iraq troops had been killed.

The domestic and foreign reaction was not as supportive as Washington had hoped for. France, Russia and China called for the ending of the sanctions programme and also for the removal of Richard Butler as the head of UNSCOM, who had been so compliant with Washington's principal aims. Republican critics of President Clinton suggested there should be hearings about the timing of Desert Fox. The military operation conveniently diverted media attention from the impeachment proceedings then being conducted against Clinton, following his testimony in the Monica Lewinsky (sex) affair. The same issue of timing was raised in Britain by Sir Edward Heath, the former Conservative Prime Minister. 'The whole setting is so dubious, especially as the President of the United States has his own domestic problems.' The aim of Desert Fox was 'not clear'. Unless, it

---

might be added, that the purpose was simply to weaken Saddam's forces. Which the attack certainly did.

It was accepted in the UN Security Council that sanctions had lasted longer than expected and caused more widespread distress than predicted. There was an embargo on all items other than medical supplies or food or other items of humanitarian necessity. The stated aim was to force Saddam to cooperate with UN inspectors. Also, according to the CIA, the sanctions would definitely hasten Saddam's replacement by some as yet unidentified rival. In the event, the protracted inspection process meant that sanctions lasted until the next US-led invasion in 2003. The long-term humanitarian consequences were grave and a gift to propagandists in the Arab world. The position was well put by Denis Halliday, who became UN coordinator of a revised and 'improved' Security Council programme allowing oil sales in return for food. He resigned in 1998 with the comment that the sanctions programme 'probably strengthens the existing leadership and further weakens the people of the country'.

The scale of the suffering has always been difficult to assess with accuracy. Halliday himself spoke of '4,000 to 5,000 children dying unnecessarily' each month. There had been a breakdown in water supplies, sanitation and power, partly through lack of maintenance and components and partly because they had been bombed in the war itself. Only medical supplies and food were allowed where they were deemed for 'relief'. The suffering was exacerbated because many items were barred since they might have a dual use: pesticides, computer equipment and at one point ambulances unless they were stripped of their normal communications equipment. UNICEF put the number of child deaths as a result of sanctions at possibly as high as 500,000.

Washington seemed strangely unmoved. Madeleine Albright was interviewed on TV. What was her reaction to those who claimed that more children had died as a result of sanctions than in Hiroshima? Her answer was memorable: 'I think this is a very hard choice but the price … we think the price is worth it.' The White House press spokesman, Marlin Fitzwalter was also blunt, sanctions would remain 'until there is a change of government in Iraq'.

The failure of the sanctions programme to unseat Saddam should not have come as a surprise. The Iraqi elite was largely insulated from the sufferings of the general population. As Halliday claimed, the governors were unaffected and the governed were weakened. In any case, Saddam's strength and obstinacy was in large part due to being a Sunni in a country where, though they formed a minority of the population, had long wielded most of the power. The majority were Shias and the religious differences were fierce. The American approach, with UK support, was singularly short-sighted. Washington seemed unable to shake off the idea that a leader who lacked popular backing and who impoverished his people was bound to fall. There is little in history to support such a notion. It is nursery politics.

The propaganda consequences were menacing. The USA and its supporters were condemned, and not just in the Arab or Islamic world, as inhumane –

and hypocritical too given the high moral tone that constantly emanated from Washington, whichever party was in power.

SEARCHES FOR AN ARAB-ISRAEL SETTLEMENT

US efforts to achieve peace – the pro-Israel problem – illegal settlements built – Clinton brings Arafat and Netanyahu together – Israel's internal politics – East Jerusalem problem – Sharon provokes riots – Moscow and Washington agree on a 'road map' – conflict continues

Throughout the Middle East turmoil, Washington persisted in its efforts, with varying degrees of determination, to find a solution for the Arab–Israel conflict. Reagan unsuccessfully proposed a plan for sharing Palestinian and Jordan rule of the West Bank. It was not to be until a conference in Madrid in 1991 that progress was made. Israeli and Palestinian leaders met secretly in Oslo and produced their 'peace accords' on 'Interim Self-government Arrangements'. They signed them in Washington amid acclamation. But in a mirror image of the fate of Sadat, the Israeli Prime Minister involved, Yitzhak Rabin, was assassinated in 1995. Progress ground to a halt. Israeli settlements were not being removed as promised. They steadily increased in number and doubled in population. When Binyamin Netanyahu became Premier again in 2009 he used the threat to increase the settlements still further and particularly in Jerusalem as a negotiating weapon. A study by the Israeli organisation B'Tselem emphasised not only the growth of the settlements but also the extent to which they were subsidised by the government. These intrusions on to what had been Palestinian land continued to be condemned as illegal at the UN without any effect. The Americans were always at hand to veto any resolution by the Security Council at the behest of the Tel-Aviv government.

There had seemed to be another chance of progress when Israel's Prime Minister Benjamin Netanyahu and Arafat signed the Wye River Memorandum mediated by President Clinton, in 1998. It was designed to bring into force the previous Israeli–Palestinian agreements on the West Bank and Gaza that had not been implemented. In fact, Netanyahu's authority had succumbed to one of the most remarkable political conspiracies. Top figures of the Israeli Left met with Palestinian leaders to place Netanyahu in as difficult a position as possible, thus allowing the Labour Party to return to power. The conspiracy provides a useful counter to the myth that leading political figures on both sides could not be dragged to the conference table because of innate personal and national hostility. In reality Arabs and Israelis are born bargainers. In this particular case, a series of meetings between them took place over dinners at the residence of the Egyptian Ambassador to Israel, with the American Ambassador kept informed.

The plot unfolded thus: details of a proposed settlement worked out by the conspirators would be presented by President Clinton as his own plan. Netanyahu would be very reluctant to defy Washington and, if he signed, his own right-wing supporters would drop him. For those anxious for both a settlement and the removal of Netanyahu it was a 'win-win situation'.[216] The plan worked. Netanyahu signed the Wye River agreement, though reluctantly. The Knesset showed no such reluctance in voting swiftly for a general election, which Labour's Ehud Barak won by a landslide. That degree of public backing plus his own natural arrogance left him in no doubt that he would succeed where so many others had failed. Initial negotiations led to an agreement at Sharm el-Sheikh, signed, impressively, by Barak and Arafat along with President Mubarak, King Abdullah and Madeleine Albright as US Secretary of State. But it was only an agenda laying out the groundwork for detailed negotiations which might provide a final settlement.

Barak's own plans made strategic sense, but with little regard to the timetable which had supposedly been agreed. He would negotiate a deal first with Syria which was after all a considerable military force. Once that had been done, the Palestinians – with Damascus more or less out of the equation – would be feeling isolated and easier to deal with. But the negotiations with Syria, even offering to return the bulk of the Golan Heights, proved harder than he expected. Damascus had been offered all of the Golan Heights by Israeli Premier Yitzhak Rabin in the 1993 negotiations and were not now prepared to settle for less. It resented the plan for Israel to retain an area which denied Syria access to the source of the Sea of Galilee and part of the Jordan River. In addition, Barak wanted an early warning station on the Golan Heights. His own plan apart, Israeli public opinion was strongly against the full return of the Heights.

While he pursued these negotiations at length – which were eventually to collapse – Arafat demanded to know why no talks were proceeding between Palestine and Israel as promised at Sharm el-Sheikh. They were resumed, after procrastination by Israel. But they promised and delivered little. An illustration of the problems of personal prestige came in negotiations between Arafat and Barak in early 2000 over three villages which bordered the boundary of East Jerusalem.

Arafat pleaded that they be returned to Palestine in the limited land transfer agreed at Sharm el-Sheikh. He needed to show his people that he had extracted a concession from Barak – who gave the impression that he was sympathetic. But the Israeli Prime Minister, considering how this might well be viewed by Israelis as dividing up Jerusalem, decided against it, angering Arafat by making his decision known in public, rather than directly to him.

The Palestinian leader responded by insisting that the proposed February transfer would be rejected without that concession. Washington, for a change, put

---

216   Ahron Bregman, op. cit., p. 28

real pressure on Barak and the transfer of the three villages was accepted.[217]

The protracted negotiations between the two sides on principal issues came to a head at Camp David in the summer of 2000. It soon became clear that the main obstacle was East Jerusalem. The Palestinians wanted it for their capital. The Israeli team was divided, with Foreign Minister Shlomo Ben-Ami leading the dovish faction which saw concessions as realistic. Barak remained the hawk. He insisted on retaining more of the West Bank than the doves suggested, as necessary to preserve Israeli settlements there.

With no success in sight, Barak came up with a radical offer. It included a 'settlement of the refugee problem' – though without any details on how this mighty aim would be undertaken. There would also be Palestinian sovereignty over 85 per cent of the Jordanian border, and Israel would quit the Jordan Valley after an agreed period. The area of land demanded by Israel to protect the settlements could be slightly reduced. Above all, he was prepared to make a complicated concession over Jerusalem in which seven of the nine outer neighbourhoods would be acknowledged as Palestinian territory while in the inner east Jerusalem neighbourhoods the Palestinians would be in charge of lesser local government matters such as planning. In the old city the Palestinian, the Muslim and Christian quarters would pass to official Palestinian control. The custodianship of the Temple Mount, or Haram al-Sharif, would pass to Palestine and Morocco acting jointly.

These were concessions on such a scale that some suspected it was a clever trap, that Barak was gambling on Arafat's instinct for regarding every compromise as a starting point for further haggling. Thus the Palestinian leader would be shown up as a hopeless fanatic. If that was the plan, it certainly met with some success. Arafat reacted with suspicion.

What was meant by the vague promise of a 'settlement' of the refugee problem? What happened to the 15 per cent of the Jordanian border that remained outside Palestinian control? What was the meaning of 'custodianship' of the Haram? To give up the claim of sovereignty over that holy site could lead, he claimed, to his assassination. On the Temple Mount and Jerusalem in general, Barak would not contemplate any further concessions. Whatever other compromises might be in the air there was no question of allowing the Palestinians a return to the sovereignty over Jerusalem exercised until the 1967 war. Arab governments had already refused a Washington suggestion to pressurise Arafat over Jerusalem. They too wanted a return to the pre-1967 status.

Clinton was angered by what he saw as foolish stubbornness. He was later to tell Barak in plain contradiction of the terms on which the summit had been convened that he need not bother about handing over those promised villages abutting East Jerusalem. The President's statement at the conclusion of the

---

217 Bregman, op. cit., p. 50

talks praised Barak and was studiously neutral about Arafat. Having warned Clinton that the failure of the summit was likely to lead to uprisings on the West Bank and in Gaza, Barak plied the President with requests for more military support.

However, it was not the absence of progress by Barak which sparked off serious violence but the activities of Ariel Sharon, leader of the opposition Likud Party and still a widely hated figure in the Arab world. In September 2000, he announced that he would tour the Temple Mount. There was no legal reason why he should not. But such a visit would enrage the Muslim-dominated area, though it would endear him to his own party's hard core.

After his tour, accompanied by 1,000 police to discourage any rioting, he announced to journalists that 'Temple Mount is in our hands and will remain in our hands'. The following day, the troubles started in what came to be known as the Al-Aqsa Intifada or uprising. The rioters' stones were met by Israeli bullets and many were killed. The troubles spread to Gaza and scores of rioters were shot in a display of overwhelming force by the Israelis who suffered minimal casualties.

Sharon was carried to power within months on a wave of violence which Israeli voters saw as demanding the firmest possible hand. The Palestinians responded with car bombs and other acts of violence, the Israelis with still more military action. Sharon sent emissaries to Arafat's staff and then to Arafat himself in an attempt to cool down a rapidly deteriorating situation. His peace proposal laid down that the Palestinian leadership must first stop the violence. But the plan was more than they could deliver, even had they wanted to. The Israelis were acting with a heavy hand, not just in shooting down rioters but also in imposing curfews, the harassment at check points and in continuing to build settlements on Palestinian land. The reaction of younger Palestinians was spontaneous. Sharon even suggested a face-to-face meeting with Arafat. But the Palestinian leader evaded it, perhaps because he no longer wanted a settlement, perhaps because he knew his power was on the wane.

In 2002, the USA, the EU, the UN and Russia outlined a 'road map for peace'. The Palestinian authorities must 'visibly' arrest, disrupt and restrain individuals and groups who were conducting or planning violent acts against Israelis anywhere. Israel was to dismantle settlements established after 2001 and remove its forces from Palestinian areas occupied after late 2000. The proposal withered on the vine. Other efforts followed but little progress was made with the hawks in the ascendant in Israel and the Palestinians themselves fiercely split. For a moment there was encouragement when Israel decided it had to withdraw from the Gaza Strip under constant attack from its inhabitants. But after attacks on Israeli settlements and the growth in suicide bombings, Israel returned to maintain their dominance over the area – before retreating yet again in the face of local violence.

Of Sharon it can be said that he constantly sought peace – but always on his own harsh terms. And when he failed to secure them he reacted aggressively. The settlement continued of Israelis within the West Bank, regularly referred to by Knesset politicians by their ancient Biblical names as Judea and Sumaria. In Gaza, extremist parties grew in strength. Hamas was later to win electoral success and fighting was to rage between it and the more moderate forces of the Palestinian Fatah movement. The election of President George W. Bush was to be a key moment in providing support for the intransigents in Israel. He described Sharon as 'a man of peace', providing him with frequent access to the White House and as much US weaponry as he desired. The Israeli leader was in command and needed to fear no pressure from Washington. The British Ambassador in Washington, Sir Christopher Meyer, told the British Foreign Office: 'Hell will freeze over before Bush shakes the big stick at Sharon.' Or, he might have said, at Netanyahu, when he came to hold the reins.

The extent of Israel's heavy hand following terrorist acts from the West Bank and the Gaza Strip can be seen in the disparity in deaths caused by each side as analysed by Btselem, an Israeli human rights group, for the period 2000–2005. It reckoned that 3,218 had been killed by Israeli security forces, plus another 100 or so deaths caused by security forces in Israel itself or by Israeli citizens in the West Bank. About 1,000 Israelis were killed by Palestinian action, including 200 from the security forces.

Throughout this period, there was a steady flow of recruits to extremist groups. Where Israel had once faced only the PLO, it came to be confronted by Hamas, Hezbollah, Islamic Jihad and other splinter groups. Since they often disagreed about their aims, sometimes violently, it could be difficult for Israel or the outside peacemakers to be sure whom they were dealing with, or whether arrangements could stick.

The other big difficulty overshadowing every attempt to find peace was the USA's relentless role as a generous supporter of Israel. In any case, as all Arabs knew, Israel was so dependent on the USA that Washington could, if it wished, impose any conditions it chose on Israel to achieve a peaceful solution. The endorsement of Israel's violent tactics reached a new level when Tel-Aviv sought and obtained Bush's sanction for the politically and militarily disastrous month-long attack on Lebanon in mid-2006 and a three-week assault on Gaza in 2008. At one time Washington would have urged the restraint on Israel's highly aggressive tactics, certainly under President Clinton. But times had changed in Washington. There was a new power in the land.

CHAPTER 32
THE RISE OF THE NEOCONS

The new conservatives - a demand for US global domination - increasing defence spending - exporting democracy - Israel strongly favoured - numerous posts for neocons - their posts in defence contractors - the industrial-military complex takes office

George W. Bush took power in 2001 – elected by the slimmest majority in American political history. He was the embodiment in spirit if not in intellect of the so-called neocons, or New Conservatives, a pressure group of long standing. They had alarmingly close links with the defence industries. In 1997, in response to what was supposed to be the feebleness of Clinton's foreign policy, the movement appeared on the Washington scene as an open, well organised and amply funded force. Advocates of a 'forward' foreign policy had always been a serious presence in various administrations, as we know from the Cold War years. Now they were to emerge as a coherent and well financed political group with extravagant global ambitions for the USA.

Their manifesto, 'Project for the New American Century' (PNAC), was a call for US dominance throughout the world. This manifesto complained that 'too few political leaders are making the case for global leadership'. Unfriendly regimes which did not respond to diplomacy, mainly aimed at the promotion of democracy and liberal capitalism, should not merely be contained but coerced – if necessary by pre-emptive action. Unwavering in their support for Israel in particular, they demanded that the Middle East should be required to undergo a democratic transformation. More widely they asked: 'Does the United States have the resolve to shape a new century favourable to American principles and interests?' They advocated the forward deployment of American forces at new, strategically placed, *permanent* bases in south-east Europe and South East Asia. Bases in Western Europe already existed. The whole world outside Russia and China should be utilised.

The dominant figures in the PNAC had held important posts under President Reagan. Their future power in government offices was no certainty at the time of their manifesto. But they went on to be important figures in the Republican Party's choice of George W. Bush as the presidential candidate for the 2000 election. Their voices and their financial support were to reap an impressive harvest of public offices.

The list of PNAC members appointed to powerful positions is so remarkable that it deserves to be quoted in full:

Elliott Abrams: Representative for Middle Eastern affairs on the NSC.
Richard Armitage: Deputy Secretary of State.
John Bolton: US Ambassador to the United Nations.
Richard Cheney: Vice President.
Paula Dobriansky: Under Secretary of State for Global Affairs.
Douglas Feith: Under Secretary Department of Defense
Francis Fukuyama: President's Council on Bioethics (but disillusioned after Iraq).
Bruce Jackson: Council member of the US Committee on NATO.
Zalmay Khalilzhad: US Ambassador to Iraq.
Lewis 'Scooter' Libby: Chief of Staff to the Vice President.
Peter Rodman: Assistant Secretary of Defense for International Security.
Donald Rumsfeld: Secretary of Defense (until forced out after the Iraq failure).
Randy Scheunemann: Member of US Committee on NATO.
Paul Wolfowitz: Deputy Secretary of Defense.
Dov Zakheim: Comptroller of Defense Department.
Robert Zoellick: Deputy Secretary of Defense

A part-time position as a member of the Defense Policy Board was also provided for Richard Perle – nicknamed 'the Prince of Darkness' for the aggressive policies he advanced as an Under Secretary in the Reagan administration. One of the fiercest and most influential of the neocons, he wrote an article in the *Daily Telegraph* after the Twin Towers event of 9/11 declaring that 'countries that harbour terrorists must be destroyed'. The links of the neocons with firms gaining government contracts, above all in the area of defence, also needs to be spelt out. The industrial-military complex did not just revive under Bush, the complex seemed to *be* the administration.

The role of the Cheney family is particularly striking. Vice President Cheney, seen as the most powerful in the whole history of that office, was formerly the chief executive of Halliburton, the principal general contractor in the rebuilding of Iraq. It was to receive some $10bn in orders. He saw the value of his shareholding rise to $8m. His wife Lynne, until her husband's appointment required her to resign, was on the board of Lockheed, the government's chief military supplier. Her daughter Elizabeth was married to Phillip Perry, a lobbyist for Lockheed, who resigned that post only when appointed by Bush to the important role of General Counsel for Homeland Security. She became Assistant Secretary of State for Near Eastern Affairs in the State Department, though criticised for lacking any previous knowledge about the region.

Donald Rumsfeld, Defense Secretary, had been a well-paid director of ABB, the European-based engineering group which sold two light-water reactors to North Korea. After his resignation on appointment to political office, his former customer was named by Bush as one member of the 'axis of evil' – because of its nuclear power programme. This appeared to do no harm to Rumsfeld. He had another business appointment, outside defence, which benefitted from government contracts. Gilead was a biotech company which he chaired and which developed Tamiflu, the bird flu drug. He made $5m dollars on the sale of some of his stock but was said in 2004 to still have stock worth $25m.

Condoleezza Rice, first Bush's National Security Adviser and later his Secretary of State, had a spell on two boards of interest. She had been a non-executive director of Hewlett Packard, a substantial contractor for military and communications equipment. She had also been on the board of Chevron, the oil giant.

The Secretary of the Air Force under Bush, James Roche, had been senior vice president at Northrop Grumman, a major defence contractor. Its rival Boeing was not idle during these times. For example, it hosted a fund-raising function for Senator Ted Stevens, chairman of the Senate Appropriations Committee. Members of the Boeing board provided $22,000 personally to help their friend. Subsequently a contract was officially proposed to lease Boeing aircraft as in-flight refuellers for the air force. The terms were so favourable to the company that Senator John McCain, the Vietnam war hero and candidate for the Republican nomination, denounced them as 'war profiteering'. He also condemned the Pentagon's business connections as 'the revolving door' – by which politicians move from business to office and then back again.

Bush also set up a presidential commission to look into the future of the government's space mission. The man he chose to head it was Edward Aldrich, a member of the Lockheed board and a former Under Secretary of State at Defense for acquisitions. Gordon England, nominated as Deputy Secretary of Defense, had worked for Litton Industries, a government contractor, and later moved to a very senior post at General Dynamics, which built warships, and then on to be president of Lockheed. Over at the Navy department, the post of Secretary went to Donald Winter, a former top executive at Northrop Grumman.

The military-industrial complex was soon to be put to the test.

AFGHANISTAN AND THE PLANNED 'WAR ON TERROR'

The twin towers attack – 'war on terror' announced – the USA's pre-prepared plans for attacking Afghanistan – success of the mission – the NATO contingent assembled – attempts at pacification and 'nation building' begun

Bush's first year proved a turning point in US history – though not quite in the way it was seen at the time. There had never been such a terrorist attack as was launched on 11 September 2001 when two seized airliners plunged into the Twin Towers in New York, a third struck the Pentagon and a fourth, thought to have been heading for the White House or the Capitol, was only brought down through the courage of its passengers. The world watched with horror as the attack was shown again and again on TV channels. Bush's instant declaration of a 'war on terror' was met with acclamation, though quite how such a vague enterprise was to be waged was not clear.

If the immediate foes were at once identified and denounced – the elusive Osama bin Laden and al Qaeda, its national host – it was hardly surprising. Action against them had in fact been planned for some time. A proposed National Security Directive arrived on Bush's desk the day before the 9/11 incident. Bin Laden and his host Afghanistan were specified as targets. Al Qaeda had masterminded two attacks on US embassies in Kenya and Tanzania in 1998, leaving 250 dead, twelve of them Americans and the remainder from the local populations. Clinton retaliated swiftly in that instance with cruise missile attacks from US warships in the Gulf on what were thought to be the terrorist sites in Sudan and bin Laden's sanctuary in Afghanistan. He was thrown out of Sudan in an effort to improve relations with the Americans and with the strong encouragement of the Saudi government, though it nervously refused the suggestion that he be allowed back to his homeland.

Clinton's Operation Infinite Reach did not live up to its name. Bin Laden remained at large and the Sudanese part of the operation miscarried through poor intelligence. A factory ostensibly producing medical drugs was said to be providing nerve gas components for Saddam's supposed WMDs. The factory was destroyed but it was later accepted that it was producing innocent drugs. In 2000, al Qaeda also carried out an attack on the USS *Cole* in Aden, killing seventeen sailors. More assaults were, correctly, expected.

The military counter-attack by the USA in 2001 in the wake of the airliner atrocities seemed to the world astonishingly swift and successful. Bin Laden remained at large but the Taliban was driven from power within a month. Had the attack been quite as a spontaneous as presented, the display of American power and reach would have been awesome. It was only to transpire a year later how the attack had been under preparation for months. The elaborate intelligence operation involved had drawn on support from Pakistan, India and Sudan. Fears of Islamic radicalism were shared by all three nations. The former Pakistan Foreign Secretary, Niaz Naik, was told in 2001 by US officials, in a Kiplingesque touch, that the attack on al Qaeda bases would be made 'by the time the snows melted'. In Afghanistan, that meant before October. The 9/11 onslaught, under preparation for years, was launched only days before the USA took the initiative.

The Bush administration did not, as was also to be the case in Iraq, bargain on a prolonged war in Afghanistan. Yet the problems in dealing with a country like Afghanistan were more challenging than in a centralised and fairly secular country like Iraq. The Taliban at least was a regime about which they knew a fair amount since Washington had helped create it to oppose the Soviets.

The country was tribally and politically complex, dominated in areas by a loose alliance of warlords. The Pashtuns were the country's largest ethnic group. The next largest groups, the Tajiks and the Uzbeks were dominant in the north. The Pashtuns had never been at peace even among themselves. Ancient tribal divisions had led to some supporting the Taliban and others the ousted monarch, King Zahir. But one of the few things which could unite the traditionally disparate forces in Afghanistan was the foreign invader. Britain had been roundly defeated twice in the 19th century and the Soviets in the 20th. The dangers of staying any length of time in the country should have been plain enough.

The al Qaeda training camps were the obvious target for the USA. They had been attended by Muslims from all over the world. The fact that so many of the camps had their headquarters in caves presented problems. Assistance from neighbouring Pakistan might be difficult since the USA had imposed economic sanctions on the country for conducting nuclear tests. General Musharraf, who had came to power in a coup, had been written off as an anti-democratic dictator. Now he became overnight a valuable ally. The 'war against terror' was under way and the sanctions were immediately lifted.

But Afghanistan was 7,000 miles away. The old rule that military power fades in proportion to distance – perhaps in proportion to the square of the distance – was one the Americans had no will to learn. They thought in this case that having no bases to hand themselves they could turn to the Gulf States. There Britain had friendly and useful relations. Bases to the north required establishing good relationships with Uzbekistan, Tajikistan and Turkmenistan which did not prove so straightforward.

A Fistful of Dollars

The first step was easy. A CIA operative was despatched with $3m dollars to distribute among potential supporters in the Northern Alliance. It was soon disbursed with few questions asked. The next move was to gather an international alliance for the US retaliation. It proved no problem. NATO countries came swiftly to the support of the Americans. The war – 'Operation Enduring Freedom' – would soon begin. Chasing bin Laden across country, from cave to cave, would be difficult however many troops might be sent in. Memories of Vietnam made Washington very cautious.

But ousting the Taliban did not prove too difficult in the end. The US total commitment on the ground by the time this initial objective had been achieved was little over 400 men. The Northern Alliance provided the manpower and the US the sorties which destroyed the Taliban's heavy weapons – tanks, ground-to-air missiles and radar. Kabul fell. Hamid Karzai, who had defected from the Taliban government some time before, found general favour with the USA and its Afghan allies. He became the newly appointed President – in little more than 100 days after the Twin Towers attack. The Americans stepped up their supplies of food and humanitarian aid. Matters seemed settled at first but almost a decade later NATO forces remained still struggling to pacify various regions of the country. The initial military victory had been straightforward enough, misleadingly easy in fact.

The dilemma for the Americans in Afghanistan, which they did not appreciate at the time, was that while a punitive expedition might succeed, a prolonged intervention was doomed to fail. The urge of 'nation-building' was to prove as irresistible as it was hopeless. By shipping in all the network of 'aid' agencies, the NATO operation was merely providing more personnel who would need safeguarding.

The moral arguments cited for nation building looked powerful in 2001. The country had been badly damaged by a Soviet invasion which Washington had actively stimulated. Democracy plus a lot of money was going to save Afghanistan. To the novel institution of an elected central government, the Afghan people seemed to assent in the election of President Karzai in 2003. But real power remained with the tribes and the warlords, some of whom could be bought, some not. When it came to money, the growth of opium could be even more lucrative than being a friend of the USA – and less dangerous, it might be argued. The Taliban had more or less wiped out the opium growing business but the vast bulk of the world's supply was soon being grown in 'rescued' Afghanistan. It was now being shipped out through Pakistan whose porous borders contained the most lawless regions of the Middle East.

Five years into the war, a conference was summoned of some sixty nations and international institutions. The security position was acknowledged to be deteriorating – a formula the Obama administration was to repeat in 2009, with an added note of despair. The 2006 conference gave the flavour of the attitudes doomed to fail. A five-year plan was adopted for the goals of: security; governance, rule of law and human rights; and social and economic development. That Afghans might have their own highly distinctive views about what constituted social and political advance was not confronted. The conference looked to new measures in such diverse fields as policing and laws on business organisation. The warlords must have been fascinated by the idea of Western-style company legislation in a country where business was conducted through family and tribal connections. The conference of 2009 went over the old ground but with less optimism.

By the end of the Bush era it was easy to see the cost but hard to discern progress. Half the country was deemed to have become too dangerous for aid workers to operate in. The elected Karzai government's writ did not run outside Kabul and not very effectively there. Corruption was notorious, opium growing flourished and was estimated to account for 90 per cent of the world's supply. The sporadic effort to curb it was not serious. A governor of Helmand Province was caught with nine tons of opium. He was forced to resign but he had his connections. So he went otherwise unpunished. Power remained in the hands of the warlords, tribal leaders and the Taliban plus its Jihadist allies. Many of these were recruits responding to the invasions of Iraq and Afghanistan – also to the continuing battles between Arabs and Israelis, with the latter seen as America in all but name.

An increasingly alarming feature of the conflict was that it was spilling over into the Indian subcontinent. Pakistan was the main supply route for the NATO forces. As such, it was also a permanent target not just for Jihadists but for any conveniently placed tribe which might exact a fee for allowing convoys through the lawless North West frontier area. Pakistan's intelligence agency (ISI) had long been an essential agency for NATO, since it provided the best information about the Taliban, al Qaeda and other Jihadist groups in the frontier areas and in Afghanistan itself. The ISI was soon regarded as badly infiltrated by Jihadists and in any case unfriendly to the USA which was ready to dabble in that country's chaotic politics. The fragile relations between Islamabad and Washington took a fearful tumble when an American drone (controlled by the CIA from Virginia) killed twenty-four Pakistani regular troops.

The ISI was fiercely anti-Indian, with the long-standing Kashmir conflict never ceasing to rile Pakistani opinion. Charges that it either supported or did little to curb the terrorists who launched their attack on Mumbai in 2008 found fertile ground in India. The war in Afghanistan certainly increased the power and importance of the ISI. An alarming deterioration in India–Pakistan relations was just one of the unlooked-for consequences of the NATO operation, though experienced old hands in the State Department might well have foreseen this.

The Bush administration remained addicted to the belief that if Afghanistan could be put on a stable, prosperous and, above all, democratic basis, it could be relied on not to offer shelter to terrorists. The ambitions for the country were in the realm of fantasy alongside a profound failure to understand the roots of terrorism – or indeed of national resistance, despite the lessons from Vietnam. National resistance is easily stirred. It is on that soil that terrorism can thrive, with or without the spur of religion. By the time that Bush left office, the country was in no better state than when American troops had arrived. Claims, such as those about the number of girls with access to better education, had to be set beside a higher level of warfare, many civilian deaths, more opium cultivation and spreading corruption.

By 2012, when Obama was facing his second Presidential election, his inheritance from Afghanistan had become very grim. His promise to end that conflict had been an abject failure. The formula he had devised (alongside the UK) of removing most troops in 2013 and all by the end of 2014 – except those required for training the Afghan army – was under severe strain. A number of incidents had led to tense relations with Kabul. These included riots following the (accidental) burning of the Koran at a US base and, worst of all, the murder of sixteen civilians by an American sergeant who apparently had mental problems. His removal to the USA for trial was also much resented since the understandable view of the Afghans was that he should be tried in the country where he had committed his crime. The promise to keep adequate troops in the country to train the new army was also called into question as the new soldiers showed a marked tendency to shoot their trainers.

Yet when it came to recruiting more Muslims to Jihadist ranks, the invasion of Iraq – which soon followed the start of the Afghan conflict – proved even more disastrous.

CHAPTER 33
<u>PLANNING TO INVADE IRAQ</u>

Washington plots the final overthrow of Saddam – the Afghanistan success seductive – alleged Weapons of Mass Destruction – NATO allies involved – Britain promises assistance – intelligence services distorted – WMD inspections – the uranium fraud – Tony Blair's dossiers – UN refuses to sanction war

The success in removing the Taliban from power proved seductive. American prowess halfway round the globe had been amply demonstrated. The messianic mission to remake other countries was as strong as ever. Now it was time to bring matters to a head in Iraq. In April 2002 the President made his first public declaration that the USA would force regime change in Iraq. There would have to be substantial build up both militarily and politically before any attack – or perhaps Saddam would crumble when he saw the force to be arrayed against him. But anxious as the hawks were to make the removal of Saddam another step in the 'war on terror', it lacked an essential ingredient. There was no evidence whatever that he had supported al Qaeda in any way. Indeed he had steered clear of it since such an alliance could invite ferocious retribution. There was also the problem at that stage for Washington that the weapons inspectors had still not found any evidence of WMDs, only of their destruction.

Powell was to object to the proposal to invade Iraq on the grounds that it would antagonise other partners in the NATO coalition. Iraq should only be a target if it could be proved to have played a part in 9/11. In this he echoed the view of General Shelton, the outgoing Chairman of the Joint Chiefs of Staff, startled when he heard from Powell of the plan to invade. 'What the hell are these guys thinking about – can't you get these guys back in the box?'[218] Evidently not.

Bush at War by Bob Woodward, Simon and Schuster, 2002, p. 61

Bush himself had momentary hesitations, not least on the grounds that the increasingly aggressive Cheney and Wolfowitz, Rumsfeld's deputy, had been involved so prominently in the 1991 Gulf War which had ended without Saddam's removal. 'He did not want to use the war on terror as an excuse to settle old scores', wrote Woodward.[219] Powell was to prove the most cautious of all. Iraq had no role in 9/11, he insisted.

Wolfowitz was not easily deterred, arguing that there was a '10 to 50 per cent chance' that Saddam had indeed been involved in 9/11 (for which no evidence was ever to be unearthed). Rumsfeld, for the moment, sat on the fence. But buoyed up by the swiftness of the Afghanistan triumph, Bush became more confident of success. In January 2002 he had laid out his 'war on terror', including his labelling of Iran, Iraq and North Korea as 'the axis of evil'. By August, Powell was complaining to Bush about the scale of the pressure for an Iraq invasion. It seemed to have occurred to some that an invasion, far from helping the 'war on terror', would act as a recruiting sergeant for terrorists. The point certainly worried the now retired Brent Scowcroft, who had been Bush Senior's National Security Adviser. He spoke publicly in August of the danger of stirring up a 'cauldron' in the Middle East which would make it harder to win the war on terrorism. This was a worry for Powell too. To his opposite number in London, Foreign Secretary Jack Straw, he at one point described Rumsfeld and Wolfowitz as 'the fucking crazies'.

Cheney was pressing for war publicly even before it was settled administration policy. Bush sided readily with the hawks. He was in part driven by the evidence that he had not been able to deliver a crushing blow to al Qaeda, only to the Taliban. Saddam had the advantage of being an easy target. There was unrest in Iraq, his brutality was notorious and he had been constantly in conflict with the UN over weapons inspectors. He was disliked and distrusted by most other Islamic rulers.

Now was the chance, as Washington saw it, to finish him once and for all and at the same time to establish the unassailable American global supremacy of the neocon dream. No country would feel safe that defied the USA. All that was needed was an excuse to go to war which would garner support from the allies who had been so agreeably forthcoming over Afghanistan. Britain's Tony Blair hurried eagerly to the President's support, apparently mesmerised by the prospect of being the USA's most important ally.

The path to war proved to be an extraordinary exercise in deception, including self-deception, by the principal actors. It was the only way to make the war with Iraq look justifiable and win allies. They seemed to be in short supply, Britain apart, as the conviction spread of Bush's intention to go to war come what may. Regime change was contrary to international law, whatever President Clinton and

---

219   Woodward, op. cit., p. 85

Congress may have declared in 1997. Tony Blair proved resolute though regularly harried by dissidents in his own Labour Party.

Yet it was from Britain that Washington received the wisest advice and the most thoughtful warnings. Blair, under pressure from his own advisers, was able to persuade the President to postpone the invasion plan to 2003. It would be necessary to 'wrongfoot' Saddam on issues of inspection and WMDs and thus to secure a mandate from the UN Security Council. This would need time. It was also important at least to try to persuade other Western nations that the USA was not hell bent on regime change at any price.

Sir David Manning, Blair's foreign policy adviser, talked at length with Condoleezza Rice, pointing out that Blair had to manage a Parliament in a critical mood, particularly within his own party. Manning wrote a memorandum for No. 10, laying out the points which Bush had to consider: 'to persuade international opinion that military action against Iraq was necessary and justified; what value to put on the exiled Iraqi opposition; how to coordinate a US/Allied military campaign with internal opposition (assuming there is any); what happens the morning after'.[220]

His caution about the exiled Iraqi opposition was all too justified. It was headed by Ahmed Chalabi, a banker who had been sentenced to a lengthy term of imprisonment *in absentia* in Jordan for fraud and was the self-styled head of the Iraqi National Congress. He received funds from a gullible Washington. He was a perfect example of supply and demand in the intelligence field. The more claims he provided that Saddam had WMDs the more generous Washington proved. In the three years from 2000–2003, his organisation received more than $36m from the government it was so effectively misleading. His group also spun a series of tales about the supposed strength of important opponents of Saddam and the readiness with which the country could be brought to order once he was removed. It was all nonsense, as the coalition was to find out. But the neocons, especially Wolfowitz and Perle, held him in high regard.

Manning also made the point that it was of paramount importance that the Allies dealt with the issue of Israel. Otherwise they could find themselves 'bombing Iraq and losing the Gulf'. He concluded: 'I think that there is a real risk that the Administration underestimates the difficulties. They may say that failure is not an option but that does not mean they will avoid it.'[221]

Bush and Blair were determined to believe what they wanted to believe. The British Joint Intelligence Committee's frank assessment was not helpful at this stage. It described the information on Iraq's WMDs as 'sporadic and patchy'. It

---

220   *War Crime or Just War* by Nicholas Wood, South Hill Press, 2005, p.70. Also provides a useful timetable of the development of the conflict.

221   For Manning and Ricketts' analyses of the pressure for invasion see http://www.acronym. org.uk/docs/0409/doc14.htm

concluded: 'We believe that Iraq retains some production equipment and some small stocks of chemical warfare agent precursors and may have hidden small quantities of agents and weapons'. It was very tentative language.

The policy director at the Foreign Office, Peter Ricketts, proffered advice to Straw. 'We can bring home to Bush some of the realities which will be less evident from Washington. He [the Prime Minister] can help Bush make some good decisions by telling him things his own machine probably isn't.' He continued: 'the truth is that what has changed is not the pace of Saddam Hussein's WMD programme but our tolerance of that, post-9/11 trends. I am relieved that you have decided to postpone publication of the classified document' (from the JIC). Another problem, Ricketts went on, was the end state: 'what sort of regime would we be left with? Regime change does not stack up. It sounds like a grudge match between Bush and Saddam.'[222]

Straw passed on his own warnings to the Prime Minister: 'We have a long way to go to convince them [Labour MPs] on: the scale of the threat from Iraq and why it has got worse recently; what distinguishes the Iraq threat from that of, e.g., Iran and North Korea so as to justify military action; the justification for any military action in terms of international law; and whether the consequences of military action really would be a compliant law abiding replacement government.' He added that there was no 'credible evidence to link Iraq with Osama bin Laden and al Qaeda … what will the action achieve? there seems to be larger hole in this than anything.'[223]

Blair flew to the USA and met Bush at his Texas ranch for talks. The pair came away with very different publicly stated conclusions. Blair told a TV interviewer that he and the President were 'not proposing military action at this point in time'. Bush told another interviewer on the same day 'I made up my mind that Saddam needs to go'. Privately, it seems, there was less disagreement. Blair told Bush that whatever the President decided, he would go along with that.

Ricketts was right to fear that Bush's own 'machine' was not feeding him with the pros and cons of invasion. The main intelligence came to him filtered through Rumsfeld, Rice and Cheney. Powell remained cautious but allowed himself to be outgunned. He had never been close to Bush; his influence and his skill in intrigue would never match that of the political veterans Cheney, Rice and Rumsfeld. In any case, the purpose of intelligence had ceased to be the provision of accurate information. As the hawks saw it, its purpose (like many of the Security Council activities by Washington) was to provide excuses for a war which had already been planned. This was to lead to serious hostility between the professional intelligence gatherers and the White House hawks, especially Cheney. There was particular resentment by him and Rumsfeld of

---

222   http://www.acronym.org.uk/docs
223   http://www.guardian.co.uk/commentisfree/2010/jan/18/straw-leaked-letter-blair-iraq

the claim made by CIA Director George Tenet – directly to Bush – that there was no connection between Iraq and al Qaeda. Cheney and Rumsfeld ordered the intelligence to be scoured for anything which might weaken the director's claim. At the same time they set about playing down the value of anything from the CIA.

What Bush himself understood about Iraq is hard to know but it cannot have been much. It was apparently news to him on the eve of the invasion that Iraq was a country deeply divided by sectarianism. He did not understand the terms Shia and Sunni, used by an Iraqi visitor, according to accounts by John Simpson, the BBC's World Correspondent.

The accusation that it was the intelligence services which misinformed the administration came to be resented, understandably. Paul Pillar, the National Intelligence Officer for the Middle East, wrote in early 2006 in the magazine *Foreign Affairs*:

> If the entire body of national intelligence of analysis on Iraq had a policy implication, it was to avoid war – or if war was going to be launched, to prepare for a messy aftermath. What is remarkable about pre-war US intelligence on Iraq is not that it got things wrong and thereby misled policy makers; it is that it played so small a role in the most important US policy decision in recent decades.[224]

A casual disregard for crucial information extended also to Congress. The legislators had asked for the NIE estimates on Iraq's WMDs in 2002, before the invasion. Pillar records that few of those for whom these confidential documents had been prepared actually bothered to read them, least of all in detail. Various aides responsible for safeguarding the items told him that no more than six senators bothered to study them and only a handful of congressmen got beyond the five-page executive summary. Pillar compares this with a similarly casual approach by Congress when it faced President Johnson's false claims about an attack on the US warship in the gulf of Tonkin.

Even where an intelligence claim was labelled as dubious or suspect, it had a way or reappearing with increasing emphasis in the claims of the hawks. One example concerns Saddam's supposed nuclear programme. In August 2002, Cheney made a speech in California saying: 'what we know from various source is that he [Saddam] continues to pursue a nuclear weapon.' Two weeks later he was enlarging the threat, claiming that Saddam had a nuclear capability that could directly threaten 'anyone he chooses in his own region or beyond'. Bush built on this, though somewhat toning down the immediacy of the supposed menace: 'Saddam Hussein has the infrastructure for a nuclear weapons programme, and has illicitly sought to purchase the equipment needed for enrich uranium for a nuclear weapon.'

In September, Blair declared in the Commons on publishing his first 'dossier'[225] that intelligence had concluded that Iraq had 'chemical and biological weapons which could be activated within forty-five minutes including against his own Shia population; and that he is actively seeking to acquire a nuclear weapons capability'.[226] In his State of the Union message in January 2003 Bush stated that: 'The British government has learnt that Saddam Hussein recently sought significant quantities of uranium from Africa.' But it had learnt no such thing. It had merely heard the American claim made ten months before – based on fraudulent documents passed to the CIA. It was another case of intelligence echoes. Something heard in one capital reaches another and when circulated is treated by the first as a new source.

The episode was in fact richly farcical. A forger, though not apparently of great talent, persuaded an Italian publication, in return for $4,000, that he could provide documents proving that Iraq was purchasing uranium from the former French colony of Niger. The documents were immediately passed from the US Embassy in Rome to Washington. The hawks were delighted. When the journalist who had been sold the material went to Niger two weeks later, she swiftly concluded that the documents were forgeries. One of the copied signatures was of a minister who had left the Niger government some years before.

But the forgery made its way from the CIA to the Pentagon. A point was made of not passing it straightaway to the less hawkish State Department. When it surfaced at the White House, the State Department's Intelligence and Research Bureau raised some doubts. But the hawks did not want to hear. Bush was keen to publicise this new smoking gun. George Tenet, the CIA Director, tried to hold him back but he spoke out and Saddam's attempts to buy uranium became a feature of the official case for war. Iraqi denials were scorned. They were 'the real untruths', according to Rice. The Niger lie was now acquiring a momentum of its own, despite the Italian journalist disowning the original document. Even Powell was to repeat the falsehood in February.

The role of the Secretary of State remains something of a puzzle to this day. He was the most sceptical of Bush's advisers. But the instinct of the military mind apparently took over, as it sometimes does when a general goes into politics. There was clearly going to be war. He felt bound to go along with the decisions made by his Commander-in-Chief. He would give him his support; he would help to make the case and seek to bring allies on board.

In the turf war in Washington between the different agencies, the CIA claimed that it had not had time to evaluate the Niger document properly. The story about

225 http://en.wikipedia.org/wiki/Iraq_Dossier
226 Blair was later to tell the Chilcot inquiry into the Iraq war that he was surprised by the strong reaction of the press to the 45-minute point. He meant only battlefield weapons, he said.

the uranium sales might be true, though it could not confirm it. The INR had made a study and found no persuasive evidence of any nuclear programme. But Bush pushed the claim all the same – which later led to an official admission that he had been mistaken. And careless, it might be added.

The matter seemed to be finally clarified by Mohamed El Baradei, head of the International Atomic Energy Agency, in March 2003, who told the Security Council that the Niger documents were fakes. But that was two weeks before the invasion began and nobody in Washington at that stage was to be deterred, and nor was the ever faithful Blair on the other side of the Atlantic.

The British Prime Minister was already in trouble at home because of his second report for Parliament swiftly dubbed the 'dodgy dossier'. It painted a dramatic picture of the menace from Iraq, showing the range of its missiles which could hit Cyprus, Turkey, Saudi Arabia, Iran and Israel. It was not so much a distillation of intelligence reports as a war cry. MPs were alarmed. Campbell's well-known hand was detected. But the scorn swiftly poured on the dossier and other evidence was never enough to prevent the Prime Minister going to war. He had the support of most Conservative MPs who were instinctively and unquestioningly supporters of the Anglo-American 'special relationship' and temperamentally inclined towards the tough approach when dealing with brutal dictators, at any rate the smaller ones.

It was claimed by both Washington and London that Iraq was in breach of its original ceasefire terms, in relation to WMDs and in failing to cooperate fully with the inspection process. It certainly failed to comply with the inspectors, as we have seen, though not because it was pursuing a WMD programme. In November 2002, Iraq accepted Resolution 1441 which demanded the return of the inspectors under the leadership of Hans Blix of Sweden. To the disappointment of the USA and the UK, they found no evidence of WMD production. On the other hand, Blix conceded they could not be sure of complete elimination of these programmes since Iraq had not fully and readily complied with the inspectors' numerous demands.

Washington and London now sought a new resolution to permit military action. But President Chirac declared in March that France would veto any resolution that would automatically lead to war. The Russians and the Chinese, less openly, indicated they would do the same. So the Americans and the British were forced back on the argument that war was legitimised under Resolution 1441. It was a patent breach of procedure since the Security Council has long ruled that it is up to the Council itself and not individual members to decide how a resolution is enforced.

But the die was cast. In March Saddam and his two sons were given forty-eight hours to leave Iraq. The demand was refused, to the relief of Bush and Blair, now straining at the leash. Had he complied he might have left a trusted lieutenant in his place and the diplomatic quadrille might need to start all over again. The invasion was launched.

CHAPTER 34
VICTORY IN IRAQ

Military success – law and order breaks down – post-war plans hopelessly inadequate – first proconsul sacked – no WMDs found – civilian and military casualties mounting – refugees flee Iraq – a prolonged search for political stability – prisoners abused and tortured

The coalition's victory was swift. It took less than three weeks for its forces to reach Baghdad. Moreover it could lay some claim to be an international force, as Washington and London were eager to stress, including 2,000 Australians, 300 Danes and 200 Poles, plus nominal teams from other countries – 'the Coalition of the Willing' as it was enthusiastically called. The propaganda campaign against Saddam had undoubtedly brought in recruits. And no doubt some of the countries which sent purely nominal contingents thought this was a costless way of keeping in Washington's good graces. Of the fighting troops, the USA and Britain contributed 98 per cent.

Pictures of delighted Shias welcoming the tanks and the toppling of Saddam's statue fired the American imagination and, for a while, sent Bush's approval rating soaring. Iraq's oil was secured at great speed by a series of commando raids. But there was also an immediate and total breakdown of law and order. Widespread looting took place of banks, official buildings, businesses and even the National Museum's ancient artefacts. Most ominous for the future was the massive looting of all arsenals. The failure to secure them at once was just one of the steps which facilitated the subsequent chaos.

Planning for the rule of Iraq had been left to Rumsfeld. It was assumed, fatally, that it would not be a particularly difficult task. General Tommy Franks, in charge of the invasion itself, had compiled a forecast which was in the realms of fantasy. After the fighting there would be a three-month 'stabilisation' phase, followed by an eighteen to twenty-four-month 'recovery' phase. Fewer than 5,000 US troops would be left in Iraq by 2006.

When Bush left office, there were over 140,000 troops still present. President Obama promised to reduce the number to less than 50,000 by mid-2010. He achieved this, though leaving a further 50,000 troops in training and advisory roles. In Baghdad however tension remained. A near fifty-fifty split in seats by the two main parties had left the balance of power in the hands of militants, some very aggressive.

Finding the Right Proconsul

Two months before the invasion itself Rumsfeld was searching for a suitable man to run post-invasion Iraq. He wanted someone who would understand that he must report only to him and not challenge his authority. Moreover the Defense Department would be the channel through which the President would be kept informed and consulted. The isolation of Bush from the reality of Iraq was to continue.

General Jay Garner seemed ideal. He had retired from the army and was – like many other retired generals – occupying a lucrative post with a defence contractor. Rumsfeld had been impressed to learn that Garner had played a considerable role in protecting the Kurds from Baghdad during the sanctions period which followed the first Iraqi war. That made him an Iraq expert in the Defense Secretary's eyes. Garner had little time to prepare for his task. But putting Iraq back on the straight and narrow would not require very long. He told his wife that he would be back for Thanksgiving. This at least proved an accurate prediction. Rumsfeld dismissed him after only two months.

Garner appreciated in the planning stage that the task would be wide-ranging. He scoured Washington for a team of experts in fields as diverse as power supply and agriculture. At the last minute, Rumsfeld challenged the list, insisting that virtually all the twenty-odd individuals should come from the Defense Department. This was simply an arrangement to ensure that Rumsfeld loyalists would control the new Iraq. It was a bad omen.

Garner, after arguing for the value of his team, accepted the decision. One result was that he arrived in Baghdad with the team still being assembled in Washington. Garner was an intelligent man but weak. Like Powell, like other generals, he allowed the excuse of 'superior orders' to overwhelm his better judgement. This supine attitude was to be displayed after his dismissal when he was called to the Oval Office for an official farewell. He knew that Rumsfeld and others were preventing an honest assessment of Iraq's problems getting through to Bush. Garner chose to say nothing.

When he arrived in Baghdad, conditions proved worse than anything he or his team had anticipated. The chaos was total. Law and order vanished, essential public services failed. Power supplies fell badly. The plants themselves were among the looted sites. For many private citizens as well as businesses, the only solution to this was to own a petrol generator. But even petrol was often in short supply.

The failure to prevent the mounting chaos and bloodshed convinced Rumsfeld that the problem was Garner himself, not the hopelessness of his mission. He decided to replace him. His choice was Jerry Bremer, a State Department ambassador-at-large on counter-terrorism. Bremer, like his fellow neocons, was not a man given to any self-doubts. Like them, he saw himself on a mission. He was however to multiply the chaos.

The new 'Presidential envoy' carried with him orders from Washington, so he said, to disband the Iraqi army – then dispersed to their homes – and remove Ba'ath Party members from government employment. Garner was stunned. He had been convinced from the start that the army had to be kept in being to have any chance of maintaining law and order – though top ranks might need purging.

The chief CIA adviser in Baghdad was also aghast. On the Ba'ath Party order, he complained : 'You will put 50,000 on the streets, underground and mad at the Americans.' He warned that they would include the most powerful and well-connected elites from all walks of life.[227]

On top of that, the disbanding of the army would affect some 150,000 men, mostly retaining weapons, being put unpaid on the streets and blaming the USA for their loss of security. A more effective plan for boosting anti-American feeling would be hard to imagine. Or indeed for multiplying breakdowns. Many of the Ba'ath Party members were simply professionals who had joined to improve their employment prospects – teachers, doctors, lawyers, government officials. Bremer would not relent. He was a new broom determined to recast Iraq in his own chosen mould. His neoconservatism had a strong Wilsonian streak.

The situation continued to deteriorate. Within three months Washington contemplated replacing Bremer. But it was concluded that two dismissed proconsuls within so short a time would undermine imperial authority. There had been no planning for civilian casualties, let alone attacks on the military, once the invasion was over. Both mounted steadily.

At first, the attacks by roadside bombs and the dreaded weapon of the suicide bomber were aimed at the troops. But soon it was predictably by Sunnis against Shias and Shias against Sunnis – in marketplaces, cafes, businesses and buses. In other cases there was an indifference to the identity of the victims. Various terrorist groups had one thing in common – a desire to make the country ungovernable. It is a known terrorist tactic. Another motive is to provoke a disproportionate response. The Americans were all to ready to provide that, placing great faith (as in Vietnam and in Afghanistan) in the supremacy and accuracy of advanced technology from the air. The clear innocence of numerous victims provided propaganda for Jihadists across the Middle East. The heavy-handedness of the troops in dealing with people of an alien culture was also evident enough.

There was another problem for Washington (and London). In early 2004, the Iraq Survey Group announced that no WMDs had been found. It concluded that they had all been destroyed years ago. Saddam's reluctance to help the weapons inspectors demonstrate this was put down to his desire to keep potential Middle

---

227 *State of Denial* by Bob Woodward, Simon and Schuster, 2006, p. 194

East enemies guessing. Intelligence also confirmed that no assistance had ever been given to al Qaeda. It is an interesting comment on the working of democracy that both Bush in 2004 and Blair in 2005 went on to be re-elected, despite such humiliation. In both cases the readiness of their opposition parties to support the invasion in the first place was an obvious help.

The Coalition lost the propaganda war, almost from the start despite the sophisticated machinery of Washington which was supposed to have learnt from Vietnam. In 2004, a newspaper report revealed the practices at Abu Ghraib prison where prisoners were held sometimes beaten, and regularly humiliated. Washington instinctively denied the report, then set up an investigation which led to nine soldiers being charged and some senior officers demoted. But no rigour in laying down the law afterwards could compensate for the huge publicity which the affair generated.

Alongside this was the much larger problem of the abuses at Guantanamo Bay which could not be written off as just a matter of some soldiers exceeding their duty. Since the base was in Cuba, in foreign indeed hostile territory, normal legal procedures did not apply. Those imprisoned there were deemed 'enemy combatants' who did not enjoy either the right of prisoners of war or those of US citizens facing charges.

By the time closure was promised (but never delivered) by Barack Obama in late 2008, some 750 prisoners had passed through. Washington had long insisted that the prisoners were treated humanely. But the UN found evidence of torture, including lengthy solitary confinement and exposures to extremes of noise, temperature and lights. More gravely, there were claims of 'waterboarding' or simulated drowning. Since figures ranging from Bush to Rumsfeld denied that the practices at the camp amounted to real torture, the world needed to have no illusions about the extent of the brutality. In 2006, Cheney said it was a 'no brainer' if it saved lives to give a prisoner 'a dunk in water'. The camp at Guantanamo Bay was a gift to Jihadist propaganda from the moment it opened.

The total of civilian casualties caused by the invasion of Iraq remains notoriously hard to assess. The figures for deaths vary wildly, ranging to the end of 2008 from nearly 100,000 to over one million. The lower figure, assessed by Iraq Body Count, is based on clearly reported and cross-checked cases. The higher figures cover deaths either assessed by pollsters' sampling or by medical estimates of mortality rates before and after 2003 which took into account indirect effects such as the breakdown of public services and food shortages. A British polling firm, Opinion Research Business, took samples of households across the country and arrived in 2008 at a figure of over a million, which was consistent with a death rate they also found through sampling in 2006. The most scholarly study appeared in a survey by Johns Hopkins University and published in the *Lancet* in 2006. It included both the direct deaths and those resulting from the collapse of sanitation, medical services, etc. and inadequate nutrition. The effect of one third of Iraqi doctors being among those fleeing abroad was a contributing factor. It arrived at a median figure of around 500,000 from the time of the invasion to the middle of 2006. The Iraqi Heath Ministry, using only official records of those brought to hospitals and recorded as dead put the number between January 2004 and February 2009 at 87,000. An accurate figure will never be known but the dramatic scale of deaths and injuries is beyond dispute.

A less disputed figure was provided for the refugee tragedy. The United Nations records in 2008 that 4.7m Iraqis were displaced, 'many in need of humanitarian relief'. About 2.7m were 'internally' displaced, i.e. they had to move from their homes to new areas. The remainder fled abroad. Other Arab countries, already with refugee problems, had to shoulder a new burden.

Together with the deaths caused by the invasion, to say nothing of so many injuries, there could scarcely be a single family in Iraq which could not record a deep grievance against the Coalition invasion. There can be no formal figures for the rise in the number of militants across the Middle East. But equally there is no doubt the Coalition's war provided a major boost in recruitment. The 'war on terror' merely served to increase the power of extremists and to increase their number in countries like Britain with significant Muslim populations.

As the number of civilian deaths kept rising alongside US military casualties, Bush decided that Rumsfeld would have to go. He was replaced by the former CIA head Robert Gates in 2006, who proved a voice for some realism. The US was not winning, he told Congress. American forces, he suggested, could be cut without contradicting the administration's declared aims. He also warned that war with Iran could produce devastating results. Stirred by criticisms, Bush ignored Gates on Iraq and decided to raise the number of troops, hopefully for a temporary period. He authorised a 'surge' of troops to Baghdad in a strategy of swamping the area of highest casualties. The officially recorded death rate fell from around 23,500 recorded in 2007 to fewer than 9,000 in 2008. To the enthusiasts for invasion, this was a simple lesson. Lack of troops had been the problem from the start. And it is true that some voices in the military had originally warned that up to 500,000, not 150,000, would be a proper number for maintaining law and order.

However, there were other factors which could explain the fall in terrorist activities. In Baghdad itself, Shias and Sunnis had to a considerable degree separated themselves into two physically divided communities and reached an agreement to curb the fighting. The Iraqi government had also reached an agreement with one group of Shia militants for a truce. Iran may also have played an important part by reducing its support for terrorists. Tehran was growing ever more interested in Afghanistan, where the fighting was more simply against the Americans and the British.

The surge was authorised in the wake of the Baker-Hamilton report, a privately commissioned bipartisan study, headed by James Baker, a former Democrat Secretary of State. Bush had been adamant that there could be no 'cut and run'. But the report, which struggled to find common ground among its ten participants, suggested that withdrawal could be contemplated if Iraq did not make substantial progress 'towards national reconciliation security and governance'. The means to achieve this were not spelt out. It was admitted that the US seemed locked in a conflict 'which has no foreseeable end'. On the other hand, said the report, there would be grave disadvantages in 'precipitate or premature' withdrawal. The President agreed with that part at least. It would destroy such as was left of the case for the invasion. All that he could do was pray for the Iraqis to rescue themselves – and him.

Building Democracy in Iraq

The build up to a self-governing and democratic Iraq was a slow one, culminating in 2008 in an agreement between Washington and Baghdad that US troops would withdraw during 2011, which they did, though a substantial number remained in a training role. Baghdad's second democratically chosen Premier, Nouri al-Malaki, had wanted less than eighteen months. Washington's eagerness to accept Iraq as self-governing did not extend that far.

The first move towards establishing representative government after the invasion was the establishment of the Coalition Provisional Authority which included twenty-five nominated leading Iraqis intended to embrace all the ethnic and religious groups in the country. Proceeding by stages, a democratic election was held in 2005 where the turnout was high despite some Sunni threats to boycott the polls. The first Prime Minister, Ibrahim al-Jaafari, proved a problem. He was seen as too friendly to Iran. In any case, he was unable to curb the mounting violence. The Americans and the Iraqi parliament both agreed that he should go and be replaced by Nouri al-Malaki. But relations were not easy with him, either. His agreement with the 'Mahdi Army' of the rebellious Moqtada al-Sadr smacked too much of compromise.

Americans like to believe that installing democratic procedures will produce America-friendly leaders. But there is no logic in this. Indeed, a popularly elected leader in a country which is occupied by American or other nations' forces will naturally set out to prove he is not a tool of the invaders. Washington's enthusiasm for their man al-Malaki abated further when he criticised the heavy-handedness of US forces as well as Washington's inability to accept early withdrawal. He was also in US eyes too ready to talk to Tehran. A campaign against him was launched in Washington with Senator Hillary Clinton prominent among them. In August 2007, according to a CNN broadcast, a prominent Republican lobbying firm, 'with close ties to the White House' had been brought into the fray against him. The explanation for this hostility became clear when he addressed Congress in July 2008. The event was boycotted by a number of Democrats because of his harsh criticism of Israel's attack on Lebanon in 2006.

Al-Malaki commented that the American refusal of an early withdrawal of forces stemmed from their stubborn view that it would be 'an admission of defeat'.

It was not clear that it would amount to much more than a slower withdrawal. But Washington's pride was being challenged. It cost many lives. Richard Armitage, a retired State Department official observed to Powell that Bush's stubborn line amounted to this: 'in honour of the memory of those who have fallen … we've got to have more men fall to honour the memories of those who have already fallen.'[228]

Absent from the Baker-Hamilton report and in nearly all other American studies of conflicts overseas is the appreciation that other countries also have their pride, never more evident than when they are resisting an invader. This is doubly true when the theme of an American invasion or indeed pressure without an invasion, is accompanied by the message, implicit or explicit, that the country in question is deemed inferior in its culture, institutions and people.

So far as reputations were concerned, casualties were heavy. Bush's standing in the opinion polls hit an all-time low for a US President by the time he left office. Tony Blair was effectively driven from the premiership which he had hoped to occupy for another parliament, at least. He was particularly damaged by the resignation of Robin Cook, Leader of the Commons, but more significantly the previous Foreign Secretary, when the invasion began. The Parliamentary Labour Party was held together with difficulty. The death rate among British soldiers serving in Southern Iraq had not been particularly high – under 200 compared to US deaths of over 4,000. The lighter touch used by the British military was much acclaimed as an example to the Americans. But Basra at first did not see the same concentration of insurgent effort as the more northern parts of the country until 2006, when an onslaught by the Mokhtar Army had to be repelled by letting US forces take over.

The chief cause of discontent in the British public was the supine attitude of the Prime Minister towards an obviously failed American adventure. Hopes that his successor, Gordon Brown, would strike out on his own were disappointed.

Another Invasion of Lebanon

Three years into the Coalition struggle for control of Iraq, Israel launched another attack on Lebanon. It was supposed to be a very swift punitive action – as was the onslaught on Gaza launched at the end of 2008. In both cases the level of resistance was underrated and the operations went on longer than expected, drawing bitter criticism from every quarter, except the faithful US government. Both operations were bound to be counter-productive, more joining the Jihadist ranks than the Israel Defence Forces (IDF) was able to eliminate.

The 2006 operation was in response to continual rocket attacks by the fiercely militant Hezbollah and the kidnapping of three Israeli soldiers. What was supposed to be finished in a few days dragged on for well over a month. The IDF once more fought its way to Beirut against stiff resistance with heavy bombing and shelling

---

228   *Defeat. Why they lost in Iraq* by Jonathan Steele, I. B. Tauris, 2008, p. 139

of areas where Hezbollah was known to exist and exercise local power. The use of cluster bombs left southern Lebanon littered, it is estimated, with over a million unexploded 'bomblets' taking a deadly toll on unwary civilians.

Any doubts about whether the attack had been sanctioned by Washington was quickly dispelled. The expedition used up vast amounts of munitions which only the USA could supply or replace. Calls at the UN for a ceasefire were opposed by Washington. Some Arab governments, notably Egypt, Jordan and Saudi Arabia, condemned Israel but would have been happy, once the attack started, to see it at least culminate in the crushing of Hezbollah which was seen as a dangerous, radical influence in the Middle East. The radical Hezbollah, founded in Lebanon after Israel's original invasion, was proving one of the most relentless opponents of an Arab–Israeli settlement. Moderate Arab governments had witnessed with dismay the party and its allies gaining increased power in the Lebanese parliament in the 2005 elections. Hezbollah had on occasions had successful indirect negotiations with Israel – over such matters as exchanges of prisoners and maps of mines left in Lebanon. But it remained a determined enemy. For its part, Israel made attempts to assassinate Hezbollah leaders, which in one case killed eighty civilians.

The assault on Lebanon in 2006 completely failed to deliver the 'clean surgical strike' which the IDF had hoped for. It seemed that Israeli intelligence, no doubt in alliance with American intelligence, had blundered. Hezbollah's armed forces could not be neatly separated from the civilians living in its areas, where it provided many of the local amenities. The sheer weight of metal used and the scale of inevitable innocent casualties was fuel for Jihadist propaganda as well as general global outrage. In the course of the conflict, some 6,000 homes in Israel were damaged. But 30,000 homes in Lebanon were destroyed. Civilian deaths in Lebanon are reckoned to have exceeded 1,100.

A year after the assault, the UN Secretary General issued a report severely critical of Israel's failure to implement the full ceasefire agreed after the month's fighting. Israel remained in a small area of Lebanon, violating the country's air space continuously with flights of up to thirty-two manned and unmanned aircraft. The UN Office for the Coordination of Humanitarian Affairs put the number of cluster bombs fired by the IDF at over 1.1m of which only 10 per cent had been cleared within the year. Israel was criticised for still failing to provide enough information on the firing data relevant to the use of (US manufactured) cluster bombs. Since much of the affected land was agricultural and since most of the country's income comes from this and from the service economy, the country's overall economic position was severely damaged. Progress in rebuilding or repairing the 107,000 homes damaged or destroyed had been slow, according to the news agency AFP. But most of the country's infrastructure was restored in due course. Hezbollah's political power rose. In 2008, a power arrangement was accepted in the Lebanese parliament which gave the party one ministry and ten of the thirty Cabinet posts.

The determination of Washington to keep the Lebanon invasion going was spelt out in an interview in the *Spectator* with John Bolton, the neocon US Ambassador to the United Nations. He acknowledged that the USA had been deliberately frustrating diplomatic negotiations to achieve an end to the fighting and was 'damn proud' of it. An uneasy peace reigned after the ceasefire was agreed by Israel. With a UN peace-keeping force bolstered by a large contingent from the Lebanese regular army, Hezbollah could be kept well back from the Israeli border but not from achieving significant power.

The attack on Gaza

There was great anger in Israel at the failure of the invasion to achieve its desired end and at the damage done to the country's reputation. The upshot was an official investigation which castigated the Premier, Ehud Olmert, the defence minister, Amir Peretz, and the IDF's chief of staff during the attack, Dan Halutz. Olmert refused to resign. Peretz lasted until mid-2007. Tipi Livzni, Foreign Minister, called openly but unavailingly for Olmert to go. He was still in power in December 2008 when Israel launched another attack on a neighbour, this time Gaza, making the most of the support it could rely on from the dying Bush administration.

Livzni was a keen supporter of military intervention. Elections were due in February. Olmert had agreed to resign in the face of corruption allegations and Livzni was being tipped as a possible Prime Minister. Gaza was the most crowded area of the occupied areas, its refugee camps seething with resentment towards Israeli rule which lasted until 2005. At that point Tel Aviv decided on a retreat in the face of violent local hostility. This included dismantling Israeli settlements which housed 9,000 and which, all too plainly, could not be protected. In theory, Gaza had some sort of independence though, since everything which entered or left the strip was controlled by Israel, it was not real. It was merely different from the West Bank where Israel operated a different form of blockade in the form of hundreds of checkpoints between towns and villages which curbed normal commercial activity and even divided families. With the 420-mile-long wall snaking in and out of the West Bank to protect the illegal Israeli settlers, this was a form of siege. Gaza had always been the most militant part of the occupied territories. This led to Hamas winning the combined Palestinian Authority elections in 2006 and becoming the governing power in Gaza. The less militant Fatah was left in power in the West Bank region.

The Gaza assault was much like the Lebanon affair. It was a calculated overkill. Hamas's military wing had kept up a continual though not very lethal rain of rockets on Israel after the war with the IDF ended. Some twenty civilians had been killed by these rockets over eight years. Some 1,300 were killed in the Israeli attack which encountered greater resistance than expected. The disproportionate response – filmed remorselessly and shown on TV all over the world – caused an international outcry and concluded after three weeks with no certainty that

Hamas had lost its popular support. Throughout the attack, the United States refused to join in the demand for an immediate ceasefire.

Thus the eight-year-long disaster of the George W. Bush presidency ended. The 'war on terror' had multiplied the number of terrorists with its closer allies, notably Britain, brought into the firing line. Iraq, though seen as somewhat a different issue, had been through horrors to achieve the democracy which Washington thought would be bought so cheaply and so quickly. No lesson was learnt, at any rate by the battered Bush administration. The mission remained unchanged, indeed emphasised. In 2008, Condoleezza Rice wrote in *Foreign Affairs* under the ironic title 'The New Realism':

> We recognise that democratic state building is now an urgent component of our national interest. And in the broader Middle East we recognise that freedom and democracy are the only ideas that can, over time, lead to just and lasting stability, especially in Afghanistan and Iraq.[229]

So the building of nations in the American image, including force as in Afghanistan and Iraq, had to continue with urgency. It was the Wilsonian mission but with gunfire. The contradictions in her words were no doubt lost on her. Nations were to be free but only with the democratic formula. The freedom to evolve governments of their own type would not be acknowledged.

This runs alongside the belief that Israel as a democracy is entitled to uncritical support. An important part of the American faith in democracy is that it will always bring reasonable, moderate men to the fore. Even if this generalisation were true, which it all too obviously is not, it would fail to take account of the Israeli electoral system which puts extremists into pivotal roles.

By contrast, there is virtually no sympathy at any level in the US for the traditional values in the Arab world of tribal loyalties built up over centuries and the continuing power of tribal elders – an inequality which keen democrats deplore. The older colonial powers, like Britain and France, were content to leave these tribal and cultural loyalties alone. The United States adopts an altogether more aggressive approach and argues that one-man-one-vote democracy is the *only* proper course in all societies.

CHAPTER 35
THE LOST PEACE

In place of the constant tension between the Soviet Union and the US-dominated Western alliance, a global divide has opened up between the USA – with less ready allies – and the Muslim world. The Cold War with the menace of Mutually Assured Destruction appeared to make nuclear war itself almost inconceivable. In its place came the more fluid menace of Islamic terrorism and the American 'war on terror', providing alarming conditions for major international conflict.

The success of the US-led First Gulf War, with its support from Arab states, seemed briefly to promise greater stability in the Middle East, perhaps progress towards a peace settlement between Israel and its neighbours. But thereafter the deterioration – through the period of sanctions leading on to the war with Iraq, the 'nation building' conflict in Afghanistan and the Israeli interventions – was continuous. US support for Israel moved from defending that country's survival to supporting its intransigence.

Matters have been made worse by the retained belief in Washington that security of oil supplies can somehow be assured by the use or threat of military action in the region, bolstered by a substantial armed presence. Spencer Abraham, Secretary of Energy, declared in 2005: 'Energy Security is a fundamental component of national security. Military force will be an *increasingly* (emphasis added) important prerequisite to safeguard the flow of foreign oil.'

It would be hard to think of a more self-defeating or dangerous doctrine. Military action has multiplied the strength of the Jihadist guerrillas and radicalised still greater numbers in the Middle East and beyond. The certainty of the oil supply has become less not more assured. A lesson should have been learnt from Saudi Arabia where the Americans had long thought they had a secure base for 5,000 troops. The Saudis labelled the second war with Iraq as illegal and told the Americans to leave, though some training personnel were left; and CIA employees continued to be used to protect leading figures in the regime. An American base anywhere in the Middle East has the potential to become a liability for host governments – richly as the Americans would be prepared to pay for that privilege.

The Pentagon became acutely aware of this and embarked in 2005 on a long-term policy of 'reposturing' its bases around the world, i.e. finding sites where the natives were friendly. It involved the belated recognition that their prominence was liable to be provocative. But bases can hardly be hidden away, nor can the stability or the friendliness of the host country be relied on. At the end of the Bush era, the US maintained bases in some sixty countries, deploying over a quarter of a million personnel. They are designed for swift expansion if necessary. A substantial fleet continues to be deployed in the Gulf. It is argued in Washington that this helps to safeguard 'moderate' governments in the Middle East. There is an obvious contradiction in this. If the US presence stimulated radicalism, as of course it did, it undermined 'moderate' governments.

Moreover the question has long arisen whether the US forces are in practice any more usable in this context than were nuclear weapons during the Cold War. If a friendly Arab government were to be overthrown, would it make sense for American forces to rush to the rescue? Would the USA seriously want to be involved in yet another bloody exercise in occupation, further feeding the recruitment of Jihadists?

Confused US Aims

In his Veterans Day speech in late 2005, Bush declared of the USA's Middle Eastern enemies 'These extremists want to end American and Western influence in the broader Middle East because we stand for democracy and peace'. Such words have worn very thin. The invasions of Iraq and Afghanistan were a spectacular blow to peace. The claim to stand for democracy was not only untrue, it left the USA open to the charge of massive humbug. The moderately inclined governments which Washington supports in the 'broader Middle East', may be benign or instinctively friendly to the West. But the Gulf States and Saudi Arabia and other US-friendly nations are hardly democratic. Popular votes in Iran, Lebanon and Palestine have seen the enemies of the USA steadily improving their position. Democracy may appeal to Americans and the West in general. But in the cultures of the Arab world, democracy has the handicap that it is an alien cult – though that does not mean it is always rejected. The structure of society is heavily based on the historical phenomenon of 'patrilineal kinship', that is the connection of men through a common male ancestor and the consequent growth of tribal groupings. This has the advantage of encouraging cohesion (though also long-lasting feuds). The tribal elders become a powerful force in a way which the democratic powers from the West, especially the USA, seem never to understand. Tribal elders wield authority in part through age in part through families' status. Afghans told that the vote of an 18-year-old man should count the same as that of a 65-year-old tribal elder would regard it as a joke. To say that an 18-year-old woman should have that equal say would be regarded as lunacy. Democracy is not a universally saleable commodity, let alone a global cure-all.

The success in Iran of outright enemies of the USA is particularly important. It is born in part of a general anti-American feeling which pervades the region. But, more significantly, it also stems from a genuine fear of a long-nurtured American plan to attack the country. It was after all part of what Bush designated as 'the Axis of Evil'. US sanctions on the country imposed after 1979 have never been wholly lifted. Fear of an American plan to take revenge one day for the events of 1979 has sunk deep into the Iranian psyche. The country is all but surrounded by American forces including a formidable US fleet. It accounts in part for the undoubted desire of Tehran to make their country a nuclear power one day – though officially denied. It also accounts for the active aid which was provided for terrorists in Iraq in the hope of forcing an ignominious American (and British) retreat. It was another example of a confrontation's long-term effect on a national and nationalist outlook.

Making Enemies in the Name of Security
It is regularly argued that a major retreat from the Middle East would produce the empowerment of governments so hostile to the USA that oil supplies would be endangered. However, a retreat from the Middle East, wholesale or partial, would not and could not alter the basic economics – before or after any politically-inspired interruption of supply. Oil producers would still be anxious to sell whether the Americans were nearby or not. This applies whether the sales produce undue benefits to the ruling few or whether they are more evenly spread. How oil revenues are disbursed throughout the population is prominent in the minds of radical Arabs wanting to change regimes, not an ending of oil production and sales.

It is the more surprising, given the obvious danger of using force, that Washington has been so reluctant to recognise the formidable and peaceful weapon it has in the Strategic Petroleum Reserve. The capacity stood at over 720m barrels in 2010. Combined with private industry's own reserves, the existing total amounts to about 150 days of supply on its own. The relevant legislation allows the official reserve to be higher. Washington keeps down the cost of SPR operation by requiring companies which receive oil from the reserve to pay it back with interest. Given the size and diversity of the international oil market there is no reason why the reserve should not be boosted when conditions are easy and depleted when times are harsh.

In short, the SPR is by far the most effective weapon against the disruption of the oil supply, but it is a process without glamour.

The Long-term Consistency of US Foreign Policy
The wider, historical question is whether the policies of sustained intervention which reached a peak under President George W. Bush represent continuation in American policy, a major departure or – in their outcomes – simply a spell of bad luck.

The period since the end of the Second World War does in fact show remarkable continuity. Clearly there are parallels between the rhetoric of the Bush Jnr and Reagan periods. One railed against 'The Evil Empire', the other against 'The Axis of Evil'. Sir Christopher Meyer concluded as Ambassador in Washington that the Republicans 'had always missed communism and the Soviet Union as the tangible Manichaean enemy'.[230]

Barack Obama's victory in 2008 no doubt owed more to Medicare than the Middle East. Nonetheless, his promises about reducing US involvement in that region were important. He had been a lone voice in the Senate against the second Iraq war. He was by instinct and calculation opposed to US interventions overseas and public opinion on these operations had been shifting his way for some time. He promised to close the Guantanamo Bay prison within a year. He would end the Iraq operation 'responsibly' and wind down the involvement in Afghanistan. He was open to suggestions that there could be negotiations with the Taliban – though never al Qaeda of course.

Among his first acts was the appointment of Hillary Clinton as Secretary of State. Her instincts were crudely aggressive, unusually so for a woman and certainly compared to Obama. But the office had been promised to her as a close runner-up to Obama in the Democratic primaries. He also reappointed Robert Gates, Bush's last Defense Secretary to his old post. This was partly in the cause of continuity and cross-party support and partly because Gates was an admired old hand, astute in the ways of Washington.

By these two key appointments Obama had tied his hands before he even got started. He may have thought that he could reach out to others and achieve consensus for his new approach. But if so he was to be sadly disappointed. It took a year and serious rows within the administration before the President could announce the specifics of his new foreign policy. Guantanamo Bay's prison would stay open – though with a less brutal regime. The President had been persuaded that closing it would leave at large a number of determined terrorists who could not be successfully prosecuted, for lack of legally obtained evidence.

The campaign promise to 'end the war' in Iraq became a plan to withdraw all combat troops by the early summer of 2011 with a start in 2010. A certain amount of verbal legerdemain arose in meeting this target since many combat troops were relabelled and relocated as 'advisers and trainers'. But their combat potential remained. It was conceded that a large contingent would have to remain in the training role. Army sources suggested anything from 10,000–50,000, depending on arrangements with the Iraqi government, itself ruling without a parliamentary majority and nervous about its future. The departure of combat units in August 2010 coincided ominously with a bomb attack which killed fifty-nine Iraqi men queuing at an army recruitment centre.

Matters proved even trickier in Afghanistan. The military establishment was

---

able to persuade the President that far from reducing troop numbers he should go for a 'surge', which would produce the pacification necessary for the Americans to depart without the indignity of defeat. The Pentagon continued to claim that the decline in civilian casualties in Baghdad in 2007 had been due to the rise in American combat troops, not the armistice that Sunnis and Shias had agreed, exhausted by so much blood-letting. Obama added to his excuse for his change of line that the failure of US forces in Afghanistan had been substantially due to the tight-fistedness of the Bush government. It had denied the military its full needs. The President was now stepping up the Defense Budget and not just for the surge.

The Afghanistan surge began in late 2009 with an extra 30,000 troops. Once that had worked as expected the withdrawal of troops could start in mid-2011 with the process of handing over security to the nation's national army and police completed by – or 'in' – 2014. But by early 2011 it was all too evident that surge had not made any serious progress. The Wikileaks underlined the continual but unacknowledged frustration of the military at the lack of success. The insurgents were like dragon's teeth. Defeated in one place, they would reappear elsewhere.

The official UN representative in Kabul claimed in March 2011 that the surge was actually working. But within a few weeks, in the hitherto relatively peaceful town of Mazar-i-Shari, a mob attacked the UN building and killed eight of its civilian staff, two of them beheaded. The attackers were protesting at the news that in an obscure church in Gainesville, Florida, an even more obscure pastor had publicly burnt the Koran. After this the prospects for pacification looked hopeless. But the Americans fought on.

By the time Obama was starting his preparatory campaign in early 2012 for nomination as the Democrat's presidential candidate, remarkably little had changed from the Bush era. Guantanamo Bay was still open. There were more, not fewer, troops in Afghanistan. The drone attacks in Pakistan's lawless North West frontier region had been sharply increased. And relations between Pakistan and the USA were oscillating between friendship and outrage. The government of Pakistan was weak. American financial aid had become increasingly important. The country's military intelligence service, the ISI, was still permeated with supporters of the Taliban, with whom various officers had formed close relations since the Soviet–Afghan war. Bush's policy alternated between threats to Islamabad, and protestations that his goodwill towards the country was deep and sincere. Islamabad countered that Bush's protestations of friendship were false since his real interest was in his close relations with the Indian government, still bitterly at loggerheads with Pakistan over Kashmir.

Obama found his dealings with Islamabad just as difficult. The drones, controlled from the USA by the CIA, recorded a regular toll of insurgents but often civilian casualties as well. The innocents' deaths were greedily recorded in the often hostile media. The President had outlined his policy as being 'to disrupt, dismantle and defeat al Qaeda in Pakistan and Afghanistan and to prevent their return to either country in the future'. Here as in other pronouncements there was little or no mention of the Taliban. Behind the scenes the Obama government, after constant arguments, had opted for opening a path to negotiation. But the Taliban, secure in the knowledge that its recruitment was continuing, despite – or because of – the drone attacks, played for time. It saw the potential for announcing a victory when the troop withdrawal began. And their popular support in Pakistan still looked secure.

Far from disengaging from the Middle East, the Obama presidency was being entangled in greater difficulties. His Middle East policy was looking like a continuation of his predecessor. The lessons of all this were not entirely lost on the President. When the uprising occurred in Libya, Washington showed no eagerness to be involved. It was left to other NATO nations to make the running, notably France and Britain. But they needed US weaponry in addition to their own. The USA joined up after a pause. But it was now in something of a junior role in that alliance. After the Afghanistan and Iraq debacles, Washington's leadership was regarded by its allies as being as unwise as it had once been thought natural.

But then in May 2011 came the sensational success of the US Special Forces in assassinating bin Laden in Pakistan by US special forces – without any warning to Islamabad on well-justified grounds of security. The Pakistan government's position fluctuated between protest and acceptance. How the al Qaeda leader had been able to live close to the country's officer training academy remained inexplicable in many minds.

In the USA Obama's popularity soared. But there was a problem as well as a benefit. Washington was encountering one of the harsh ironies of imperialism. Displays of a powerful reach were as likely to conjure up as discourage more enemies. There was also the problem in the wake of this success: how would he now approach the electorate in 2012? Being a hawk paid off with the voters. But it had been his hope that in the presidential contest he could return to his natural role as a dove – the man who would lead the USA away from confrontations with Islamic states.

A good case for the latter approach arose from the stern fact that the money was running out. The Defense Budget by 2011 had become higher in real terms (allowing for inflation) than at any time since the Second World War, exceeding the worst periods of the Cold War missile race and Vietnam. A prolonged programme of cuts in this department's spending, up to 2024 (!), was promised. But such a leisurely approach could not impress the voters or the USA's creditors. The combined effect of massive overseas spending plus major increases at home – not least in health provision – had weakened the USA's financial position to an extent unseen in the post-war years.

American public debt had reached spectacular proportions during the Obama regime. In figures which do not mean much to non-economists, the national debt stood at nearly $14.3 trillion. In figures which mean a little more, the deficit amounted to about 100 per cent of GDP. In terms which all can understand, the International Monetary Fund calculated that the existing proposals for debt reduction, such as they were, would leave it 10 per cent higher in five years' time. It also declared that there was no 'credible' official strategy for stabilising the position.

So bad was the outlook that the credit rating agency Standard & Poor's announced in April 2011 that it was considering removing the top rank AAA rating for US official borrowing (Treasury Bonds). If that downgrading took place, by this or any other credit rater, the cost of debt repayment would rise significantly. This news item was received on Wall Street with initial alarm – and within days it was all shrugged off. It felt sure that the dollar would remain the world's safe-haven currency, whatever S&P or anyone else might say.

However, the USA's geopolitical role remains strongly dependent on its spending power. Not least of the costs it has incurred are the overseas bases which have ballooned in number – though to precisely what total is curiously difficult to discern. Different departments provide different numbers. Many bases in Afghanistan and Iraq – so the pious hope remains – will naturally be closed or will diminish in number as the withdrawal from the two countries proceeds. There are, however, no known plans to leave the Bagram base near Kabul, eight square miles in size.

The USA's global reach and power is taken for granted by most Americans – and much treasured. But it will have to suffer as Washington cuts back, both domestically and internationally. This will be on a scale which few voters envisage or will readily come to terms with. The USA is now in the position that China, with its ever-growing economic strength, has been the saviour of the Treasury Bonds market. The People's Republic is the biggest buyer of these securities, though occasionally overtaken by Japan. So large is this stake that the Beijing government openly rebuked Washington for financial imprudence when it was faced with the S&P re-rating.

Stern rebukes have long flowed the other way as well since China has a massive trade surplus with the USA, through its constant ability to undercut American goods. It means that American jobs are being exported to China, runs the complaint. Beijing refuses to revalue its currency. It feels that the country has earned its export strength by its own prowess.

Overall, the current position over currencies and trade underlines a decline in US power and influence and a rise in China's, still on a clear economic growth path. It still has a huge rural population which, as it shifts towards the cities, can provide an almost endless supply of cheap labour, the key to economic expansion.

The judgement of a World Bank report in mid-2011 was that the traditional dominance of the USA of the global economy would be over by 2025. By then, a new international system would gradually evolve wiping out the US dollar's position as the world's main reserve currency. The Chinese renminbi and perhaps the euro would share that position.

And the USA remains for the time being without that 'credible' policy to clear up its immense debt problem. The fragility of its banking system has not gone away. The USA can be charged with having caused the world's banking crisis of 2008. It arose from the collapse of the huge American housing market, caused over time by Washington's legally backed insistence that mortgages should be made available to those with poor credit ratings. No more discrimination on grounds of race, colour, creed or sex – the basis on which US banks had previously avoided 'sub-prime' loans. When the soaring house market collapsed like a spent rocket, banks collapsed like dominoes, refusing even to lend to each other, a normal practice in everyday business for large lenders. Numerous global financial instruments based in the last resort on American property prices were wiped out. The sector will take years to restore, perhaps with another crisis on the way.

Significantly China has avoided much of this crisis. We do not know how the minds of the Chinese leaders are working, only that the economy is. The path to a new, possibly hostile rivalry has clearly opened up. The boast of the neocons that they could make the 21st century 'the American century' failed. There is a better chance that it will prove the Chinese century.

✪

Explaining It Away

After more than half a century of American post-war foreign policy, missionary and so often high-minded in principle though not in practice, President Bush faced the TV cameras after the 9/11 attack to answer as best he could the question uttered by a stunned New Yorker and much publicised on TV: 'Why do people hate America?'

It was a grossly over-simplified question, inviting a grossly over-simplified answer; which is no doubt why his speech writers urged its inclusion in his broadcast. 'People' is studiously vague as is 'America'. Bush's answer to the question was a revealing simplicity: 'Americans ask "why do they hate us?" They hate our freedoms – our freedom of religion, our freedom of speech, our freedom to vote and assemble and disagree with each other.'[231]

A more searching question would have been why had policies based on noble institutions, left Americans facing enemies ready to commit suicide in their profound hatred of the USA. After all, there was no fundamental reason why foreigners, least of all those thousands of miles away and with their own faiths, should loathe the USA's institutions – though they might scorn them – so long as they remained institutions for Americans in America. The trouble only arose because the USA tried to export these values and impose them on other countries from the barrel of a gun, or more dramatically with often indiscriminate bombing from high altitudes.

---

231   Bush address to Congress, 21 Sept 2001

The authors of *Why Do People Hate America?*[232] offer an elegant analysis:

> Many of the worst effects of American power are the results of the best-intentioned action. As a result, the animosity in other parts of the world seems unaccountable in the USA and makes it difficult for well-meaning Americans to conceive of an effective change of policy.[233]

The fundamental lack of change in Washington's approach since 1945 remains striking. The sense of mission has never faded. The arrival on the scene of the Jihadists saved many from making a badly needed mental readjustment. Clearly these enemies could be written off as driven by a profoundly hostile religion, manifesting itself in rule by clerics, hostile to American and Western values. Analysis of their hostility could stop there. There could be no reasoning with religious maniacs who are also suicide bombers. Since they were dealing with irrational people, there was little point in attempting a rational analysis of their motives. If there is no reasoning with them, there is little point in reasoning about them. Serious reassessments of US policy were needed. But it was the neocons who carried the day and made policy more assertive than ever.

---

232 *Why do People hate America?* by Ziauddin Sardar and Merryl Wyn Davies, Icon Books, 2002, p. 7
233 Ziauddin Sardar and Merryl Wyn, op. cit., p. 7

CHAPTER 36
BEING TOO POWERFUL FOR ONE'S OWN GOOD

Power can corrupt a nation as surely as it corrupts an individual. To borrow from Lord Acton's dictum, power corrupts and superpower corrupts absolutely.

When the Second World War ended, the military and economic supremacy of the USA was without parallel in history. The military superiority did not only turn on the A-bomb but on the power of every other arm. The Russians, though they might put formidable numbers in the field, had forces which were exhausted, ill-equipped in many areas and no longer able to draw on the US for material. Above all, Russia had been economically and physically devastated by the war.

Britain's position was better. But its national income had declined sharply and so many of its overseas commercial assets had had to be sold off. Efforts to police a dissolving empire were more than Britain could afford – though successive governments refused to admit it. Continental Europe was in poor shape. France had suffered badly during the occupation. It was no longer a serious military power. Its colonies were giving trouble. Germany's condition spoke for itself.

The fact that the USA's wealth had soared during the war underlined the country's global superiority in every field. It was a natural source of pride to all Americans. It was also corrupting. It fulfilled Senator Fulbright's warning that power was assumed to arise from virtue, from God's favour, with a mission to remake other nations 'in its own shining image'.

The USA became imbued with the idea that not only was their way of life the best solution for the world's problems, it was the only solution. True, there were some European nations which had long-standing democratic institutions. But they were not seen as comparable in value or scale to the great freedoms of the US constitution, or so Americans believed. Moreover, while Europe was generally understood by Americans to have some admirable (though often quaint) institutions, it lacked economic competence. So here too was another aspect of the American mission. It had also to teach the world about business. This fitted very conveniently with the American doctrine of the 'Open Door' which it had operated since the 19th century. Other nations were in both American and their own interests supposed to open up their markets to foreign investment and competition. Truman pressed very hard at Potsdam for the Danube to be made an open waterway along which and around which the USA could trade.

It was not surprising that Americans resented seeing their power challenged, especially by small nations. Many of them, of whatever size, were seen as ingrates after clamouring for and receiving American financial assistance. To know that the USA was the greatest superpower the world had ever seen and then be faced with defiance was hard to bear, especially humiliation at the hands of what President Johnson called 'raggedy-arsed little countries'. American hegemony had constantly to be reasserted. Presidents who failed to follow this were branded as weak. Promises to restore and enhance American prestige in the world have been the common currency of challengers in every presidential election and always effective in garnering votes.

This same attitude has come to dominate American policy towards China during the Obama administration. Under previous presidents, Washington has shown no hesitation in criticising Beijing's human rights record, wholly undeterred by the charges it came to face over American actions in Iraq and Afghanistan, the issue of Guantanamo Bay and the readiness to sanction torture there. At first Obama muted the administration's criticism of Beijing. But by 2011 a new policy was developing which accorded with the belligerent instincts of Hillary Clinton at the State Department and with the need to show that China's ambitions or its human rights record were not being appeased. American policy, she announced in an article for *Foreign Affairs*, would in future 'pivot' towards Asia. In military form this was later to result in the deployment of 2,500 marines to a new base in Darwin which the Australian government had agreed to provide.

At the same time Clinton challenged China's claims to sovereignty of a number of islands in the South China Sea. These islands ranged from little more than rocks to substantial land masses; their ownership had long been disputed by China, Taiwan and Vietnam.

The fact that arguments over navigational and territorial rights have continued for so long and been settled by the nations concerned speaks for itself. Why should Washington get involved? There is no sensible answer to this beyond the American desire to show that its military power is truly global: apparently no part of the world should be allowed to escape the net.

On both military and political grounds this display of power makes no sense. The marine base at Darwin underlines this. Were there to be a resort to force over whatever issue, China's multimillion-strong forces would clearly win. The willingness of the USA to adopt a hostile attitude has no point, other than satisfying a domestic demand that the country be seen as a truly global power. A willingness to treat a nation as an actual or potential enemy serves only to make it such.

The American Personality

We need to understand reasons for the incomprehension and belligerence which are such unfortunate characteristics of US foreign policy. On the first issue, it used to be a regular source of scornful amusement in the Old World to quote the number of American senators and congressmen who did not even possess passports. That at least has improved. Nevertheless, general ignorance about the globe over which the USA holds sway persists. Presidential candidate Newt Gingrich, when challenged in early 2012 about having no foreign policy, replied that his first act would be to go to the United Nations and demand that Israel be recognised as a sovereign nation. It had of course enjoyed this status since 1948. In fairness the average American's ignorance of the outside world might be attributed, at least in part, to the very success of America at home. E Pluribus Unum – one nation out of many. The American 'melting pot' had succeeded, though not perhaps to the extent it boasted, in uniting so many national groups and varying creeds into one mighty identity – the US citizen imbued with a fierce sense of patriotism. In economic terms it was the world's greatest success story, an abundant country carved by the adventurous out of a wilderness.

Those who were sufficiently interested in the outside world to travel to Europe were rarely interested in the people (unless seeking out their ancestors) or the nature of their governments and institutions which could not, in any case, be more wisely contrived than their own. Their sense of curiosity was concentrated on the one thing that the USA lacked – buildings and monuments of serious antiquity. Even today, little real interest is taken by Americans in the outside world they believe they are destined to lead. Their media contain remarkably little foreign news. The study of history is largely confined to studies of their own national success. It might be claimed that there are excuses for this lack of interest beyond their own shores. The average American has everything he needs on his own doorstep. The country has every variety of climate and he has little need to travel abroad. The country produces everything from superb technologies to fine wines. Every hobby, sport or pastime is easily and cheaply indulged. Magnificent scenery is never far away. Rivers and lakes abound. It is a country of extraordinary abundance. It is constantly tempting to think that the rest of the world needs no more than a cursory glance.

American Standards

Principles and methods in foreign policy are not the same thing. The methods often used by America cast grave doubts on the principles allegedly at stake. Various countries resort on occasion to brutality. The USA is unusual in denouncing infringements of liberties and human rights in other nations despite its own record. Imprisonment without trial and torture, for example in the record of Guantanamo Bay, existed and to some extent still exists, alongside denunciations of human rights infringements by China.

The Carter Presidency was the first administration in the world to declare that its aims overseas would be motivated by a desire to spread human rights abroad, 'an ethical foreign policy'. This claim to righteousness has coloured US foreign policy ever since. Thus there could still be lectures to China on infringements of human rights even though Washington was prepared to sanction the use of torture on those it claimed were terrorists.

The CIA and military handbooks of the 1960s and beyond outlined useful methods of interrogation. They had subsequently to be released under the Freedom of Information Act. They provided such useful tips as checking on the electrical power in the site to be used for torture in case such items as transformers might be needed. Most of the manuals are devoted to forms of psychological torture including threats to an individual's family if he did not talk. The manuals were extensively used in the School of the Americas where Latin Americans were trained in more than the military skills supposed to be a principal purpose of the institution.

The activity of US employees themselves has to be seen alongside the assistance given to various military rulers in Latin America to bring them to power – with few worries about the sort of regimes they might prove to be. Washington could always be relied on to defend the regimes against charges of torture – in many cases extensive. Protests were liable to be dismissed as untrue and merely the squawks of Communist sympathisers or 'bleeding heart liberals'. The crushing evidence of widespread torture in Argentina and Chile produced no protests from Washington. Less had changed than people thought when Guantanamo Bay became an issue.

The Religious Element

The American outlook on the world has remained strongly coloured by a fervent Christianity. In a Gallup Poll in 2003, samples in the USA, Canada and Britain were asked to rank the significance of religion in their lives. Some 60 per cent of Americans ranked it as 'very important' compared to 28 per cent and 17 per cent respectively in the other two nations. Another poll claimed to find the alarming information that 60 per cent of Americans believed in the Genesis account of the creation. A recent poll found, though perhaps this was not related to religion, that one in five Americans believe that the sun revolves around the world, the pre-Copernicus doctrine of the Church.

A poll also unearthed the remarkable information that 71 per cent said, or claimed, that they would die for their God or their religion. It is also significant that among the evangelical Protestants, the fastest growing section of American religion, nearly all believed in the literal truth of the Bible, (which includes the divine purpose of a greater Israel). Such fervour is hard to match – outside the world of Islam. Inevitably, it makes it easy, even necessary, for American foreign policy to be enunciated in Manichaean terms. There are enough votes among the Protestant evangelicals to turn a presidential election. And every candidate invokes God's support and/or blessing in a way which is strange to European ears.

The Puritan inheritance handed down ever since the colonisation of America has also played a role. The USA is the only country in the world which has banned alcohol by public demand. It is hard to think of any other government which would dare to do it. As the McCarthy era was to demonstrate, if witches were no longer to be burnt, at least the eager search for them could continue.

Washington's unquestioning political, military and political support for Israel, reveals much about the driving forces of American policy. The Jewish and usually Zionist lobby itself is extremely powerful in the US. This inevitably means that the cause of Zionism is a constant in American politics, whoever occupies the White House.

But religious Zionism is by no means confined to Jews. In a detailed analysis in *Foreign Affairs*, titled 'The Deep Roots of Zionism', Walter Russell Mead wrote:

> Widespread Gentile support for Israel is one of the most potent forces in US foreign policy and in the last sixty years there has never been a Gallup poll showing more Americans sympathising with the Arabs or the Palestinians than with the Israelis.[234]

He traces American Zionism's roots back to the 19th century and beyond. Remarkably, he points out, instruction in biblical Hebrew was compulsory for much of early US history at Columbia, Dartmouth, Harvard, Princeton and Yale. The Old Testament (the New was written in Greek not Hebrew) with its tales of the ferocious battle by Israel to acquire its new and 'promised' land has always been a widely and reverently read book in the USA. In the earlier years, he suggests: 'Americans found the idea that they were God's new Israel attractive partly because it helped justify their displacement of Native Americans.'

Mead also stresses that Zionism has come to flourish among Republicans and in the American heartland. The turning point of the 1967 war and the apparent military supremacy of Israel fitted in with a series of religious revivals, evangelical and fundamentalist, which swept across the USA at that time.

It would be foolish however to ignore what Israel gained from a powerful secular force – the world of film and TV. Jewish strength in Hollywood is highly effective in portraying Israelis favourably and Arabs unsympathetically. The IDF fighting man is seen as a fine fellow. It is an echo of the view handed down since the 1948 war among Israelis themselves. In *Israel's Wars* the historian Ahron Bregman wrote: 'The Israeli soldier emerging from this war was portrayed as a fighter always playing a fair game – a sort of English gentleman who even in the heat of battle never stabs his enemy in the back.'[235] Whether the English gentleman was quite so gallant is arguable but the picture the screen provides of Israel has certainly had immense influence.

---

234   *Foreign Affairs*, July/August 2008
235   Bregman, op. cit., p. 17

Quite why the USA should contain so much fervent religion is difficult to say. No doubt, the lack of a common cultural heritage among the immigrants who swarmed into the country played a part. Their native languages and cultural habits varied extensively. But a shared religion could provide an invaluable bond. It could also provide certitudes in a new nation where the pattern of life was only slowly being established. In this way, the habits of religion became a major feature of the earlier generations of settlers and immigrants and was transmitted by them to later generations.

However, that is to put a favourable gloss on what has often proved an unhealthy trend. There have long been strains of paranoia in American religion. Some of the early churches leant heavily on their value in resisting the menace of the negroes or the Jews – often both. The Catholics were another threat which only protestant churches could resist, or indeed comprehend. Another danger denounced from a variety of pulpits was the Freemasons, as secret as they were sinister. They were a particular threat denounced by the Catholic priest and broadcaster, Father Coughlin, with his massive audience for his radio programme in the 1930s.

Religion became not just an affirmation of faith and Christian values but also a refuge for fanaticism. It remains a distinct phenomenon in American politics. Being a 'born again' Christian (as well as a reformed alcoholic) was seen as a bonus for George W. Bush's campaign for the White House – more likely by contrast to arouse suspicion in European countries. Both he and Reagan started their official day with a Bible reading. Quite what they read or whether it came from the Old or the New Testament is not recorded. Less privately, Reagan would sometimes quote from the darker passages and direst prophecies of the Old Testament. Most remarkably, he arranged for the Rev Jerry Falwell, his favourite evangelist, to meet the NSC after writing a pamphlet titled 'Armageddon', envisaging a nuclear end of the world – but naturally on God's terms. The reactions of the NSC members are not recorded.

Politics and Guns

The fervour of religion and the evangelical outlook sit easily alongside the US belief in its own triumph as the consequence of American traditional values – democracy, liberal capitalism and the rule of law. It seemed logical to believe that if these values were be exported to other countries, they too are bound to share in the triumphant consequences. This has been a constant underlying theme in the American mind. Moreover, Washington politicians have long been prey to the belief that democracies are so deeply averse to war that, with enough of them, peace could be assured in the world. This attitude can certainly be traced back to President Wilson.

Yet Hitler came to power by a democratic vote and promptly abolished the system. There can however be no doubt that had he held a normal election in the mid-1930s he would have won easily. Today, the call for Middle East countries to adopt democracy remains a regular theme in American policy. The result of popular votes in Iran, Lebanon and Palestine fail to disillusion Washington.

President Wilson also believed that the old, conflict-prone world of ancient feuds had been handed a clean slate for the first time in history. Naturally it would be for the USA to write its own great message on it. Truman's good intentions are rarely questioned. But the regular readiness to resort to force, whether in a major or minor way, needs some explanation. The military-industrial complex for whom war represented good business was obviously one factor. But also important has been a cultural issue – the glamorisation of force through the cinema and the TV screen.

The Western hero is always a man with a gun on his hip. He is always the fastest on the draw. Crime films habitually end in a hail of gunfire or violence of some sort. The heroic policemen is also fastest on the draw or the better marksman; or he and his comrades simply overwhelm criminals by sheer physical force. The more prosaic and more common process in, say, British drama of Inspector Plod simply handcuffing the criminal – and perhaps not even that – and leading him off to the police station is unsuited to popular viewing in the USA. America at large may see itself as a peace-loving nation. Yet the reality is that it has a love affair with guns and violence. It may be said that this is spreading elsewhere in the Western world, but there is no doubt about its origins in the USA and it is bound to play a part in the minds of the country's rulers. And in no state of the union, it might be noted, is the image of the swaggering gunman – the John Wayne syndrome – more potent than in Texas, from which the country gained two of its most aggressive presidents: Lyndon Johnson and George Bush Jnr.

Where Next?

Over the years since the end of the Cold War, seen as the great moment of triumph for the USA and its nobler ambitions, Americans may have been disillusioned about the outside world but not enlightened. There is of course a widespread realisation that various interventions over the years went badly wrong, as in Vietnam or Iraq. But much of the analysis still tends to be concentrated on detail not principle. Over and over again, failures are explained away as due to bad organisation: not enough troops, inadequate follow through, poor planning or clumsiness in capturing hearts and minds. Anyway, the hostile populations involved are the prey to a strange and hostile religion. The notion that foreign intervention is naturally wrong or that the world can get along without the USA playing its historic superpower role is simply unacceptable.

For Americans to admit that its interventionist, superpower role is unwise, dangerous and self-defeating would require a Damascene conversion. Besides, to pull back the troops and the aircraft carriers, to dismantle the great array of global bases would involve a scarcely bearable humiliation. Moreover, it would excite the ever popular cry, that a retreat means 'appeasement' and therefore more likely to increase attacks on the American homeland than curb them. And what is the point of the country building itself up to be a global superpower if it does not exercise that power?

A retreat from empire is always liable to be painful. Britain softened the blow for itself with the pretence that the Commonwealth was somehow a new force in the world of which it was the leader. British governments also found it difficult to admit that its various bases East of Suez, remnants of the empire, were pointless. Britain had long ceased to be a global policeman or even its traffic warden.

France also had problems in imperial retreat. French pride was badly dented at Dien Bien Phu. The retreat from Algeria was much more painful and deeply divided the country. It needed exceptional statesmanship and courage, found in President de Gaulle, to accept that there was no alternative to retreat. There is no de Gaulle in prospect in the USA. There is no American Commonwealth which can be conjured up as a pretence for continued empire, though of course Washington always likes to play up its role in Latin America. But even that still produces more resentment than gratitude.

The basic conflict in the USA's foreign policy is between idealism and realism. The idealists have certainly had a bad time in the Middle East. The region as a whole is threatened by the confrontation with Iran. In the Indian subcontinent, Islamic fundamentalists make progress.

The alternative to realism is a vicious circle of confronting those who oppose America with increased force which can only lead to increased attempts to undermine the power of the USA by whatever means possible. If the Americans could accept retreat from Vietnam, why not from the Middle East? Of course, that former retreat inflicted damage on American pride from which it took a generation to recover. Another major retreat would be hard to bear. But at least it would be better than conflicts which the USA can never win.

As we have seen, the issue of 'safeguarding' oil by military means is deeply counter-productive. It is all the odder given that Washington has a peaceful solution at hand in the SPR. However, such a policy lacks the essentials of glamour and spectacle. Huge aircraft carriers, soaring jets, zooming helicopters and rumbling tanks make good TV. They remind America of the nation's immense power and global reach in a way that nothing else can. Oil storage offers no spectacle whatever. One might as well replace the Western gunslinger with a chartered accountant. And the military – plus its immensely powerful lobby of weapons contractors – will always resist any suggestions that it should be reduced in size, importance and expenditure.

The popular appeal of national and especially imperial power has always depended on theatre and spectacle – today as it once did in ancient Rome. The British Empire at its zenith, then the world's only superpower, provided displays of grandeur which could always be relied on to stir the hearts of British citizens from the wealthy to the poorest. The components were striking. An endless line of warships were laid out for review on Queen Victoria's jubilee. The spectacle of Durbar in India showed another long line (this time rajahs and maharajahs) pledging their loyalty to the King Emperor. Accounts of how single British imperial servants maintained peace in vast areas with just a handful of local troops were truly remarkable. All these inspired pride and a sense of righteousness – just as Fulbright commented of America, this realisation of power was seen as a gift of God and an inspiration.

As in Britain in former times, the USA can offer imperial spectacle through the sheer scale of its military power patrolling all parts of the globe. In the nature of things, this display cannot be lightly put aside. Aircraft carriers which merely patrolled in home waters would be derided. An American politician who declared that the globally deployed warships and the long line of overseas bases were more a threat to than a safeguard of national security might be facing reality. But it would be too much to ask his electorate to forego the spectacle and theatre which they have long seen as the outward sign of the nation's manifest destiny. The USA is the victim and even the prisoner of its own power – as other empires have been before. Withdrawal can never be popular.

A sea change in American policy cannot be sudden. That is not in the nature of politics. But a gradual retreat from the nation's immense overseas commitments and from interventionism remains essential. Americans need to understand that the end of empires throughout history has a common theme: over-extension. The Roman Empire was a good example. It could have remained, for much longer, by far the greatest power in the world had it not tried to conquer so much of it. But it was constantly adding new territories with ever more demanding frontiers to defend. It was the empire's unwieldy size which led to its division and final fall. The tale has been much the same ever since. The world has witnessed the rise and fall of the empires of Spain, France, Portugal and Britain, each of whom found the imperial role too costly or too difficult to maintain. The rise of nationalism among the ruled sapped the resources of the imperial power.

It is also an important fact of history that the last kicks of a declining empire can be – usually are – violent. Governments accustomed to a great role do not give up easily. An acknowledgment of declining power is essential to global stability. There are very few signs that the USA has been ready for this.

Obama

At the time of writing – mid-2012 – Obama's message for his foreign allies and his domestic supporters remained ambiguous, something for both hawks and doves. For the hawks he promised that if the US detected other terrorist sanctuaries in Pakistan like bin Laden's he would be prepared to launch a similar assault (despite its perils for relations with Islamabad). For the Europeans there was some assurance that the relationship with the USA would be less over-bearing. For Britain in particular there was the helpful promise that the two nations could operate a joint security group to liaise on the Middle East and to share information. This was seen, or at any rate presented as, a tribute to the 'special relationship' between the two countries.

The USA would also come closer to the European point of view on the Arab–Israel problem. Peace negotiations must be based on the 1967 boundaries and Israel must make a meaningful start. Netanyahu went to Washington and emerged grumbling and unhappy – an essential precondition for tackling the age-old problem. Just how much pressure Obama would apply, given the strength of his Zionist lobby, remained to be seen. The rapturous reception given to the Israeli Premier by Congress suggests little prospect of progress.

As far as its general outlook on Islamic countries is concerned, US policy is to warmly encourage the Arab Spring and the advance of democracy. In short, Washington seemed happy that it had now identified the winning side in the region's upheavals. Support for US-friendly but democracy-unfriendly rulers would no longer play a serious part in Washington's foreign policy.

The problem which remained notably untackled was Pakistan. The Taliban and other extremist groups were active and even growing in strength. Suspicions of the ISI's loyalties remained. The Islamabad government remained weak. Henry Kissinger in his retirement spelt out a dire message as Obama embarked for Europe: 'If we let matters drift … India-Pakistan could become the Balkans of the next world war.'

After more than six decades of American foreign interventions, the world has been left a more unstable and dangerous place.

APPENDIX

Canada's tar sands hold oil reserves second only to Saudi Arabia. But they are extremely expensive to work compared to the Middle Eastern fields. The development of deep sea drilling is expected to yield large reserves outside the Middle East but the costs in exploration and drilling are high.

The Middle East producers did business until 1960 through the so-called Seven Sisters: Exxon, Mobil, Chevron, Texaco, Gulf, BP and Shell. The producing nations were in the happy position that they could sit back and let the companies extract, ship and market oil while their governments could sit back and draw what were by their standards huge revenues. The companies did not form an actual cartel. That would have produced legal problems with the USA's anti-trust laws, five of them being also dominant suppliers to the American market. But the sisters had few secrets from each other and rarely disagreed about their interests.

The price arrangement was that the producer nations received 50 per cent of the value of the extracted oil, less the cost of production, all based on the prevailing 'posted' price. Everyone seemed content. Oil was cheap to consumers, the companies made handsome profits and the Middle East governments had only to spend their revenues on domestic programmes which however became increasingly ambitious. All seemed well until a world glut of oil developed, despite the rapid rise in its use throughout the Western world. In 1960, led by Exxon, the sisters accepted with varying degrees of reluctance, that a cut in the posted price was necessary. Exxon led with a 17 per cent reduction in 1960. It was alarm at the fall in revenue that made the principal suppliers form the Organization of Petroleum Producing Counties which soon added to its original members Indonesia, Libya, the Arab Emirates, Algeria, Venezuela and the new producer Nigeria.

But Libya, which had become an oil producer in the late 1950s and a very large one in the 1960s, proved troublesome. The sisters had been trying to reduce oil output to keep up an already faltering price. Libya proceeded to undermine the united front that OPEC was trying to present. It called in independent oil operators who sold openly and freely at well below the posted price. A completely free market for buyers was developing through Rotterdam. Oil was now on offer at around $1.20 a barrel, down from $2. Libya's new ruler, Colonel Gadaffi was now in a powerful position to set his own terms with his own producers. The country was supplying a significant proportion of Europe's needs. He insisted on a massive increase in royalties and his producers, principally the independent Occidental, had little choice but to pay up. Single-handedly he had achieved what OPEC apparently could not.

At its 1970 meeting, OPEC called for similar terms from the sisters. They tried to resist, agreeing to unite against this demand. Any company which found its output reduced by an OPEC government would be able to gain supplies from its other sisters, who in any case had operations outside the region. Since this put the companies clearly in breach of US anti-trust laws, they asked Washington for an exemption. It was granted. An Under Secretary of State was despatched to the Gulf to try to dissuade OPEC members from their demands but failed.

OPEC's share of global oil production fell from over 50 per cent in 1973 to 30 per cent in 1985 and rising somewhat to 35 per cent by 2005, the group has always remained a key source. It is the 'swing producer'. The price of oil, like that of any other commodity or product in what is essentially an auction, is decided by the final bidder.

The fear that oil will 'run out' is an interesting aspect of the human capacity to prefer bad to good news. Alarm about a prospective shortage has been commonplace ever since oil was first put to industrial use. The conversion of the Royal Navy to oil before the First World War was accompanied by worries that oil might run out within thirty years and thus that it was essential to establish control, direct or indirect, of the Middle East's supplies – a precursor of the pattern of American political intervention we have seen in recent decades.

The figure, which was down to twenty years in 1948 rose to thirty-five in 1972 and was put at forty years in 2003, even more by 2010, despite a dazzling rise in oil consumption. A reason for the rise was not just the discovery of new fields but also improved technology. In the last two decades of the last century, extraction rates worldwide rose from 22 per cent to 35 per cent. Indeed, it is arguable that the real problem in oil is not a physical shortage but the menace – at any rate to the producers – of a glut. It is not generally realised that various oil fields in the Middle East are under-exploited for fear of a surplus. It costs money to exploit them fully. Meanwhile a certain shortage keeps up the price and the revenue that supplier governments can enjoy.

The world is in any case facing major changes in the pattern of production. Vast new oilfields are being explored not least because the high price of recent years has made the search worthwhile. In the former Soviet Union, Kazakhstan, a newcomer to the oil business, has enormous potential. Azerbaijan embraces the traditional and large Baku oil fields but the infrastructure there is badly in need of expensive modernisation. The tar sands in the USA as well as those in Canada have immense possibilities but capital and environmental costs are a barrier to proper exploitation.

The position of Azerbaijan does however illustrate how political the world's oil supplies remain. The easiest route for Azerbaijani oil is through Russian pipelines to the Black Sea. But that allows an unwelcome degree of control from Moscow. A connection to Iran would be logical but the Azerbaijanis and the Iranians have never got on. A pipeline through Georgia would make sense but that country is politically unstable and very susceptible to Russian influence. Through Armenia to Turkey is another possibility but the Armenians are hereditary enemies.

A delight to catastrophists is the claim that 'peak oil production' will very soon be reached. This may or may not be true. It depends on many factors including the lifespan of various existing oil rigs and platforms, the scale of recent new exploration, the rise of alternative sources of energy (such nuclear power) and the campaign to reduce the world's 'carbon footprint'. But it has nothing to do with the level of reserves. It is rather like assuming that if an individual reduces his spending, it must mean that he is short of capital. The opposite may be true.

BIBLIOGRAPHY

Adamthwaite, Anthony P., *The Making of the Second World War* (London: Allan & Unwin, 1979)

Agee, Philip, *Inside the Company: CIA Diary* (New York: Bantam, 1986)

Aldrich, Richard J., *The Hidden Hand: Britain, America and Cold War Secret Intelligence* (New York: Overlook Press, 2002)

Ambrose, Stephen & Brinkley, Douglas, *Rise to Globalism: American Foreign Policy Since 1938* (London: Penguin, 1985)

Armstrong, Hamilton Fish (ed.), *Fifty Years of Foreign Affairs* (New York: Praeger, 1972)

Bailey, Thomas A., *A Diplomatic History of the American People* (New York: Appleton-Century-Crofts, 1958)

Bailey, Thomas A., *Woodrow Wilson and the Lost Peace* (Chicago, IL: Quadrangle Books, 1963)

Birkenhead, Frederick Winston Furneaux Smith (Earl of Birkenhead), The Life *of Lord Halifax* (London: Hamish Hamilton, 1965)

Blum, William, *The CIA: A Forgotten History* (London: Zed Books, 1986)

Blum, William, *Rogue State: A Guide to the World's Only Superpower* (London: Zed Books, 2003)

Boaz, David (ed.), *Assessing the Reagan Years* (Washington DC: Cato Institute, 1988)

Bown, Colin & Mooney, Peter, *Cold War to Détente, 1945–1980* (London: Heinemann, 1978)

Bregman, Ahron, *Elusive Peace: How the Holy Land Defeated America* (New York: Penguin, 2005)

Bregman, Ahron, *Israel's Wars: A History Since 1947* (London: Routledge, 2004)

Cantor, Norman & Werthman, Michael S., *The Twentieth Century: 1914 to the Present* (New York: Thomas Crowell Co., 1971)

Carlton, David, *Anthony Eden: A Biography* (London: Allen Lane, 1981)

Carmichael, Joel, *A History of Russia* (New York: Hippocrene Books, 1990)

Caute, David, *The Great Fear: The Anti-Communist Purge under Truman and Eisenhower* (New York: Simon & Schuster, 1978)

Charmley, John, *Churchill: The End of Glory* (London: Hodder and Stoughton, 1993)

Churchill, Winston, *The Second World War, Vols. 1–6* (London: Cassell, 1950)

Cohen, Warren L., *Empire without Tears: America's Foreign Relations, 1921–1933* (Philadelphia, PA: Temple University Press, 1987)

Colville, John, *The Fringes of Power: Downing Street Diaries* (London: Sceptre, 1986)

Cooley, John J., *Unholy Wars: Afghanistan, America and International Terrorism* (London: Pluto, 1999)

Dallek, Robert, *Nixon and Kissinger: Partners in Power* (London: Allen Lane, 2007)

Damms, Richard V., *The Eisenhower Presidency, 1953–1961* (London: Longman, 2002)

Dilks, David (ed.), *The Diaries of Sir Alexander Cadogan, 1938–1945* (London: Cassell, 1971)

Djilas, Milovan, *The New Class: An Analysis of the Communist System* (New York: Praeger, 1957)

Donovan, John, *The Cold Warriors: A Policy-Making Elite* (Boston, MA: D.C. Heath, 1974)

Donovan, Robert, *Conflict and Crisis: The Presidency of Harry S. Truman, 1945–1948* (New York: W.W. Norton, 1977)

Dulles, Foster Rhea, *America's Rise to World Power, 1898–1954* (New York: Harper & Row, 1963)

Feis, Herbert, *Churchill, Roosevelt, Stalin: The War They Waged and the Peace They Sought* (Princeton, NJ: Princeton University Press, 1957)

Fenby, Jonathan, *Alliance: The Inside Story of How Roosevelt, Stalin and Churchill Won One War and Began Another* (New York: Pocket Books, 2006)

Fisk, Robert, *The Great War for Civilisation: The Conquest of the Middle East* (London: Harper Perennial, 2006)

Fitzpatrick, Sheila, *The Russian Revolution, 1917–1932* (New York: Oxford University Press USA, 1982)

Fleming, Donald F., *The Cold War and Its Origins, 1917–1960, Vols. 1 & 2* (London: Allen & Unwin, 1961)

Fraser, Geoffrey & Natanson, Thadée, *Leon Blum: Man and Statesman* (London: Victor Gollancz ,1937)

Fried, Richard, *Nightmare in Red: The McCarthy Era in Perspective* (New York: Oxford University Press, 1990)

Fulbright, J. William, *The Arrogance of Power* (New York: Random House, 1966)

Gaddis, John L., *The United States and the Origin of the Cold War* (New York: Columbia University Press, 1972)

Gaddis, John L., *We Know Now: Rethinking the Cold War* (New York: Oxford University Press, 1998)

Gardner, Howard, *Leading Minds: An Anatomy of Leadership* (London: Harper Collins, 1996)

Gardner, Lloyd, *Spheres of Influence: The Partition of Europe, from Munich to Yalta* (London: John Murray, 1993)

Gilbert, Martin, *Prophet of Truth: Winston S. Churchill, 1922–1939* (London: Minerva, 1990)

Griffith, Robert (ed.), *Major Problems in American History Since 1945* (Lexington, MA: D.C. Heath, 1992)

Halle, Louis, *The Cold War as History* (New York: Harper & Row, 1975)

Hanna, George H. (trans.), *Outline History of the USSR* (Moscow: Foreign Languages Publishing House, 1960)

Hargreaves, Robert, *Superpower: American in the 1970s* (London: Hodder & Stoughton, 1973)

Harriman, W. Averell, *Special Envoy to Churchill and Stalin, 1941–1946* (New York: Random House, 1975)

Heffner, Richard D., *A Documentary History of the United States* (New York: New American Library, 1965)

Herz, Martin F., *Beginnings of the Cold War* (New York: McGraw-Hill, 1969)

Hiden, John, *Germany and Europe 1919–1939*, 2nd edn (Longman, 1993)

Hofstadter, Richard, *The American Political Tradition and the Men Who Made It* (New York: Vintage Books, 1948)

Hofstadter, Richard, *The Paranoid Style in American Politics and Other Essays* (Chicago, IL: University of Chicago Press, 1979)

Hoopes, Townsend, *The Devil and John Foster Dulles* (London: Andre Deutsch, 1974)

Horne, Alistair, *Macmillan: The Official Biography*, Vols. 1 & 2 (London: Macmillan, 1989)

Hoyt, Edwin, *Pacific Destiny: The Story of America in the Western Sea from the Early 1800s to the 1980s* (New York: W.W. Norton, 1981)

Hull, Cordell, *The Memoirs of Cordell Hull* (New York: Macmillan, 1948)

Johnson, Rossiter (ed.), *The Great Events by Famous Historians* (New York: The National Alumni, 1905)

Kalb, Marvin & Kalb, Bernard, *Kissinger* (Boston, MA: Little, Brown & Co., 1974)

Kennan, George F., *American Diplomacy 1900–1950* (New York: New American Library, 1962)

Kennan, George F., *Realities of American Foreign Policy* (New York: W.W. Norton, 1966)

Kennan, George F., *Russia and the West under Lenin and Stalin* (Boston, MA: Little, Brown & Co.,1961)

Keppe, Norberto, *The Decay of the American People (and of the United States)* (London; Proton Publishing, 1985)

Kirkendall, Richard S., *The Global Power: The United States since 1942* (Boston, MA: Allyn & Bacon, 1973)

Kissinger, Henry, *American Foreign Policy: Three Essays* (New York: W.W. Norton, 1969)

Kornilov, Alexander & Bass, Robert (ed.), *19th Century Russia: From the Age of Napoleon to the Eve of Revolution* (New York: Capricorn, 1966)

Krock, Arthur, *Memoirs: Intimate Recollections of Twelve American Presidents from Theodore Roosevelt to Richard Nixon* (London: Cassell, 1970)

LaFeber, Walter, *America, Russia and the Cold War, 1945–1966* (New York: John Wiley & Sons, 1967)

Lanyi, George & McWilliams, Wilson (eds.), *Crisis and Continuity in World Politics; Readings in International Relations* (New York: Random House, 1973)

Leopold, Richard, *The Growth of American Foreign Policy: A History* (New York: Alfred A. Knopf, 1962)

Lepgold, Joseph, *The Declining Hegemon: The United States and European Defense, 1960–1990* (New York: Greenwood Press, 1990)

Liddell Hart, B. H., *History of the Second World War* (London: Pan Books, 1978)

Llewellyn Woodward, Sir (Ernest), *British Foreign Policy in the Second World War* (London: H. M. Stationery Office, 1971)

MacArthur, Douglas, *Reminiscences: General of the Army* (New York: Fawcett World Library, 1965)

Macmillan, Harold, *At the End of the Day, 1961–1963* (London: Macmillan, 1973)

Macridis, Roy (ed.), *Foreign Policy in World Politics* (Eaglewood Cliffs, NJ: Prentice-Hall, 1972)

Maier, Charles S. (ed.), *The Cold War in Europe: Era of a Divided Continent* (New York: Markus Wiener, 1996)

McDonald, Iverach, *A Man of the Times: Talks and Travels in a Disrupted World* (London: Hamish Hamilton, 1976)

McGeough, Paul, *Kill Khalid: The Failed Mossad Assassination of Khalid Mishal and the Rise of Hamas* (London: Quartet Books, 2009)

McNamara, Robert, *In Retrospect: The Tragedy and Lessons of Vietnam* (New York: Random House, 1995)

Medvedev, Roy, *Khrushchev: A Biography* (New York: Anchor Press/Doubleday, 1983)

Medvedev, Zhores & Medvedev, Roy (eds.), *N.S. Khruschev: The Secret Speech* (Nottingham: Spokesman Books, 1976)

Mee, Charles L., *The End of Order: Versailles, 1919* (New York: E. P. Dutton, 1983)

Mee, Charles L., *Meeting at Potsdam* (New York: M. Evans & Co., 1975)

Meyer, Christopher, *DC Confidential: The Controversial Memoirs of Britain's Ambassador to the US at the Time of 9/11 and the Run-Up to the Iraq War* (London: Phoenix, 2005)

Moran, Charles McMoran Wilson, Baron, *Churchill: The Struggle for Survival, 1940–1965* (London: Sphere, 1968)

Morris, Roger, *Haig: The General's Progress* (New York: Playboy Press, 1982)

Mosley, Leonard, *On Borrowed Time: How World War II Began* (London: Pan Books, 1971)

Nicolson, Harold, *Peacemaking, 1919* (London: Constable, 1937)

Nicolson, Nigel (ed.), *The Diaries of Harold Nicolson: The War Years* (London: William Collins, 1967)

Northedge, F. S. & Wells, Audrey, *Britain and Soviet Communism: The Impact of a Revolution* (London: Macmillan, 1982)

Overy, Richard, *Russia's War* (London: Penguin, 1997)

Patterson, Thomas G. (ed.), *Major Problems in American Foreign Policy: Documents and Essays* (Lexington, MA: D.C. Heath, 1989)

Payne, Robert, *Life and Death of Lenin* (New York: Simon & Schuster, 1964)

Pilger, John, *Distant Voices* (London: Vintage, 1992)

Pope, Arthur Upham, *Maxim Litvinoff* (London: Martin Secker & Warburg, 1943)

Reeves, Richard, *President Reagan: The Triumph of Imagination* (New York: Simon & Schuster, 2005)

Regan, Donald T., *For the Record: From Wall Street to Washington* (San Diego, CA: Harcourt Brace Janovich, 1988)

Ricks, Thomas E., *Fiasco: The American Military Adventure in Iraq* (New York: Penguin, 2006)

Ritter, Scott, *Iraq Confidential: The Untold Story of America's Intelligence Conspiracy* (London: I.B. Tauris, 2005)

Robinson Beal, John, *John Foster Dulles, A Biography* (New York: Harper, 1957)

Sardar, Ziauddin & Wyn Davies, Merryl, *Why do People Hate America?* (Cambridge: Icon Books, 2002)

Schechter, Jerrold & Luchkov, Vyacheslav (trans. and ed.), *Khruschev Remembers: The Glasnost Tapes* (Boston: Little, Brown & Co.,1990)

Scheer, Robert, *With Enough Shovels: Reagan, Bush and Nuclear War* (New York: Random House, 1982)

Service, Robert, *Stalin: A Biography* (London: Pan Macmillan, 2004)

Sherwood, Robert E., *Roosevelt and Hopkins: An Intimate History* (New York: Harper, 1950)

Shirer, William L., *The Collapse of the Third Republic: An Inquiry into the Fall of France in 1940* (New York: Simon & Schuster, 1969)

Shirer, William L., *The Rise and Fall of the Third Reich: A History of Nazi Germany* (London: Book Club Associates, 1971)

Sivachev, Nikolai V. & Yakovlev, Nikolai N., *Russia and the United States* (Chicago, IL: University of Chicago Press, 1980)

Spengler, Oswald, *The Decline of the West* (New York: Oxford University Press, 1991)

Steele, Jonathan, *Defeat: Why They Lost Iraq* (London: I.B. Tauris, 2008)

Stettinius Jr, Edward R., *Roosevelt and the Russians: The Yalta Conference* (New York: Doubleday, 1949)

Stoessinger, John G., *Crusaders and Pragmatists: Movers of Modern American Foreign Policy* (New York: W.W. Norton, 1979)

Stokes, Gale (ed.), *From Stalinism to Pluralism: A Documentary History of Eastern Europe since 1945*, 2nd edn (New York: Oxford University Press USA, 1996)

Sumner Welles, Benjamin, *The Time for Decision* (New York: Harper, 1944)

Taylor, A. J. P., *The First World War: An Illustrated History* (Harmondsworth: Penguin, 1966)

Taylor, A. J. P., *The Origins of the Second World War* (New York: Atheneum, 1962)

Thompson, W. Scott (ed.), *National Security in the 1980s: From Weakness to Strength* (Oakland, CA: Institute for Contemporary Studies, 1980)

Truman, Harry S., *Memoirs, Vol. 2: Years of Trial and Hope* (New York: Doubleday, 1956)

Truman, Margaret, *Harry S. Truman* (London: Hamish Hamilton, 1973)

Walker, Martin, *The Cold War and the Making of the Modern World* (London: Vintage, 1994)

White, Theodore, *The Making of the President, 1960* (New York: Atheneum, 1961)

Williams, William Appleman, *The Tragedy of American Diplomacy* (Cleveland, OH: World Publishing, 1959)

Wolfe, Alan, *The Rise and Fall of the Soviet Threat* (Cambridge, MA: South End Press, 1984)

Wood, Nicholas, *War Crime or Just War?: The Iraq War* (London: South Hill Press, 2005)

Woodward, Bob, *Bush at War* (New York: Simon & Schuster, 2002)

Woodward, Bob, *State of Denial* (New York: Pocket Books, 2006)

Zeman Z. A. B., *The Making and Breaking of Communist Europe* (Oxford: Blackwell, 1991)

INDEX

Also available from Biteback

THE WORDS OF OUR TIME

JOHN SHOSKY

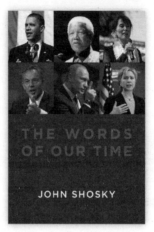

This is a book of the most influential speeches given since the new millennium. It is a timely book, capturing contemporary and powerful expressions of ideas and reasoning. Global in perspective, these speeches stand as unmediated and authentic testaments to the profound impact of great words and persuasive vision. Our ideas, mindset, politics and culture have changed to reflect national and global events of immense magnitude, such as international terrorism, the rise of new wealth in the developing world, austerity in Europe and the United States, shifting global power arrangements and new opportunities for investment and influence. These speeches define our present history and will be used by historians to understand us in the years and centuries to come. These are the words of our time.

400pp hardback, £20
Available from all good bookshops or order from
www.bitebackpublishing.com

Also available from Biteback

THE PALIN EFFECT

SHANA PEARLMAN

A US presidential election is, quite simply, the greatest show on Earth. In the battle to occupy the most important seat in the world, in which power can be bought and sold, forces on either side hoodwink the public and claim their political victims. Witness the age of the Palin Effect. An extraordinary exposé of the political depravities and media-proliferated inequalities of the entire electoral process, *The Palin Effect* sheds light on an ugly phase of American politics hell bent on slander and spurious belittling. Revealing an increasingly greedy war based on class, sex and money, former Fox News and BBC journalist Shana Pearlman looks at what motivates the protagonists in the electoral circus – the media, the people, the money, the candidates themselves – and wonders how free this star-spangled land really is.

288pp paperback, £12.99
Available from all good bookshops or order from
www.bitebackpublishing.com

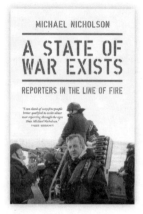